AMERICANNESS

Americanness: Inquiries into the Thought and Culture of the United States analyzes several core themes that connect Americans because of, and despite, their pronounced diversity.

The book investigates shared ideas and ideals, such as individualism, mobility, materialism, and future-orientation, that drive an overarching American worldview. Simon J. Bronner begins with ideas of space and time as they formed and changed through the history of the United States, before moving to the emergence of modern American culture. He examines reasons America is characterized as having a "victory culture" that extends to the American legal, military, and business complexes. This victory culture is further analyzed by looking at the country's relationship with the game of football—a sport that thrives in America but has not caught on in other countries. Finally, the volume probes American consumerism driven by a desire for individual prosperity in a supposedly egalitarian society. Using interdisciplinary approaches drawn from psychology, sociology, ethnology, and history, Bronner seeks explanations for people invoking, and evoking, ideas that they perceive as American.

This book would be an invaluable addition to courses on American history, sociology, cultural studies, and American studies.

Simon J. Bronner is Dean of the College of General Studies and Distinguished Professor of Social Sciences and Business at the University of Wisconsin-Milwaukee, USA. He is the author or editor of over 40 books and served as the editor of the *Encyclopedia of American Studies* and *Youth Cultures in America*.

AMERICANNESS

Inquiries into the Thought and Culture of the United States

Simon J. Bronner

NEW YORK AND LONDON

First published 2022
by Routledge
605 Third Avenue, New York, NY 10158

and by Routledge
2 Park Square, Milton Park, Abingdon, Oxon OX14 4RN

Routledge is an imprint of the Taylor & Francis Group, an informa business

© 2022 Taylor & Francis

The right of Simon J. Bronner to be identified as author of this work has been asserted by him in accordance with sections 77 and 78 of the Copyright, Designs and Patents Act 1988.

All rights reserved. No part of this book may be reprinted or reproduced or utilised in any form or by any electronic, mechanical, or other means, now known or hereafter invented, including photocopying and recording, or in any information storage or retrieval system, without permission in writing from the publishers.

Trademark notice: Product or corporate names may be trademarks or registered trademarks, and are used only for identification and explanation without intent to infringe.

Library of Congress Cataloging-in-Publication Data
Names: Bronner, Simon J., author.
Title: Americanness : inquiries into thought and culture of the United States / Simon J. Bronner.
Description: New York, NY : Routledge, 2022. | Includes bibliographical references and index.
Identifiers: LCCN 2021006656 (print) | LCCN 2021006657 (ebook) | ISBN 9781138320994 (hardback) | ISBN 9781138320987 (paperback) | ISBN 9780429452970 (ebook)
Subjects: LCSH: National characteristics, American. | United States--Civilization.
Classification: LCC E169.1 .B79824 2022 (print) | LCC E169.1 (ebook) | DDC 306.0973--dc23
LC record available at https://lccn.loc.gov/2021006656
LC ebook record available at https://lccn.loc.gov/2021006657

ISBN: 978-1-138-32099-4 (hbk)
ISBN: 978-1-138-32098-7 (pbk)
ISBN: 978-0-429-45297-0 (ebk)

DOI: 10.4324/9780429452970

Typeset in Bembo
by Taylor & Francis Books

For Michael Barton—Friend, Colleague, and Americanist

CONTENTS

List of illustrations   *viii*
Preface and Acknowledgments   *x*

Introduction   1
1   Space   9
2   Time   47
3   Winning   101
4   Money   142

References   *195*
Index   *231*

ILLUSTRATIONS

Figures

1.1	Reconstruction of Plimoth Plantation, Plymouth, Massachusetts, 2005	14
1.2	"The Old Plantation." Lithograph. C. 1880	15
1.3	Wainwright Building, St. Louis, Missouri, 1891	26
1.4	"Fall Plowing" by Grant Wood, Oil on Canvas, 1931	27
1.5	Levittown, New York, houses, 1958	30
2.1	"Fortuna and Her Wheel" (28v), Illustration from John Lydgate's *Siege of Troy* (England, mid-fifteenth century), showing the Wheel of Fortune turned by the Quene of Fortune. On the left, Dame Doctryne is accompanied by two male figures, Holy Texte and Scrypture, and two female figures, Glose and Moralyzacion	71
2.2	"The Voyage of Life: Childhood" by Thomas Cole, oil on canvas, 1842	72
2.3	"The Four Seasons of Life: Middle Age. The Season of Strength." Lithograph. Charles R. Parsons and Lyman W. Atwater, artists	74
2.4	"The Life and Age of Man, Stages of Man's Life from the Cradle to the Grave."	75
2.5	"The Life and Age of Woman, Stages of Woman's Life from the Cradle to the Grave."	76

2.6	Quinceañera Corte de Honor, Santa Fe, New Mexico, 2014. Traditionally made up of 14 damas (girls) and 14 chambelanes (boys)	83
2.7	Performers demonstrate traditional African song and dance at the Booker T. Washington National Juneteenth Celebration of Freedom, 2019	91
2.8	"Our Country: Uncle Sam." 1898	92
3.1	"Yale-West Point [Army]: Yale's Line-Up," showing the perpendicular lines forming the "gridiron." October 17, 1908	122
4.1	Wanamaker's Department Store, Philadelphia, c. 1896. Photographic print on stereo card	165
4.2	In the foreground is the "lower" farmers' market house or "shed" on Market Square, Harrisburg, Pennsylvania, prior to 1889 when the market houses were razed (originally erected around 1792). Behind it is the "upper" house on the north side of square, known as the "butchers market" dominated by sales of meats and sausages	178
4.3	Sales clerks and stockroom boys in front of Fahnestock's Department Store on Market Street, downtown Harrisburg, Pennsylvania, probably upon its opening in 1894. Owner William E. Fahnestock is the man with a Bowler hat and bowtie in the middle. In 1922 the property became part of Woolworth department store chain	179
4.4	Sales clerks with furniture, toys, and display cases in front of the shop windows of Robinson's Department Store, uptown Harrisburg, Pennsylvania, 1902. A reflection in the window on the right includes the Broad Street Farmers' Market across the street. The site at the end of the twentieth century became part of an independent bookstore complex	180

Tables

2.1	Opinions of the Opportunity for Next Generation to Live Better than Parents, 1992	59
3.1	Syntagmatic Morphology of American Football	125

PREFACE AND ACKNOWLEDGMENTS

Hearing how people both within and outside the United States of America identified objects, events, and individuals as *American* sparked the project that led to this book. While the use of *American* could be about location, the adjective often connoted a distinguishable style, manner, and appearance. I took notes on the impulse to categorize phenomena as American and attribute traits to the definition of "America," which, after all, is the entity, whether simply geographic and governmental or more deeply philosophical and psychological, that comprises the states. With heightened awareness in the world since the beginning of the new millennium of the globalization of American culture and democratic institutions, it is even more imperative to put the very idea of America on the table for discussion. The essential question I am posing here moves beyond the objectivist query of what defines an American that occupied a previous generation of Americanists to probing how and why people engage the idea of America as a subjective or perceived experience. That is, I not only ask how people live in the United States, but also how and why global observers think *with* America. These questions do not imply an unanimity of thought or reductionist reasoning. Rather, they suggest an introduction to a broad inquiry into various patterns, perceptions, and themes associated with American thought and culture, past and present. They further summon use of the results of this foundational survey to comment on American local, national, and global futures.

Leading up to this project, I contributed many localized case studies on American things, events, and individuals and this book is an opportunity to address the larger pictures of which they are a part. It is more broadly reflective and cumulative than my previous works, but it maintains a special attention to the significance of cultural evidence as expressions of shared ideas. I rely on the writing strategy of the thematic essay, although my field research in the far reaches of the nation and world certainly fed into the present interpretations.

I am grateful to Steven Drummond, the executive editor in history at M.E. Sharpe for encouraging me early on to take this project and Emily Irvine of Taylor & Francis for her incredible patience. I appreciate the many conversations with friends and colleagues about my views of Americanness. I have dedicated the book to one of my senior Penn State professorial colleagues, Michael Barton, who dispensed keen insights whether in the hallway, cafeteria, or classroom. He was the first colleague I recall who insisted on the comparative study of the United States in both its local and global dimensions. Others deserving of praise for stimulating my thinking from many years at Penn State University in an American Studies Program in alphabetical rather than priority order are Erin Battat, Emily Bernard, Anthony Buccitelli, Gary Cross, Jessica Dorman, John Gennari, Theodora Graham, John Haddad, Charles Kupfer, William Mahar, John Patterson, and Karin Thomas. At the Historical Society of Dauphin County in Harrisburg, librarian Ken Frew was immensely helpful for the research on the city in this book and on other local projects of national importance. I benefited from Penn State's American Studies Distinguished Lecture Series that brought visiting professors and researchers from abroad who enlivened our seminars on the meaning of America. All of them were special, but I want to mention a few who became especially attentive to the questions I raised: Haya Bar-Itzhak from Israel, Lei Cai from China, Paul Oliver from England, Valentina Plavinskaya from Russia, Werner Steger from Germany, Ivana Takacova from Slovakia, José Vargas-Vila from Venezuela, and Harika Zöhre from Turkey. Conversations always took in the influence of brilliant students on our perspectives. I can honestly say that the students' feedback, and their piercing questions about American identity and experience, greatly influenced my writing.

At Missouri University of Science and Technology, I was fortunate to be named Maxwell C. Weiner Distinguished Visiting Professor of Humanities. This opportunity gave me ample time for study and writing in addition to engaging faculty and students about their research. Among the many fine colleagues I met there I am especially grateful to Emilia Barbosa, Trent Brown, Eric Bryan, Gerald Cohen, Anne Cotterill, K.C. Dolan, Kate Drowne, Shannon Fogg, Larry Gragg, Patrick Huber, Irina Ivliyeva, Alanna Krolikowski, Audra Merfeld-Langston, Kathryn Northcut, Justin Pope, Daniel Reardon, Jeff Schramm, Kathleen Sheppard, Kristine Swenson, and David Wright for their hospitality and insights. Following the inquiry into material and physical culture that I began there I had the good fortune to receive a Lemelson Center Fellowship from the Smithsonian Institution that allowed me to work in the Smithsonian's tremendous archives and collections. This research informed particularly the section on the body in this book.

Headed north to the University of Wisconsin-Milwaukee (UWM), I added a professorial title in social sciences and business to widen my portfolio and perspectives. There I am beholden to Provost Johannes Britz who encouraged my scholarship and with his anthropological background shared with me his views of American culture. I owe a debt to executive assistant Brenda Dugan for keeping me organized and Amy Ronner for keeping my nose to the grindstone. I cherished stimulating discussion at UWM on non-administrative matters with professors Greg Ahrenhoerster, Julianna Kwapil Alito, Rachel Baum, Joel Berkowitz, David Clark, Lisa Hager, Margaret Hankenson, Gregg Jamison, Jonathan Kasparek, Nan Kim, Dean Kowalski, Ellyn Lem, Courtney O'Connell, Lou Pech, Mark Peterson, Paul Price, William Schneider, Tait Szabo, Tim Thering, Millie Wenzel, Anika Wilson, and W. Warner Wood, among others. The Southeast Wisconsin Festival of Books sponsored by the UWM at Waukesha Foundation provided me with memorable occasions for authors from many backgrounds to reflect on American experience. At Harvard University as a visiting professor of History of American Civilization and Folklore, I was exposed to the kindness and brilliance of Daniel Aaron, Lawrence Buell, Deborah Foster, Joseph Harris, Werner Sollors, Laurel Thatcher Ulrich, and Ruth Wisse, who welcomed me to campus with open arms. They provided great opportunities to tackle ideas, and I am grateful for the opportunity to address the Charles Warren Center for Studies in American History there. At the American Studies Program at Dickinson College where I was also a visiting professor, I benefited from time with faculty members John Bloom, Amy Farrell, and Sharon O'Brien. I wish I could name all the students in my seminars at Dickinson, Harvard, and Penn State. More than sounding boards, the students served to vet and add to the ideas presented here.

I could not have written this book if I did not have opportunities to live and teach abroad to think about cultural difference and the input of international students. I want to acknowledge the Fulbright Program for granting me the opportunity to teach at Osaka University in Japan and Leiden University in the Netherlands, and to the Meertens Institute within the Royal Netherlands Academy of Arts and Sciences in Amsterdam for a research fellowship that bore fruit in work I produced and lifetime friends I made. I thank the Baltic-American Freedom Association and Rūta Muktupāvela, Rector of the Latvian Academy of Culture (LAC) in Riga, Latvia, for their support of my scholarly residence at the LAC and an eye-opening excursion to the University of Tartu in Estonia, where I engaged in lectures about American thought and culture. I also benefited from generous invitations to have extended stays in countries while participating in international lecture series at Beijing Normal University, Hong Kong University, Oxford Brookes University (England), Ritsumeikan University (Japan), University of Aberdeen (Scotland), University of Helsinki (Finland), University of Tartu (Estonia), University of Turku (Finland), and University of Wrocław (Poland). Indeed, seeing the United States from afar put its people and the ideas they hold into sharper focus.

INTRODUCTION

I was telling a friend living in Europe that because of restrictions on gatherings during the public health crisis of 2020 over the Independence Day holiday, a neighbor arranged a drive-through celebration in which she dispensed hot dogs and burgers to automobile passengers. "How American!" my correspondent exclaimed. "What do you mean?" I asked. "You know, cars, barbecues, and defiance. You're not about to let a little thing like a pandemic deter you," he said sarcastically. More than referring to the iconic foods featured at the event as what made it American, he detected an idea conveyed in the constructed social act of a drive-through event to mark a holiday. He identified a way of thinking American as well as acting it, or maybe he had an idea of America that did not necessarily jibe with what Americans would say about their organized event. Even without stepping foot in the United States, he had a sense of an Americanness and an engagement with the symbolism of America that constitute the subject of this book. Was he right that the drive-through was distinctively American, or is that beside the real point of why and how he used *American* metaphorically? To address the question, my goal in this book is to evaluate judgments of Americanness, and interpret the apparent need for a cognitive concept of Americanness.

Americanness refers to the basis of phenomena that draws attention to themselves as American. Americanness represents ways of thinking and acting shaped by history, society, politics, and geography connected to the United States, and is associated with people identifying as Americans. Its significance is that it drives perceptions and outlooks that people hold and affects personal actions and public policies. It has a portable and often imitable quality, and comes out as a sign of difference for residents of the United States living in foreign lands or non-Americans who mimic American behavior and attitudes. Although significant to a national sense of self, Americanness usually escapes definition because it is not easily materialized. It is typically expressed as a demeanor or sensibility rather than an artifact. It frequently enters the emphatic rhetoric of national political campaigns in the United States in pithy slogans such as "This is America" or "We Are Americans" although politicians usually do not pin down what this quality is. They appeal to a perceived intellectual unity out of social and geographic difference. Americanness becomes most discernible as an undertone of sayings, customs, arts, and cultural expressions that can be called "loaded" with meaning (Garber 2012).

Americanness as a concept points to ways of thinking in and about America. Drawing on the symbolic anthropology of Claude Lévi-Strauss I would emphasize further that the cognitive concept of Americanness entails the ways that people think *with* America, typically outside of their awareness (Lévi-Strauss 1963, 89; see also Culler 2013; Garber 2012, 94–103; Leach 1989). By this is meant that beyond the literal inventory of American things such as hot dogs and hamburgers, the evocation of the meaning of being American is itself a mutable idea that comes into play in different settings and is variously perceived. Americanness produces symbols and metaphors meant to comfort or disturb and it directs awareness to shared ideas and ideals, and indeed worldview as an overarching outlook or belief system. Yet as a mode of thought, Americanness does not signify a total identity exclusive of others. It can be conveyed in various situations and moments that in themselves reveal thinking not only about the present but also the varied historical legacy of the United States across time and space for diverse groups and environments. It overlaps with other identities and the challenge for analysts is to untangle the complex relationships and sources of national feeling with other outlooks that might be considered local, regional, religious, occupational, ethnic, gendered, and racial, among others.

A thematic organization of this book around Americanness is different, therefore, from a historical, sociological, or geographical textbook survey, and yet it incorporates all those kinds of knowledge. An Americanness approach is more cultural, rhetorical, and ethnographic—and perhaps above all psychological—rather than chronological or demographic. This approach has a goal of explaining reasons for people invoking, and evoking, ideas that they perceive as American. The affirmation of Americanness is complicated by the fact that the people of the United States of America, many coming as immigrants and those who are indigenous, have struggled with the country's balance of nationalism and localism, in addition to the composite picture of its mixed ethnicities, religions, and races. Yet that has not stopped Americans from defining variously characteristic American traits, its national "heartland" and "mainstream," over the country's centuries of existence. Or maybe the ambiguity of the overall image in such a cultural collage prompts vigorous posturing and abundant folklore of American identity. This discourse has contained both shared and contested ideas that I seek to reveal, and understand, and lay a groundwork for future investigation. I am not after a fruitless delineation of what is unique about Americans but rather concerned with interpreting the patterns and perceptions that drive a sense of Americanness. At stake in the question of Americanness now and in the past is the process of cultural affirmation and reproduction of what America is, and what it should be. Without reducing Americanness to a single trait, exploring the tangled qualities of the American frames of mind leads me to especially map the concepts of individualism and future-orientation underlying my friend's exclamation of "How American!"

Let me expand on my use of cultural, rhetorical, and ethnographic methods and the ways that they invoke psychological perspectives to chart the embodied ideas of Americanness.

Cultural

Those things labeled American are usually cultural in the sense of being expressive, socially shared, and symbolic. They include the visible foods, dance, gestures, houses, and crafts and audible slang, proverbs, stories, and music that manifest traditional knowledge. And the process of tradition involves transmittal of belief and values across space as well as through time. To find patterns, analysts compile collections of cultural expressions, usually emphasizing form because this component is the most structured and comparable. Because *form* tends to be stable compared to other components of construction and use, when noticeable changes occur to form in time and space, it is usually a sign of a deep social change or division that bears explanation (Glassie 1968).

Construction refers to how cultural expressions are formed rather than the form they take. This component of analysis therefore takes into account the people who construct culture and the procedures and materials they employ. Especially with material aspects of culture, construction involves inquiries into local environments and the way they influence the final product. Yet even with oral and social traditions, construction is evident in often localized settings and the way that communities exert influence on the way that people communicate and the appropriate content. *Decoration* of objects, and for oral and social traditions *stylization*, are often subsumed and in fact neglected under the rubric of construction, but I tend to treat them separately so as to draw analytical attention to the way that artistic and ritual framing provides an overlay to material that can reinforce or change its meaning.

Use is the least stable and shifts attention from the constructers to the consumers of cultural expression. Another way to conceptualize this shift is that in construction, people encode intentions and in use, or practice, meaning is decoded. For considerations of construction and use as part of discerning cultural patterns, analysts will often work with individual practitioners and artists and localized events and settings to discern the encoding and decoding process. This work will include those incidents that appear unusual as well as everyday to view the social negotiations to establish culture, determine meaning, and constitute norms.

In this book, I follow the convention of using adjectives of folk, popular, and elite to describe cultural processes. As processes of learning and production, they can be types of action that are not mutually exclusive. They should not be construed to be hierarchical divisions. Indeed, most people have combinations of folk, popular, and elite ideas in their heads. The analytical terms are useful to draw attention to different modes of learning and transmitting culture and the social and environmental contexts associated with them. *Folk culture*, for example, refers to practices drawing on knowledge gained from tradition and often transmitted orally. Learning and engaging tradition in verbal, social, and material forms suggests transmission through the variable repetition of expressions by word of mouth, imitation and demonstration, and custom. Typically localized or associated with group identity, such ordinarized traditional knowledge usually varies across space and is stable over time. I caution against the use of *vernacular* to describe such knowledge because the components of learning and transmission are typically absent from its analysis and it falsely connotes a crudeness and simplicity to folk forms. When I use vernacular, it follows published references to language and architecture that are considered to be colloquial, rather than implying an aesthetic or cultural judgment (Vellinga 2011).

Popular culture refers to expressions that are widely distributed, usually commercially, and tend to be standardized. It might also have an aesthetic connotation as "low-brow" but the significant factor for analysis here is the negotiation of corporate interests and those of consumers. Packaged artistic forms such as films, television shows, songs, and memes that are called popular tend to be stable across space and vary over time. Following the analytical attention in folk culture to modes of learning and transmission, popular forms often emphasize visual communication and corporate rather than group organization. Even before photographic and broadcasting technology became broadly available in the twentieth century, popular culture was associated with standardized media reproduced with mechanical forms of printing and imaging (such as the eighteenth-century production of silhouettes). One might argue that popular culture is therefore not tied to place, and less adaptable to region or nation, as folk culture usually is. Yet popularity refers to the widespread consumption of expressive arts and part of cultural analysis is to trace the diffusion as well as ubiquity of such material. Although one thinks of popular culture in terms of period-based fads, there can be different spreads of popularity, with attendant state, regional, and nationalistic symbolism, such as recorded southern "hillbilly" music that became a national phenomenon as country music, or the "popular" dining experience of the Friday fish-fry in Wisconsin that did not diffuse outside of the state (Hagen 1999; Malone 2018). Whereas tradition-driven folk culture is viewed as the intellectual property of a group, commercial popular culture is typically connected to a producing and distributing organization seeking users who are unfamiliar with one another. That something is popular does not mean that everyone in a wide geographic expanse has it, but they are probably aware of it. When referring to commercial productions that are mass-produced and owned on a global scale, such as clothing items I will discuss in Chapter 4 on the body, I refer to them as part of *mass culture*.

Elite culture no doubt implies a connection to social class because of educational as well as economic attainment. Yet one does not need to be rich or have a college degree to be culturally informed by elite expressions of art, music, and theater. In relation to learning and transmission, elite productions are refined through academic training and organized artworld networks. Analytically, one can detect aesthetic judgments that emphasize perceived refinement in labeling of *fine* arts, *fashionable* dress, and *serious* theater. More so than folk and popular culture, elite culture promotes individuality and expressive originality. Less tradition and nation oriented than folk and popular culture, elite culture embraces the avant-garde and futuristic, even though the creativity of elites generates traditions (often described as "movements" and "schools") and communities of practice much as folk and popular artists. Of significance to the understanding of Americanness, national leaders often lay claim to the status given to fine arts and academic achievements as markers of nationhood. Given that Western education and art have emphasized European civilization, the standards of elite culture are often based on European aristocratic legacies and hence Americans have often felt self-doubt in a democracy about the status of a comparable American high art of literature and music. References to elite culture in folk and popular culture thus often reflect both an aspiration to and antipathy for elitism.

Even the concept of national culture has a European standard to contend with. Modern ideas of national identity are rooted in the philosophy of Romantic Nationalism attributed to Jean-Jacques Rousseau and Johann Gottfried von Herder in what is now France and Germany. Anti-monarchical in its intention, Romantic Nationalism asserted that the boundaries of a political state should be based on the cultural unity of the people it governs. The longstanding or organic culture that provides the poetic soul of a nation is rooted in those groups closest to the land, namely peasants reflecting a folk culture. Influenced by this political view, Jacob and Wilhelm Grimm in the early nineteenth century famously collected and presented folktales they attributed to peasants to make a case for a German cultural nationalism. Other efforts to locate national cultures followed in Italy, England, Scotland, Ireland, Poland, Finland, Norway, and Denmark, among others. The cultural nationalists pointed out factors supporting a culturally supported nation-state including a uniform geography, shared language, ancient historical legacy, rooted native peasantry living off the land, and common racial and religious stock—attributes that the new nation of the United States lacked. As I will elaborate in Chapter 1, American leaders adapted the concept of cultural nationalism to a future rather than past-oriented individualistic ethos of nation-building with a constructed frontier and regional mythology, urban-industrial pluralistic vision, and popular arts of landscape vistas and social mobility.

Rhetorical

To identify the systems of thought and culture that evolved over time and space in the United States, I read oral, written, material, visual, bodily, and event texts for rhetorical content. More than a selection of key phrases in political speeches and literary works, this kind of rhetorical reading locates repeated components of communication that condense layers of meanings with strategies of persuasion in action as well as text and images. Self-identifying as a student of culture, Americanist Alan Trachtenberg (1982) aptly called this expanded form of rhetoric, "vehicles of self-knowledge, of the concepts upon which people act" (8). Examining cultural expressions for cognitive concepts that are communicated symbolically in images, sounds, and objects as well as words, I find, for example in Chapter 1 on space, uses of machines for displaying relations of nature and humans in an American democratic ethos in addition to serving instrumental ends. And in Chapter 4 on money, I look at the way that the body has been rhetorically imagined as a machine within an industrialized country and how that representation in art, work, and action adjusted to a service and information economy.

Ethnographic

Cultural and rhetorical approaches typically analyze what people say and write and ethnographic methods fill in the picture of what people do and chart the cultural scenes or frames that give meaning to their actions. A central task of the ethnographer, then, is to identify and code the cultural scene and its participants. The scene might be bounded socially rather than physically. In such cases, the observer notes the actions, props, and communication that becomes symbolic in the scene. For comparison, the ethnographer should observe the differences of similar events outside the social frame of the action. Interviews with participants can shed light on their awareness of their symbolic gestures in and out of the scenes in addition to their backgrounds that inform their actions. Polls and surveys such as those in Chapter 2 provide a broader cultural context that in the spirit of ethnography provide "emic" or native views. In this book, I use them to reveal American attitudes and beliefs toward the future and tradition that can be compared longitudinally. The point of ethnographic microstudies and macro-surveys for the analysis of Americanness is that they provide evidence of the ways that ideas associated with the nation are enacted in the rounds of daily and ceremonial life and in American thinking. They can be effectively used to comment on how socially shared ideas translate into actions, and resistance, on the street and in the home as well as in the halls of government.

Drawing on these methods, I guide readers to interpret thought and culture that Americans have confronted in word and deed through their history as part of a fragile, and often divided, nation. And I bring in what people outside the cultural scenes in the United States have constructed or perceived as American. I begin with "space" (Chapter 1) because that was the first point of comparison for travelers and natives in what was first mapped as "America" by German cartographer Martin Waldseemüller in 1507 (Allen 2016). It appeared as a vertical sliver of the northern hemisphere from the eastern shores that had been sighted by Europeans. He named the space on a world map after Italian explorer Amerigo Vespucci for the revolutionary concept that the lands that Christopher Columbus observed in 1492 were part of a separate continent. He thus visualized a binary of a *New* world contrasted with the *Old* of Europe. He raised images of an untrodden wilderness affording new settlement and transformation. Biblical rhetoric continued to describe the flora and fauna of the land as Edenic, and its inhabitants as belonging to nature. In this chapter, I describe the development of frontier mythology as issues of space and mobility, and consider the often neglected ideas of urban and suburban space in relation to a pastoral ideal established early in American history. These often conflicting developments are couched in the growth of regional cultures that had to be negotiated with national unity. I move then in the second chapter to the concept of American time with which space is often paired. I identify a rhetoric of a non-sectarian busy as well as business culture that often was at odds with Christian structuring of the work week and seasonal cycle.

In Chapter 2 I move from questions of space to those of time, particularly American attitudes toward the future and past. In this analysis I use statistical evidence from polls to view attributed characteristics of optimism at times of stress such as the turn of a new millennium in 2000 and global pandemic in 2020. I also discuss time in relation to the ritual year and life course with holidays and rites of passage as frames for paradoxes of Americanness that celebrate individualism simultaneously with community. A tension that I analyze within many practices of tradition in the United States is one arising from the perceived absence of a shared, exclusive ancient historical legacy with a desire for an inclusive cultural past. A way that time was marked in American thought and culture was with constructed and adapted American holidays and ritual customs that raised basic questions about what constituted national traditions and an American sense of tradition in relation to its predominant future and commercial orientation.

Americans are often characterized as obsessed with sports which reflects a "victory culture" that extends to the American legal, military, and business complexes. The belief system underlying victory culture is also responsible, I contend, for the winner-takes-all mentality in America's binary election system and agonistic politics in the country. In Chapter 3 I take a closer look at the American style of winning as manifested in "America's game" of football and contemplate the reinforcing power of sporting conquest rituals in American institutions.

Related to the enactment of sports and the Americanness of winning is the role and perception of the enculturated body in thinking in, about, and with America. Although references to bodily issues intrinsic to race, ethnicity, gender, sexual orientation, occupation, class, age, and disability pervade this book, in Chapter 4 I focus on the body as a culturally constructed and cognitively perceived object in metaphorical uses of masculine strength. At a macro-level, I examine the visual and verbal rhetoric of obesity and on a micro-level a cultural account of cosmetic surgery as an American expression of attitudes toward physical appearance. I find linkages in the way that Americans perceive fat according to factors of gender, ethnicity, and race.

I close the book with an interpretation of the dramatic intellectual and cultural shift in the United States from a producer economy to a consumer society. American capitalism takes a distinctive form in the world economy and there is frequent satirical reference to cultural imperialism in the "McDonaldization" on a mass global scale. In Chapter 4 I examine the roots of consumer culture and ways that it informed the rise of modern America and the "American Dream" of attaining wealth and social mobility known internationally. I continue the theme of individualism and future-orientation in Americanness by focusing on the prominent cultural history of American technology for domestic consumption to interpret the theme of pragmatic ingenuity in American thought and culture. Besides investigating evidence for the view that technological progress in the United States owes to ordinary individuals with an intrepid "pioneer" spirit, I examine the belief system that holds that technology is an answer to social problems and its consequences.

While I do not claim this as a comprehensive survey of things and ideas American, taken together the chapters provide an overview of major concepts that compose Americanness in mind and body. They also offer a primer of approaches to analyzing American thought and culture that I hope will inspire future contemplation on thinking in and with America.

1
SPACE

Eyeing their destination for the first time after an arduous voyage from England, Puritans aboard ship were not much impressed by the shore. But once inland, they waxed poetic about the glorious wooded lands that stretched out for what seemed like eternity. Francis Higginson, a Puritan minister, upon arrival at the Massachusetts Bay Colony in 1629 wrote:

> here wants as it were good company of honest Christians to bring with them horses, kine [cows], and sheep to make use of this fruitful land. Great pity it is to see so much good ground for corn and for grass as any under the heavens to lie altogether unoccupied, when so many honest men and their families in old England, through the populousness thereof, do make very hard shift to one by the other.
>
> *(Higginson 1950, 78)*

For his followers convinced to become settlers in strange surroundings, the value of the New World space was in the familiarity of cleared, arable land that could be made into property. Property marked wealth, and was largely inaccessible to their common sort back home. They described much of the shoreline as wooded "wilderness," but crediting the indigenous population with their agricultural skill Higginson gushed, "a man may stand on a little hilly place and see divers[e] thousands of acres of ground as good as need to be, and not a tree in the same" (72). The new spaces seemed more fertile, more wondrous than what they remembered in England. He observed, "This country aboundeth naturally with store of roots of great variety and good to eat. Our turnips, parsnips, and carrots are here both bigger and sweeter than is ordinarily to be found in England," and added:

DOI: 10.4324/9780429452970-2

> the abundant increase of corn proves this country to be a wonderment. Thirty, forty, fifty, sixty are ordinary here; yea Joseph's increase in Egypt is outstripped here with us. Our planters hope to have more than a hundredfold this year, and all this while I am within compass; what will you say of two hundredfold and upwards? It is almost incredible what great gain some of our English planters have had by our Indian corn.
>
> *(72)*

With this vast expanse of fecund space to be had, the settlers were puzzled that the natives "had no certain fixed place of abode" and did not lay out property in private lots (Hennepin 1950, 294). They appeared to be more communal and have far more fidelity than the settlers to preserving their natural surroundings. In the settlers' perception, the natives viewed space as what one could see as a broad landscape rather than as private, finite plots of land. The Puritans considered their social as well as spatial differences with the Natives based on the Puritans' European experience. Compiling a guide to the language of the New England Natives, Puritan minister Roger Williams speculated that perhaps their unusual beliefs and migratory ways owed to their being one of the lost tribes of Israel, and called them a "Folke," in recognition of their communal social structure in contrast to the hierarchical settlers' society (Williams 1643, 7). Louis Hennepin, a Belgian Franciscan missionary accompanying La Salle in 1678 on an expedition to the western part of New France, echoed Williams's comparison of natives with Jews as the European racialized "others" and pointed to their use of space as evidence:

> One would be apt to suspect that these savages of America originally sprung from the Jews, some of whom might casually have been wrecked and cast upon that part of the world, for they have several customs not unlike theirs. They make their cabins in the form of tents, like as the Jews did. They anoint themselves with oil, and are superstitiously addicted to divination from dreams.
>
> *(Hennepin 1950, 294)*

Although a false claim, the symbolic equivalence of Jews and Natives by Williams and Hennepin in different locations of the North American continent underscored the centrality of individually owned property and the dependence on boundaries—social and physical—to the settlers' conception of New World space.

The growth of the New World land to the settlers was often framed in biblical terms of the Garden of Eden, which now could be reclaimed (Smith [1950] 1978). Listening to the stories of the Illinois nation, Hennepin took note of the contrast of Christian and Native creation beliefs. He wrote:

> They say, much like the former, that a woman came down from heaven and hovered awhile in the air, because she could find no place to set her foot

upon. The fish of the sea, compassionating her, held a council to determine who should receive her. The tortoise offered himself and presented his back above water. The woman placed herself upon it and stayed there. In time the filth of the sea, gathering and settling about the tortoise by little and little, formed a great extent of land, which at present is that we call America.

(Hennepin 1950, 293)

Hennepin, as a missionary wanting to convert the natives, tried to explain the land-based idea of the Garden of Eden as paradise, from which they were expelled (Hennepin 1950, 292). Instead of Eve made from Adam's rib, the Illinois related the story that "some time after the spirit came down again to the woman, she brought forth a daughter from whom…is descended that numerous people who now take up one of the largest parts of the universe" (Hennepin 1950, 293).

Early on in the history of North America, colonists divided the space "that we call America" into South and North east of the Appalachian Mountains and the West beyond them, before referring to the "Far West" beyond the vertical marker of the Mississippi River. From a political or commercial standpoint, region might be an official unit that designates a section of a country below the nation, or state. It might combine states or suggest service areas within a state. In this kind of organization, the justification for drawing boundaries is of coverage from an administrative or distribution center. The lines of demarcation might be variously planned by population density, geographic markers, or travel routes. Sometimes boundary lines become disputed and need to be settled administratively as was done by the survey of the famous "Mason–Dixon Line" between 1763 and 1767 that originally settled a conflict between Maryland, Delaware, and Pennsylvania, and later was socially perceived as the dividing line between North and South. More often, the state represents official boundaries that do not necessarily follow cultural connection, while region connotes from residents' viewpoint the place with which people feel socially and environmentally familiar beyond the neighborhood, town, and city.

In contemporary America, when questions of place are raised, people usually reply with reference to physiographic characteristics—high mountains, deep valleys, and extended plains—that become noticeable to one's view, and residence, because they are different from others surrounding them and presumably affect those who interact with them. Travelers might use region as a frame of reference for geographic location and direction, such as indicating that a place can be found to, and therefore in, the south or west. Although appearing to be a way to get one's bearings rather than referring to cultural difference, designations such as southern and northern California can evoke folklore defining their differences in a large expanse of coastal land in a state. There might be an allusion to northern California slang in a variation of a traditional riddle-joke "How many northern Californians does it take to screw in a light bulb? Hella!" [probably a contraction of "hell of a," it is an intensifying adverb usually substituting for "very"]. There is the southern California equivalent in the parodic answer, "They don't screw in light bulbs; they screw in hot tubs" (or the variation, "one to screw it in and six to share (groove on) the experience"), suggesting an unconventional hedonistic, affluent lifestyle (Dundes 1981). The unofficial division of North and South spaces in this case conveys the view that one affiliates with a regional culture. More so than describing a nondescript "area" or "state" for habitation, region often suggests a social as well as geographic cohesion, a historic and cultural "sense of place," in an extensive environment.

Region and its relation to nation as a larger unit and locality as a smaller one are significant factors of constructed and inherited cultural identity that are expressed through various traditions and practices. In the United States this is more of an issue than in other countries because the nation had a colonial past of settlement, an indigenous population that established living patterns on the land, borders marking a western frontier that continuously expanded, and a varied landscape and demographic profile. It was not composed of kingdoms that could provide borders based on areas of control, but when compared to the ruling powers of Europe, Africa, and Asia, the United States also was lacking in an ancient lineage that could contribute to regional and national consciousness. Much of the political attention in forming an American "New Republic" in the eighteenth century was therefore cultural and concerned with whether a unified national identity could be maintained while allowing strong pastorally based regional roots to sprout. The dividing line between sectionalism, considered negative, and a healthy regionalism as part of a national whole, cultural as well as political, continued through the divisive Civil War and Reconstruction era in the nineteenth century, the civil rights era in the twentieth century that raised a discourse of race and ethnic domination in regional self-identity in the North and South, the federal "War on Poverty," also in the twentieth century, that focused on conditions in the Appalachian region, and in the twenty-first century an added awareness of border culture and Southwest history in immigration conflicts at the border. Thus regional culture, usually based on a pastoral ideal established during the colonial period, informs political as well as psychological issues on American places and their relation to the nation and those surrounding it.

A cultural region is one in which residents over a geographic area share a number of expressive features that differ from others. Language, food, and architecture are often the most noticeable cultural expressions that tend to follow regional lines, but queries related to the land might also include place names and legends, festivals and customs, hunting and fishing practices, and agriculture and animal husbandry. Cultural geographers refer to folk regions as native or "emic" perceptions of place beyond the immediate community or residence (Clements 1979; Nicolaisen 1976a). Richard M. Dorson, for example, drew attention to "Little Egypt" as a folk region, and regional identity, in southern Illinois recognized by residents and expressed in various forms of folklore such as speech, games, and songs (Levin 2006). Although there is a historical explanation for the name owing to establishment in 1818 of Cairo, Illinois, because of the analogy between the Mississippi and Nile rivers, a better-known migratory legend relates the regional cohesion of the area when it boasted a plentiful harvest of corn that rescued people to the north suffering from a drought or frost (Dorson 1964, 296–97).

From an ethnographic perspective, a folk region is one associated with a tradition-centered group that dictates much of the round of life in a place. Dutch (or Amish) Country in Pennsylvania, Cajun Country, and the Upland South have all been described as folk regions in this sense, because the dominance of a way of life is more apparent and goes beyond uses of oral tradition to include occupational foodways and architecture that suggest an immersive "cultural landscape." Indeed, the association of these places with "country" suggests a separatist "sense of place." Self-identification as being regionally distinctive, and exoteric names for residents as a group, can reinforce this view. For example, in the mostly rural Pine Barrens of New Jersey (Hufford 1986), residents referred to themselves proudly as Pineys to mark their difference from industrialized, urbanized New Jersey to the northeast and metropolises of Philadelphia and Baltimore to the south, and in the multi-ethnic Upper Peninsula of Michigan, folklorist Richard Dorson ([1952] 2008) heard the slang term of "Yoopers" that appeared to him to be both self-deprecating (in response to outsiders' perceptions of backwardness) and boastful (taking what others hold as negative to be positive and a sign of social belonging).

The operative question in American thinking about region as "homeland" while nation is "country" is how the connection that people make to space is cultural and is sustained through interpersonal, intergenerational transmission, practice, and especially in a mobile society such as the United States through diffusion and hybridization of traditions. A theory that is frequently tested about American regional formation concerns the mixing of ancestries and the formation of new identities in homelands. Questions arise about the ways that European settlers adapted Native-American traditions or rejected them as they took control of the land culturally as well as physically. Another issue was that as the Eastern Seaboard became dominated by white English rule, and a split in economy grew between the plantation South (using slave labor from Africa) and the North (with its yeoman tradition), there was a relative integration of African and non-English patterns (particularly of the German, Celtic, and French) in the westward movement. There was also a different kind of mobility from the Caribbean up the Mississippi River. When the United States annexed former Mexican areas in 1848, another ethnic-regional mix emerged that led to recognition of the "Spanish Southwest" as an extensive cultural or folk region.

A way that perceptions of space shaped regional identity and a difficulty with national unity was in the association of plantation economy with the Lowland South. The idea of the plantation derived from an English farming system of working an agricultural estate with resident labor. Puritans famously established

FIGURE 1.1 Reconstruction of Plimoth Plantation, Plymouth, Massachusetts, 2005.
Source: Photo by Muns. Creative Commons Attribution-Share Alike 3.0 Unported license.

their New England settlement as Plimoth Plantation but their single-crop plantations were on a smaller scale than in the South and could not be sustained into the nineteenth century. Eyeing what they perceived as an undeveloped wilderness further inland, settlers looked beyond their religious enclaves to individualistically farm their own properties to the west, expand their domain, and cultivate wealth (Bercovitch 1975; see also Miller 1956). This land grab had tragic consequences for the Native-American population whose communal claims to hunting grounds obstructed the colonialists' individual aspirations for property ownership (Lepore 1999). Indeed, it marked a shift from the communal ideals of the Puritans to what historian Sacvan Bercovitch (1975) describes as the roots of capitalist individualism in America. It further marked New England as a distinct region of small-scale farms and crossroads villages and port cities. When textile mills created an American system of manufacturing in the early nineteenth century, they drew on the farms for their labor (Hounshell 1985). Although the yeoman ideal was popularly associated with New England "pioneers" clearing the land and forming a backbone of small-town life, the region also was significant in the growth of urban-industrial centers that affected a paradoxical image of city wage-earners from varied immigrant and racial backgrounds.

Demand in industrialized Europe for raw products from the New World such as sugar, indigo, and tobacco supported the plantation economy and landscape. Attracted by the moist soil and long growing season of the South, plantations were organized with states specializing in different crops. Virginia led in tobacco cultivation while rice prevailed in South Carolina. At first planters relied on

FIGURE 1.2 "The Old Plantation." C. 1880.
Source: Lithograph. Prints and Photographs Division, Library of Congress.

indentured labor, but that was expensive and it became increasingly difficult to compel Europeans to come to the difficult conditions of southern climate and disease. Lured by the promise of land, many indentured servants often sought out farms of their own rather than stay in service. Planters turned to African slavery to fill in labor shortages. By 1840, the U.S. Census counted 2,312,352 slaves in the Lowland South or 47 percent of the area's population. The Upland South in contrast was half that number. The plantation system in the American South peaked in the mid-eighteenth century but had a resurgence with the spread of cotton plantations in the Deep South in response to increasing demand from European countries. After emancipation, the dependence on the plantation landscape and master–servant relationship continued with tenant farming and Jim Crow laws that created a racialized debtor underclass and limited mobility. With depletion of the soil because of single cash crops such as tobacco, many white farmers, turned pioneers, were impelled to migrate west across the Appalachian Mountains to find new lands. The South did not build the concentration of industrial-urban centers as the Northeast and the Old Northwest did. Based upon this heritage of plantations reliant on large, flat expanses of land, an elite white planter class, and African slavery, the South, divided between the Lowlands and Uplands, developed a strong regional identity indicated by the political rhetoric of the "Solid South" that suggested a national unity and white master class worldview (Fox-Genovese and Genovese 2005; Grantham 1992; Taylor 1961).

If "worldview," i.e., a general outlook that reflects an internalized value system, is subjective evidence from expression of beliefs and customs, objective evidence in the form of dialect, housing, and gravestones has been used to map smaller regional affiliations then the meta-region of the South (Dundes 1971; Marshall and Vlach 1973). Examples of regions named by this process are the Pennsylvania Culture Region (PCR) that crosses state lines and the Mormon Culture Region (MCR) in the American West (Gastil 1975, 165–74, 237–43; Glass 1986; Meinig 1965; Yorgason 2003). Analysts use this procedure to identify exceptions to regional formation in which "isoglosses" or subregions form (e.g., "Delmarva" also known as the "Eastern Shore" between the PCR and Lowland South and the "Down East" culture extending from coastal area of northeastern Maine into Canada's maritime provinces that show differences, some of them ethnically and linguistically based, from the larger New England region). They also will try to assess areas of ethnic mixing and cultural exchange that could result in hybridized, urbanized, or creolized regional cultures emerging (e.g., the "Metropolitan New York Region" and Creole or Cajun culture of Louisiana).

Subjective approaches base regional influence, and indeed individual and social agency to create or "perform/practice" place-based identity, upon the "esoteric" self-perception of residents and the "exoteric" rhetoric of outsiders to the region who identify a cultural difference between themselves and others, even though they might live in close proximity. For example, researchers might ask interviewees their subjective views of their regional and local affiliation in addition to documenting their official postal address. In aggregate, the answers can give clues to the relative strength of regional identity and test views that the South and New England have the strongest regional identity and other designated areas such as western New York, Pennsylvania, and Ohio purportedly lack a regional consciousness (Zelinsky 1980, 13). Perception of region has also been relevant to areas like Texas and Oklahoma that appear to be between regional cores of the South and Southwest, and raise questions of whether they are part of a geographically defined "Great Plains" or constitute a separate nationalistic identity (Blevins 2014; Brands 2004; Grider 2001; Zelinsky 1973, 119). In border states such as West Virginia and Missouri, residents often have mixed responses that suggest "inter-regions" or interior border cultures (Lowry and Zonn 1989). In Missouri, for example, residents refer to "Little Dixie" which actually lies in the northcentral rather than southern part of the state, the Ozark region that stretches into Arkansas, and the flat "Bootheel" section on the edge of the Mississippi Delta region (Marshall 1981). Cultural geographer Wilbur Zelinsky (1980, 12) pointed out in his study of regional identifiers for businesses that although the area designated as the Middle Atlantic region covers several states on the Eastern Shore from New York to Virginia, the only locality in which "Middle Atlantic" was dominant was the inland city of Harrisburg, Pennsylvania. Further, the only regions in which residents referred to themselves as "eastern" were separated in an arc from the New Jersey coast to western New York (Zelinsky 1980, 14).

Life stories often relate the ties of residence within regional culture to one's outlook. Ex-patriates of a region hold on to regional identity through various customs such as Groundhog Day celebrations with traditional regional foods of shoofly pie and chowchow in California for former residents of Pennsylvania and Pioneer Day gatherings of Utah Mormons outside of the West. Family reunions (Henderson and Bronner 2013) and regional celebrations such as Decoration Day (Jabbour and Jabbour 2010), concentrated in the Appalachian region, and Juneteenth festivals (Abernethy 2010; Wiggins and DeNatale 1993) also serve as public events to reinforce regional cultural roots. In digital culture, another example of esoteric lore that indicates regional affiliation is the production of memes along the lines of "You Know You're [regional group]" or "You Might Be From [region as a proper noun]" or the variable quiz "How Are You A [regional group]?" Birthday parties and sports events can become traditionalized with parties emphasizing regional ties to teams and can be ethnographically analyzed.

Cyberlore, as well as orally told jokes and slurs, can also be exoteric, that is, used to communicate stereotypes of a regional cultural personality (this derisive humor is also known by the French term *blason populaire*; see Wehse 2014). In so doing, the expressions presume that the regional characterization is a sign of groupness, and backwardness, in comparison to the regional affiliation of the speaker. Sigmund Freud ([1918] 1957, 66; Freud 1959, 42–43) was puzzled by rivalries created by such regionalization or utterances, and called them "narcissism of minor differences," suggesting that because the groups were typically close together, the use of folklore psychologically serves to create separation and borders. Among the most popular in American folklore are Kentucky-Indiana jokes. Although concerning states, they relate to regional analysis because of the ambiguity of regional identity in both places. Historically, migration into Indiana came from the South and southern Indiana boasts southern patterns in foodways, architecture, and speech. Although connected by southern heritage, Indiana joketellers might express superiority associated with a northern affiliation. Back in the border state of Kentucky, Indiana migrants were known as "Hoosiers," which folklorist Ronald L. Baker (1986, 109) defines as "a derogatory epithet suggesting rusticity and is roughly synonymous with such terms as hillbilly, hayseed, and hick." Many of the Hoosier jokes told by Kentuckians reinforce the view that Indiana residents put on false airs and deny their proud regional identity while Kentucky humor told by Indianans in the fashion of traditional numskull tales conveys Kentuckians as ignorant southern rustics. Some narratives are about telling such jokes, and often can interchange the butt of the humor. An example from the Indiana side in Baker's collection is:

> Three or four guys were sitting around telling jokes. This one started telling a Kentuckian joke. The joke started going against the grain of a Kentuckian in the group. The Kentuckian said, "Hey, wait just a minute. I'm a

Kentuckian, you know." So the person telling the joke said, "Oh, I'm sorry. I'll talk a little slower."

(Baker 1986, 111)

In a sign of the joke's traditionality and variability as narcissism of minor differences, the punchline also shows up in Vermont/Maine-Massachusetts humor (often with the onomastic slur of "Masshole" for an uppity Massachusetts resident and rube identity of "Down Easters" for Mainers, even though they supposedly share a New England identity). The humor further appears in cyberlore as variable memes in regional sports rivalries.

Humor of state/regional rivalries suggests that the place and space with which one associates culturally is important in the United States, and yet it might appear more indefinite than other kinds of identity. Or is it significant in a few places and as a type of regional experience such as southern, southwestern, or Yooper? What does it mean, then, to grow up in a state that is not known for regional identity, or do all places have regional consciousness in one form or another? Much of regional cultural theory is formed on the assumption that people rooted in the area (and therefore have not traveled extensively outside of it) primarily interact in face-to-face communities and inherit as well express their regional and national identities from social exchange in familiar communities throughout their lives. With accelerating relocation and global media communication arguably producing less connection to place in the twenty-first century, a major challenge emerges to reassess American regional influence and identities of place and space on individual lives as well as national culture.

Regional Thought and Rural Culture

A historical perspective on American cultural experience argues that early colonial experience of agrarian expansion from locations separated by spans of distance on the Eastern Seaboard largely determined the formation of distinct regions. Colonization meant that settlers were imprinted in the idea in Europe that they were transplanting their culture, and encounters with indigenous populations and what appeared to be strange, varied environments forced adaptations to both the social and natural landscape. Although the British came to dominate the eastern coastline, they featured some socially distinctive backgrounds. The first permanent English settlement was the Jamestown settlement in the Colony of Virginia, that took hold after 1610, and added Africans in 1619, which would have a profound effect on the social economy and racial composition of the area. To the north, Puritan separatists in 1620 established the Plymouth Colony on Cape Cod and a larger group still aligned to the Church of England created the Massachusetts Bay Colony in 1629. The Pennsylvania Colony under British rule was the last to be formed in 1681 and featured a mix of German pietists and English Quakers. Adding to the diversity of the area were remnants of a Swedish colony in the

Delaware Valley and to the north the establishment of New Netherland by the Dutch, who surrendered it to England in 1664. As a result, questions arose whether the different ethnic mixes would create several different cultural hybrids along regional lines or be variations on an English-dominated colonial identity.

Cultural geographer Wilbur Zelinsky (1973, 13) proposed the "Doctrine of First Effective Settlement" to be tested historically and geographically. He defined it as an inevitable process:

> Whenever an empty territory undergoes settlement, or an earlier population is dislodged by invaders, the specific characteristics of the first group able to effect a viable, self-perpetuating society are of crucial significance for the later social and cultural geography of the area, no matter how tiny the initial band of settlers may have been.
>
> *(Zelinsky 1973, 13)*

He added the corollary that appeared to diminish the cultural contributions of later urban immigrants:

> in terms of lasting impact, the activities of a few hundred, or even a few score, initial colonizers can mean much more for the cultural geography of a place than the contributions of tens of thousands of new immigrants a few generations later.
>
> *(Zelinsky 1973, 14)*

To view cultural process and test this doctrine, analysts document the material culture in the emerging colonial centers located near major ports of entry in the Tidewater South, New England, Pennsylvania, and New York. This inventory of forms in historical context often leads to comparative analysis of, on the one hand, European precedents, and on the other, material in other regional centers to determine the structure and process of hybridization, if it occurred. Zelinsky (1973, 84) also extrapolates a political thesis that New England through the nineteenth century "was clearly the most fecund and powerful, setting an example for the whole country in many departments of higher human endeavor." As seen in the holiday customs of Thanksgiving, the prominence of New England led to the perception that national culture was dictated by northeastern or Yankee societies. Later historical investigation of traditions in the southern and middle colonies often challenges this view or suggests a stronger regional division in the United States that explains a different perception of cultural separation in the nation's geographic parts. It also can reveal the ramifications of "folk identities," often suggesting stigmatization of language and customs, associated with southern and Pennsylvania cultures (Goldstein and Shuman 2012).

Instead of a view of national unity, four major centers of cultural dispersal for regional development are usually identified in the eastern United States: southern and eastern New England, southeastern Pennsylvania, Chesapeake Bay area, and the coast from southern North Carolina (Fisher 1989; Glassie 1968; Leach [1966] 2002). In those areas, different social mixtures and agricultural adaptations came together and diffused along identifiable paths inland. The result was the creation of hybridized cultural regions of the Lowland South, Upland South, North, and Mid-Atlantic. The Upland South has a smaller westward branch that Henry Glassie called "Upland" in the Ozark area of Missouri and Arkansas. The Mid-Atlantic, while being perceived as possessing the least regional identity, could be the most influential geographically because its culture radiated south, north, and west to form the Midwest, often associated with general American culture. Evidence for the diffusion is apparent in the highly comparable and quantifiable evidence of folk architectural forms to objectively map these formations, but other concentrations are notable in foodways (molasses for sweetening in the South and maple in the North) and craft (French-influenced pirogue boat building in Louisiana compared to the Chesapeake log canoe). The cultural divisions became less clear inland, however, at points of encounter that formed some of the first American border cultures in places such as Indiana, Kentucky, Ohio, and Illinois. Arguably, the regional cultures that formed during the eighteenth and nineteenth centuries continue to affect a twenty-first century sense of space and place that is simultaneously in concert with and a barrier to nationalism.

Complicating this picture of regional formation are types of cultural material that did not diffuse west such as connected farm buildings of New England (Hubka 1984), or those that reportedly did not regionalize such as quilts (Milspaw 1997). Subregions and isoglosses, or in some cases claims for separate cultural regions with folk cultural features, came forward (Bronner 1986b). Examples were the creolized culture of the Cajun region, or Acadiana, renowned for a persistent French dialect, gumbo foodways, shotgun housing, and Cajun/Zydeco music (Ancelet and Edwards 1991). An implication of this work was to assess the impact of New Orleans as a cultural entry and encounter point for Acadian, French, Spanish, British, and African influences and the way that the creolized results diffused northward up the Mississippi River and beyond. Isoglosses often formed with racial and occupational variables as well as environmental factors that led to comparative questions about pressure for, and resistance against, processes of regional acculturation and massification, and the forces of creolization in various locations (Haas 2008; Mieder 2012). Because of the emphasis on inland diffusion, maritime cultures in American thought are typically not well accounted for. Examples of intersections of space and race that stand out as different are the African-influenced Gullah and Geechee cultures arising out of the Sea Islands on the Atlantic Ocean coast of the southeastern United States and spreading to the Lowcountry region of South Carolina and Georgia (Cooper 2017; Jones-Jackson 1997; Morgan 2010). The combination of traditions, including songs, Anansi folktales, and games, and customs raises numerous questions about the role of the coastal region in what has been called the Atlantic World because of interconnections between Africa, Europe, and the Americas (Brown 2012; Harris 2014; Joyner 1985; Morgan 2010).

When extending the cultural dispersal model for the eastern United States to the West, problems arose, because migration to the area was inconsistent and derived from land travel in addition to sea travel to ports of entry on the Pacific Coast, environmental barriers to agricultural settlement in arid and mountainous areas were more severe, indigenous populations were more resistant, and European ethnic-linguistic patterns became more complicated. With a far different landscape than the wooded East, the West challenged the colonists' view of fecundity of the land and its treasures for human control. Although the reality was that the arid Great Plains with extreme temperature swings was not as hospitable to European agricultural settlement as the East, and Native-American nations resisted subjugation, migrants had faith that the previous wonderment of fertile growth of the Eastern Seaboard could be gained with technological ingenuity and human industriousness. Through the nineteenth century new cohorts of immigrants from Scandinavia and northern Europe took the chance that life would be better on the Plains. They thought prosperity could be willed from the dry ground, and emboldened by opportunities for individual gain were awed by the great expanse of the country they thought of as "unoccupied."

Reflecting this view of the special circumstances of the European-American power to tame the wilderness with divinely inspired expansion, journalist John L. O'Sullivan in 1845 wrote an editorial for the magazine he founded, *United States Magazine and Democratic Review*, arguing for the annexation of Texas by the United States. His argument was that adding this land is "our manifest destiny to overspread the continent allotted by Providence for the free development of our yearly multiplying millions" (O'Sullivan 1845a, 5). It was not the first time O'Sullivan invoked the homiletic rhetoric of destiny. Six years earlier, he contended that the key characteristic of the new nation as a result of its break with the European past was its commitment to "futurity." O'Sullivan declared that "Our national birth was the beginning of a new history, the formation and progress of an untried political system, which separates us from the past and connects us with the future only." He continued with a flourish that:

> we may confidently assume that our country is destined to be *the great nation* of futurity. It is so destined, because the principle upon which a nation is organized fixes its destiny, and that of equality is perfect, is universal.
>
> *(O'Sullivan 1839, 426)*

He followed later with a claim for the annexation of Oregon on the basis of "the right of our manifest destiny to overspread and to possess the whole of the continent which Providence has given us for the development of the great experiment of liberty and federated self-government entrusted to us" (O'Sullivan 1845b). Catching the attention of Congressman Robert C. Winthrop of Massachusetts who exclaimed it a week later three times in a debate on the floor of the House of Representatives about Oregon, "manifest destiny," according to historian John Carl Parish, then "began echoing back and forth across the country" (Parish 1932, 2; see also Pratt 1927, 795). To Parish:

> this imperial vision was not so much a cause as it was a product of our early westward expansion. Nevertheless, once it had taken form in the minds of Americans, it stimulated in extraordinary fashion their movement across the continent.
>
> *(Parish 1932, 1)*

Although viewed as a jingoistic battle-cry connecting biblical prophecy to American imperialism and national unity, "manifest destiny" was more evident in the emergence of sectionalism, states' rights, and western regionalism (Cherry 1998, 117; Wilsey 2017). Its contribution to the developing ideas of Americanness is its reference to futurity and inevitable progress represented by exclusive technological control of space, even if that meant destruction of natural and indigenous cultural resources. When the conservation movement arose in the late nineteenth century, activists such as Henry W. Shoemaker and Gifford Pinchot tried to counter this faith with an alternative progressive argument that nature constituted a manifestation of the divine in need of protection for the public good (Bronner 1998b). Acknowledging the lure of the land for individual gain and freedom, they campaigned for a cultural as well as political change that would view preservation of nature as part of a better future, mutual aid and cooperation as part of a restoration of communal values, and instill a shared commitment of the state to enforce cultural as well as natural conservation. Rather than viewing progress as inevitable, Shoemaker and Pinchot offered a doomsday scenario if action was not taken and they advocated for the federal government to address what they viewed as a moral as well as environmental crisis with a national policy. A source of division through the twentieth century, the question of reimagining the environment, particularly after the supposed close of the frontier in 1890, nonetheless reinforced the worldview of America as "the great nation of futurity."

Within western regionalism, an emergent American religion of the Church of Latter-day Saints, also known as the Mormons, constructed a distinctive cultural landscape that spread from a core settlement in the arid environs of Salt Lake City. Cultural geographers have called the domain and wider sphere of Mormon cultural diffusion the Mormon Culture Region (MCR) (Eliason 2006; Meinig 1965; Zelinsky 1973, 115–16). Mostly of English background from New York State, Mormons had migrated from previous settlements in Ohio, Missouri, and Illinois to the Great Salt Lake in present-day Utah. Their settlement plans had a distinctive layout of a numbered rectangular grid system of north and south streets instead of names. They also built open irrigation channels following main streets in towns, planted windbreak rows of Lombardy poplars, and grouped stone houses in agricultural villages instead of isolated farmsteads, and used wooden hay derricks (Eliason 2006, 868; Fife 1988, 133–216). This pattern outside the core in a narrow strip by the Wasatch Range was evident in a domain that stretched throughout Utah, southern Idaho, and southeastern Nevada. Church members diffused to clustered communities within the Southwest, Pacific Northwest, and Rocky Mountain West, and thus show several cultural features in a sphere that extends to Oregon to the northwest and Arizona and parts of western New Mexico to the southeast. As the region developed, use of folk cultural expressions on the landscape was not restricted to church members, and agricultural and architectural practices became part of the round of life of residents in the region. The area thus created a paradox of a socially shared worldview that is at once nationalistic, often espousing a fundamental Americanness, alongside a self-image of themselves as "peculiar" or separate in belief from other regions (Campbell, Green, and Monson 2014; Fluhman 2012; White 1978).

In several regions, cities are associated with the "heart" of the region such as Boston in New England and Philadelphia in the PCR. A frequently given reason for not considering cities in regional cultural analysis is that they do not have the spatial stability of agricultural areas and are too multifarious. Yet some sprawling metropolitan areas appear to emanate from an urban core and constitute regions that differ from those that surround it. The most commonly cited example is the New York Metropolitan Region (NYMR) that extends to northern New Jersey, eastern Long Island, and suburbanized areas along the Hudson River. The cultural status of the area raised questions because of a highly recognizable dialect that pervades a Metropolitan Core District in the city's boroughs (Gastil 1975, 162; Labov, Ash, and Boberg 2006, 233–35). Although dating back to the seventeenth-century Dutch colony that extended up the Hudson Valley and down into New Jersey, New York City takes much of its character from successive waves of immigration since the nineteenth century, which has resulted in large concentrations of people of German, Irish, East European Jewish, and Puerto Rican backgrounds, among others, that scholars tie to the "New York" or "Brooklyn" accent (Bronstein 1962; Hubbell 1950; Thomas 1932).

Historically, these cultural formations bring into question the pastoral ideal associated with the American origin story that later informed narratives of frontier expansion. One might reasonably argue that cities and their promise of socioeconomic mobility were magnets for immigrants as well as American migrants. Boston, New York, Philadelphia, Baltimore, and Charleston formed during the colonial period and entered into popular imagination as locations for a fresh start and social progress that composed aspects of the emerging "American promise," an important aspect of the perception of Americanness. Countering this view was a depiction in realistic literature and graphic art of cities as dingy, dark, and corrupt. They were also portrayed as being disturbingly multicultural, full of diseased immigrant "races" with criminal elements. Popular magazines touted a strong moral case for working off the land outside of the cities and celebrated frontier heroes. Throughout political campaigns of the nineteenth century, supposedly having grown up in a log cabin and working on the farm were important appeals to the voting public even though candidates typically were of substantial means (Gunderson 1957; Pessen 1986).

Considering the emphasis in regional thinking on a ground-level expansion of land, how do cities, arguably central to modern American culture, figure into Americanness? Into the twenty-first century, American cities composed less than 4 percent of land area in the United States but were home to over 70 percent of the population. The U.S. Census counts over 80 percent of the population as "urban" and 41 urbanized areas have more than a million people (United States Census Bureau 2018). Geographers refer to urban concentrations as metropolitan regions unto themselves. In everyday conversation, however, people reveal perceptions of sharp divides between urban and non-urban areas in talk of "living outside the city." Concerned about the divide also constituting a racial division, for example, residents of Milwaukee told reporters that "There's still that sort of almost invisible, but known barrier between Milwaukee and adjacent Wauwatosa" (Dennis and Maternowski 2017). Aware of the sprawl of metropolitan areas such as Houston, pollsters asked locals to locate the boundaries of the city. They concluded "It's hard to rein in 655 square-miles of city in the minds of residents. Most Inner Loopers only think 'real' Houston is inside Loop 610, while even others would say Houston is inside Beltway 8" (Hlavaty 2018).

Even more extreme, in New York City, the largest in the United States for population and density, residents refer colloquially to "going into" or "working in the city" as being in Manhattan, giving the surrounding boroughs the image of the city as a commercial center and other spaces defined by residence.

Urban cultures such as New York City that entered into the popular imagination through media and literature, if not based in landscape features, are culturally recognized in distinctive foodways and festivals, and in fan cultures surrounding city-based sports teams. Countering the nationalistic opprobrium for "inner" cities as locations for crime, illicit sex, and drugs, music and art often labeled "contemporary," "modern," "avant-garde," and "chic" celebrate city life as a stimulating and fashionable experience that suggests an accelerating future. Cities are thought of as timeless: reflecting a notion that cities operate on a business/machine cycle of 24/7 rather than a human sleep cycle, promoters will claim their urban areas as places that "never sleep" and hence offer the ultimate defiance of nature. The cities are depicted as bustling and people as constantly busy as well as moving at a fast pace (Harris 1987). Metropolitan regions such as New York and Los Angeles are culturally constructed as disconnected islands that have unusual properties—of physical space as well emotional pace—and yet represent the power, energy, and commercial centers of American culture. Yet based upon the yeoman and pastoral ideal in American intellectual and settlement history, they vie still with rurally based regions for the moralistic political, if not pluralistic, social core of America. Since the beginning of the twenty-first century, political pundits often comment on the patterns in presidential elections of rural and urban voters as a symbolic polarization of rooted conservative, white, and past-oriented residents on the rural side, and mobile liberal, multicultural, and future-oriented voters on the urban end, respectively (Gimpel, Lovin, Moy, and Reeves 2020; Oberhauser, Krier, and Kusow 2019; Scala and Johnson 2017).

One visible way that the city promotes its claim for cultural and political dominance of America is through the regnant protrusion of vertical rather than horizontal space. Cityscape photographs feature towering "skyscrapers," starting with the Home Insurance Building in Chicago that stood at 180 feet tall in 1890 and was soon outdone by the Chrysler and Empire State buildings in New York by 1931 at over 1,000 feet. The skyscraper was hailed as an engineering marvel with the use of fireproof structural steel and reinforced concrete. Devoted to business office space, the original World Trade Center (WTC) in New York City stood as the tallest building in the world at the height of 1,368 feet in 1972, and was outdistanced two years later by Chicago's Willis Tower (named the Sears Tower until 2009) which reached 1,450 feet (Gillespie 2002). The publicity for the Willis Tower emphasized its representation of urban power and modernism in claiming that it stood in the "heart of downtown Chicago and the *future of work and play*" (Willis Tower 2020; emphasis added). In the aftermath of WTC's destruction in 2001 in the terrorist attack of September 11, 2001, the One World Trade Center (OWTC) in its place, also known as the Freedom Tower, was set at 1,776 feet; a symbolic reference to the year of the signing of the Declaration of Independence. At that height the OWTC reclaimed the distinction of being the tallest building in the western hemisphere and representing "the top of America," as a headline in *Time* magazine blared (Sanburn 2014).

Back in 1883, the *Chicago Tribune* labeled the building of "skyscrapers" more than eight stories tall a current "craze" and "mania" (New York Gossip 1883). The newspaper described conservative elites who preferred buildings closer to the ground at human scale and protested the trend. "They were mostly old fellows," the anonymous reporter wrote, and portrayed them as "slow of speech, cautious of action, into whose brains new ideas trickled slow" (New York Gossip 1883). Citing the skyscraper as "a building of the future," adapting well to the cramped conditions of the rising city, the story concluded with a tribute to the intersection of commerce and technology in expensive elevators servicing the buildings that creates an urban version of "Alp…added unto Alp" (New York Gossip 1883). And it was fitting, the reporter thought, that America's greatest city of New York should have more "high buildings…than in all the rest of the country put together" (New York Gossip 1883).

A prominent architect of the skyscraper, Louis Sullivan, thought about the cultural meaning of the "lofty construction called the 'modern office building'" (Sullivan 1896, 403). His answer for the skyscraper as a democratic American feature was ironically based on its "loftiness." "This loftiness is to the artist-nature

FIGURE 1.3 Wainwright Building, St. Louis, Missouri, 1891.
Source: Adler, Sullivan, and Ramsey Architects. Missouri History Museum. Public Domain.

its thrilling aspect," he wrote, and added that for architects working toward a modern urban vision, the vertical space is "the true excitant" of their imagination (Sullivan 1896, 406). Beyond its commercial function of holding multiple offices, the skyscraper must, according to Sullivan,

> be tall, every inch of it tall. The force and power of altitude must be in it, the glory and pride of exaltation must be in it. It must be every inch a proud and soaring thing, rising in sheer exultation that from bottom to top it is a unit without a single dissenting line,–that is the new, the unexpected, the eloquent peroration of most bald, most sinister, most forbidding conditions.
> *(Sullivan 1896, 406)*

Responding to critics that the skyscraper was unnatural, and therefore lacking art and culture, Sullivan answered that the tall building represents change and individuality (Sullivan 1896, 409). Invoking Abraham Lincoln's democratic clarion call issued at the Gettysburg battlefield, Sullivan mounted a moral as well as aesthetic defense that skyscrapers constituted "an art that will live because it will be of the people, for the people, and by the people" (Sullivan 1896, 409).

The trouble with Sullivan's claim for the inclusiveness of the skyscraper is that the "high-building" also marked the rising power of corporate organization and the office emblematizing a hierarchical bureaucracy (Trachtenberg 1982). Arguably, the prominence of the office as a work space encouraged the growth of a middle class, but it also disrupted the traditional integration of home and work that led to the concept of urban "divided space" between the upper propertied class and a renting and homeless under class pushed out to the margins of the city, made famous in the photographs of tenement buildings and street life in New York City by Jacob Riis under the title of *How the Other Half Lives* (Barth 1980, 28–57; Riis 1890).

With America's urban population surpassing the number of rural residents in 1920, an artistic and intellectual agrarian movement tying cultural regionalism with closeness to the land pushed back against the triumph of urban imagery as the future. Sullivan's upward facing worldview had artistic detractors who disputed the modernist label of the cosmopolitan city. Aptly named Regionalist art,

FIGURE 1.4 "Fall Plowing" by Grant Wood, Oil on Canvas, 1931.
Source: Deere and Company, Moline, Illinois. Public Domain

influenced by an artworld folk art movement of the 1920s, artists such as Grant Wood, Thomas Hart Benton, and John Steuart Curry used modernist painting styles to celebrate rural and small-town America within recognizable regional demarcations to claim the democratic and ethical influence of the soil and simplicity of the *heartland* (Burdan et al. 2016; Dennis 1998). In literature, regionalists and local-color writers sensing the lure of the alienating, corruptible city exuded a nostalgia for the traditional values growing out of America's country roots. Iowa-born Ruth Suckow, for example, drew literary attention in 1924 to *Country People*, an epic narrative of three generations of a German-American family who lost their identity as they gained wealth. Indeed, her narrative is representative of feelings of loss—of farmland, of family, of community—expressed by Regionalists (Boyer 2019, 549–53; Ochonicky 2020, 29–54). Reflecting on a regionalist worldview informed by a sense of open space, she writes of a traveler who:

> has caught varied glimpses of the spirit of the country in the settled prosperity of the plain frame houses of the Middle West…At the end of such a journey, the much talked-of standardization of gasoline-stations and chain stores seems nothing but a hasty superstructure erected of necessity coupled with energy to bridge the mighty gaps of an overwhelming variety.
> *(Suckow [1930] 2002, 148)*

When she looks at a skyscraper, she sees "the hasty superficialities of standardization" (Suckow [1930] 2002, 160). The ethical alternative, she declared, is "bound up with the American soil," which provides social intimacy, generosity, and "a greater and greater inclusiveness" (Suckow [1930] 2002, 160; see also Omrčanin 1972).

Suckow was well aware of the hold of the "rags to riches" motif in popular literature such as Horatio Alger's *Ragged Dick* novels that portrayed poverty-stricken boys who rose to middle-class security in the crowded, competitive urban environment. Moralists interpreted the message of these plots and settings as rewards for hard work and living ethically, but typically Alger described significant barriers to social mobility in the city that are overcome through a stroke of luck often arising from a chance meeting or incident in a heartless environment filled with strangers (Tebbel 1963). Defenders of the cultural and moral effects of the city, who viewed a pluralist mix of national ancestries, religions, and races and were able to gain upward social mobility, imaginatively entrenched the lines between the yawning countryside characteristic of America's regions and the imposing towers of the city that belonged to the modern individualized world of tomorrow. They touted the high-rise apartment building that fostered independent living, especially for unmarried residents, and could promote neighborliness. It framed life in neighborhoods that often had a historic ethnic legacy and street culture. Although some historically ethnic areas such as Chinatowns formed because of discrimination, some urban enclaves embraced the identity of ethnic villages such as Hasidic sections of Brooklyn, Little Bangladesh in Los Angeles, and Little Ethiopia in Denver. Questions of socioeconomic class and displacement of residents arise from accusations of gentrification of old urban neighborhoods from "young urban professionals," many of whom came from the suburbs. In the "back-to-the-city" and "urban homesteading" movements of the late twentieth century, the sought-after structure that combined privacy with urban cosmopolitanism was the rowhome or townhouse over the high-rise (Bronner 1986a, 62–86; Hyra 2014; Schuerman 2019; Moskowitz 2018). These "yuppies" represented a new urbanized socioeconomic class more oriented to the multicultural and artsy neighborhood, and working from home, rather than in the downtown corporate skyscraper.

The 'Burbs

Despite Louis Sullivan's *fin de siècle* praise for skyscrapers and the "office" as the icons of future American democratic aspirations, through the twentieth century the major landscape change around the city was the suburban development marked by the sprawling ranch or Cape Cod house that spread out rather than up. As Ruth Suckow was critical of the standardization of gasoline stations and chain stores across the country, the Regionalist in her was also skeptical of the claims of wholesomeness for suburbia. Suburban "cookie-cutter" homes, as they were derisively called in reference to their repetitive production, appeared to have little relationship to the land or region, even though they brandished lush lawns that distinguished the suburban material culture from the rural farmstead and the urban townhouse. Without that relationship, critics asserted, suburban designs lacked cultural roots, community connection, and aesthetic appeal. Yet many Americans, and developers, hailed them as the materialization of the "American Dream" of propertied comfort and status.

A suburb literally refers to a spatial category under the domain of the city. Sparked by the rise of trolleys and light rail lines at the end of the nineteenth century, residential areas arose for commuting workers from home to work downtown. Houses built in these outlying areas could be larger than what was feasible in the city and this attracted a wealthy clientele to construct elaborate structures that departed from the traditional symmetrical Colonial-era facades. The expansion of car ownership and creation of highway systems along with the rise of a professional class in the mid-twentieth century sparked middle-class attraction to areas on the outskirts of cities. With the development of easily reproducible balloon-frame construction and the rise of a service and information economy, entrepreneurs saw the opportunity to build whole communities of similar-sized buildings in volume rather than the occasional custom-built home for the wealthy.

One such entrepreneur was William J. Levitt who saw a robust market after World War II of returning veterans who were quickly creating families. He had served in the Navy's construction battalions called Seabees and became familiar with building of military housing with uniform and interchangeable industrially produced parts. Selling houses in a planned community he called Levittown on Long Island, east of New York City on prospectus in 1947, Levitt sold 1,400 homes during the first three hours after they went on sale. On October 1 the same year 300 families, all white because of covenants excluding people of color, moved into their homes with street names suggestive of rural life such as Old Farm Road and Green Lane. New housing laws passed during the civil rights era ended the racial covenants, although many of the suburbs still had a reputation for being most welcoming to whites.

The original Levittown lots included a 750 square-foot house built on a concrete slab (25 x 30 feet) with ground for a front lawn and back yard. Workers completed a home in one day following 27 steps with specialists trained to perform one step. The standard house had two bedrooms, one small bathroom, and an eat-in kitchen. In 1949, the company adopted a "ranch house" label for the homes. The footprint expanded with the growth of a "living room" and the structure added an expandable attic and carport. The one-story ranch house floor plan designed for arid environments could be a problem in cold weather and central heating was a technological innovation that helped make it more suitable to any climate.

The term *ranch* suggested the vast open space of the frontier West, integration of exterior and interior environments, casualness of life, and a great expanse of propertied land. In keeping with the pattern of increasing living space, in 1963 the average new house had 1,450 square feet compared to 2,000 square feet

FIGURE 1.5 Levittown, New York, houses, 1958.
Source: Gottscho-Schleisner, Inc. photographer. Prints and Photographs Division, Library of Congress.

during the 1990s, and 2,430 square feet by 2010 (Muresan 2016). Living area per person for other countries pales by comparison to 807 square feet in the United States: Nigeria's 65, Turkey's 194, Russia's 237, Brazil's 258, China's 323, Germany's 484 (McCarthy 2020). Compared to available, newly built homes in 1910, the average American living in a newly built home enjoys 211 percent more living space a hundred years later. And the suburbs, with the growth of multi-car garages, playrooms, theater rooms, and finished basements, have led to the replacement of the ranch house label for suburban houses with the pejorative term "McMansion" referring to the mass-society scale of McDonald's hamburgers (Wagner 2017). The growth and variety of the suburban floor plan by the start of the twenty-first century suggested that rather than conforming to a house type, suburban spaces represented a widening range of income and social needs. Suburbia, if not the suburban house, became more of the residential standard.

Although suburban homes of various shapes and sizes typically have lawns and foyers as neutral spaces to reinforce the impression of the house's spaciousness, the utilized living space is in the back and represents an inward orientation away from community. The symbolically private house, in which children each have their own rooms, implies an emphasis on private property and individualism. Yet the social convention of the suburban house and its typical setting also allow for adjustment to necessary and frequent moves. Suburbs are largely interchangeable, so that if a family moves in or near another urban center, suburbia and its structure will be familiar. The order of the suburban plan is more than a response to movement and a desire for distinct private spaces. It also bespeaks conditions of change underlying suburban life for both parent and child. Architect William Hubbard has speculated that the shape of differentiation in the house has something to do with authority: "In a more authoritarian society, the children might have to pass through the parent's room to reach theirs—or at least symbolically to pass by their door. Neither happens in the typical suburban house-plan" (Hubbard 1981, 29). Within the home, space is divided between public and private space. The living room is typically a display piece, while many homes have a separate family room for social purposes. Eating might also be divided between a public dining room and a private kitchen space.

Instead of being oriented toward the entrance of a person, the suburban house welcomes the car. Despite the pivotal position of the car in suburbia, streets often curve in the manner of the countryside and take on bucolic names of trees and rural locations. They also want to suggest the intimacy of a village environment even though the structure of daily life orients residents socially inward. In Harrisburg, Pennsylvania, for example, suburban developments carry rustic names such as Paxton Hollow, Village Knoll, Lakewood Hills, and Tree View. Yet advertisements for these developments also underscore modernity and technological progress with rhetoric such as "contemporary," "the latest," and "completely equipped" (Bronner 1986a, 59). The fast construction of the suburban house made possible by technology also accommodated the newest appliances and private entertainment in the house's interior. That might appear to simulate urban space, but through the lawn the suburban house conspicuously projected the image of the country estate.

Sociologist Thorstein Veblen featured the distinctive American lawn and suburban space in his argument expressed in *Theory of the Leisure Class* (Veblen [1899] 1979) for "conspicuous consumption" in the United States social system. His theory was that in the suburban landscape in which middle-class neighbors are uncertain about their social standing, residents will reach for higher status by displaying their consumption of objects that represent their capacity for leisure. The consumables represent their ability to spend money on other people providing labor for them and the extent of equipment expended on work. According to Veblen, the American lawn symbolizes a "cow pasture," which would have been a status symbol in a rural economy. Maintaining the lawn in a suburban setting, however, requires human labor and assorted tools to keep it cropped, weeded, and lush. He wrote that "The close-cropped lawn is beautiful in the eyes of a people whose inherited bent it is to readily find pleasure in contemplating a well-preserved pasture or grazing land" (Veblen [1899] 1979, 134). At first glance, the lawn serves an aesthetic purpose, but Veblen thought that because it did not serve a pragmatic utility, the attainment of a technologically maintained green lawn filled a need to display social status to viewers. Its "expensiveness of the attendant circumstances bars out any imputation of thrift," he asserted (Veblen [1899] 1979, 134). With the visible signal of the lawn, conspicuously put in front of the suburban home, owners broadcast that they consume services and control property as well as people below them.

The representation of pastureland probably means less to twenty-first-century viewers of the suburban landscape than it did in the nineteenth century. As suburban development has grown, so too has the widening obsession with a manicured lawn serviced by a growing lawn-care industry worth 100 billion dollars, and over 500 dollars per household at the start of the second decade of the twenty-first century (Jenkins 1994; Mazareanu 2019; Steinberg 2006). Indeed, the expectation for the aesthetic "curb appeal," as realtors refer to the look of well-maintained house fronts, has expanded in suburban tracts with elaborate flower beds, garden paths, and lawn ornaments. Rather than pastureland, the representation of many lawns, particularly with the growth of McMansions, is the European manor house. Early in American colonial history, land grants given to favored gentry evolved into large agricultural estates reminiscent of feudal English and Dutch manor houses (Desmond and Croly 1903, 41–96). The lawn became infused into American imagination with the design of the White House in Washington, D.C., which *Architectural Record* editor Harry W. Desmond and *New Republic* founder Herbert Croly described as "the reproduction of a planter's manor-house, in a different material and on a somewhat larger scale" (Desmond and Croly 1903, 98). The officially named North Lawn described as the front lawn of the White House was redesigned in 1902 by Frederick Law Olmstead to restore the grounds to more of the function of a lawn that rises to the entrance and enhances the imposing nature of the house over the landscape (Pliska 2016).

Desmond and Croly reported that the prevalent tradition at the time of Olmstead's simpler design was an adaptation of English manor gardening to create "a big expanse of lawn, no straight lines, and an occasional shrub or tree. What flowers there were grown as a rule in circular beds or borders near the house" (Desmond and Croly 1903, 393–94). As early as 1918 the International Harvester Company advertised its products to new homeowners to "Make the Place Homelike" and warned that property is not homelike or healthy without a lawn, adding with patriotic fervor that "the strength of a nation lies in its homes" (International Harvester 1918; see also Lands 2008). Recognizing that in the "modern period" of the twentieth century constructed houses and acreage surrounding them were smaller than during the colonial period, the lawn created the effect of the occupants of the suburban house as "lords of the manor." The front lawn served the function of extending the approach to the house and widening the land for middle-class residents aspiring to upper-class control. As a space, suburbia also provided a barrier to what was viewed as moral threats of urban popular culture, including youth gangs, drugs, and violence (Riismandel 2020). The symbol of the gated community gave the impression of keeping out low-income urban trouble, and perhaps racialized others. In popular movies such as *The 'Burbs* (1989) and *Neighbors* (2014), suburbia raises mistrust of younger troublemaking strangers moving next door. Pictured as artificial and lacking in the grounding that a traditional small town or neighborhood in a city provides, an increasing number of horror films used suburbia as a backdrop for deviant behavior behind the facade of ordinary-looking residents (Bryant 2020; Siegel 2008). Filmmakers played off the commonly held image of suburban serenity and repression captured in the satirized name of *Pleasantville* (1998), for example, to show a dark underside of mayhem bursting out under stress (Muzzio and Halper 2002).

Yet for most Americans, suburban space still represented their ideal location when given a choice of city, country, and suburbs. In 1987, a Harris poll asked a sample of Americans about what they considered their "dream home" or ideal primary residence. Fifty-eight percent of respondents chose a "house on its own lot in the suburbs" (Roper Center 2021, 8/6–9/22/87, ID: USHARRIS.87HOME.R12A01). Asked to clarify in the same poll the attractive features of a dream home, the context of the land came immediately to mind. The top four choices were "A home with a great view" (16 percent), "More property/acreage" (13 percent), "Near places offering recreation such as beaches, mountains, or golf courses" (11 percent), and "More space/room" (11 percent). Seventeen years later, 51 percent of respondents still preferred the suburbs over the city (13 percent), although more people longed for a larger expanse of land in a rural community (35 percent) (Roper Center 2021, 8/26–9/6/2004, ID: USBELDEN.04COMMUN.R04). A Gallup poll in 2018 gave respondents more choices of big or small city, suburb of a big city, suburb of a small city, town, or rural area (Roper Center 2021, 11/13–11/18/2018, ID: 31115657.0011). Although the highest percentage of respondents chose a suburb, they showed a strong preference for living in a suburb of a big city (21 percent to 10 percent preferring a suburb of a small city). Twenty-seven percent selected "rural area" while those preferring an urban residence were divided between 17 percent in a small city and 12 percent in a big city (12 percent chose "town"). Reflecting on the growth of the suburbs in the United States as a major change during the twentieth century, most Americans responding to a Pew Research Center poll said that it was a "change for the better" (52 percent compared to 21 percent who thought it was a change for the worse) (Roper Center 2021, 4/6–5/6/1999, ID: USPSRA.070399.R12NF2). They held this opinion even though they told pollsters that the "big city" offered the best access to good healthcare, public services, and entertainment (Roper Center 2021, 2/18–2/22/2015, ID: USFTI.030915.R77). It appeared that the lure of containable property outside the city swayed them in their preference for suburbia. Rural areas had a hold in their thinking as the best place to raise children or grow old, but despite their attraction of open space, pragmatically Americans turned to the suburbs. They questioned, however, the Americanness of the suburbs in their answer to the question of what kinds of space represented the "real America." On that issue of authenticity—presumably referring to the relevance of cultural experience to the present—suburbs scored lowest at 10 percent. The highest was "big cities" (27 percent) followed closely by "rural areas" (22 percent) and "small towns" (21 percent). Interpreted another way, the result indicates a split in American worldview between the perceived wholesomeness of its landed heritage and the accelerated future-facing pace of urban progress. The suburbs appeared to be a hybrid of both, but its "betwixt and between" status and its artificiality left its cultural position uncertain.

Aware of the concern for the appearance of cultural authenticity, a twenty-first-century development is the construction of planned communities that invoke regional-ethnic culture, convey a small-town feel, and offer more social inclusivity (Argeros 2019; Li 2012; Roberts 2010). Part of this movement is triggered by the attraction of new immigrants to suburbs as gateway communities to what they think of as the American Dream or Promise of social mobility (Stanton 2020). Noticing suburban ethnic clusters of residences and businesses in large metropolitan areas, geographer Wei Li (2012) called these enclaves *ethnoburbs*. Although the ethnic suburban communities she observed in Los Angeles included a concentration of Chinese Americans, they did not compose the majority and other ethnic groups were also attracted to these suburban locations because of strong ties to the globalized economy of surrounding businesses and services. Although a development such as Hacienda Heights suggests a higher Hispanic connection, immigrants born in Taiwan were the largest minority group (Li 1998, 494–96).

In other metropolitan areas, developers have turned to names as well as designs that convey a regional cultural connection. For example, Rancho Sahuarita in the

Tucson, Arizona, metropolitan area is a planned community that opened in 2002 with buildings in a Spanish colonial design. It provides, according to a report on the new suburbs, "a cohesive sense of place" and "a sense of character that is largely absent from other MPCs [lifestyle master-planned community] in the region" (Urban Land Institute 2016, 27). The gated Preserve at Little Pine outside of Asheville, North Carolina, offers mountaintop vistas of the Blue Ridge Mountains from homes with log facades that suggest early American pioneers. Although the material culture is rustic, the audience is economically upscale. Spaciousness is emphasized in rhetoric such as "a preserved sanctuary as vast and varied as the great outdoors" (Preserve at Little Pine 2020). For most Americans, the image of the suburban space is more nondescript. They perceive it as a modern development, and maybe containing a sparse contemporary facade and plenty of consumer technology. They are hard-pressed to describe its features beyond the lawn and garage that could be replicated in any place in the country. Lodged in popular imagination as serene family havens privatized in the orbit of hectic cities, suburbia is tied to American ideas of economic attainment and social mobility by lording over manorial property.

Traditionalizing Space and Place

Defining freedom as living where one wants, Americans in their speech often brandish a paradoxical manifest destiny of free movement from shore to shore and simultaneously searching for roots in one's region to create a sense of place. Americans invoke region at certain moments and in selected places, and with certain people and settings. In reference to life "around here," wherever that is, people define place for themselves, since as folklorist Suzi Jones (1976, 106) suggests, "almost any culture group may be defined as regional, and the designation becomes so ubiquitous as to have little meaning." Often rejecting the thesis that region and community grows out of provincial isolation, analysts look for subjective evidence for the strategies that drive spatial thinking and action (Jones 1976, 107–10).

Jones (1976, 111–14) observes that legend telling is an ideal communicative frame for the strategy of regionalization in American culture because legendary material is often migratory and tellers make their narratives more compelling by including local and regional references. According to Jones's rhetorical reading of legends in context,

> A legend often begins with some measure of regionalization, with some reference to the specific environment (usually quite local) which is the setting for the legend. Such regionalization is a common feature of legends, for associating the event which is the subject of the legend with a specific locale is a means of asserting the reality of the event.
>
> *(Jones 1976, 112)*

One can usually hear many etymological stories of place names and natural features as part of growing up in a place, and the question Jones (1976) poses is when are they enacted and to whom—and perhaps most importantly, for what purposes (see also Nicolaisen 1976b, 1977). The preponderance of place-name and feature legends is arguably a function of historical settlement legacy and developed trait of mobility in the United States because of the view that American settlers were always the strangers on the land, and therefore the story of living in a region involves uncovering a hidden or ancient past. Indeed, one might venture the thesis that there is a psychological need to constantly narrate, and construct, region to verify a group or community's right to live there.

Other events besides legend telling bring out the process of, or need for, regionalization. Jones, who lives in Oregon, observes, for example, that people who live west of the Cascade Range are not assigned a regional identity or are lumped together by geographers with a large, vaguely cultural expanse called the "Pacific Northwest." Yet in her fieldwork, she identified folk speech such as "going to the coast" (rather than "to the ocean" or "to the beach" that outsiders use) and heard references to Oregonians living east of the Cascade Range as "bunch-grassers" (the westerners self-identify with the nickname of "webfoots" (Jones 1976, 107)). Further, they tell jokes about the constant rain and check insider status by the way they pronounce Willamette (one of many traditions of a pronunciation test often accompanied with narratives about its use including Lancaster, Pennsylvania, and Versailles, Indiana).

Some festive frames in which strategies of regionalization occur that might not be viewed as regional traditions often revolve around holiday customs. The celebration of New Year is an international event and is epitomized in the United States by the nationally televised "ball drop" in New York City's Times Square. Maybe in response to the massification of the holiday, or a need for community at a time of uncertainty for the future, in many places, it is an occasion to promote regional identity. In the PCR, it is common for residents to partake in a ritual meal of pork and sauerkraut on New Year's Day. The custom derived from Pennsylvania-German traditions of mid-winter feasting after butchering family hogs (Weaver 2013, 43). The celebratory dinners included the German specialty of sauerkraut as a symbol, like the pork, of abundance, because both the hog and the cabbage with which that tangy sauerkraut is made grew quickly to the point of excess. It attached to Pennsylvania communities after the heyday of home butchering in line with other expressive means to ensure luck in the new year. Often the belief would be explained with a traditionalized explanation, or metafolklore: pigs root forward, or make progress, the same direction that people want to go in the new year (Stonebeck 2018). The custom took on a regional association because to the South residents would eat black-eyed peas on New Year's Day. The symbolism of pork and cabbage for future good fortune, and a strategy of regionalization, was apparent in its serving along with the peas, supposedly because the peas represent coins and cabbage dollar bills. Expressing folk names for the special dishes can further regionalize the event; in the Carolina Lowcountry, the peas are served with rice and called "hoppin' John" while in Texas, cooks prepare a salsa called "Texas caviar" (Chavis 2007, 126).

Lyrics of many folksongs and their performances often evoke and reinforce regional associations (Cohen 2005). Folk material signifies traditions that are rooted in place, and raising voices in song together signals social learning as well as expression rooted in place. Folksongs are often commercialized about different regions, but the settings for various genres of music can be ritualized around region. Bluegrass festivals across the country, for example, although named for the bluegrass region of Kentucky, often celebrate Appalachian Mountain heritage in song, dress, and dance (Adler 1988; Rosenberg 2005). Blues festivals meanwhile pay homage to African-American regional roots in the Mississippi Delta and Chicago (Erlewine 2010). The social interaction in them and the performances of regionalized blues material often create the feeling of framing familiar space with representations or staging of Mississippi and Louisiana "juke joints," dance halls, homecomings, and family picnics (Cook 2012).

Less public musical events that ritualize family tradition steeped in place, such as the one I documented near the Mason–Dixon Line in Lancaster County, Pennsylvania, provide a sample of the regionalization strategies in a mobile society. I first interviewed Philip Owen (1928–2018) from Lancaster County, Pennsylvania, for his wooden cane carving (Bronner 1996, 169–74). Keeping to the theme of men's creativity in old age, I focused on his individual artistry and asked him questions about the social worlds that set him apart from his present surroundings. It became clear to me that he identified with his Appalachian upbringing in western North Carolina and a way that he related to feelings of disconnection was participation in regular family gatherings at the home of his sister, also in Lancaster County. Coming from a family of 12 siblings, he saw in them a simulation of his childhood environment, even though the circumstances were vastly different. Several generations were represented at the events who had no direct experience in the North Carolina mountains and were skeptical that this background constituted a special identity. Food was served but it was not regionally distinctive. There were occasions when quilting was done, but this did not involve everyone who came to the house. A way to inculcate a feeling for the past was to sing what the Owen siblings referred to as "old songs."

Although musicologists classify many of their ballads such as "Black Jack Davie," "House Carpenter," and "Barbara Allen" in their gatherings, the Huber-Owen singers thought of the songs as reminders of their homeplace in North Carolina. I noticed that they contextualized the singing in its connection to the family and their place in the land, and not of historical or musicological interest. They provided cues for storytelling about the family roots in the mountains and in the South. Most attendees, especially the younger ones, personalized their reason for being there—filial devotion to grandmother or great-grandmother—rather than out of a commitment to cultural preservation.

In the past, at least two members of the clan, Eva (Owen) Girvin and her husband Clarence "Doc" Girvin, also of Lancaster County, had taken to the stage, albeit in a limited way, to perform the songs. Ironically, at the Smithsonian Institution's Festival of American Folklife, the Girvins were contracted to represent the traditions of Pennsylvania, although their performance was billed as "Mountain Songs and Ballads" from the southern Appalachians (Smithsonian Institution 1969). They were joined at the festival by fellow North Carolinians Ola Belle and David Reed who also relied on their "mountain songs" to alleviate feelings of alienation in their new Pennsylvania home (Glassie, Murphy, and Peach 2015). Both families had migrated from rural enclaves in Ashe and Alleghany counties, North Carolina, to southcentral Pennsylvania factories during the Great Depression for economic reasons, and stayed in the area through the 1950s with development of large public works projects that attracted more southern migrants. Arguably there would be merit in analyzing their songs to note their persistence despite popular predictions of their doom, and posit the social psychological functions they provided for migrants as audience as well as performers of the music. The fact remained, however, that more family members were not motivated to perform publicly, and yet the family continued to assemble and sing together even after most of the Owen siblings had died.

Given that younger family members were born in Pennsylvania, why did they come back together for this celebration of a distant land, often travelling significant distances, in the midst of dramatic life changes? One answer is the creation of a shared social space within their dispersed, individualistic lives. The gatherings were ritualized as family events with expectations of being served food followed by unison singing. Packed into the dining room where photographs of the extended family hung on the walls along with religious artifacts, family members viewed food on the table as a symbol of shared sustenance offered in abundance. In this way the event fit into what folklorist Lin T. Humphrey (1979) identified as a "small group festive gathering" (SGFG) to create a sense of community out of members of a dispersed society. The SGFG arose conspicuously in the late twentieth century, she theorized, as a result of individuals who were alienated from one another by modern economic forces organizing repeated festive frames in which eating communally drove, or simulated, a social environment characteristic of a family unit or folk society. She, along with other ethnographers, viewed these gatherings as integrated into the "'ordinary' life of Americans" because they often served to metaphorically substitute a family away from the cognitive idea of home as where one grew up (Humphrey, Samuelson, and Humphrey 1991, 1). For the descendants of the Huber-Owen family, the action of singing together more than eating, or storytelling, gave them ownership of the practice to sustain the regional identity of the original family.

An important rhetoric of the occasion was that coming to the house was not considered "visiting"; it was a repeatable practice as much as going to church or work. Of course, one might inquire about the effectiveness of the strategy and the ways that it translated into a shift from an informal meeting to maintain a memory culture to an organized frame for social action within an understanding that outside the frame life is more individualized and heterogeneous. The praxis of mutual aid and hospitality also could be discerned to convey the idea that outside the frame, life is inharmonious and alienating. Without expressing their wishes to prioritize family identity, the elders had created a reproducible environment in which singing of "old songs" symbolized their plan for the future. Watching who was seated near the matriarch and delegated responsibilities, I detected that certain younger individuals were designated to "carry on tradition." I realized that their idea of tradition would involve more than gathering together; it required a social action recognized among the participants for its symbolism and practicality. And there was the strong possibility that despite the connection that the elders had built to their mountain roots, the meaning of the event would shift to one more about family cohesiveness in Pennsylvania rather than roots in North Carolina.

The rhetoric regarding the family's southern roots as a basis for the contemporary identity in traditionalized events such as the Huber-Owen gatherings and the processes and practices of singing, storytelling, and dining together that bonded them, imagined a regional "homeland" as relevant in collective memory as countries of national ancestry across vast oceans for immigrants. Huber-Owen family members do not have to step foot back in the mountains to use the homeland idea rhetorically, culturally, and psychologically. Richard Nostrand (1992, 14) defines the concept of a perceptual or subjective homeland as "emotional feelings of attachment, desires to possess, even compulsions to defend." Nostrand together with geographer Lawrence E. Estaville went on to identify 14 prominent homelands that have this kind of emotional, psychological function in the United States: New England Yankee, Pennsylvanian, Old Order Amish, Plantation South, Creole Coast, Nouvelle Acadie, LaTierra Tejana, Anglo Texan, Kiowa, Highland Hispano, Navajo, Deseret Mormon, Russian California, and Montane Montana (Nostrand and Estaville 2001). Based on rhetorical evidence, they mapped these areas that for the most part (exceptions are the Pennsylvanian and Mormon regions) have markedly different boundaries from the image of regional distribution created from objective cultural data. Drawn from perceptual and behavioral information, the boundaries, and designations, are highly variable. Noticeably left out of their list, for example, is a "mountain homeplace" (e.g., Appalachians to which the Huber-Owen family cling and Ozarks) often apparent in American folk narrative, architecture, and song (McNeil 1995a; McNeil 1995b; Williams 2004). Many of the homelands are based on ethnic-linguistic heritage and Nostrand and Estaville (2001, xxi) hypothesize that feelings of attachment to the homelands are strongest among ethnic groups whose folk cultures have been in decline (e.g., New England Yankee, Pennsylvanian, Russian California).

Mapping regional homelands is less of an outcome of rhetorical and ethnographic analysis than the assessment of settings and practices in which homelands are imaginatively remembered, forgotten, traditionalized, maintained, and constructed. Frequently presented research goals are to explain the role, and "sense," of place on the identities of a community and individuals within it; locate functions, strategies, and psychological motivations for participating in, and organizing, homeland-inflected events; evaluate interrelationships of ethnicity, religion, language, race, gender, and other social factors with locality, region, state, and nation; and interpret the effect of homeland thinking in the source area in addition to environments outside of it (see Diner 2000; Ferris 1982; Jabbour and Jabbour 2010; Ryden 1993). An example is the "dinner (picnic) on the grounds" in southern tradition that often accompanies family reunions (Camp 1989, 60–64). Organized as a cultural throwback to an earlier time, typically with familiar regional dishes of barbecue, fried fish, and hushpuppies, the dinner is ostensibly about reaffirming family members who have dispersed, particularly among African Americans since the period of the great northward migration between 1916 and 1970 (Wilkerson 2011; Yates 2006). The attendees at the dinners also connect a dislodged community that is seemingly "out of place" and probably have negative feelings about the historical conditions of the region, to a cultural source area or homeland. The dinners are often regular features of annually scheduled reunions, but can also be a part of a late-decade birthday party or golden anniversary for family members that underscore the southern homeplace as a cultural root. They create special cultural frames in which storytelling and singing are encouraged around the convivial function of providing "down-home" food in abundance, and consequently an emotional tie, if not social attachment, is developed. The reunion events frequently have a link to churches, and follow up with members through digital media. Variations abound of the festive reunion event connected to homeplace and provide an occasion to engage the distinctive American practice of the picnic, which in action fosters an appreciation, if not ownership, of the land as home (Camp 1989, 55–82; Edison 1988; Wachs 1988).

Border and National Culture

The designation of a national culture suggests clear distinctions between countries on either side of a boundary, but the shifting political, social, and natural lines that mark the southwestern border of the United States have raised questions about the cultural status of borderlands in relation to their administrative units. Walter Prescott Webb ([1931] 1959, 208), one of the first western American historians, delimited a special diamond-shaped region with San Antonio at the apex and an area across the Rio Grande border at the bottom. Known for its mixture of Mexican and American, or "Anglo," societies, cattle-raising according to Webb is its social as well as economic heart. What was different there from the Great Plains to the north and the forest and farm of the East, he observed, was the blending of northern Mexican ranchero with British-American stock farming that occurred in the course of building a cultural landscape based on the life of cattle ranching. Folklorist Américo Paredes ([1978] 2002, 201) later elaborated that "cattle and horses, as well as land, were Mexican to begin with; and when the Anglo took them over he also adopted many of the techniques developed by the ranchero for the handling of stock." The "culture of the border," while born of the union of Mexican ranchero culture with technological improvements brought by the "Anglos," carried over into a number of cultural expressions and the border culture of Mexico and the United States expanded in the Southwest in Texas from the Rio Grande and Nueces valleys to Baja and southern California (Graham 1991; Griffith 1995; Griffith 2011; Nájera-Ramírez, Cantú, and Romero 2009). In some historical conceptualizations that include Spanish colonial influence, the area extends even further east to the Carolinas (Hurtado 1996; Weisman and Dusard 1991).

The rise of hybridized border cultures based upon conflict of nationalities is hardly unique, as in historical examples in the lines between Scotland and England and Greece and Turkey (Buchan 1972; Kassabova 2018). American thinking about the U.S.–Mexico border might be distinctive, however, because of being wrapped up in the mythology of the frontier, racial overtones, and frequently shifting political boundaries (Baud and van Schendel 1997). Paredes theorizes a liminal "in-between existence" not only in place but also in levels of cooperation as well as conflict that engenders cultural expressions to address or resolve social and political paradoxes ([1978] 2002, 203). The area also has a background as a liminal frontier space rather than a precise line suggested by the rhetoric of border. In light of a long history of treating the area as remote from the political rule of both Mexico and the United States, the region is generally perceived as an inchoate frontier in which residents can shape its own culture. Paredes ([1978] 2002, 205) also notes historically that the partition of the Lower Rio Grande communities fostered a "set of folk attitudes" that included "a favorable disposition toward the individual who disregarded customs and immigration laws, especially the laws of the United States." Despite blending of ethnic traditions along the border, the cultural process, according to Paredes, cannot be recognized as fully hybridized because of socialized divisions between Mexicans and Anglos. Carrying a distinct identity of Mexicans because of language and racialization, in Paredes's words, they have "always been on the defensive in the border situation, afraid of being swallowed whole…The folklore shows [their] preoccupation about remaining 'Mexican' even when [they are] becoming most Americanized" (Paredes [1978] 2002, 213; see also Cantú 2002, 2005; Limón 1983; Villarino and Ramírez 1992).

Especially expressive of Mexican-American views of border cultural liminality has been the *norteño corrido* (northern ballad) (Herrera-Sobek 1993; Paredes 1995). Often traced to medieval romances set in ballad form, *corridos* about folk heroes and legendary events with political overtones in the contested border region of the American Southwest circulated widely in oral tradition among Mexican Americans. Paredes found special significance to songs and stories of Gregorio

Cortez (1875–1916) born on the Mexican side of the border but raised in Texas (Paredes 1958). "El Corrido de Gregorio Cortez" first circulated orally in the early twentieth century and continued to be sung into the twenty-first century (Chávez 2012). According to the legend that inspired the ballad, Cortez was unjustly accused of horse theft by a gringo sheriff and violence erupted when the law moved in to arrest him. A long chase ensued that added to Cortez's mystique as possessing extraordinary strength and perseverance. Stories circulated that he had walked 100 miles, ridden more than 400, all the while being pursued by a posse of 300 men. Eventually Cortez was caught and put on trial. He was acquitted for the murder of one sheriff but not the other. He was sentenced to life in prison, but when pardoned by the governor, his Mexican-American admirers interpreted the events as a triumph of justice for oppressed Mexicans at the hands of gringos in the border region. Indeed, the *corrido* form calls for a moral lesson and farewell from the singer after giving a salutation and relating the story.

Although *corridos* became commercialized by recording companies and broadcast on television and radio, many folklorists point out that the folk process is still evident in an evolution of the folk hero *corrido* into the *"narcocorrido"* (McDowell 2012; Morrison 2008; Wald 2001). Emerging in the 1970s, the *narcocorrido* features the traditional tripartite *corrido* structure of salutation, description of events, and moral lesson to relate legends of fabled drug smugglers and dealers and their brazen exploits. Folklorists listen for circulating motifs in the lyrical content within the context of shared folk performance styles. For example, in 2015 when drug lord Joaquin "El Chapo" Guzman escaped from Mexico's most secure prison, songs quickly circulated outside of media outlets that portrayed him as a Robin-Hood figure, rags to riches mythology, his braggadocio in declaring that the authorities could not keep him, and his vanity, or cunning, in escaping without messing up his hair (Martinez et al. 2015). Ambivalence could be heard in the moralizing typical of the genre, including questioning the power, and obsession, with having more money than one could possibly use. As with other popular expressions of ethnic groups with a persistent community presence, folk aspects are couched within an older tradition and the content compared with earlier themes, often to bring out the resistance to assimilation and hybridization with other traditions within the massified American experience.

The undefended northern border of the United States presents a different cultural situation from that of the Southwest. Folklorist Robert Klymasz (1983) reports cultural awareness of the border especially among indigenous groups who as part of the Jay Treaty of 1795 were granted unrestricted travel across the U.S.–Canada border (Klymasz 1983). The claim to the region is dramatized, and folklorized, every July with a border-crossing parade that, according to Klymasz (1983, 228),

> by force violates the values of both the laws and the nationalism of Americans and Canadians. As parade, festival, and mass-media drama, the event helps to set the native people apart from all others, in a symbolic act that

validates their identity. It also serves as a social event and annual holiday ritual for Indians in the border area.

After the parade, Native folk artists demonstrate traditional crafts and foodways to symbolize the persistence of their culture in the face of pressure from both countries. Indeed, the border-crossing event and others based upon the relationship of indigenous nations that pre-existed Canada and the United States can be analyzed rhetorically and ethnographically for their use of festival and performance to frame views of region, tradition, and nationalism.

An ethnic borderland that compels more cultural attention is the area between Quebec and the northeastern states of the United States extending into the Canadian maritime provinces. From Maine on up, the border-transcending term Acadia is colloquially used to refer to the French-influenced culture that has roots in the colony of New France. Yet even across the northern tiers of New York, New Hampshire, and Vermont, the Francophone connection can be discerned that suggests a development of cultural exchange characteristic of border culture. According to cultural geographer Peter M. Slowe (1991), this transnational exchange is not fostered by ranching as it was near the Rio Grande, but they share a legacy of smuggling. Traffic across the Canadian border increased dramatically as a result of the prohibition of alcoholic beverages during the 1920s. Certainly before then there was cultural exchange among the English and French-speaking groups that worked the forestry industries, and later hunting and recreational activities, especially in Maine and New Hampshire (see Bethke 1981; Dan Kirk 2018). Smuggling is still apparent, notably for cigarettes across the boundary of the Mohawk Indian reserve that spreads out at the junction of New York, Ontario, and Quebec, and adds an indigenous factor into the ethnic mix of the region. Back-and-forth traffic that fostered a borderlands identity is most evident, according to Slowe, in modern consumer culture. In the twenty-first century, as the borderlands in Maine and New Hampshire are mostly uninhabited, in the towns and villages of northern Vermont and New York, sometimes colloquially called the "North Country," a social economy arose around cross-border shopping because of different tax laws (Slowe 1991, 193). Beyond the association with bilingualism in the region, folkloric evidence indicates regionalization of cultural expressions such as jokes, foodways, music, and legends rhetorically designating a borderland (Fox 2007; Slowe 1991, 196–97; TAUNY 2016).

That borderlands are dependent on the integration of the nations surrounding them raises the question of the strength of a national culture for the relatively young United States with its pluralistic ethos. Given the regional and ethnic diversity that has been described, how does border culture convey commonalities for people calling themselves Americans? Commenting on the founding of the New Republic in 1789, which established unity to offset sectional divisions, Richard M. Dorson argues that writers, artists, and civic leaders mythologized a pantheon of national heroes beginning with George Washington in the early nineteenth century (Dorson 1966). With a lack of a national epic or aristocratic legacy, many heroes that became legend were cast as earthy comic demigods, including Davy Crockett, Daniel Boone, and Kit Carson. In story and song, they were rugged individualists, scrapping for a fight, and ready to expand the frontier. Using print and visual sources, Dorson (1973) connects them to the social construction in folklore of later heroes that exemplified a national future-oriented spirit of optimism and expansive pluck (Dundes 1969). In postindustrial America, folklorists point out that for contemporary legends and rumors, thematic shifts are apparent when examining them in aggregate. Narratives of celebrities, if not hero tales, exemplify conversations about the relations of ordinary individuals to a national mass culture. They often enter into discourse on the effects of commercial culture and fame (e.g., celebrity death hoaxes for Miley Cyrus, Michael Jordan), race and violence (e.g., rumors of how riots began), and government conspiracy and political leaders (e.g., a cabal of Satan-worshiping pedophiles plotting against the president, COVID-19 vaccines containing aborted fetal cells), and concerns for differences between the promise and reality of an open society such as the United States that should be different from the less tolerant rest of the world (Fine 1994; Fine and Turner 2001; Turner [1920] 1996).

The Americanness of Mobility

In 1981, journalist Joel Garreau scored a national bestseller with *The Nine Nations of North America* in which he included a map of the northern hemisphere that would anticipate the political news of the day. It was based upon reporters' perceptions rather than objective cultural evidence, and yet its boundary lines paralleled results of many geographers' regional analyses based upon objective data. The familiar label of New England was there, although Garreau extended its influence well north into Canada. One could see the conventional outline of the South in the nation he dubbed "Dixie" but he omitted distinctions between upland and lowland regions. The location of the PCR was displaced with an economically driven region of the "Foundry" extending into the Midwest. Another economically driven region of gargantuan proportions was the "Breadbasket" that spanned most of the West. The borderlands that Webb identified had grown substantially into "MexAmerica." Absent was the MCR, replaced with a vast area that Garreau apparently dismissed as "The Empty Quarter." He completed the survey of North America regions with a coastal area stretching from California to Alaska that he dubbed "Ecotopia" and a maritime region from Florida to the Caribbean that he simply called "The Islands." Other Americanists revised his map of regional cultures, often adding sections while maintaining the rhetoric of distinct and often rival "nations." (Woodard 2011, for example, surveys 11 regional "nations" in North America.)

Garreau's rhetoric of nations signified that despite the massification of the United States resulting from rapid industrialization in the twentieth century, and its supposed homogenization of American culture, region and a sense of place still mattered to Americans. With another dramatic change in the twenty-first century ushered in by a reported revolution of digital communication, rapid transit, and an information/organizational economy, cultural criticism again was leveled against Americans that they no longer cared about place as an identity marker or a nexus of their daily lives. After all, websites upon which people rely are not bound by place (indeed it is often difficult to find an address on a "homepage"), advertisers promote the boon of being "mobile" and going "wireless" as liberating for a better life, and youth become accustomed, in conversational rhetoric, to "pick up and go." Although the Pew Research Center which monitors American social and demographic trends recognized that Americans in the wake of the digital age are portrayed as "restless and rootless," census data indicated that a longing for community was manifested in declining rates of relocation (Cohn and Morin 2008; see also United States Census Bureau 2016). Still, around 11 percent of all Americans move in any year, amounting to over 45 million people (with around two million emigrating outside of the United States). The U.S. Census has noted increased out-migration from the North to the South and West that affects regional perceptions of habitation (62 percent of Americans lived in the North in 1900 compared to 39 percent in 2015, while the South hosts 38 percent of the U.S. population) (Devine 2017). These trends indicate a new twenty-first-century regional demarcation of a "Sun Belt" stretching from southern California to Florida that suggests shared bodylore of leisure activities and health into old age. They also raise questions about "snowbirds" with multiple residences and their regional affiliation and ritual year practices. But even if Americans are not moving as much as pundits predicted, does not digital technology encourage people to be alone more and not interacting with community and gaining a sense of place and home space (Franzen 2000; Katz and Aspden 1997; Mesch 2001)?

Asked whether the observation of a regional cultural layout of America still applied in the wake of a new age marked by dramatic technological and economic changes, Garreau responded:

> More than three decades after publication, two things amaze me: how little the boundaries have changed and how much chatter this idea is getting recently. Much of the online discussion in the last few years has been spurred by dismay over American national gridlock and the 'nine nations' divisions that fuel it.
>
> *(Garreau 2014)*

Despite recognizing heightened mobility, if not relocation, and communication that seemingly obviates the need for rooting one's self, and culture, in a region, Garreau (2014) finds that:

> every North American also knows a place where, on your way back from your wanderings, surroundings stop feeling threatening, confusing or strange.

Ultimately, that is the reason we are nine nations. When you're from one, and you're in it, you know you're home.

Added to the kinds of evidence usually considered in historical and geographic approaches in the twenty-first century are digital images, texts, and processes that define groupness around space and place (e.g., regional dialect and character memes, email humor, video posts of regional legend trips); creation of "networked" participants into a virtual region; material and organizational culture of incipient places and cultural scenes that apply or distort regional practices (e.g., housing developments, regional and urban planning, summer camps, and other temporary environments); festivals, heritage and nostalgic events, vacations, sporting events, political campaigns, and community celebrations—popular sites of traditionalization—in which region and nation play a central role. Representation of regional experience in touristic landscapes additionally contribute to homeland consciousness and construction. With these different trajectories, the perception of America among residents of the United States, if not from abroad, is informed by the complex American space that stretches outward on the land and upward toward the sky.

2
TIME

Elected in 1996 to serve as President into a new century, Bill Clinton announced a national mood of expectation in his second inaugural address:

> It is our great good fortune that time and chance have put us not only at the edge of a new century, in a new millennium, but on the edge of a bright new prospect in human affairs—a moment that will define our course, and our character, for decades to come.

It was a moment, in short, when Americans, used to thinking ahead, were asked intensely about the future. Clinton's homespun message in his second inaugural address called on Americans planning their individual destinies to think collectively when he said simply, "[T]he future is up to us." As the year 2000 approached, American polls repeatedly measured the national "mood" in light of individual beliefs about the future. Gallup, Torrance, Zogby, CNN, USA Today, ABC News, and the Pew Research Center, among others, polled Americans about their feelings for the impending millennium "event" and their hopes and fears for the next year, generation, and century. Based on the experience of the last turn of the century, many publishers, educators, and politicians encouraged reflections on the century just past as much as the era ahead. But it was a rare poll as the twentieth century ended that actually asked Americans about their view of the past. To be sure, authorities were queried for the greatest events, presidents, books, films, and television shows of the last century, but it was as much a sign of the difference of their historical perspective from the man or woman on the street as it was some national reflective urge. To get at attitudes toward the future, polling organizations sampled everyday Americans, presumably because everyone had their eyes on the millennial horizon. And more of them asked about views in

DOI: 10.4324/9780429452970-3

the United States than for any other country in the world. Judging from publication records such as the electronic database of Periodical Abstracts, more magazine covers and book titles on American shelves probed or predicted the future than for any other nation.

It is hardly news to say that Americans as a whole are relatively future-oriented, but what is more novel is to explore the various meanings of the future they hold in light of not only comparative polling data, but the process of polling in America, which has become part of the nation's popular culture. Further, this exploration suggests the question of whether a future-orientation necessarily displaces fidelity to tradition, or whether the distinctive American attitude, if one can be identified, rather complicates the American idea of tradition. In this chapter, I review the past contributions from several disciplines toward a definition of American future-orientation and examine the attitudes toward the future and tradition apparent in polls at the pivotal moment of the new millennium. I choose a moment such as the dawn of the new millennium for my baseline evidence because it was then that the future became especially open for national reflection.

Questioning the Future

A future-orientation is apparent in the fever for polling around the time of the millennium, since in asking repeatedly about the future, pollsters assumed that Americans were thinking about it. Or did pollsters create a sport of predictions of the future? Historically, polls arose primarily to gauge opinions about the present, but surveys of attitudes toward the future can be traced to the 1950s. Checking the database of the Roper Center for Opinion Research (2021), for example, one can locate 597 polls with the keywords "future" and "mood" for the 40-year period between 1948 and 1988. The 11-year period of 1989–2000, when *fin de siècle* reflections accelerated, generated 690 hits. Between June 1998 and June 2000, when news reports of the coming of the new millennium were most apparent, a surge occurred of 151 polls and surveys on Americans' feelings about the future. Using evidence from polls conducted between 1948 and 2000, I review the answers to questions of the future as a guide to an American worldview generally. I check these results with polls in 2020 when effects of a global pandemic, economic struggle, divisive presidential election, and race relations crisis could have potentially dashed Americans' optimism for the future and their supposed "can-do" attitude.[1]

Cultural critics often tie future-orientation of Americans to a view of inevitable progress. Related to expansionist ideas of Manifest Destiny and celebration of individual ingenuity, the future is expected not only to be an improvement on the present but also larger in scale. Sociologist Florence Kluckhohn, for example, commented that "Americans, more than most people of the world, place emphasis upon the future—a future which we anticipate to be 'bigger and better'" (Kluckhohn 1953, 349; see also Mead 1951; Williams 1952, 405). Alan Dundes used the evidence of comparative folklore as expressions of deep-seated beliefs to make the case for "the tendency of Americans to look, think, and plan ahead." If proverbs reflect collective wisdom, then common American sayings such as "The ends justify the means," "The best is yet to come," and "Tall oaks from little acorns grow" in Dundes's collection show that "Americans look into the future in part because they are end oriented" (Dundes 1969, 57). Beyond the conditioning of an inherited value placed on ends, Dundes argued that American folklore, based as it is on tradition, ironically repudiates the past. In sayings such as "Let bygones be bygones" or beliefs that retracing one's steps is bad luck, the message resounds that looking back is counter-productive.

Viewing the future as positive set against a negative feeling for tradition is often incorporated into characterizations of American personalities. Guidelines sent to international students sent out by Cornell University and other institutions, for example, include belief in "progress and change" as fundamental to answering the question "What is a US American?" The guide explained:

> Most people in this country accept change as an inevitable part of life. Non-western people tend to look upon their traditions as a guide to the future. Americans are more inclined to make decisions based on the anticipated or desired immediate future. Achievement, positive change, and progress are all seen as the result of effort, hard work, and the control of nature and one's destiny or future.
> *(Cornell University 2000)*

In this explanation, the definition of the future is attached to feelings of control over destiny. If America encourages individualism (another American trait highlighted in the guide), there is risk, even anxiety, that one's goal is not tied to a public destiny. That suggests the need to worry about controlling one's "anticipated or desired immediate future," and implies a constant concern for how the future can be shaped to meet *one's* desires.

Supporting the idea that Americans are obsessed with the future, economist Robert Heilbroner qualified Americans' view of the past by asserting that Americans are not so much against following traditions and honoring heritage as they are uncomfortable with the determinism of the past. American future-orientation in his view is about youth breaking away from their parents and getting a "fresh start." In addition, America is a "land of opportunity" with entrepreneurial innovation and many choices among infinite possibilities. He wrote:

> We are naturally sympathetic to ideas which stress the plasticity and promise, the openness of the future, and impatient with views which emphasize the "fated" aspect of human affairs. We strive to see in the challenges which beset us not obstacles but opportunities. In a word, we are an optimistic people.
> *(Heilbroner 1960, 16)*

The call for a changeful future, of feeling optimism for the different road ahead, especially resounds through American politics. To cite one prominent example, Ronald Reagan, often pegged with promoting "traditional values," nonetheless used the purportedly national trait of optimism in his second inaugural address when he declared, "Voices were raised saying we had to look to our past for the greatness and glory. But we, the present-day Americans, are not given to looking backward. In this blessed land, there is always a better tomorrow" (see Bronner 1998a, 55–68).

While Reagan, Dundes, and Heilbroner paint America with broad cultural brush strokes, Evon Vogt claimed ethnographic documentation of the attitude toward the future as crucial to the life of a single community in Texas he called "Homestead." He generalized that:

> to look forward to the future, to forget or even reject the past, and to regard the present only as a step along the road to the future, is a cherished value in American culture and a conspicuous feature of life on the frontier.
> *(Vogt 1955, 93)*

He pointed to evidence from high school student autobiographies, and correlated a future-orientation with prominent values placed on progress, optimism, and success. In his reference to the frontier is a historical argument for the influence of western expansion to American character commonly attributed to historian Frederick Jackson Turner:

> Each frontier did indeed furnish a new field of opportunity, a gate of escape from the bondage of the past; and freshness and confidence, and scorn of older society, impatience of its restraints and its ideas, and indifference to its lessons, have accompanied the frontier.
> *(Turner [1920] 1996, 38)*

The hold of the idea of the frontier in American imagination is strong evidence for future-orientation, since the frontier implies the fresh start for new settlers as they moved west toward a promised future with new opportunities. Even the move from Old World to New announced a sense of a future, different from what occurred before, as Hector St. John de Crèvecoeur implied in his famous question posted in 1782, "What then is the American, this new man?" that "a modern society offers itself to his contemplation, *different from what he had hitherto seen*" (Crèvecoeur [1782] 1971, 39, emphasis added). The future is broadly defined and apparently open-ended as a matter of a break from the past rather than a planned venture.

Yet it may be argued that the frontier also represented a move toward the primitive past, away from the progressive bases of industrial development. For many observers, America's future-orientation in a modern society emerged from its rapid industrialization and urbanization after the frontier closed. The link of technological advancement with a sense of progress in the future became pronounced in American popular literature, art, and architecture by the end of the nineteenth century, according to historians Joseph Corn and Brian Horrigan ([1984] 1996, xii). They point out, "Since at least the late nineteenth century, a portrait of the future as a secular utopia erected on technological and scientific innovation has loomed large in our culture." Henry Adams set a literary tone for this view in *The Education of Henry Adams* ([1918] 1931) with a reflection on the Great Exposition of 1900 in which he saw the dynamo on exhibit as a symbol of sudden, profound change in the new century and a symbol of power for a decidedly new era. The change was to a long period of classic civilization epitomized by the virgin goddess with "natural" qualities of innocence and virtue. Inspired by Adams one hundred years later, literary critic Sanford Pinsker nervously declared the microchip as the herald of the next futuristic era (Pinsker 2000). The microchip draws even more awe because on the space of a fingertip it holds the power of the huge dynamo needing a building to house it. The era it signals appropriately magnifies the resources of energy developed since the dynamo because it enters a new millennium. The implication in the millennial era is that the advancement of the chip over the dynamo in a short time signals an ever-advancing, even more imposing future. In this type of thinking, the future appears closer, and probably more powerful, because it means immediate changes in structures of life. The theme, as stated by journalists such as James Gleick in *Faster: The Acceleration of Just About Everything* (1999), is "Technological change just keeps getting faster, and it speeds up everything else in life with it" (Allen 2000, 18). Indeed, in millennial thinking the past seems less and less distant as each new mark of the future in technology promises a radical break from tradition.

Forming the future may appear easier in the United States than grasping its tradition. The function of tradition as helping to form a national heritage has been problematic because of the lack of an ancient historic lineage, common racial stock, and consistent geography (see Bronner 2002). Public concern in the twentieth century for locating a common American tradition based on a shared heritage could be interpreted as a response to a lack of feeling for a collective American past, especially in light of growing racial, ethnic, and class conflicts. A national profile based on a future-orientation was one way to summarize American ascension. Historian David Potter's *People of Plenty* (1954) tied the orientation to the future as a function of the promise of success and abundance in America, especially within family contexts. As he explained, the American

> is keenly aware of class distinctions and class levels, which are powerful realities in America, though they lack the tangibility of such distinctions in the Old World, but he conceives of the class hierarchy as a ladder whose rungs are to be ascended rather than as a set of pigeonholes whose compartments

are identified with permanent status. Projecting this success drive to his children, he expects them to have a different future and an achievement greater than his own. Mobility and change are natural by-products of his quest for success, and departure from the patterns of the past is a matter of course.

(Potter 1954, 48)

The conditions of the 1950s, including America's post-war prosperity and technological advancement, raised the future as political ground, for scenarios of peace and destruction became commonly debated in light of the Cold War tension, nuclear arms buildup, and space technology development.

Coinciding after World War II with the growth of scholarship on a national future and tradition characteristic of a leading country in the world, some of the first polls on confidence in the future emerged. Rudimentary polls to that time had primarily been used to measure political and economic trends, but because of interest in post-war cultural change in addition to recovery, some polls focused on social/psychological attitudes as well as economic/political values. The wording was often vague as polls struggled to measure feelings about events that had not yet occurred. Although not explicitly tying the confidence in the future to the state of the economy or political stability, they nonetheless referenced that view because of the context of the questions. In February 1948, *Time* magazine asked 1,000 adults "Five years from now do you expect to be better off than you are now, worse off, or about the same?" Overwhelmingly, Americans thought they would be "better off." Only 11 percent thought they would be worse off, as compared to 56 percent who thought their lot would improve. When the Roper Organization polled 3,014 adults with a similar question in July 1948, in the midst of inflation worries and widespread labor unrest, the results were significantly different. Asked "Do you expect that the next few years are going to bring better times, worse times, or do you think we'll go along about as we are now?" 31 percent thought "worse," 39 percent replied "go along the same," and only 19 percent said "better." Repeating the survey two straight months resulted in similar results. By the beginning of the decade, a trend had been set. Rather than ask what kind of future Americans beheld or wanted, pollsters sought replies measuring optimism in the form of opinions for a "better" or "worse" future. "The future," however, was not stated, probably because it implied an era more distant in time. Pollsters' corporate clients interested primarily in short-term returns wanted to plan their moves in the "next few years." In June 1951, the National Opinion Research Center asked, "Looking ahead about ten years from now, do you think things will be generally worse, than they are today?" Forty-four percent thought better, 30 worse, and 11 about the same. What is not clear is whether the respondents meant better or worse economically, socially, or personally. Gallup joined the National Opinion Research Center three years later to refer to "life" as a measure of well-being: "On the whole, do you think life will be better or worse, in the next few years than it is now?" The sample at this point had ballooned to almost 5,000 and the questions were directed toward an interpretation of concerns about communism, conformity, and civil liberties on quality of life. The answers were led by 57 percent who replied "better," while 13 percent said "worse" and 22 percent told interviewers "about the same."

In the responses to the polls of the 1950s, a confidence could be detected that American progress could not be stopped. Still, the references seemed based on contemporary conditions rather than a broad philosophy of the future. One indication was the question of the National Opinion Research Center offered in 1948 and 1952: "Many people say that they can live from one day to another at this time. Do you think this way too, or do you believe that you can make plans for the future?" In both years, nearly seven out of ten Americans in the sample thought one could make future plans. The view that the future can be planned implies that the future, or change associated with it, is imminent, and therefore can be discovered and exploited for those having foresight and initiative. A *Washington Post* poll conducted during the summer of 1999, just before the new millennium, continued this line of inquiry by asking respondents their level of agreement with the statement "It doesn't do any good to plan for the future because you don't have control over it." Nearly eight out of ten respondents disagreed, indicating their view that the future was steered rather than awaited. Indeed, one could argue that this planning for the future was part of the American optimism frequently referred to as part of a national trait. An NBC News/ *Wall Street Journal* poll in September 1999 even used this optimism as an assumption when it asked: "In the twentieth century, America has been marked by a can-do spirit of optimism. Looking ahead to the next hundred years, do you think that this spirit of optimism will increase, stay about the same, or will decrease?" Corroborating the results of the *Washington Post* poll, 72 percent of the more than 2,000 respondents said the spirit will continue or increase. Only 22 percent thought the spirit would decrease and 6 percent were not sure.

Beginning in the 1960s, more polls could be found implying awareness of rapid changes in technology along with changing urban patterns. Gallup reframed its earlier questions about life with specific reference to the future. It also encouraged respondents to think philosophically, to counteract the tendency to have a rosy view of the future based solely on the prospects for a rise in income. Seeking to identify American "hopes and fears," Gallup asked "Here's a somewhat philosophical question. In general, are you completely satisfied to be living now in the present—or would you prefer to have lived sometime in the past, or to live sometime in the future?" Eighty percent of a national sample of 1,564 adults answered "now," while 10 percent preferred the "past." Only 8 percent wanted the future, while 3 percent said "don't know." On its surface, the response negates the assumption of a future-orientation, but the context of multiple problems that provided fears and worries may have led many respondents away from choosing the future. Especially on the minds of Americans was "living in fear of war; devastation from war's consequences; nuclear war" (51 percent). Even their wishes and hopes were expressed in terms of war; 54 percent offered that their hope for the United States ten years into the future was "peace; no war or nuclear war; freedom from fear of war or devastation." Another interpretation is that if the future is imminent, then Americans think of the present as full of change, and consider philosophical references to the future as meaning a distant, uncertain vision that cannot be easily planned. An argument could be made that Americans were optimistic about the future pragmatically conceived, because when asked where in ten years the United States would be on a ladder where the top rung of 10 represents the best and 0 represents the worst, 57 percent answered between 8 and 10. Americans often voice practicality as an American trait and a reasoning behind their answers to survey questions as well as life choices. Channeled into a home-grown tradition of pragmatism, many Americans tend to voice an emphasis on future beneficial outcomes, prioritizing problem solving over ideology and success over status, working together with people of differing opinions on solutions that will often involve compromise, or as stated bluntly by a team of researchers advocating to add pragmatism to liberty and freedom as basic American values, "Value that which works, discard that which does not" (Norwine, Bruner, Ketcham, and Preda 2000, 29; see also Koppell 2019; Mieder 2020, 155–84).

When questioned where the United States was five years before, at the end of the Eisenhower Administration, only 24 percent of respondents in the previous Gallup poll answered in the top range. And personally, they felt good about their prospects. When asked where they stood on the "ladder of life," the largest percentage (21 percent) chose the fifth rung. When queried on their best guess about where they will stand five years from now, the largest percentage chose the top rung (22 percent). In responses to the "ladder questions," the sense is evident that when Americans thought about the future, they considered their prosperity first and health second. They said so in answer to the question "When you think about what really matters in your own life, what are your wishes and hopes for the future? In other words, if you imagine your future in the best possible light, what would your life look like, if you are to be happy?" Forty percent answered "improved or decent standard of living for self or family," while 29 percent said "one's own health." When the question substituted "the country" for "you," the answers were more varied. While 24 percent said "improved or decent standard of living," 50 percent chose "peace," and other matters such as "national unity" (13 percent) and "improved education" (9 percent) drew substantial affirmation.

Fast forward to the end of the century. Dramatically, "peace; no war/freedom from fear of war or devastation" was the choice of only 1 percent of the sample. Reference to the standard of living was divided between those who hoped for "greater national prosperity" (15 percent) and those who sought "improvement of present standard of living through technological advances/increase in rate of mechanization, use of modern scientific advances" (36 percent). Only 1 percent was concerned about "national unity," but significant percentages wished for "economic stability" (13), employment (14), and improvement of labor conditions (8). Social and ethical issues were more noticeable at the end of the century: "eliminate discrimination" notched 10 percent and "morality and/or religion among the people" attracted 8 percent of the sample. Although previous polls showed correlations between the self-perception of personal "quality of life" and the country's status, by century's end the ladder image showed differences between perceptions of personal and national futures. The mean for personal "quality of life" projected five years from 1999 was 8.2; the average for ratings of the country was 6.6. Eight years earlier, Roper collected similar information when it asked "How do you feel about the future?" When respondents were asked about their "personal future," 64 percent replied "generally optimistic" while only 6 percent said "generally pessimistic" (27 percent were uncertain). When considering the nation's future, however, the numbers dramatically changed: the largest portion, 49 percent, was uncertain, while 36 percent reported generally optimistic and 13 percent said pessimistic. These numbers could be compared with Roper's results in 1979 when 57 percent of respondents were optimistic about the country's future, while 23 percent were uncertain and 17 were pessimistic.

The difference between projections of personal and national futures seemed to stem from the view that the economy was solid but the culture was not. Shortly after the New Year of 2000, a poll by the Tarrance Group tried to get specifics on the attitude toward the future of the country. Asked "When you say the country is off on the wrong track, what in particular are you thinking about?"; the highest percentage answered "lack of moral values/incivility in society." The closest other categories were "government not working" (7) and "general rising crime." Yet for those who thought the country was headed in the right direction (39 percent; 49 percent thought it was on the wrong track), the meaning was simple: "the economy" (47 percent). Roper's general questioning about the country's future supported the interpretation of lack of cultural confidence when it found that 43 percent of its sample were "pessimistic" about "the moral and ethical standards in our country" (26 percent were optimistic, 27 percent uncertain, 3 percent did not know).

Even though questions about "direction," "five years from now," and even "a decade" purport to be about the future, the polling data indicate that respondents answered with reference to their present situation. So when is the future? Did the publicity for the new millennium encourage millennialist thinking of "1000" years ahead? Is American "vision" more generational, or limited by centuries, or quarter-centuries? Or if the future-orientation of Americans is a reality, is it less of a matter of time and more of an attitude?

The unusual high number of polls sponsored in 1999 and 2000 helps to answer these questions. A distinctive feature of polls during this time was questioning about the next century. Although the new millennium loomed at the time, pollsters considered a new century more graspable. Compare these two independently sponsored polls released the same month in 1999.

Survey Sponsor: NBC News/*Wall Street Journal*	
Organization Conducting Survey:	Hart and Teeter Research
Release Date:	September 1999
Number of Participants:	2,025
Interview Method:	Telephone
Population:	National Adult
Do you think the next hundred years will be better or worse for America than the last hundred years were?	
Will be better	55%
Will be worse	33%
Will be about the same	7%
Not sure	5%
Organization Conducting Survey:	Zogby International
Release Date:	September 1999
Number of Participants:	1,008
Interview Method:	Telephone
Population:	National Adult
Overall, in the next century will life be much better, somewhat better, somewhat worse, much worse, will it be a century of devastating changes which may bring an end to human history, or will it not be much different from life as it is now?	
Much better	12%
Somewhat better	30%
Somewhat worse	12%
End of history	6%
Not much difference	31%
Not sure	5%

The answer of "end of history" referenced apocalyptic biblical prophecies about the "end of days" in the new millennium. Despite religious and secular predictions of a natural disaster or technological catastrophe because of computer glitches, the majority of respondents in the latter poll thought that life would be much or somewhat better (42 percent). The first poll reported more negative comments on the future, but the question framed the answer in relation to the last hundred years.

Respondents indicated elsewhere that the twentieth century had indeed been America's century, when the nation exerted great political, cultural, and economic influence. The NBC News/*Wall Street Journal* poll focused more on potential lifestyle changes in the next hundred years. It divided changes between those respondents expected and those they desired, or detested. The poll asked, for example, "Which one or two of the following aspects of daily life do you expect will change the most in the next century, that is, the next hundred years?"

42% The number of hours people work
37% The way people shop
25% What people eat
15% How much people exercise
7% The number of hours people sleep
4% The sports people play
6% All
2% None
3% Not sure

Changes in working and shopping, expected by the majority of Americans, also entered into answers for what excited Americans the most. The themes of speed and global reach, provided by transportation and computers, were evident in the answers.

28% The opportunity to live and work throughout the world
24% Faster or more convenient forms of transportation
17% Greater integration of home and office
8% A wider variety of consumer products
7% The ability to make almost all your purchases over the Internet
4% All
8% None
4% Not sure

What worried respondents in the next century of post-Cold-War America? An entry that had not shown up significantly in Cold-War era polls was "loss of privacy." It was on the minds of Americans because of alarming media reports of computer hacking, surveillance culture, and Internet information gathering. The largest number of respondents (29 percent) thought that loss of privacy would be the great concern in the twenty-first century. Percentages for other problems were fairly evenly distributed:

29% Loss of privacy
23% Overpopulation
23% Terrorist acts on American soil
17% Racial tensions
16% World war
14% Global warming
13% Widespread availability of guns
13% Economic depression
4% None
3% Not sure

It is an indication of the future-orientation of the poll that a question about the past referred to what respondents wanted to "bring back." The pollsters asked "Thinking about the way of life one hundred years ago, which one element of that lifestyle would you most like to bring back?" The implication was that the future naturally displaced the past; it appeared that the future was a break from the past, rather than an outgrowth of it. The answers were:

38% A more family-centered life, rather than a work-centered life
19% Greater emphasis on religious values
14% Greater sense of community and ties to neighbors
9% Less media influence
8% Less emphasis on material wealth
1% Less travel and instant communications
9% All
1% None
1% Not sure

Family, religion, and community emerged as signs of tradition and hence stability, while technology and economy arose as realms of change, and therefore emblems of the future. Americans apparently were weighing both in the perceived rush to the future brought by science and technology. While 68 percent of the respondents agreed that "science will solve many of the world's problems," 37 percent also agreed with the statement "science imposes major risks to humanity." Asked in what areas they expected the biggest changes in the next century, respondents noted the technological fields of medicine (46 percent) and communications (24 percent). They did not expect much change in work life (13 percent) and politics (11 percent).

Perhaps the potential conflicts of tradition and future come even more to the fore when Americans are questioned about the time of the future, and its implication of change, as the "next generation." The explanation is the referencing of social time measured in family lineage rather than calendrical cycles. Americans responded less confidently to the future when measured in generations than in centuries or portions of centuries. Several polling organizations use generational questions. In December 1991, NBC News/*Wall Street Journal* asked "Do you feel confident, only fairly confident, or not at all confident that life for our children will be better than it has been for us?" The largest response was "not at all confident" (51 percent) followed by "only fairly confident" (35) and "very confident" (9). CBS News/*New York Times* received similar results in a series of polls that asked "Do you think the future generation of Americans will be better off, or worse off, or about the same as life today?" In June 1990, 36 percent thought "worse" (28 percent for better); in March 1991, the same percentage came in for "worse" while the number for better dropped (26); in October 1991, the number for worse jumped to 52 percent (20 for better). The following year, CNN/*USA*

Today rephrased the question and reported demographic breakdowns: "Are you satisfied or dissatisfied with the opportunity for the next generation of Americans to live better than their parents?" Dissatisfied respondents outnumbered satisfied ones by percentages of 61 to 36 percent. Shortly after the turn of the century on January 7, 2000, the same organization asked a similar question but allowed respondents to answer "somewhat satisfied" or "not too satisfied." Then the highest percentage was "somewhat satisfied" (43), but 20 percent reported being "not too satisfied" and 9 percent checked "not at all satisfied." Twenty-six percent told pollsters "very satisfied." Only 2 percent had no opinion.

In the demographic breakdowns for the 1992 data, surprisingly little variation was reported according to income, religion, region, and gender. Variations can be noticed, however, for race and ethnicity, education, and age (as shown in Table 2.1).

In the categories of race and ethnicity, the largest expectation of improvement in the next generation came from Hispanics, and all minority groups outdistanced whites for their optimism. Harvard's Latinos Survey conducted in 1999 suggested that the optimism expressed by people of Hispanic background may stem from the strong favor for planning for the future because one could indeed control it. The economic groups that expressed the most optimism were at the bottom and top of the scale. Those making less than $15,000 a year notched a 43 percent satisfaction rate, and those making over $75,000 had a 37 percent satisfaction rate,

TABLE 2.1 Opinions of the Opportunity for Next Generation to Live Better than Parents, 1992

	Satisfied	*Dissatisfied*	*Don't Know/Refused*
Race and Ethnicity			
White	34	62	3
Black	39	56	4
Hispanic	47	51	1
Asian	38	62	0
Education			
Some HS	37	60	3
HS Graduate	39	58	4
Some College	36	61	4
College Grad	30	68	2
Age			
18–29	43	54	3
30–39	36	63	1
40–49	31	65	4
50–59	31	66	2
60–69	30	65	6

the same rate reported for incomes between $15,000 and $19,999. The lowest came in the groups between $20,000–$49,999, perhaps indicating frustration over economic mobility. College graduates at the time were not confident about their job prospects, although surveys closer to 2000 showed more optimism, especially in growth sectors of computers and communications. A strong correlation in the 1992 data existed between age and optimism for the next generation. The generation embracing more of computer and communication technology marking the future expressed their confidence in the improvement of life in the next generation.

The contrast of the progressive future for the nation and person with the traditional past for family and community in the minds of Americans comes through in several polls referencing "tradition." In 1992, Roper asked parents of children through age 17 the following:

> We hear a lot these days about family values. Family values can mean a number of different things to people. Taking that into account, please tell me which of the statements on this card best describes what family values mean to you personally? A. Are a set of beliefs that promote togetherness or unity among members of one's immediate family. B. Are a set of beliefs which emphasize the importance of the conventional family structure, that is, a mother and father who are married to each other and living with their children. C. Mean adherence to *traditions* that have been passed down from one generation to the next. D. Mean putting the desires and needs of one's children before one's own desires and needs. E. Mean adherence to religious beliefs. F. Mean the same thing as basic American values, like hard work, responsibility, and working to make life better for your children than it was for you.

The selections that received the most affirmations were probably the broadest: beliefs that promote togetherness (54 percent) and basic American values (47 percent). But a significant percentage, 19 percent, chose adherence to traditions. And there is an indication from another source that indeed "family" means "tradition" to most Americans. Pollsters in Mass Mutual's American Family Values Study asked adults whether "has traditions" describes their families. Over 80 percent answered "very well" or "pretty well." Only 19 percent thought "not too well" or "not well at all." Americans told pollsters that they valued tradition for raising a family. When the Institute for Social Inquiry in 1996 asked a sample of American parents of children younger than 18 how important they thought "a sense of local history and tradition" are for raising a family, 76 percent answered "very important" (26) or "fairly important" (50). Yet generational differences are apparent. The perception is strong in America that one's parents' generations always followed traditions more than the present generation. A *Rolling Stone* survey in 1987 revealed that 77 percent of respondents thought that their parents' generation "follows traditions." Only 8 percent described their own generation that way. When the Veterans Administration polled Americans about "the Vietnam Generation" (between 25 and 35 years old in 1979), over 63 percent thought that its main characteristic was that it was "not willing to keep traditions, too interested in changing things."

If Americans told pollsters that tradition was indeed desirable—it meant family, and their parents had more of it than they did—they also felt that they came up short on tradition compared to other nations. In answer to the question posed by Harris pollsters whether the Japanese have a stronger sense of family tradition and parental authority than Americans, an American sample in 1982 overwhelmingly responded that the Japanese do (87 percent). Further, when asked in the same poll whether the statement "has a unique culture and tradition" characterizes Japan, China, or the United States, 63 percent of the American sample applied that statement to Japan, 45 to China, and only 29 to the United States. Given a series of descriptive characteristics besides "unique culture and tradition," respondents thought that the United States was best described by the statements "major economic power" (33 percent) and "major military power" (21 percent), sectors that do the most future planning. For that question, only 1 percent chose "unique culture and tradition." Yet for Japan, the highest percentage chose "unique culture and tradition" (37 percent) followed by major economic power (22 percent) and "financial situation is the highest priority" (13 percent). The connection of "tradition" with "old" was apparent in the *New York Times*'s question to a national adult sample in 1983 "Do you think that Japan is still a feudal kind of society bound by old traditions and customs, or not?" (34 percent thought so). One could further look at the implication of tradition in this context as a "medieval" mindset associated with feudal society. That may explain the tendency of Americans to view tradition positively for their own families and communities, but negatively for nations. Consider the views of Americans toward other countries in handling social and economic issues. When Greenberg Research in 1994 asked a national adult sample about the forces that "hold back" other countries economically, 56 percent said "their own traditions, cultures, and customs" while 23 percent noted "financial institutions restrict progress." When Gallup in 1992 asked a national adult sample to comment on reasons for overpopulation in developing countries, 79 percent thought that "cultural traditions" were very or somewhat important (only 16 percent thought it was not too important or not at all important). Americans viewed tradition-centered nations negatively, even as they sought to instill more traditional values into their social lives.

Responding to the perception that Americans are separated from their national past, historians Roy Rosenzweig and David Thelen in *The Presence of the Past* (1998) offered a survey to show more of a past orientation for Americans than had been previously acknowledged. Their effort was inspired, in fact, by the lack of questioning by polling organizations on popular history making. They took heart in the response that between 53 and 57 percent reported reading any book about the past or visiting any history museums or historic sites. Yet the largest connection to the past is again associated with family: 91 percent said they "looked at photographs with family or friends." Measured another way, "gathering with your family" was given the highest score of various choices showing "connection to the past" on a scale of 1 to 10. Respondents were more likely to put their trust in "personal accounts from grandparents or other relatives" (8 on a scale of 10) than they were in high school teachers (6.6) or non-fiction books (6.4). Although the authors used the data to make the overly broad claim that Americans "make the past part of their everyday routines and turn to it as a way of grappling with profound questions about how to live," their finding of history's popular function of "maintaining family and community ties" leads me back to the observation of a separation of a national future-orientation from localized social tradition (Rosenzweig and Thelen 1998, 18). Commenting on the data and what he calls the "rose-colored glasses" through which Rosenzweig and Thelen view them, historian Michael Zuckerman reads a "pathological, nonparticipatory, and ahistorical culture." He writes of Americans that "so far as they told interviewers, they care only for themselves or, at best, for their families…They cannot get out of self, and they cannot get out of the present" (Zuckerman 2000, 19).

Extending the argument for the past being used to explicate the polling data showing self rather than communal interest of Americans, it is possible to view individualism as a foundation for both a national future-orientation in which moral and political connections are unnecessary and a localized social tradition in which the individual is at a center of communities with legacies to be discovered. In either case, connection is discoverable rather than prescribed. With the present more certain than the past or future, individuals define the past and future for themselves, and plan accordingly. The evidence also suggests that Americans are more likely to look broadly ahead, particularly early in life, than to look back for community. In childhood, a favorite question to pose in conversation is "what do you want to do when you grow up?" suggesting thinking ahead about many available choices (Dundes 1969, 57–58). Dundes claims that

> Americans judge one another, not on the basis of what an individual *is*, but on the basis of what he *will do or become*. Evaluation and decision making is very different in past and future oriented societies. In a past oriented society, one acts and judges others in accordance with the presumed wishes of one's ancestors, that is, according to a paradigm of the past. In a future-oriented society, one acts in accordance with how one thinks one's parents or more probably one's peers (or one's children) will judge or react to the planned action.
>
> *(Dundes 1969, 68)*

Ethnographers also note American greeting and leave-taking rituals that emphasize future action. Upon meeting acquaintances, people are likely to say "What's new?," "What's up?," "What's happening?," "How are things going?" and upon departing, might say "See you later," "Looking forward to seeing you again," and "Take care" (Dundes 1969, 58–59).

On the eve of the new millennium, 61 percent of Americans, according to Gallup, indicated they were reflective, and probably considering what had transpired in their lives. Yet a higher percentage used "excited," embracing the changeful future, to describe the way they were likely to feel as the calendar turned to a new era. The lowest percentage used "apprehensive or fearful" to describe their feelings. The Pew Research Center Millennium Survey conducted in 1999 divided the views of the future between "Self and Family" and "Nation [United States]." The poll found that Americans were more "optimistic" about self and family than about nation with percentages of 81 and 70 respectively. This result may suggest the tie between individualism and future-orientation, or read another way, that the basis of tradition in self and family offers security and hence optimism, while national problems cited of the potential for terrorist attacks, medical epidemics, natural disasters, nuclear wars, and energy crises caused concern for progress in the future. Yet the pollsters were generally surprised that the optimism for the future was as high as it was. They commented,

> Americans anticipate many perils in the next century, but none of them, no matter how grave, can dim the public's positive view of the future. Despite consensus forecasts of natural disasters, environmental calamities, and international terrorism, Americans are near unanimous in their confidence that life will get better for themselves, their families and the country as a whole.
> *(Pew Research Center 1999)*

A major disaster such as the September 11, 2001 terrorist attack on the World Trade Center may be thought to dash this reported optimism, but pollsters addressed American future-orientation quickly after the tragedy and Americans apparently stuck to their confidence in the future. The *Los Angeles Times* queried 1,995 adults between November 10 and 13, 2001:

> Generally speaking, would you say the attack on September 11th (2001, on the World Trade Center and the Pentagon) and the events that followed have contributed to your feeling more hopeful about the future, or less hopeful, or have those events not changed your hopes for the future?

Although a significant number of respondents felt "a little less hopeful" (14 percent) or "a lot less hopeful" (4 percent), 27 percent felt "a lot more hopeful" (14 percent) or "a little more hopeful" (13 percent). Indeed, the small percentage that reported feeling "a lot less hopeful" appears significant. The largest percentage by far reported "no change" in their hope in the future. Thinking of a generational view of the future, the poll also asked the same adults about their children's future. In answer to this question, a larger percentage reported feeling "a little" (19 percent) or "a lot" (8 percent) less hopeful (8 and 9 percent, respectively, felt a lot or little more hopeful), but even more respondents (53 percent) felt "no change" in their hopeful view of the future. This is not to say that they felt that the tragedy, and other present conditions, did not have an impact on their lives. When a sample of Americans were asked by Harris pollsters in November 2001 how much the attacks "will impact your life in the future: a great deal, somewhat, only a little, or not at all?" the largest percentage said "somewhat," followed closely by "a great deal"; 12 percent said "only a little" and a small group at 5 percent said "not at all." Yet their minds remained focused on the future.

Judging by the number of talk-show discussions as well as polls on the future of the United States, the end of 2020 ranked high as another significant time for many Americans to pause to reflect on Americanness. They welcomed the new year after recounting on the year that passed the surging death toll and economic turmoil resulting from the COVID-19 virus, people taking to the streets to protest racial injustice, and a divisive presidential election. Days before the race to the White House between incumbent Donald Trump and former Vice-President Joseph Biden, the overwhelming reaction to the question "When you think about the divisions in our country, do you think they are deeper than they were in the past, less deep, or about the same?" was that 7 out of 10 Americans felt that the fissure was "deeper" (Roper Center 2021, Suffolk University/USA Today, 12/16–12/2020. ID: 31118141.00038). Americans were evenly split as to whether this division would remain. In a Quinnipiac University Poll taken in December 2020, 49 percent thought that the nation would unite while 45 percent thought it would remain divided for the "foreseeable future" (Roper Center 2021, 12/1–12/7/2020, ID:31118123.00010). In late June of 2020, 74 percent of Americans told Monmouth University pollsters that the country was headed in the wrong direction (Murray 2020). It would be easy to imagine that the previously heralded American optimism and progressive worldview would be greatly diminished if not extinguished.

American self-confidence in its technological and economic prowess took a hit that year as multiple reports emerged of the image of the United States suffering across many regions of the globe, largely because of its handling of the pandemic and social unrest over racial incidents (Wike, Fetterolf, and Mordecai 2020). The positive ratings for the United States of a traditional ally, the United Kingdom, plummeted from a high of 83 percent at the turn of the new millennium to 41 percent, and Germany dropped even lower to 26 percent from a high of 78 percent. In Asia, Japan tumbled from 77 percent to 41. Clearly, world powers openly criticized the United States as a paragon of progress and as a result of media coverage Americans became more aware of their country's relative ineffectiveness in curtailing the spread of the virus as a measure of its worth. In June, respondents to a Kaiser Family Foundation poll were split between describing their view of the "future of America" as "hopeful" or "fearful." While 49 percent were somewhat or very hopeful, 46 percent were "somewhat" or "very fearful" (Roper Center 2021, 6/8–6/14–2020, ID:31117492.00044).

By year's end, undoubtedly buoyed by the announcement of vaccines produced by American pharmaceutical firms and a dramatic change in leadership after the election, most Americans reported being more hopeful and indeed optimistic about the future. In October 2020, an Associated Press-NORC survey reported that 55 percent of Americans thought that "America's best days are ahead of us" while 42 percent considered them "behind us" (Roper Center 2021, 10/8–10/12/2020, ID:31118004.00028). The Pew Research Center found similar results when it reported that 51 percent of Americans held the opinion that "future generations of Americans will enjoy about the same or better life than today" (Roper Center 2021, 6/16–6/22/20, ID: 31117509.00053). A Marist Poll recorded that 6 out of 10 Americans agreed with the statement that their "children and grandchildren will have a better life than you" (Roper Center 2021, 11/16–11/18/2020, ID: 31118101.00016). At the same time, Marist discovered more of a gap between those Americans who considered themselves more optimistic or pessimistic as a result of the events of 2020. It reported 56 percent being "more optimistic" while 38 percent said they were "more pessimistic" (6 percent were unsure). To be sure, the spread of the pandemic, and the consequent curtailing of mobility, was a cause of major concern for Americans affecting their view of the future, but it appeared that Americans remained forward-looking. For race relations marking perhaps the most conspicuous divisions in the country that had plagued the United States for centuries, Monmouth University pollsters, after a number of tragic racial incidents in 2020, questioned a sample of various people of various backgrounds and found that 83 percent of Americans were somewhat or very "hopeful," if not optimistic, about improvement (cf. 15 percent were "not too" or "not at all" hopeful; Roper Center 2021, 9/3–9/8/2020, ID: 31117681.00048). Although Americans, whether white or "of color," in the wake of the incidents recognized anew that the civil rights movement of the 1960s did not resolve racial inequities in the United States, and that race relations needed to be a national priority, there was evidence of the fabled "can-do" attitude in fixing the problem labeled "systemic racism" which is often traced to cultural and psychologically rooted attitudes (Payne, Vuletich, and Lundberg 2017; Salter, Adams, and Perez 2017). Many respondents thought that the worsening of racial relations was owed to the Trump Administration, and would improve with different leadership (Horowitz, Brown, and Cox 2019). Understandably blacks, Hispanics, and Asians told pollsters that more attention to race was needed in the United States but that overall intergroup relations were positive (Horowitz, Brown, and Cox 2019, 21–22). Not long before the shocking outbreaks of racial violence in 2020, prominent African-American historian John Hope Franklin had reminded Americans of the fundamental "American idea" of "freedom, equality, and justice" that needed re-assertion as the country's "rightful heritage." These outbreaks were shocking because many Americans had thought that more progress than the incidents indicated had been made toward the goal of building an equitable, civil society. Calling out the gap between political ideals and the daily conduct, Franklin wrote, "The American idea is the nation's holiday garb, its festive dress, its Sunday best. It covers up an everyday practice of betraying the claims of equality, justice, and democracy" (Franklin 2007). Racial prejudice—indeed the Americanness of various inequities related to bodily attributes and physical location including anti-Semitism, Islamophobia, sexism, and homophobia—could not be denied and a Black Lives Matter movement calling for change became mainstreamed during this period (Miller 2020; Serwer 2020). No doubt shaken, American idealism nonetheless arose in the 2020 presidential election when a majority of voters rejected Trumpism—a right-wing populist movement that Trump as well as presidential historians compared to nineteenth-century Jacksonian political philosophy revolving around a nationalist authoritarian ideology and nativist white racial dominance (Bartlett 2020; Cha 2016; Fraser 2018; Holland and Fermor 2020; Inskeep 2016; Mead 2017; Purnell 2020). Even though political observers remained worried by the fervid, unapologetic "base" of Trumpist supporters who stormed the U.S. Capitol under the nationalist banner of "Make America Great Again" on January 6, 2021, the prevailing American faith in the "American idea" of social equality and liberal democracy was bent but not broken (Kunzelman and Seitz 2021). In the aftermath, the public and political reaction to Trump's incitement of the mob with conspiracy claims and rallying cries of "taking back our country" was resoundingly negative. It was a historic crossroads moment of nationalist and pluralist streams in American political culture in conflict that resulted ultimately in a re-assertion of a progressive pluralist path.

Yet that rejection of Trumpism did not mean it went away or was a fleeting moment of intellectual history. The conflict of nationalist and pluralist streams could indeed be interpreted along the lines of Vernon Louis Parrington's thesis of the longstanding Americanness of conceptualizing an oppositional cultural as well as political paradigm of a conservative tradition based upon Hamiltonian federalism locked in an ongoing battle against a coalition of grassroots groups growing out of Jeffersonian social politics working on behalf of the common people (Parrington 1927–1930; see also Bush 1996; Hofstadter 1968, 349–436). Parrington described the dialectic polarity as "largely a struggle between the spirit of the Declaration of Independence [by Jefferson] and the spirit of the Constitution [Hamiltonian], the one primarily concerned with the rights of man, the other more practically concerned with the rights of property" (Parrington 1927–1930, 3; see also Peterson 1954; Reinitz 1977). This binary model that appears to undergird the modern two-party system in the United States and the country's constant social as well as political divide strains to account for the twenty-first-century populism that Parrington aligned with the Jeffersonian liberal tradition but seems to have evolved into a libertarian revolt while still supporting an authoritarian figure such as Trump. Racial-ethnic politics, that polls strive to uncover, complicates the picture with evidence of an urban concentration of African-American and Jewish voters identifying with liberal democratic policies while Latinx and Asian voters show splits in their avowed political leanings. Regional differences are also apparent in a southern embrace of conservatism, although in the 2020 election the big news was the flipping of Georgia in senatorial as well as the presidential election to the Democratic side. Another paradox is that for elections, even before Trumpism came on the scene, the rural vote that supposedly was the heir to the Jeffersonian liberalism swung to the conservative side. This paradox came to the fore in the 2020 siege of the U.S. Capitol because Trump campaigned on the rhetoric of "law and order" (a Hamiltonian, Constitutional trademark) although the mob that advocated for Trump evoked libertarian, even revolutionary rhetoric of "Don't Tread on Me," and rural resentment of urban, centralized power (Beauchamp 2021; Barry, McIntire, and Rosenberg 2021; McGreal 2021; Pettigrew 2017).

Heightened polling of the nation during frequent election cycles verifies the binary division inherent in American society because respondents are asked to couch their outlooks by choosing Democratic or Republican sides. And in the twenty-first century that divide appeared more distinct because of widely reported rural–urban, black–white, and regional differences along liberal–conservative lines or political cultures. This attention to the intensity of the division became especially evident in the rhetoric of "battleground" states (concentrated in a belt from Pennsylvania to the upper Midwest with a mixed rural–urban demographic). Considered as a process, and an increasingly daily one in digital culture, polling in the nation suggests ways that Americans in a pluralist society have a cultural as well as psychological need for prediction and forecast—and a desire for resolution (see Cooper and Layard 2002). Polling data as evidence have to be approached cautiously, not only because of the sampling errors that can occur, but because they are by their very structure future-oriented and culturally constructed. Yet the demographic clustering questioned by new polls offers more of a multidimensional view of American society than the narrowly defined national samples of the 1950s. As a cultural influence, polling and forecasting can be seen more pervasively in society as advisers in an atmosphere of expanded possibility of choices and directions. In the absence of national unity, polls have helped entrench a social category called "the general public" that increasingly over the twenty-first century has been viewed as splintered. This public is bound by adulthood and Americanness; its significance comes from its ability to vote and shop. To be sure, its preferences and tastes change, and therefore it needs to be measured often, but over time, the assumption is that consistent trends can be detected.

Despite a scholarly skepticism of generalizations of national profile based on statistical opinion data (the public urge to grasp the "average American" is often tempered by the celebration of diversity reflected in demographic breakdowns for American minorities), the popular press regularly features reports on surveys purporting to identify distinctively American trends and changing qualities, and offer predictive forecasts.[2] Television networks frequently highlight sections of broadcast to report opinions of their viewers. Indeed, polls in American media encourage the democratic idea of voicing difference and the expected outcome of division. Poll results get in the news when there is consensus and national leaders' responses of calls for unity. Polls draw attention to the perception that America is intrinsically about division, in a strained, paradoxical relationship between individual, region, and mobile, diverse nation (Kammen 1972). One might speculate whether this expectation of division, and the struggle to overcome it as a nation, is a natural outcome of the sectional/regional composition of American culture, an emerging American brand of representative democracy divided into majority and minorities, longstanding racial/ethnic divisions exemplified in the rhetoric of distinct colors (black, white, red, and yellow) and native/resident and immigrant/outsider, and a political system based upon the entrenched two-party system of oppositional winners and losers, or more likely, a combination of all of these historical factors. Affected by the past, including a tradition of breaking with it, polls constantly ask whether the future will be different.

The interactive quality of the Internet makes it especially ideal for surveys and several prominent sites have highlighted electronically administered surveys of opinions about future directions—personal, national, and global. Many popular sites feature "polls of the day." Putting the power of polling in individuals' hands, several apps such as Poll Everywhere, SurveyMonkey, and Outgrow allow users to create surveys to distribute. In addition to having a global reach, the Internet encourages consideration of a wide array of special-interest groups. This revised demographic picture of "clustering" (rather than the common designations of race, ethnicity, gender, and age) comes through in examination of the variety of discussion lists on sites encouraging formation of electronic communities. They offer daily polls and group-specific surveys that can be designed by moderators. The opportunity to respond to polls, even if unscientifically, recognizes the therapeutic value of expressing opinion in a society growing beyond community scale. Polling thus becomes a daily experience to reinforce individualism and realize the acceleration of change. This empowerment to tally opinion is especially important to balance fears of losing the personal voice, and democracy, in a technological society such as the United States. It further reinforces the sense of an imminent, accelerating future filled with change, an open future forcing daily decision-making and opinion-formation. Sources of tradition in family and locality, pollsters learned in the new millennium, are another place for this personal voice. This interpretation supports arguments that a pronounced future-orientation in a technological society heightens rather than displaces a sense of tradition, although the conceptualization of tradition and the past may shift to more symbolic uses, such as Richard Hofstadter's identification of the "agrarian myth" representing the ironic or compensatory interest in rural folkways during the American period of rapid industrialization in the nineteenth century or the rise of interest in rural America in the Regionalist movement (see Chapter 1) during the urbanization of the early twentieth century (see Hofstadter 1997; Bronner 1986a, 2002).

The United States is hardly alone in the popular consumption of future-oriented polls, but there is evidence that Americans particularly relish surveys or they interpret them as a priority for a leading commercial and political power. By regularly seeking views of, and confidence in, the future, polls presume that Americans need information on a planned future more than a usable past. Polls commonly focus on economic, political, and technological topics that presumably drive an ascending society. That Americans are accustomed to polls and surveys, particularly at moments of change, is itself a sign of future-orientation. In providing data to forecast trends, they contribute to the thinking that discovers, even invents, the future. With the expectation that more dramatic moments of change and crisis are bound to increase at an even faster pace as the twenty-first century proceeds, America and the countries that look to it as a model, can anticipate more questioning of the trajectories of the accelerating future and reflections on the functions of the social present, suddenly converted to the past. Just as American ideas of the future need clarification as a result of what polling data reveal about the time and areas of concern represented by futurist thinking, so too does past and a sense of tradition for its late twentieth-century reference to generational time (see also Bronner 1998a, 2000). Evidence to examine this counter to American future-orientation and individualism can be found in the American definition of the ritual life course and year.

The Time of Your Life

Referring to the American life course as extending from the "cradle to the grave," most Americans express a linear rather than cyclical view of life (Dundes 2004; Lee 1950). In modern parlance, life constitutes a "course" evoking images of an obstacle or variable course, rather than a naturalistic rigid "cycle" as it might have been described in preindustrial life, because people in an individualistic society presumably have more choices to decide when major milestones of education, marriage, and parenthood occur (Elder and Shanahan 2006; Elder and Giele 2009). One has the power to "change course" that suggests moving ahead, even if it curves, whereas one is governed by or "caught up in," as the saying goes, a repeated, and sometimes "vicious" cycle. Yet the course has a basic structure dictated by the realities of birth and death of a beginning, middle, and end. The cultural construction that has evolved over time is the marker for those phases of life and the social expectations for conduct within them. A cognitive trichotomy is evident in the division of the life course into childhood, adulthood, and old age. In the United States, the extension of years in school since the early twentieth century at the front end and longer life expectancy at the back has informed the addition of liminal categories of adolescence, or the transitional adult years, and senescence, or "old, old age" in modern life. A cultural factor in the vagueness of these relatively new phases is the lack of rituals compared to other cultures for entering adulthood and old age (Raphael 1988). The additional modern perception of a lengthening "middle age" which is visualized as a long unchanging plateau contributes further to the paucity of ritual passage.

Amid a transition from an agricultural producer to urban-industrial consumer society during the nineteenth century, Americans witnessed an evolving self-perception of a life cycle to course in graphics and literature. A dominant image in feudal Europe was the wheel of life or fortune (Cole 1992, 15–18; Sears 1986, 144–50). In its many variations, the consistent character was a ruler identified by a crown at the top of the wheel. Related members of the aristocracy are situated at other spokes. A mysterious non-aristocratic figure representing fate stands next to the wheel and with his or her hand turns the wheel, indicating that suddenly the king can be at the bottom. Although apparently a political statement about the fragility of power, the wheel was also a metaphor for life that assigned roles by class and assumed that people stayed within that circle. Common people appreciated and circulated the image because it suggested that the high and mighty could fall even though it also underscored the lack of social mobility of those stuck at the bottom (Hallgren and Söderberg 1970, 5–19; see also Bringéus 1988, 6; Sears 1986, 144–50). In an American twist on the various versions of the television program *Wheel of Fortune* (debuting in 1975, it is the longest-running syndicated game show in the United States), the king is absent and the contestant from ordinary circumstances controls the spin of the wheel to gain money, although he or she can at any time go bankrupt. Money rather than title bestows status, and in a capitalist framework, players purchase vowels to solve a word puzzle.

The European wheel expresses a sense of fatalism which is famously evident in Shakespeare's theatrical metaphor of life spoken by the cynical nobleman Jaques in *As You Like It*. The character contemplates regularized "seven ages" beginning with infancy and closing with the "last scene of all," of inevitable death (Bringéus 1988, 23; Cole 1992, 24–37; Sears 1986, 38). Seven in Abrahamic religions often symbolized perfection because of its relation to the week of creation in Genesis (see also the practice of an agricultural sabbatical in Leviticus 25) and the idea that critical points in the life cycle occurred at intervals of seven years (Landau 1920; Sears 1986, 38). The combination with official sounding number "ten" translated into a life span of 70 in many broadsides. For example, "The Age and Life of Man, perfectly showing his Beginning of Life, and the progress of his Dayes, from Seaven to Seaventy" printed in London between 1650 and 1665, composer Peter Fancy wrote "At ten times seven his Glasse is run" (English Broadside Ballad Archive n.d., 31654). Jaques's monologue inspired visual culture in the form of a series of paintings in England such as "The Seven Ages of Man" (1798–1801) by Robert Smirke that depicts a male figure's linear life journey in sequential order through settings, rather than theatrical stages, of being an infant, schoolboy, lover,

FIGURE 2.1 "Fortuna and Her Wheel" (28v), Illustration from John Lydgate's *Siege of Troy* (England, mid-fifteenth century), showing the Wheel of Fortune turned by the Quene of Fortune. On the left, Dame Doctryne is accompanied by two male figures, Holy Texte and Scrypture, and two female figures, Glose and Moralyzacion.
Source: Artist unknown. University of Manchester Library. Public domain.

hot-headed soldier, judge, silly pantaloon, and tamed old man (Smirke 1864). Other comparisons in popular street literature were to the 12 months of the year starting with January as the time of beginnings and the cyclical clock. June was equated with adulthood as the most comfortable period of life. By December, the body was withering and bent from the cold (Sears 1986, 113–20). The procession through the year was often accompanied with religious symbolism, indicating that the cycle was ordained by God. For example, using the often-cited title of "The Age and Life of Man," a ballad broadside printed in multiple versions from the late seventeenth to early nineteenth century distinguishes its content from other organizing principles of life with the description, "A short description of the NATUR [sic], RISE, and FALL, according to the Twelve Months of the Year." It suggested a peak at the age of 35 coinciding with July, although the text gives the possibility of the man "creepeth up and down till he come to fourscore [80]."

In a bow to a divine plan, a closing line in a verse reads "Ah! Christ on high have mind on me, and learn me for to die" (Bodleian Libraries n.d., Broadside Bod5563; Roud Folk Song Index n.d., V9249).

As an agricultural producer society, the citizens of the New Republic descended from Europe and influenced by the driving principle of a divinely provided natural bounty of the land for their benefit, preferred the imagery of life following four seasons or a voyage through four natural environments over the conceptualizations of seven and 12 stages (Kammen 1979, 38–45; Kammen 2004, 75–95). Four, derived also from biblical sources (in Genesis 1:14–19, God finished the creation of the material universe on the fourth day), was a quantity that represented completeness and the "fourscore" as the ballad "The Age and Life of Man" indicated referred to 80 as the extent of life (Brandes 1987). To fill out the sense of a linear space as well as time divided into four episodes or quarters equaling a whole life, early American authors created picaresque narratives with a four-phase journey as a process of maturation (Freese 2013, 253–63). Rather than being stories of directionless wandering, fictional plots such as Edgar Allan Poe's *The Narrative of Arthur Gordon Pym of Nantucket* (1838) involved coming-of-age voyages of a boy that take him on three ship adventures before heading south toward death in a pirogue. This is one of the stories that literary critic Peter Freese calls "a particularly American variant" of the mythical goal-directed quest by emphasizing not only the maturation of the youth but a secular search for individual self-discovery in a new, strange land (Freese 2013, 255).

FIGURE 2.2 "The Voyage of Life: Childhood" by Thomas Cole, oil on canvas, 1842. *Source*: National Gallery of Art. Public Domain.

The four-phase division of life as a water journey was spread in the United States through elementary education. A common text in American schoolbook anthologies of the early nineteenth century was Samuel Johnson's "The Voyage of Life" which described life as a turbulent journey through the "the stream of time…full of rocks and whirlpools" first in childhood, then youth, manhood, and finally to old age (Kammen 1979, 41–42). The imagery of the sea voyage "courting the gale with full sails" evoked memories of travel across the ocean to a new life. Picking up this theme, painter Thomas Cole who had emigrated to the United States as an 18-year-old in 1819, soon after arriving envisioned a series of pictures to be called an "Allegory of Human Life." Receiving a commission in 1839, Cole retitled his series as "The Voyage of Life" and painted a male figure in a boat apparently moving toward a celestial kingdom with an angel standing on the shore to direct the voyager. The first scene shows the sitting child amid confining rock formations but a pastoral vista lies beyond his view. In "youth," the stream opens up with lush trees and a mountain on the horizon. "Manhood" is a darker scene with decaying trees and threatening skies. In the last painting of old age, the man is sitting again and looking out to open waters and the angel pointing to the sky. The series was exhibited widely after 1842 and reproduced in numerous engravings after Cole's death in 1848. One might view Cole's imagery as drawing a compromise between the cyclical and linear view of life. While it showed the boy venturing out on his own through four environments that suggested especially bright prospects in youth, the constant presence of the angel as a hand of fate suggested a predestined rise and end.

Although sharing the four-phase characterization of life's journey, the immensely popular Currier and Ives lithographs titled "The Four Seasons of Life" (1868) populated their scenes with people and lacked the guiding divine hand. The "Season of Joy" is childhood which is symbolically equivalent to the bloom of spring. Playing children and sheep are in the foreground in front of a two-story house. They are looking toward the viewer rather than toward the pastoral vista that is in the background. They do not appear concerned with journeying on. The well-dressed couple who are strolling in summer along a path alongside growing wheat are also more preoccupied with each other than with getting to work. Currier and Ives labeled this lithograph "The Season of Love" and instead of a sole house, a church and surrounding community representing maturity is behind them. This is hardly the depiction of scruffy, rebellious youth who populated late twentieth-century films and television. But what they share is a recognition of youth, identified later by age as "teens," as a distinct age. Film critic Steven Goodman discussing how to teach 1950s movies such as *Rebel Without a Cause* and *The Wild One*, for example, pointed out that "James Dean's and Marlon Brando's tragic but appealing characters represented the possibilities open to the new American teenager, an independent lifestyle that promised thrills, danger, and even premarital sex" (Goodman 2003, 26). With the advent of electronic media, the adolescent time of life between childhood and adulthood raised questions about its empowerment and its increasingly central position in popular culture.

FIGURE 2.3 "The Four Seasons of Life: Middle Age. The Season of Strength." Lithograph. Charles R. Parsons and Lyman W. Atwater, artists.
Source: Currier and Ives, publisher. Prints and Photographs Division, Library of Congress.

In the Currier and Ives series of the 1860s, adulthood, and particularly non-agricultural manhood, appeared to predominate life. Instead of Cole's "manhood," the Currier and Ives print drawn by Charles R. Parsons and Lyman W. Atwater depicted a domestic family scene in autumn titled "Middle Age: The Season of Strength." Four children are in the household and walls of the house block much of the view of the outdoors. The scene is also transitional in presenting a home and dress that do not show a garden or farm. There are ample signs of "settling down" and material development including wallpaper, rugs, top hat, cane, and painting in the house. A significant fixture is a hall mirror and stand that in the Victorian period was a location for self-admiration and accumulation of consumables (Ames 1978). The designation of "middle age" was relatively new and evoked a connection to the growing "middle class" who were also consumers of the popular prints. More consumable goods are contained in the final season of life: "old age, the season of rest." One can barely view what is outside through a window with curtains, but the scene is clearly winter. Inside, flames from the fireplace provide warmth and lies opposite a large cabinet expanding the display of goods. The artists also included a grandchild in the scene to indicate a continuity of the family into the future. Although tied to the regularity of the seasons, the phases in the prints depict material progress, presumably from the work of the white male breadwinner, and a reward of rest in a darkened space for one's labors. The seasons are not equal. With the emphasis on the "fresh start" and break with the past, the influential prints placed a cultural emphasis on youthfulness while also encouraging domestic harmony of the family.

More individuality of increasing importance in a mobile nation was conveyed with a host of widely circulating prints on the theme of a stairway of life from the cradle to the grave. It has a European source in the first illustrated textbook for children, *Orbis Sensualium Pictus* (Visible World in Pictures), by Czech educator John Amos Comenius in 1658, who included a drawing of a male and female beginning in a cradle and then ascending to the wide fourth step before descending to old age back on the ground. On the fourth step was a mathematical combination of 4 x 10 representing 40 as the pinnacle of life (Comenius 1810, 63; see also Bringéus 1988, 24). It was widely used as a children's schoolbook and republished in multiple languages, including English in the United States through the nineteenth century. Whether Comenius was influenced by images included in broadsides and almanacs available on the street or vice versa is hard to say (see Bodleian Libraries n.d., Bod23541; English Broadside Ballad Archive n.d., 31654; Roud Folk Song Index n.d., V21053). Regardless, the ascending and descending stairway motif in depictions of one's life became part of the popular culture of the United States with countless reproductions and wide circulation of prints by Currier and Ives.

FIGURE 2.4 "The Life and Age of Man, Stages of Man's Life from the Cradle to the Grave."
Source: James Baillie, publisher, 1848. Prints and Photographs Division, Library of Congress.

FIGURE 2.5 "The Life and Age of Woman, Stages of Woman's Life from the Cradle to the Grave."
Source: James Baillie, publisher, 1848. Prints and Photographs Division, Library of Congress.

In the United States, the stages of life from the cradle to the grave became standardized as representing increments of ten from 0 to 100 familiar in the commercial rather than religious world, with 50 being at the peak. The Americanness of this regularized progression was indicated with the United States flag at the pinnacle. Nature in the form of foliage was pushed aside; the changing bodies and their varying dress dominated the frame. On the left was a blooming tree and on the right was a weeping willow. Various versions included animals associated with the ages from the infant kid or lamb to the old goat or even ass. Verses at the bottom of "The Life and Age of Man, Stages of Man's Life from the Cradle to the Grave" (published by James Baillie, 1848) explain the symbolism for the rising man of the animals: "At forty nought his courage quails, But lion-like by force prevails, Strength fails at fifty but with wit, Fox-like he helps to manage it." Unlike many of the European prints that centralized religious symbols undergirding the climb and descent to indicate the hand of God in the aging process, American prints tended to have secular symbols of a grave or cemetery (hence the reference of "cradle to the grave"). The grave and flanking trees are shared icons of the American print "The Life and Age of Woman, Stages of Woman's Life from the Cradle to the Grave" (published by James Baillie, 1848) but differ in the landscape features shown under the steps. Her climb toward reaching 50 when she is "A busy housewife full of cares, The Daily food her hand prepares" is connected to images of a growing fruit tree with the analogy of "Now bearing fruit, she rears her boys, And tastes a mother's pains and joys." Reflecting the imagery of separate spheres of the Currier and Ives Seasons series, the woman is shown ascending to marriage and childbearing, representing a "sparkling fountain gushing forth." But as "age creeps on," the scenes turn to church and houses, where finally she sits still in her chair and "listless knits till death appears," according to the accompany verse. Besides indicating the expected *busy*-ness as well as business of adulthood, the prints suggested progression as individuals rather than fated lives.

Popular American board games arising during the Civil War era that were meant to be played in the middle-class parlor reinforced the availability of choices in a life course. An element of fate was still evident in the throw of a numbered teetotum which dictated the moves that players made (Asbury 2015, 3). The *Checkered Game of Life* (1861), designed and manufactured by Milton Bradley, reportedly sold over 40,000 copies a single year after it was released (Asbury 2015, 14). Instead of a circular route in the manner of a chasing game such as *The Mansion of Happiness* (1843), Bradley used a checkerboard with spaces for good and bad traits that could propel a player forward or backward. The goal was to receive 100 points and reach "Happy Old Age." Instead of the aim of ascending into heaven in *Mansion of Happiness*, Bradley's game invited players to use strategy to choose directions to acquire points, and thereby achieve physical longevity and financial prosperity (Asbury 2015, 14). The popularity of the game inspired variations such as the rags to riches narrative of *The Game of District Messenger Boy or Merit Rewarded* (1886) distributed by the McLoughlin Brothers played on a checkerboard featuring boys who climbed the corporate ladder to receive rewards. It was, as the narrative suggests, informed by the popular literature of Horatio Alger, Jr., with themes of self-reliance and social mobility in urban settings. *The Game of Life* manufactured by Milton Bradley in 1960 was a version of the *Checkered Game of Life*, updated for post-war suburban America. Players move an automobile piece on a track a number of spaces numbered 1 through 10. The game refers to the older conceptualizations of life with the spin of the "Wheel of Fate." On several spaces the spinner is forced to make a decision on different life options, such as retiring to the countryside, that translates into taking a direction. Players place pegs in the car to represent milestones such as marriage and career. Although the course appeared circuitous, success followed a linear pattern of taking individual paths that involved risk-taking (Canary 1968, 431). During the 1990s, updated ethical issues came into play such as helping the homeless on the board game and a video version was released. By 2007, the game replaced cash with credit cards; accordingly, a player could still advance even in debt. Game designers reduced the idea of a lucky break, or fate, to move ahead and included more opportunities to enact success strategies by adding the subtitle "Twists & Turns" (Lepore 2007). This postindustrial image of each person following different paths was based on the Americanness of having choices and separating oneself individually.

A host of popular self-help books during the late twentieth century visualized the life journey as an upwardly inclining straight or "life" line replacing the stepped ascent and descent metaphor with protrusive, twisting, and branching trajectories along a straight line (Bolles 1978, 359–63). One of the best-selling was *The Three Boxes of Life* (1978) by Richard Bolles, which underscored individual agency on the cover by advertising that the book was "an introduction to life/work planning." It offered a guide to change one's life or course. Planning ahead suggested a confidence in the probability that taking strategic paths would ensure material progress and that an individual could take control of one's future rather than submitting to the hand of fate. The title of the book referred to restrictive boxes that constituted predominant activities at different stages of life. In childhood, one was absorbed in the box of education, followed by the largest box of work. The third box with a size matching that of education is retirement with the expectation that it is spent idle or in leisure activities withdrawn from a job and learning. The result of not integrating education, work, and leisure, Bolles asserted, was personal dissatisfaction with life and socioeconomic malaise. The solution, he proposed, was for persons to do a life review along a single axis visualized as a forward pointing arrow divided into time segments of five years from 5 to 80. A reviewer maps decisions that have been made and their impact. Then on the remainder of the life arrow, one can forecast the future with slanted trajectories to actualize success. Fitting this plan into a service and information economy are various services and specialists to enable individuals to meet their goals.

Despite the conceptualization of old age in books, games, and humor-filled "retirement parties" in corporate offices as a drop off a corporate cliff rather than part of a gradual descent, other visualizations in the postindustrial age smoothed the steps into a hill and used the age of 40 as the plateau of life after which one is "over the hill" (Brandes 1987; Druckerman 2018). Many Americans upon turning 40 were feted with parties with banners announcing a "mid-life crisis," black balloons, and mock gravestones for the end of youth. Other social occasions marked 50 as the bottom of a U-curve of happiness (Rauch 2014). However, the number was symbolic rather than serving as a statistical mid-point, since the average American life span was in the 70s. Precedents could be discerned in the organization of a complete life in quantities of four and the visualization in popular prints of the pinnacle of a climb as 40. But the representation of mid-life as a long period of stagnation, or a plateau of life, appeared to be ushered in by a twentieth-century postindustrial service and information economy and its dominant image of the office building. Mid-life crisis was reported especially in men expected to be on "top of the heap" or "king of the hill." With the emphasis on promotion to levels of bureaucracy, 40 was imagined as the point at the peak of advancement, the spot from which "it was all downhill from there" and anxieties arose about being displaced by younger ambitious workers. Among the jokes made about this time was the need for 40-year-olds to ponder career changes, have romantic flings with younger partners, take up odd hobbies or purchase fast and expensive sports cars, and take off on a long journey. It was perceived as a long plateau because of the view that middle age extended interminably with few if any rites of passage. There was also a social reason. It was considered a time of settling, often with a lonely "empty nest" caused by children leaving the childhood homes, and therefore it marked the segment of life in which individuals had the least social support (Jackson 2020). Although this psychological perception of a culturally determined mid-life filled with malaise was attributed to Western middle-class corporate systems, the expectation, if not biological reality, of stress at 40 or 50 was highest in the United States and there was an element of Americanness evident in the connection to competitive individualism and consumerism (Wethington 2000).

Considering the orientation of visual culture in the "cradle to the grave" metaphor to white middle-class America, one might look for alternative visions from people of color, women, gays, and other stigmatized groups concerning the lack of barriers to an easy climb upward toward the American cultural expectation, or dream, of success and social mobility. Rhetoric of an obstructive glass, and even concrete, "ceiling" abound in economic and political discourse to signal the difficulty of ascent in corporate America (Babers 2016; Hines 2019). Still, the metaphor suggests a stairway or climb upward within a bureaucratic structure. In many African-American folk cultural expressions that take a horizontal view of the street, the life journey can end at any moment and is full of ups and downs until the final fall. In America, it is filled with violence and racial prejudice. During the 1960s and 1970s, reflections on the shape of African-American life were evident in narrative folk poetry known as "toasts." They were often shared and performed in prisons, bars, and street gatherings by and for African Americans. Although frequently framed by stories of legendary badmen such as Stagger Lee and settings of jails and saloons, the toasts had floating verses that could be inserted in various performances. Common to these was reference to the "daily (steady) grind," "early death," and fate of street life. Describing the opening line of "Do Your Crying for the Living" as "proverbial," collectors for the anthology *The Life: The Lore and Folk Poetry of the Black Hustler* (1976) recorded:

> Do your crying for the living, hustling their butter and lard,
> 'Cause dying comes easy, but it's the living that's hard.
> It's an everyday grind for that rice and grits,
> A constant watch for that number that never hits.
> *(Binderman, Newman, and Wepman 1976, 164)*

Instead of a future-orientation, one can read in the rhetoric of "grind" an existence of survival. To be sure, many toasts relate "Well, it's all the same, 'cause it's all in the Game…You had your fun, but now you're done" (Binderman, Newman, and Wepman 1976). "It" in the Game is being a winner one minute and losing it all the next. There is no steady climb in this scenario. Although protagonists strive to succeed, fate, police, or prejudice brings them down, and they try to get back up to play the Game again. In "The Fall," the character of a black street hustler relates,

> Well, I'd like to tell of how I fell
> And the trick *fate* played on me;
> So gather around, and I'll run it down
> And unravel my pedigree.
> *(Binderman, Newman, and Wepman*
> *1976, 79; emphasis added)*

In the dramatic performances of toasts, black male speakers often relate adventure and thrills on the street before being derailed by prison and violent death. In a toast titled "The Junkie," the male speaker describes having a prize within view, only to be tripped up by the invisible hand of fate.

> Then I saw a young girl who was out of this world,
> With her purse swinging real nice,
> I got ready to swing and snatch that thing,
> But *fate* had me slip on the ice.
> *(Binderman, Newman, and Wepman 1976, 101;*
> *emphasis added)*

The street poet also refers to another difference between the white stepped image of the life course and the expressive characterization of male fatalism in the Game. Many toasters describe the black world as a matrifocal one in which women have more control of their destiny. Unlike many depictions with whites in four seasons or ten steps of life centrally showing the succeeding public man, women in the street poetry hold power in black settings and are resented for it. Although clearly not speaking for all people of color, and despite the closing gap in mortality and life expectancy between white and black Americans (Achenbach 2017), an outlook persists of a rough road to travel that could be blocked or ended at any moment. Unlike the increasingly individualized trajectories in self-help books and board games, black oral narratives repeatedly express worry about a lack, or suppression, of individual agency as a result of controlling systems of society and government (Rogers 2006).

Popular hip-hop lyrics continued these themes through the twenty-first century, often with commentary on the illusion of a long peaceful life in the phrase "cradle to the grave." In "Cradle to the Grave" by Thug Life, which sold over half a million copies in a single year, the singer opened with lines that throughout one's life, from the cradle to the grave, it is hard to get out of the ghetto (Thug Life 1994). Female rapper Foxy Brown at the start of the twenty-first century described "roadblocks" and short-term outlook in life in the soundtrack to the successful action film *Cradle 2 the Grave* appealing to urban black theater audiences, as she sang that she lived in fear of losing her life at any moment (Brown 2003). Although many critics have noted the fatalism and untimely, violent death as a reality in hip-hop lyrics, there is also, according to rappers, a strong twenty-first-century message of taking control of one's own circumstances that appears to differ from the toasts of the 1960s and 1970s (Ayers 2012). In "The Fire" by The Roots who appear as the house band on the Tonight Show, lead singer Black Thought signals an individual's path for a better life by reaching for the skies (Ayers 2012). And with reference to the entrapping boxes of life, Lauryn Hill sings of getting out of the boxes that keep her in social bondage. Rather than submit to the restrictions, she calls for change (Ayers 2012). Her lyrics address what she perceives to be a white-controlled superstructure, system, or state that keeps African Americans from being more mobile, self-determined, and future-oriented.

In the United States, the institution that counselors say will catapult them to success as well as maturity is college. Indeed, the structure of status by years—freshman, sophomore, junior, and senior—uses the four-stage model of ritual passage. The prescribed length of time to graduation does not owe to cognitive science on the acquisition of knowledge but rather to the symbolism of four as completion or thoroughness. Before the 1960s it was common to represent this ritual passage materially. First-year students wore infantilizing caps called "dinks" or "beanies." With each stage, they would acquire a more substantial hat, often accompanied by a "moving up" ceremony or identity ritual (Bronner 2012, 114–62). In the process, they would be reminded of the social hierarchy with seniors at the top, and strive to advance to gain control of the campus. The decline of the centralized common curriculum for each class and the growing affiliation of students with the major rather than the class led to an individualization of courses of study. Not coincidentally, advising centers increasingly referred to the choices that students had for scheduling as "pathways" much in line with the modern concept of the linear life course as a series of individually determined trajectories.

With the relative lack of rituals for teenagers to enter adulthood, and the growth of university enrollment as an extension of adolescence, American higher education institutions acquired more functions of emotional as well as intellectual growth. As more than half of all high school graduates go on to post-secondary education, the ritual for high school graduation in the United States appears to be more of a stepping stone than a leap to an adult career. Proms and parties often are about separation from one's friends and family and less about pursuit of the box of work. With adulthood being vaguely defined or associated with pressures to be economically independent, universities added offices of counseling services, campus residence, and student activities that were charged with keeping students on the track to independence beyond graduation. Unlike many countries for which admission to a university is highly selective but easy to complete once accepted, the American public university system is more accessible and more difficult to finish (Baseel 2015; Bronner 2012, 6). Accordingly, the American college commencement ceremony is filled with references to the ordeal through the long road to graduation. Graduates signify this journey on many campuses by climbing steps from the right of the stage, receive their diploma as they walk across a plateau of adulthood, and then proceed down steps on the left. As they leave, graduates move their tassels on a mortarboard from the ordinary position hanging on the right to a special status on the left (Bronner 2012, 377–406). Dressed in ceremonial robes, students are reminded that they have completed a phase of their life as well as education and now having left the campus community are on their own.

Rituals earlier in life with references to adult responsibilities in the United States typically belong to ethnic groups rather than a public national occasion, such as Coming of Age Day in Japan (White 1994, 207). Even though Jews represent less than 2 percent of the United States population, the Jewish coming of age ritual of bar and bat mitzvahs is widely known, in image if not in practice. Even if one has never attended the event, it is a safe bet that the person has been exposed to it in popular television and film. Jonathan and Judith Pearl, discussing media portrayals of Jewish themes in *The Chosen Image* (1999), claim that "of all the Jewish rites of passage depicted on popular TV, none has received more attention than the *bar mitzvah*" (Pearl and Pearl 1999, 16). Since their book has come out, the bar mitzvah has been the most dramatized, or spoofed, Jewish ceremony in popular movies such as *Keeping the Faith* (2000), *Glow Ropes: The Rise and Fall of a Bar Mitzvah Emcee* (2005), *Keeping Up with the Steins* (2006), *Sixty Six* (2006), *Knocked Up* (2007), *Two Lovers* (2008), *A Serious Man* (2009), and *Donny's Bar Mitzvah* (2021). Television series including the depictions of the bar/bat mitzvah include *Sex and the City* (2000), *Frasier* (2002), *Lizzie McGuire* (2002), *The Simpsons* (2003), *Entourage* (2005), *Unfabulous* (2005), *Bernie Mach Show* (2006), *Naked Brothers Band* (2008), *American Dad!* (2009), *Black-ish* (2014), *Crazy Ex-Girlfriend* (2017), and *Transparent* (2017), to name a few. The bar mitzvah has been the butt of many jokes and cartoons among Jews and non-Jews alike, many of which concern the apparently young age, 13, when the boy is pronounced to be entering manhood or which question the Jewish boy's claim to manliness. In the *Naked Brothers Band* episode "The Bar Mitzvah," for example, wordplay is evident when a parent commands the bar mitzvah boy to join his friends with the Yiddish word *gey* meaning "go," but the Americanized boy understands the word as questioning his masculinity for acting "gay." Related to this humor in a surfeit of comic graphics and mocking photographs is the common theme of discomfort for the boy in the fabled misfitting bar mitzvah suit (also the subject of barbs by television character Murphy Brown to her younger Jewish boss Miles Silverberg on the hit show *Murphy Brown* from 1988 to 1998). The humor depends on the perception that the Jewish boy is uncomfortable in, or not ready for, the commanding pose of an adult suit, and mature authority over non-Jews (Bronner 2021, 206–36). With an elaborate catered party after a synagogue service held in a rented hall, there is a perception of the ritual as a symbol of social arrival for a marginalized ethnic group and recognition of ethnic identity along with participation in American status given to commercial success. It can carry different meanings for Jews in practice than it does in representations of the media. For Jewish families, the event often questions the maintenance of religious and ethnic identity later in life, whereas in popular culture the emphasis on material excess signals a non-Jewish concern for social and economic independence in the vague notion of American adulthood.

The kind of bar mitzvah commanding popular culture attention is likely of non-pietistic Jews, often called liberal or assimilated. In such satirical portrayals, viewers become aware of anxieties, not just for the bar mitzvah boy's relation to his faith or ethnicity, but also for the modern consumer society of which he is a part. Depictions of the bar mitzvah in popular culture focus primarily on the party because of the broader societal interest in modern materialism, or parental indulgence, that it raises, but contextualizing the celebration within traditional practices and symbols for the bar mitzvah boy leading up to, and during, the event sheds light on the inherited, and invented, meanings for the bar mitzvah.

FIGURE 2.6 Quinceañera Corte de Honor, Santa Fe, New Mexico, 2014. Traditionally made up of 14 damas (girls) and 14 chambelanes (boys).
Source: Christopher Michel, photographer. Creative Commons Attribution 2.0 Generic license.

The other conspicuous rite of passage in the United States that has entered popular culture is the Quinceañera celebrating a Latinx girl's 15th birthday. The ritual beginning in the church and extending to a celebratory dance party marks the transition from childhood to womanhood but an equivalent ceremony is not part of the culture for boys. Quinceañera has roots in Mexico but like the bar and bat mitzvah it has been described as taking additional significance and visibility in the United States. Formerly representing the readiness of the 15-year-old woman for marriage, ethnographers beginning in the late twentieth century noted its function of social bonding for local Mexican-American communities and expression of positive ethnic values for an often stigmatized bilingual group making a claim for status as Americans (Gonzalez 2016). It begins with a mass of thanksgiving and initiation of the girl into womanhood. At the dance hall, there is a formal Quinceañera presentation with a procession of a court of honor with ethnic music. The members of the court are dressed formally, and the honoree wears an elaborate dress. Decorations and props with a Cinderella theme are common to represent the flowering of the girl into a woman, and a meal represents the traditional roots of the families (Cantú 1999). While often involving community participation in the food preparation, decorations, and dressmaking, the production of the Quinceañera has also become a commercial enterprise with stores and advisers devoted to materials and planning as the scale of the events have grown (González-Martin 2020).

In 2006, Quinceañera drew media attention with the release of the movie *Quinceañera* about two Mexican-American female cousins named Magdalena and Eileen who break from the behavioral expectations of their families that are conveyed in the ritual. As with other representations of coming-of-age events, the movie announced the tension between an upwardly mobile immigrant culture wanting to preserve its culture and the pressures of becoming homogenized into norms they recognize as national (Holden 2006). The movie opens with the Quinceañera and the camera's focus is on the princess attire of the honoree. The movie uses the event to generalize for non-Latinx audiences who do not have a culturally dictated ritual passage of coming of age for adolescents who question what the future will hold. The movie broadly questions the role of marriage in one's life and highlights the way the ceremony presages a wedding in a Latinx life course. *New York Times* film critic Stephen Holden observed, "Magdalena and her teenage friends are already living the American dream but on a limited budget, and their expectations for a brighter future are high" (Holden 2006). Following the movie was a host of representations, and many ethnographers would say exaggerations, of the ceremony viewed from different angles but the theme of its drawing attention to itself as a gendered spectacle frame to address paradoxes of American coming of age in a multicultural society was consistent (González-Martin 2016).

The Ritual American Year

If Americans have an elastic set of rituals to variously define and navigate the life course, their holidays, also filled with ethnic components, ritually organize time from year to year. The Gregorian calendar used in most of the world does not follow seasonal cycles and much of the need of transition that people experience from one season to the next through the year is fulfilled by holidays. It is common to hear of Christmas–Hanukkah–Kwanzaa and Easter–Passover–Ramadan–Holi marking secular as well as religious holiday seasons, respectively, as cultural occasions to tame winter and hasten spring. The intensity of their observance suggests the extra significance of these seasonal adjustments in the ritual year. Another point of stress related to the negative associations of winter to death in life course visualizations is the calendrical New Year on January 1 which differs from many traditional interpretations of annual cycles renewing in spring and fall. The distinctive American cultural framework of calendrical time is the spectacle of "America's game" on Super Bowl Sunday, construction of a playful nationalistic "summertime," and the compensation for the decay of autumn with symbolism of abundance and mobility at Halloween and Thanksgiving. The Americanness of these events is especially evident in their forging, and questioning, of nationally shared values in relation to the highly varied local and ethnic basis of American society.

Culturally, the start of the New Year anticipated with wishful commands of "Have a good new year," signals an adjustment to change from the burdens of the past to the uncertainties of the future. In the American context of individualism, the New Year is an occasion to shed guilt over indulgence in dangerous behavior with promises of reform in the "new year resolution." Whereas spring festivals among Southeast Asian groups, for example, reflect more on the past and mark growth with signs of seasonal transition, fertility, and greenery, the designation of January 1 in the standard Gregorian calendar is based on human rather than natural control. One indication of the New Year as a turning point in Western tradition is the naming of January after the Roman mythological figure of Janus, the god of beginnings and endings, depicted as having a double-faced head looking back and forward. Yet as it is practiced in American culture, New Year is a time of looking forward with a fresh start. Reflections on the past are discouraged with derision for the figure of an old stern "Father Time" and the welcoming of the frolicking New Year baby. The vigil for the New Year is represented by the symbolism of December, a long month at 31 days; it is the 12th month, suggesting the end of a clock cycle, and its linguistic root is the Latin *decem*, for completion of a unit of ten. Further emphasizing the cultural association of the New Year with birth is the celebration of Christmas—commemorating the birth of Jesus—one week before.

In modern American culture, often characterized by its emphasis on the future, the turn of the calendar is vigorously celebrated, marked by celebrations "ringing in the New Year" on the evening of December 31. Many other New Year customs are observed in America during the course of the year, often with more somber rituals for reflecting on the past. Examples of ethnic differences in calendrical celebrations are the Jewish New Year (held on different dates each year between September 5 and October 5), the Chinese and Vietnamese New

Year (held on different dates each year between January 21 and February 21), and the Cambodian and Thai New Year held from April 13 to 15.

On New Year's Eve across the United States, municipalities sponsor public celebrations (often called "first night" parties) involving the dropping of an electrically lit object—typically a civic symbol—one minute before midnight. Atlanta, the capital of Georgia (the Peach State), drops an 800-pound peach; and Miami, Florida, counters with its 35-foot Big Orange. But by no means is the custom limited to large cities: Dillsburg, Pennsylvania, drops a pickle to draw attention to the town name, while nearby Mechanicsburg drops a wrench. Brasstown, North Carolina, building on its hillbilly self-image, eschews modern lights and mockingly lowers a live opossum in a cage to affirm its claim to fame as the possum capital of the world, supposedly because of the large quantity of roadkill in the area.

Widely imitated and satirized, the custom of dropping an object on New Year's Eve derives from the world-renowned (and internationally broadcast) New York City tradition of lowering a 1,070-pound illuminated Waterford crystal ball, initiating a countdown to midnight by up to two million revelers in Times Square. The ball was first dropped in 1907, following the New Year's Eve tradition of dropping balloons, streamers, and other objects on celebrants' heads. The crystal ball symbolizes anticipation of the future, and its illumination represents the ever-promising transition from the darkness of sleep and winter to the vitality of light and revelry. The joyous blaring of noisemakers typically accompanies the celebration and is based on the traditional idea of scaring away demons and spirits at times of change, especially when there is hope and glee in the air. In some parts of the country, the noisemaking tradition derives from an old German holiday ritual in which bands of young men fired their guns while traveling from farmhouse to farmhouse; along the way, they would be invited into houses and recite New Year wishes, receiving food and drink in exchange.

The New Year's toast is also typical of congratulatory libations for symbolic births, frequently offering thanks to fate or a higher power. The modern addition of fireworks, such as the large display in Brooklyn's Grand Army Plaza, comes from displays among the Chinese for their traditional New Year. Toasts and celebrations are typically accompanied by the singing of "Auld Lang Syne," a Scottish traditional song adapted by poet Robert Burns in the eighteenth century. The title means "for times gone by," and the opening verse poses a question with the approach of each New Year: "Should old acquaintance be forgot and never brought to mind?" Often undermined in modern performance, the original message of the song is to reflect on the past rather than forget it in embracing the future as Americans tend to do.

Although the noisemaking and libation traditions in some cultures may mark trepidation about embarking on something new, New Year's Eve celebrations in the United States welcome the new and express hopes for the future. Wishes for a "happy, healthy, and prosperous New Year" are commonplace. One sign of

American optimism, for example, is the annual "polar bear dip" by bathers emboldened by the New Year in the cold Northeast, representing with their bravado defiance of the cold and a signal of human control over the environment. Giving birth to the first baby of the New Year is a fortuitous sign in any community and widely reported in the local press. Likewise, the media inevitably broadcast a sampling of New Year's resolutions by local inhabitants, a tradition that declares American confidence in progress, enlivened by the fresh start of the New Year. It is a sign of shared American guilt and the belief in the capability of the fresh start that the most common New Year's resolutions are to lose weight, exercise more, get out of debt, quit drinking alcohol and smoking, and spend more time with family. Surveys show that 80 percent of Americans who make New Year's resolutions drop them by February, but it appears that announcing goals for change with the start of the New Year is important as an American announcement of self-determination (Mills 2020).

Game watching, traditionally associated with revelry, takes the distinctive form of college football "bowl" games on the New Year. The tradition derives from games of ritual combat and tests of power among the youth of the nation, a cathartic public ritual that marked the New Year's festival as a special time apart from everyday life. It also signified hopes for the period to follow—triumph, strength, and determination—symbolized by the rise of a new champion and the slaying of an opponent, who was then relegated to the past. Americans most likely derived this cultural expectation from festivities in the British Isles, where Highland games and rugby tournaments were commonly held on New Year's Day. In modern America, the oldest college football bowl game (referred to as the "Granddaddy of Them All") is the Rose Bowl in Pasadena, California, first played in 1902. In cities that host bowl games on New Year's Day—such as the Orange Bowl in Miami, Cotton Bowl in Dallas, and Sugar Bowl in New Orleans—the contest itself is the focus of festivities, which include parades, parties, and public revelry. Although the number of postseason bowl games has proliferated over the years, a place in one of the New Year's Day games remains a lofty honor for top college teams. The festivity and celebration of American prowess culminates with Super Bowl Sunday originally held in mid-January during the late 1960s and scheduled in February after 2002. Families and friends host Super Bowl parties with a range of unhealthy foods such as pizza, potato chips, and Buffalo wings that break earlier resolutions to lose weight and eat healthy (Price 2016). The traditionalized foods also point to the Americanness of the game as one of taking risks and moving across territory (see Chapter 3 on Winning). It is a mass-mediated spectacle revolving around television, and sales of televisions before "the big game" spike annually (Ortega 2017). Not coincidentally, consumerism is elevated in American awareness with attention to newly broadcast commercial spots for brand-name products during the Super Bowl.

Balancing the framing of New Year's Eve as a national event are a number of customs on New Year's Day that boost regional and urban identity. A prominent example is the Mummer's Parade in Philadelphia, first held in 1901. The procession features strutters in elaborate sequined and feathered costumes, along with floats and movable scenery. They are joined by string bands, often with more than 50 members playing banjos and glockenspiels. In keeping with the New Year tradition of comic reversals, a separate division of the parade is designated for prancing clowns, some dressed in drag carrying three-tiered parasols. Various floats in the comic division playfully satirize modern everyday life and mockingly make reference to current events. The parade combines elements of the British New Year's mumming tradition brought by early settlers and nineteenth-century American minstrelsy. Typically performed by masked or costumed young men as part of end-of-the-year festivities, traditional mummer plays often include the killing and restoration to life of one of the characters. The strumming banjoes and skits of the parade originated in minstrel shows, and, before a ban on blackface in 1964, many comics would dance in greasepaint as a sign of the ritual reversal and revelry of the festival. Still, a theme song of the parade played by the string bands is "Oh Dem Golden Slippers," written in 1879 by African-American songwriter James Bland for the minstrel theater and satirizing the black spiritual "Golden Slippers" popularized by the Fisk Jubilee Singers after the Civil War; the tune entered oral tradition played by fiddlers and string bands as an accompaniment to square dances. For paraders, the refrain of golden slippers "to walk the golden street" and the call to "have a good time when we ride up in the chariot in the morn" suit the boisterousness and future-orientation of the occasion.

Encompassing various traditions and celebrated on various dates, New Year's in America is viewed as a transition zone between the past and future; folk ceremonies associated with it signal change and serve the purpose of pushing celebrants forward. With globalization, New Year's Eve parties are broadcast around the world and the visibility of similar features remind many Americans that regional and ethnic customs not only help in adapting to change but also provide a conspicuous source of regional and ethnic identity.

Although summer solstice occurs in the northern hemisphere on June 20, Americans define summer beginning with the Memorial Day holiday at the end of May and ending on Labor Day in September. Beginning on May 30, 1869 as Decoration Day as a solemn occasion for honoring the graves of the Civil War dead, Memorial Day evolved into a patriotic display for military personnel who died in all American wars. After passage of the Uniform Monday Holiday Act in 1968, Memorial Day became nationally observed as part of a three-day weekend in May. With fewer Americans having a personal connection to the military and stores promoting holiday sales for summer activity, the holiday signaled the start of a summertime defined as filled with vacations and leisure. Community pools typically opened for business on Memorial Day weekend. Although most children no longer worked on the farm, schools maintained an agrarian schedule of a summer break to facilitate labor for harvesting. A growing number of summer camps filled the void for many non-agrarian children and marked summer as a getaway time.

Labor Day also is observed as part of a long holiday weekend and became the unofficial end of summer. Pools closed after the holiday and schools traditionally began classes afterward. Although promoted in the late nineteenth century by organized labor, the holiday evolved as did Memorial Day into a vacation period and consumer time to prepare for autumn as a time to get back to work and classes. Ironically, Labor Day after the 1970s celebrated leisure more than labor, and pointed to a decline of a working-class consciousness in favor of enjoying and aspiring to join the social mobility of white-collar management (Aronowitz 1992; Cowie 2012). Whereas earlier the holiday venerated the tradesperson and industrial worker who worked with their hands, in an economy turning toward professional services and information-driven businesses, Labor Day recalled the many professions that made summer leisure possible. Although unions still parade on the holiday, many communities host carnivals and fireworks displays with the closing of the weekend to celebrate summer fun as a reward for enduring the daily grind of corporatized work rather than the noble labor of blue-collar work. In many regions, communities extend the promise of leisure as a reward by organizing outdoor entertainment fairs for those at home in place of the traditional harvest festival of the agrarian economy (Grames and Vitcenda 2012). In keeping with the American connection of seasons with sports, Labor Day weekend trades in the leisureliness of baseball in the park for the opening of the fall football season, and its representation of renewed strenuosity and organizational complexity on the gridiron (see Chapter 3).

Mid-summer is marked by the "Fourth of July," the folk term for Independence Day. Although established to celebrate the nation's founding narrative of revolution, national unity, and liberty, it also has evolved into a vacation period, although it is not officially designated as part of a three-day weekend. In keeping with its patriotic theme, most municipalities organize parades, sporting events, political orations, band concerts of nationalistic tunes, and elaborate fireworks displays. To the present day, prominent events commemorating the Fourth of July are played out against a backdrop of historic sites associated with the American Revolution in Philadelphia, Boston, and Yorktown, or symbols of American liberty such as the Statue of Liberty in New York City and the Washington Monument in Washington, D.C. With its historical theme of freedom from tyranny, represented by public readings of the Declaration of Independence—highlighting the theme that "all men are created equal" and the concept of the "inalienable rights" of "life, liberty, and the pursuit of happiness"—the holiday in the American spirit of dissent has also been occasion for protest movements to stage counternationalistic events. For example, New York City, Philadelphia, and other cities have been frequent sites of anti-war rallies and protest demonstrations with themes of "Call to Liberty" and "Save America." Such events underscore the political legacy of Independence Day as a time to reflect on the paradox of a nation born out of revolution while striving for stability.

As a major secular holiday in midsummer for an increasingly mobile, dispersed society, Independence Day is often perceived as a time for family and town gatherings and reunions—especially at picnics, baseball games, and outdoor barbecues—and frequently for vacation getaways at beaches, mountains, and parks. Coinciding with reflections on national heritage, the Fourth of July is also considered a prime opportunity to celebrate America's traditional roots and cultural diversity. Thus, it has been the date around which America's largest folk festivals, including the Smithsonian Folklife Festival held on the National Mall in Washington, D.C., have been scheduled. A musical tradition of the holiday is the discharge of cannon during the outdoor orchestral playing of the "1812 Overture," composed by Pyotr Ilich Tchaikovsky in 1880. Although the performance has entered American memory as a patriotic piece commemorating U.S. victory in the War of 1812 (often referred to as the "second war of independence" from Britain), Tchaikovsky was actually inspired by the victory of Russia in the Napoleonic Wars in 1812. If Americans have adopted the piece as their own, they also have a repertoire of patriotic songs written by Americans: "You're a Grand Old Flag" (1906), by George M. Cohan, who claimed to be born on the Fourth of July; "America the Beautiful" (1893), by Katharine Lee Bates; and "This Land Is Your Land" (1940), by Woody Guthrie.

In a Fourth of July oration in Rochester, New York, in 1852, antislavery leader Frederick Douglass picked up the theme of the unfulfilled promise of freedom for slaves. It was among the first and most prominent protests of a holiday he called a "sham" and the "hypocrisy" of celebrating liberty and "national greatness" in a nation that condoned slavery. In 1866, African Americans in Texas began holding a separate celebration on June 19 called "Juneteenth," referred to as the black Fourth of July. June 19 marked the day in 1865 on which Union General Gordon Granger marched into the Texas city of Galveston and announced the news of the Emancipation Proclamation freeing the slaves. The measure had been signed by President Abraham Lincoln on January 1, 1863, more than two and a half years earlier.

Over the course of a few years, the Juneteenth celebration diffused to other states and became an annual tradition. Festivities mirrored Fourth of July celebrations for whites, with religious ceremonies and readings of the Emancipation Proclamation, followed by speeches, family picnics, theatrical reenactments of emancipation, heritage education programs, music, dancing, fireworks, and sporting events such as rodeos and baseball games. "Lift Every Voice," written by James Weldon Johnson in 1899 and called the African-American national anthem, is widely sung. Food symbolic of the southern experience, particularly barbecued meats, became central to the event.

During the early twentieth century, celebrations of Juneteenth declined as blacks shifted their festivities to national commemorations on July 4. The civil rights movement of the 1950s and 1960s, however, fueled a resurgence of Juneteenth as Freedom, or Emancipation, Day. In 1980, Texas became the first state to recognize Juneteenth as an official state holiday, and the state is still a focus for national activities. The site of the first Juneteenth celebration in Galveston remains the backdrop for organized parades, picnics, gospel music festivals, zydeco

FIGURE 2.7 Performers demonstrate traditional African song and dance at the Booker T. Washington National Juneteenth Celebration of Freedom, 2019.
Source: Tim Ervin, Photographer. National Park Service. Public Domain.

and blues concerts, and a reunion of former city residents. Houston since 1974 has designated Juneteenth as Emancipation Proclamation Day and has held a major parade and heritage festival. Among the larger Juneteenth festivals in the North is that held in Minneapolis, Minnesota, established in 1985, which attracts 60,000 participants in parades, cooking contests, sporting events, community forums, and exhibitions of black history and culture. Although since 1983 the federal holiday of "Birthday of Martin Luther King, Jr." observed on the third Monday of January often features celebrations of African-American expressive culture, its occurrence in post-New Year winter and conceptualization as an occasion for community service and an alternative labor day to counter the leisure-oriented summer holiday muted its cultural connection. As a marker of time, it more often signaled the end of winter break and the start of a new academic semester in many colleges and universities. African-American arts as a central influence on national culture are much more evident in Juneteenth festivals. Although Juneteenth is primarily a celebration of African-American heritage, since the late twentieth century its predominant theme of social freedom (often distinguished from the Fourth of July theme of political liberty) has also attracted those protesting war, the death penalty, and the abuse of workers' rights.

Amid festivals through June and July that boost ethnicity and region, the nationalism of Independence Day, and to an extent the triumphalism of the United States, is publicly visualized in the plebeian image of Uncle Sam, portrayed as an imposing if

FIGURE 2.8 "Our Country: Uncle Sam." 1898.
Source: Joseph Randall Blanchard, photographer. Prints and Photographs Division, Library of Congress.

comical tall and thin figure with a beard and a stars-and-stripes top hat and red-and-white-striped pants. He did not appear in Fourth of July celebrations until the latter part of the nineteenth century when many Americans became aware through the Progressive era of the widening gap between "robber-baron" wealth of monopolies and a growing industrial working class. Too, it was an era when with the closing of the frontier the United States embraced imperial expansion during the Spanish–

American War and in Pacific territorial acquisition. Uncle Sam appeared to be the everyman with big aspirations of social mobility and national power represented by his height and self-assured gait. Until that time, it was common for Independence Day celebrants to evoke memories of colonial revolution by carrying poles with "liberty caps" (shallow, limp hats that, according to legend, were worn by freed Roman slaves). The most common explanation of Uncle Sam's emergence as a national symbol for the future rather than the past owes to folklore. According to legend, American soldiers during the War of 1812 stationed in upstate New York began using the name Uncle Sam to refer to shipments of meat stamped with the initials (U.S.) of the supplier, "Uncle" Samuel Wilson of Troy, New York. According to another narrative, a military unit called the United States Light Dragoons went by the acronym "USLD"; when asked what the letters stood for, the reply was "Uncle Sam's Lazy Dogs." The folksy figure of Uncle Sam, popularized by the political cartoonist Thomas Nast during the 1870s, was intended as a counterpart to the British male caricature of John Bull. Bull is usually depicted as a bloated dandy in a top hat and long-tailed coat, and distinguished as a nationalistic folktype by a Union Jack flag design on his vest and white pants tucked into riding boots. Uncle Sam has more of the look of a lanky, ready to move commoner and is often displayed in parades as towering above the crowd by walking on stilts.

"All-American" foods representing American national unity, particularly the hot dog (a sausage placed in a tubular bun), are featured on the Fourth of July. Although many Americans consider the hot dog or frankfurter (named after the city of Frankfurt, Germany) to be uniquely American, it owes to the bratwurst and kielbasa shapes developed in central Europe during the seventeenth century. A hot dog is distinguished from the European versions, however, by its smaller size (usually six inches in length, although some "big American" versions, representing American optimism and aspiration, are advertised as "footlong" hot dogs) and relative lack of spicing. Americans customarily "dress" the hot dog with mustard, onions, sauerkraut, and relish. It is often grilled on the Fourth of July in outdoor barbecues, that evoke frontier images, but the hot dog can also be boiled, steamed, or deep-fried. Consuming them has American associations with Independence Day because they are a portable street food, suited to an expansive nation on the go. Another American association of the hot dog is with ballpark food; hot dogs began to be sold at St. Louis Browns baseball games in the 1880s and now are staples of stadium vendors nationwide. Many food historians associate the popularity of the hot dog as an American icon to the memorable St. Louis World's Fair (Louisiana Purchase Exposition) in 1904, where other Fourth of July favorites such as hamburgers and ice cream cones were also canonized as festival fare.

The consumption of hot dogs as a demonstration of nationalism and American abundance is symbolically enacted in hot-dog-eating contests across the country. The best-known event is held in the Coney Island section of Brooklyn, New York, where an early amusement park was built in the 1880s. According to legend, four immigrants in 1916 staged a hot-dog-eating contest at Nathan's

Famous Coney Island restaurant to show who was the most patriotic. Since that time, the restaurant has been the site of a noontime contest awarding a trophy to the person who can eat the most hot dogs in a 12-minute span. The event grew in visibility during the late twentieth century, with national television coverage and more than ten thousand spectators on hand. Other eating contests, cooking contests, and "bake-offs" represent regional and national folk identities, such as chili and barbecue (particularly in the South and West), baked beans and chowder (in the Northeast), corn on the cob, watermelon, and pie, washed down with the quintessentially American summer drinks of lemonade and iced tea.

Many Fourth of July festivals celebrate the heritage of "small-town" America with self-consciously old-fashioned entertainments including barbershop quartets, band concerts, flag-carrying color guards, square dances, vintage car shows, carousels, and children's games set against the backdrop of flags displayed on Main Street porches. As America has become more urbanized and dispersed, many small towns promote their Fourth of July celebrations as occasions for "hometown reunions." Large urban centers such as Miami, Detroit, and Los Angeles advertise their Fourth of July festivals as occasions to celebrate ethnic diversity and civic pride in local traditions. To encourage the values of citizenship since a wave of new immigration from Latin America, eastern Europe, Africa, and Asia in the late twentieth century, a number of Fourth of July festivals also feature naturalization ceremonies for immigrants. Cities with professional baseball teams once recognized the holiday with a traditional doubleheader, signaling indulgence in the pastoral sport known as "America's pastime" that evokes a double meaning of something of the past and a way to leisurely pass the time.

Quickly after Labor Day, stores begin selling candy and costumes for Halloween, and communities sponsor events with haunting themes. Halloween is not an official holiday, but "trick or treat" hours are regulated by municipalities, and communities sponsor Halloween parades. In the absence of holidays celebrating children that are common in other countries, Halloween emerged in the United States as a time to indulge children with sweets. Once meant to engage neighbors in a gesture of community, trick or treaters increasingly seek out areas known for troves of candy givers. The decorative themes of the holiday feature autumn colors and harvest symbols that suggest the holiday as an adjustment to the lengthening darkness and cold of fall days (Santino 1994, 145–67). Participants in the holiday play with death in the form of ghosts and witches to confront the decay of foliage and chill in the air. Children, a theory maintained, especially need adjustment because of the attention to youthful activities during summer, and Halloween fit the bill. A growing phenomenon in the twenty-first century, however, is the expansion of holiday celebration to adults, which also explains growing consumer spending on the holiday, amounting to over eight billion dollars in 2020. Surveys reported an increase from the start of the century of a 50 percent participation rate among adults to over 70 percent in the second decade (Owens 2018). The largest portion of revelers is between 18 and 34 years old, and is the holiday's biggest spending group. These adults are purchasing costumes and decorations, and specialty stores have opened to serve them. Besides the Halloween dance party, another emerging custom for adults is the costume contest in which one's creativity can be publicly displayed, often with commentaries on popular and political culture that goes beyond the traditional themes of death and decay. Replacing candy among adults is consumption of alcohol, often in bar events, although distribution of sweets at work are more ubiquitous for adults in office settings than they were. The reasons for this phenomenon relate at least in part to the emerging centrality of youth in the life course and the perception of Halloween as a secular escape from daily routines, particularly for corporatized office work in a liminal space between summer and fall. With the view in a vague transition to adulthood from adolescence that one needs to get serious, Halloween is an opportunity to extend youthful joy. In the holiday's playing with the uniformity of death is also an opportunity for adult party-goers to perform their vitality and individuality as they have been forced to get down to business and the prospect of a long plateau of repetitive work. It is as if Halloween for adults, unlike for children, serves as a ritual death so as to be reborn and regain one's youthfulness.

Many countries have holidays intended to show gratitude for the bounty of the land after the harvest. The American Thanksgiving is distinctive in its strong associations with American patriotism, family bonding, and prosperity in the given context of a mobile, dispersed society. In the United States, Congress fixed the holiday in 1941 as the fourth Thursday in November. The holiday has been associated since the late nineteenth century with the story of a shared meal after the first harvest in 1621 by the Wampanoag and the Puritans who settled in Plymouth, Massachusetts. It was a founding narrative promoted during the mid-nineteenth century to reaffirm the ancestry and ideals of the New England Pilgrims, particularly at a time of sectional disputes. Although the iconography of the holiday in contemporary America reflects the Pilgrim mythology, for many people Thanksgiving is a secular occasion for homecoming, affirmation of family, and social connection that compensates for American individualism. It is unique among American holidays in that for many celebrants it extends over a four-day rather than a three-day weekend. For many students in the Northeast, the holiday may be even longer in school districts that close for the beginning of hunting season accompanied by an image of pioneer heritage, usually beginning the Monday after Thanksgiving. Unlike most holidays that include a festive meal as a component, for Thanksgiving the meal itself defines the observance. With the growing emphasis in the twentieth century on shopping for Christmas, Thanksgiving has also emerged as a seasonal marker of the beginning of the Christmas season; the day after, the busiest single shopping day of the year, has come to be known as "Black Friday."

The story of the Pilgrim harvest celebration was chronicled in journals by Puritan leaders William Bradford and Edward Winslow, published in *Mourt's*

Relation by George Morton in London in 1622. Their accounts described a feast with Native Americans lasting several days after a successful harvest; the fare included fish (cod and bass), venison, waterfowl, and "Indian corn." Bradford mentions "a great store of wild turkeys" and recounts that the celebrants "took many" of them. Scholars have speculated that the feast of 1621 drew on English church-based harvest festivals often held in September (called "harvest home" in many areas), and perhaps the events surrounding Michaelmas, held around the same time, but the separatist Pilgrims are known to have eschewed the celebration of saints' days and church feasts. Since they lived for 11 years in Leiden in the Netherlands before embarking for the New World, they may have been influenced by Leidens Ontzet (the relief of Leiden), a public thanksgiving celebration featuring local foodways (herring and white bread). The Pilgrims' desire to preserve at least some measure of Dutch tradition in their collective memory is evidenced by the presence of a Leyden Street in the early Plymouth Colony, the first street laid out by the Pilgrims.

Puritan Thanksgiving became a regional commemoration in the Massachusetts Bay Colony in 1630 and frequently thereafter until about 1680, when it became an annual festival in that colony; it was also observed in Connecticut as early as 1639 and annually after 1647 (Baker 2009). The Pilgrims were not alone in holding a Thanksgiving celebration after the harvest—earlier feasts with Native Americans were recorded in Virginia and St. Augustine (in present-day Florida), and the Dutch in New Netherland appointed a day for giving thanks in 1644—but these celebrations were remembered regionally in oral tradition and from Bradford's chronicle. Thanksgivings were proclaimed by Presidents George Washington, John Adams, and James Madison during the early years of the New Republic, and by 1858 the governors of 25 states and two territories had declared Thanksgivings (although most were not connected to the Pilgrim story). Reflecting the sectional rivalries of the period, some southern states objected to a New England connection; Pennsylvania Germans called for a model based on their harvest home observance in September, involving redistribution of harvest foods to the poor. During the Civil War, President Abraham Lincoln proclaimed a national Thanksgiving Day as a sign of unity to be observed on the final Thursday of November—on which it continues to be observed. During the late nineteenth century, in the face of mass immigration, many nativists promoted the Pilgrim story as a founding narrative for the "birth of America" and advertised Plymouth as "America's hometown." Thanksgiving was made an integral part of Americanization programs for newcomers, and the New England feast became a national icon of the Puritan work ethic and commitment to an Anglo-white Protestant norm.

During the twentieth century, with the growth of the consumer culture, the day after Thanksgiving came to be identified as the first day of the Christmas shopping season. Together with the New Year and other religious-ethnic celebrations, the months between November and January became known as the "holiday season." As a custom of adjustment, the abundance of holidays during this time in many locations compensates with symbols of light and expressions of joy for the darkness and cold of winter. For the United States, the holidays are a paradoxical mixture of excess consumerism and compensatory social charity. They are occasions to simultaneously reinforce ethnic and nationalistic values, and counter narratives of conflict between indigenous and settler peoples.

A challenge to the nationalistic mythology of Thanksgiving erupted during the late twentieth century concerning the representation of Native Americans in the nationalistic mythology of the Pilgrims (Silverman 2020). In 1970, at the 350th anniversary of the landing of the Pilgrims, Native Americans staged a protest on Thanksgiving Day that featured a ceremonial burial of Plymouth Rock. Since then, Thanksgiving has been an occasion for Native-American activists to declare a "National Day of Mourning" for the tragedy that befell their ancestors with the arrival of white European settlers. Protestors often call for a march to counter the Pilgrims Progress Parade in Plymouth, held annually on Thanksgiving to commemorate Pilgrim experience in the "founding" of the nation. In 1998, after disruptions and violence the two previous years, the Plymouth Historical Alliance agreed to erect a plaque that revised the Pilgrim story to include a narrative of suffering by Native Americans. The society continued to sanction its annual procession, however, which featured muskets and halberds (interpreted by the Native-American activists as symbols of violence and oppression).

At the national political level, Thanksgiving has been an occasion for presidential proclamations of the principles of freedom that form the foundation of American democracy. Prior to the proclamation, in a ritual of mercy begun in 1947, the President spares the life of a turkey and declares it free to live the rest of its days peacefully on a farm. In addition, the National Turkey Federation presents the President with two large dressed turkeys as a sign of American abundance. And in another public gesture associated with the holiday during the late twentieth century, civic leaders and other prominent figures help serve Thanksgiving dinners to the homeless at soup kitchens and missions for the inner-city poor.

The stuffed plump turkey is the centerpiece of the holiday meal, and compliments are generally extended to the cook for its crisp, brown skin, juiciness, and oversized breasts. Indeed, American slang for Thanksgiving is "Turkey Day." Usually the bird is roasted in the oven for hours, although deep-frying is an alternative technique that has some favor in the South. Southerners generally make their stuffing from cornbread, while in other parts of the country white bread is the base, to which oysters, apples, chestnuts, sausage, or the turkey's giblets may be added. The growth of the animal rights movement and vegetarianism in the late twentieth century has prompted some to use meat substitutes such as "tofurky," made from the soy product tofu; others maintain that this merely perpetuates the symbol of the killed bird. Some vegans (who abstain from eating any food derived from animals) use homemade bread or butternut squash instead. Groups who use the occasion to reflect on the Native-American experience feature foods such as the "three sisters" (squash, corn, and beans) and Pueblo corn pie.

Also popular at the Thanksgiving dinner table are candied sweet potatoes (also called yams) and cranberry jellies. The former dish most likely represents a southern contribution, while the latter derives from New England. Regional blending into national tradition is also evident at dessert, when pumpkin pie, associated with New England, is served together with pecan pie, connected with the South. Other regional dishes include sweet potato pie (South), shoofly pie (Pennsylvania), sauerkraut (Maryland), Dungeness crab (West Coast), turducken (Louisiana), and corn pudding (South). Mashed potatoes, creamed cauliflower, turnips, and radishes are passed around in large serving dishes, appropriate to the communal character of the meal.

Rituals and activities other than sitting down to the meal mark the social significance of Thanksgiving, particularly in defining family and gender roles. It is common practice for the woman of the house to cook the turkey and for the man to carve it ceremoniously at the table. The normative seating pattern has the elders of the family at the head and foot of the table. Family bonding is emphasized by the saying of grace (or a secular expression of gratitude) and eating from communal dishes. After the meal, usually held in the late afternoon, a common tradition is to watch professional football games on television; since 1934, the Detroit Lions located in "middle America" have been perennial Thanksgiving participants. Before football became the dominant sporting holiday event in the mid-twentieth century, it was common in local communities to hold Thanksgiving shooting contests testing manly target skills, such as pigeon shoots and turkey shoots. The shoots were also warm-ups for the big-game hunting season, which opened in Pennsylvania and other states on the Monday after Thanksgiving. Many hunters trekked to hunting camp on the weekend and engaged in another seasonal tradition: a venison or steak dinner as a wilderness hunting parallel to the farm harvest theme of Thanksgiving. For Christmas shoppers, the hunt is for bargains at stores that open early in the morning on the Friday after Thanksgiving. Gifts and cards as part of the Christmas "shopping season" become especially important in a dispersed mobile society such as the United States because of their use to mediate social relations among family and friends in various locales and also forge a sense of community in modern work settings where workers tend to be strangers to one another (Bronner 1986a, 20; see also Chapter 4 in this book).

Signaling the transition to Christmas is the Macy's Thanksgiving Day Parade in New York City, which traditionally ends with Santa Claus on a reindeer-led float bedecked with elves, gumdrops, candy canes, wreaths, ribbons, ornaments, and gifts. The parade is traced to street performances by immigrant employees of Gimbel's in Philadelphia and Macy's in New York City during the early 1920s. Following eastern European harvest festival traditions, they created a carnival atmosphere with a holiday costume procession. The parade evolved over the years into a high-profile marketing and media event that celebrates consumer culture and is aimed at children. The main attractions are huge floating balloons of popular animated characters and comic superheroes and appearances by celebrities from the world of popular entertainment. Similar formats are followed in rival Thanksgiving parades in Houston, Philadelphia, and Detroit.

Although many Americans attend a parade or watch a football game on Thanksgiving, the important gesture of the holiday is to come home, often their parents' house or the town in which they grew up. Indeed, Thanksgiving is often referred to as America's "homecoming" and family celebration. Transportation providers often tout it as the busiest travel time of the year as a result. Thus, an important function of the holiday is to provide communal identity for an increasingly mobile, dispersed society (Anderson 2015). Since the twentieth century, young people are more often expected to leave home and seek opportunities outside the communities where they were raised. And even if they are not able to come home for the holiday, many Americans create a sense of family and community by sharing the holiday with "second families" of friends, neighbors, and co-workers. The customs and traditions associated with Thanksgiving refer to social connections at both the local and national levels—reflecting the immediacy of family and community, while invoking narratives of the nation's founding and ideals.

Both the American ritual year and life course venerate beginnings and emphasize the finality of the end. In their linearity, both encourage people to set their own paths while moving forward. Both are tied to metaphors of seasons and at the same time declare defiance by acts of human control. Because of the individuality and future-orientation that symbolic treks through the year and life course conceptually normalize, various markers create spaces and times for social connection and regrouping, often in response to a perceived routinization of modern daily life. Challenges to the normalized and naturalized march, and conceptualization, of time are apparent from various groups that vie to share the road, and progress, toward the future. Balancing values of equality and hierarchy in their political and cultural history, Americans negotiate their access to the middle of the avenue and revise the national and local heritage—indeed the Americanness—on which it is based.

Notes to Chapter 2

1. Polls and surveys cited in this chapter were obtained from the Roper Center (2021) database. The keywords "future" and "mood" generated the 1,287 polls and surveys between 1948 and 2000. The polls and surveys on future mood were concentrated, however, in the final decade of the twentieth century. While 597 polls and surveys were found between 1948 and 1988, 690 were identified between 1989 and 2000.

2. A number of examples can be given for the polling fever in American popular consciousness. Magazines such as *American Demographics* and *The Futurist*

are specially devoted to reporting trends and making forecasts. *Megatrends* by John Naisbitt (1982) was on the *New York Times* bestseller list for over a year, and it was followed by the successful *Megatrends 2000* by John Naisbitt and Patricia Aburdene (1990). Other books that profile the "average American" are *American Renaissance: Our Lives at the Turn of the 21st Century* by Marvin Cetron and Owen Davies (1989), *American Averages* by Mike Feinsilber and William B. Mead (1980), *Who We Are* by Sam Roberts (1995), and *Values Matter Most* by Ben Wattenberg (1995). Within the scholarship of American Studies, the use of polling data to test American exceptionalism and gauge "American character" has generated a lively methodological and theoretical debate about whether such a cultural profile is scientifically or humanistically possible. See, for examples, Barton 1982; Cooper and Layard 2002; Inkeles 1989; Lipset 1996; Murphey 1965; Stannard 1971.

3
WINNING

Even though Hollywood actors are allowed their eccentricities, the statements made in 2011 by Charlie Sheen seemed strange. In an interview on the television show *20/20* in answer to a question about his daily life, he blurted,

> Every day is just filled with just wins. All we do is put wins in the record books. We win so radically in our underwear before our first cup of coffee, it's scary. People say it's lonely at the top, but I sure like the view.
> *(Canning, Wallace, and Sher 2011)*

Sheen's reference to *winning*, and its interpretation, received so much press coverage and social media comments that *Time* magazine named it the number two "buzzword" of the year, second only to "occupy" which dominated headlines that year because of the "Occupy Wall Street" movement (Steinmetz 2011). Although prompted by the celebrity quotes, the Americanness of the loaded term *winning* and status of being a singular triumphant winner at the top of a social hierarchy drew commentary for years. Perhaps best known is a twist of a traditional proverb famously attributed to Green Bay Packers coach Vince Lombardi, "Winning isn't everything, it's the only thing" (earliest documentation of the saying was by UCLA football coach Henry Sanders in 1950; Doyle, Mieder, and Shapiro 2012, 278). And if you come in second place in this mindset, you are a loser, according to the adage "There's just winning and losing" (Doyle, Mieder, and Shapiro 2012, 199) dating back to the 1920s in the United States.

On the Internet, memes with Sheen's image and statements on winning went viral. The varied captions accompanying his smiling face included "The only thing I'm addicted to right now is Winning," "All I do is win win," "Winning at Everything," and "Duh Winning." Even the Internet's most famous baby, the

DOI: 10.4324/9780429452970-4

"Success Kid" showing a baby clenching a fistful of sand (usually interpreted as a triumphant fist pump), got into the act with memes announcing "Epic Win," "Uh Winning," and on Independence Day, "Winning a War with the Stinky British, Yay I Did It." The symbolic equivalence of "Winning" with the original caption of "Success" from 2007 was clear, often with the narrative that the boy's triumph resulted from destroying another child's sandcastle (McCoral 2009). The image was of "total" victory which the meme suggested was the most satisfying. It evoked a military metaphor of there being "no substitute for victory" (Doyle, Mieder, and Shapiro 2012, 244).

The American two-party election system is based on total victory. The winner in a presidential election takes all; power is not shared proportionally as it is in a parliamentary system. It is a startling case in which coming in second is indeed losing. It became an issue in the 2020 presidential election when the Republican presidential candidate Donald Trump claimed victory although the vote count indicated otherwise. Moreover, it was not enough to be voted into office; he pronounced that he won in a landslide, suggesting the eliminative metaphor of total victory (Wilkie 2020). Previous to the election outcome he harped on his winning ways, as making good on his promise to "Make America Great Again" (echoing Ronald Reagan's 1980 campaign slogan) and validate his aspiration to be a national leader. Indeed, those quotes became both satirized and glorified as memes (Scrapbooker 2017). In 2016, he asserted on the campaign trail,

> We're going to win. We're going to win so much. We're going to win at trade, we're going to win at the border. We're going to win so much, you're going to be so sick and tired of winning, you're going to come to me and go "Please, please, we can't win anymore." You've heard this one. You'll say "Please, Mr. President, we beg you sir, we can't want to win anymore. It's too much. It's not fair to everybody else." And I'm going to say "I'm sorry, but we're going to keep winning, winning, winning. We're going to make America great again."
>
> *(Lutey 2016)*

He claimed to be winning a war against the coronavirus and a trade war with China. Trump's successor Joseph Biden also declared war on the virus, but in the aftermath of a contentious election appealed to Americans to end to "this uncivil war that pits red against blue, rural versus urban, conservative versus liberal." Acknowledging the agonistic binary structure in the American system of winner-takes-all, he called for "the most elusive of all things in a democracy: unity" (Hunnicutt, Zengerle, and Renshaw 2021).

So who does not like to win? And who relishes a painful schism? How is this rhetoric American? And is this the price to be paid for participant democracy? My point is that the discourse, even if exaggerated by Trump, reflects an outlook of dominion that does not leave much room for sharing of power or negotiation of values. Although the ideals of liberal pluralism implied reaching consensus and compromise to accommodate the many groups that have stakes in policy, the American electoral process discouraged bipartisan action. Another problem that has especially come to the fore since the civil rights movement of the 1960s is the lack of representation for marginalized groups and financial as well as social barriers to election and acquiring governmental posts. The democratic answer is to provide checks and balances with different branches of government providing a hedge against authoritarianism. A question remains whether the political "victory culture" is an outlier in liberal American democracy or if it carries over into other realms. Economic observers have noted, for example, that American business seeks domination over spheres of the economy in a form of American unilateralism rather than sharing markets with other powers in a globalization movement (Klein and Pettis 2020; Litan 2000).

A cultural and psychological question is the source of American victory culture and the way it is perceived and reinforced. American children's games are often noted for being competitive, and especially for boy's games, emphasize social dominance (Dundes 1997; Oates and Kusz 2019). I contend that the growth of football as "America's game" exemplifies and undergirds the Americanness of victory culture. It demands closer scrutiny for the way it reflects and influences national political and economic systems. Americans are often considered to be obsessed by sports, giving them front-page attention, along with pressing political and economic news of the day. Yet why has American football risen to a level of popularity above the rest and why has it not caught on in other parts of the world where soccer tends to predominate?

Football is America's colossal spectacle of triumphalism to behold, if not to play. It is a game of elimination cheered by the largest number of fans in giant stadiums. The 17 most-watched programs in television history are all football games, and the Super Bowl is annually the most watched television event in the United States (National Football League 2009, 2). No other spectator sport commands that kind of intense popularity; opinion polls taken in the first decade of the twenty-first century show that fans name professional and college football as their favorite sport by a margin of more than three to one over other sports (National Football League 2009, 12). Much of that appeal, observers relate, is its violence, of triumphantly and symbolically slamming an opposing quarterback to the ground as a symbol of elimination, to have him "eat dirt," to lord over him as the "last man standing," and infantilize/feminize him as his "daddy" (Bronner 2019, 117–33; Brown 2007). Yet this adoration of punishing intimidation in sport appears to go against outcries in society against violence and bullying. "Are you ready for some football?," the opening theme hollered by country music performer Hank Williams Jr. for *Monday Night Football* beginning in 1989, implies that other sports have appeal, but football is the ultimate crowning contest of brute force, at least for Americans. The theme song is unapologetic in its celebration of the sport's destructiveness—"Time to get all the hits, the bangs, and the blocks" —and its macho context—"All my rowdy friends are back for Monday Night!" Is that message a reflection or a distortion of everyday life?

Football imagined as a grand festival, or spectacle, emerged in the twentieth century as a bolstering of American triumphalism in the wake of a Cold, and Vietnam, War as well as global economic competition that shook its self-confidence gained after an "all-out" victory over a despised enemy during World War II (Engelhardt 2007). In an editorial for the *Los Angeles Times*, Mark Edmundson explained the rise of football (and concomitant decline of baseball) by declaring "Football is a warlike game and we are now a warlike nation. Our love for football is a love, however self-aware, of ourselves as a fighting and (we hope) victorious people" (Edmundson 2014). He thought this is the reason that the game would not catch on in Europe, despite valiant attempts. And it is also the reason why football needs to be understood as what modern America is all about. He averred journalist Mary McGrory's often-repeated quote that historically, "Baseball is what we were. Football is what we have become" (Edmundson 2014).

In affirming the Americanness of a relative latecomer to the big-time sports world of football, Edmundson and other sportswriters noted the entrenchment of the game by traditionalizing it. In 2010, the massive superstore chain Walmart helped by launching an advertising campaign to encourage consumers to stock up for the weekend as a time for the "big game" of football. A maternal voice narrates a domestic scene: "Game time is all about the tradition. It's all about the tackles, the touchdowns, and watching my boys do what they do." Everything else going on in the house paled in comparison to sitting down to watch the game. With the invocation to tradition, promotional videos for individual teams often feature rabid fans as well as players; two representative examples are the University of Michigan that blares the message "Tradition Lives Here" and Purdue University that hails its toughness and competitiveness represented by football's "One Tradition."

In its unabashed staging of hypermasculine contests of strength and size, and in its dramatic rise to prominence in terms of attendance and media coverage, football appears to deny the thesis that play involving manly values of aggression and social dominance have been sublimated or discouraged as American culture became feminized from the nineteenth century to the twenty-first century (Douglas 1977). Despite the egalitarian spirit heralded by Title IX in the 1970s and the rise of women's sports, football is dominated by men as both players and spectators, and yet broadcasters hail it as "America's game," with its crushing blows eclipsing the public's fondness for the more leisurely, and sanitary, actions of baseball out at the pastoral park (MacCambridge 2004; Mandelbaum 2004; National Football League 2009). While thinness and speed marked the successful basketball player, the football player was epitomized in the image of an oversized hulk. The mixed message for boys is that American society disapproves of the veneration of brute force to exert social dominance, but it nonetheless extolls football players as "take-no-prisoners" gladiator-heroes amid the mass spectacle of football battles royale. While exercise gurus after the 1960s preached an aerobic gospel of non-competitive fitness involving losing weight and shedding body fat in the American body prone to obesity, media and businesses exalted linemen on either side of the scrimmage line for their excess bulk (McKenzie 2013).

Despite its tremendous popularity in America, football has not fared well in the rest of the world the way the American imports of baseball and basketball have. The cultural puzzle of football as a distinctively modern American obsession is to find the source of its popularity in the United States and at the same time its lack of appeal abroad that suggests football's Americanness. The label of "America's game" implies that it is a microcosm of national values and yet its prominent features defy social historical trends in its period of dramatic growth since the 1960s. The scholarship proposing that football is not "merely a game" and actually a prime cultural metaphor, or anti-metaphor, dates to the sport's emergence in the late nineteenth century as the trophy event of college athletics, coinciding with the start of the academic year (Krout 1929, 232–58). Youths' fondness for the sport's brutality sparked harsh newspaper editorials and banishment by some college presidents, especially among the elite institutions of the Northeast, where football had become all the rage among student bodies. Much of the critical concern was related to its ferocity and gore, which appeared to go against the image of the life of the mind in advanced education. Yet many pundits viewed it not as a reflection of life but as a necessary release from reality for adolescent boys making the transition to adulthood. They promoted its roughness as a necessary antidote to the enervating effects of modernization and industrialization on American manhood, particularly among the sedentary upper class. Offsetting teenagers' tendencies toward self-absorption and laziness, they mused, football would also transmit the values of teamwork, perseverance, and grit, which were supposed to be the keys to success in the professional world (Watterson 2000, 9–98).

The late-nineteenth-century public understood football as a participant sport associated with the high school and college years. However, with media coverage of professional football in huge stadiums before national audiences, football played by college graduates rose to the pinnacle of spectator sports during the 1960s. With replays of head-on collisions on the field and scans of rabid fans in the stands braving the elements to cheer their team on, football appeared to be tailor-made to the visual medium of television (Mandelbaum 2004, 175–79; Oriard 2001, 11–12; Rader 1999, 255–56). In 2010, football again took the lead among major American sports by being broadcast in 3-D, a viewing experience fans embraced for its ability to make the action "jump off the screen" (Pucin 2008). Viewers reported that the close-ups made them feel like they were in the midst of battle, and they praised the exaggeration of bulky, grappling bodies (Staples 2010). Unlike baseball and basketball, with many games stretching over a long season, football's relatively few games carry high stakes, and each one is cast as a major eliminative spectacle with "make or break" consequences of a "fight to the death" (Oriard 2007). Indeed, in NFL games, victory in overtime periods after ties during the regulation 60 minutes of play is decided by "sudden death" (Hume 2008). The inauguration of the Super Bowl in 1967 and the consequent construction of Super Bowl Sunday as a national festival sent signals that football deserved the crown as America's obsession as well as its prime-time sport (MacCambridge 2004).

Through the twenty-first century, reports of football scores and standings took on unprecedented public urgency as the pursuit of championships by urban teams was treated as pressing issues by big city dailies. Meanwhile, congressional hearings dragged on about the fairness of the Bowl Championship Series and concussions suffered by players; football coaches and star players became glitterati admired for their tough, aggressive attitudes, and yet they were also mercilessly incriminated for bad behavior off the field. Pundits contemplated whether the bruising game of football was a better metaphor for America than other sports were (Austin 2008). Disagreement prevailed among scholars, however, about what it was a metaphor for. The following is a list of the most common views:

1. Football is a metaphor for war and violence. As a distortion of culture, it became especially popular as America became less powerful militarily; alternatively, as a reflection of culture, it became more popular as America prepared for war (Cunningham 2004; Davison 2008; Mandelbaum 2004, 128–42; Stempel 2006; Trujillo 1995). A subset of this argument is that football was tied historically to the Cold War culture, and the sport became culturally crucial to magnify American distinctiveness and tout American values in response to communism and other perceived anti-democratic threats (Kemper 2009).
2. Football is a metaphor for corporate organization, drawing on its historical connection to industrialism and urbanism (e.g., the specialization and management of a large number of players, attention to the clock, a platoon system, ethnic participation, and collective rather than individual performance). As a reflection of culture, football became especially popular as the American economy became more service and information oriented, and football sustained the excesses of capitalism (Belliotti 2008; Hartmann 2003; Lindquist 2006; Mandelbaum 2004, 119–27; Norwood 2004; Riesman and Denney 1951; Robertson 1980, 253–57).
3. Football is a metaphor for the massification of American society. As a distortion of culture, it became an outlet for individuals to express local loyalties. Football grew in popularity as people expressed their frustrations with a society distended beyond the community scale, or the mass media seized on football (more so than other sports) as a way to construct a mass society. Related to this view is football's representation of a post-ethnic society in which helmets and alliances to the "unit" hide or sublimate players' racial and ethnic backgrounds, although some critics have complained that the rituals surrounding football reproduce patterns of inequality (Bissinger 1990; Foley 1990; Lindquist 2006; Oriard 1993, 2001; see also the message of

football players battling racial prejudice as well as athleticism of opponents in the popular movies *The Blind Side* [2009] and *Remember the Titans* [2000]).
4. Football is a metaphor for civil or folk religion, which arose with the decline of organized religion as a moral arbiter and communal institution in America (Forney 2007; Hamilton 2008; Jones 2018; Price 2001). Noting the pinnacle of professionalism given to "playing on Sunday," proponents of this concept view the ecstatic participation in the game by spectators as a transformative ritual experience in which ethical values, indeed a faith, are inculcated. In this interpretation, the football game is a national secular church.
5. Football as a framed celebration of hypermasculinity is a metaphor for sexism and homophobia in American society. Fitting in with the idea of play as a distortion of society, football became a compensation for women's increasing power in society by becoming an instrument to sustain male, heterosexual hegemony (Falk 2005; Foley 1990; Hardin 2000; Kimmel 2008, 136–38; Nelson 1994).
6. Football is a metaphor for male adolescents' anxiety over developing and repeatedly proving their masculinity. In a society lacking rituals to become an adult, participation as players enduring a dangerous ordeal of pain is a test of one's worth and passage to separation from maternal control as an adult. As a reflection of culture, football valorizes manliness by feminizing the opponent or withstanding homoerotic attack (Dundes 1978).

Methodologically, the first four views provide rationales for the rise of football, whereas the fifth and sixth are distinguished by offering psychological explanations for the American attraction to football. They seek the sources of football in boys' play development, while contextualizing the sport historically and sociologically in American experience. The last explanation, championed by folklorist Alan Dundes, shares with the fifth perspective the view that male anxiety originates in a feminizing social context, but it extends the interpretation (some critics say too far) by positing that developmental aspects of the homoerotic component of male display in big-time organized sports are rooted in male-dominated children's folk games such as "smear the queer," "piling on," and "king of the hill" (Dundes 1997). Dundes's unprecedented contention, fitting in with his broader theory that traditions persist to provide socially sanctioned outlets for conflicts and ambiguities within a society, is that football is the American version of a ritual drive, found internationally among adolescent males, to display masculinity more than femininity by engaging in homoerotic activity within this frame of initiatory play. In his words, "The object of the game, simply stated, is to get into the opponent's endzone while preventing the opponent from getting into one's endzone" (Dundes 1978, 81). Using expressive evidence in speech and custom to draw this conclusion, he theorizes that sport can be linked structurally to war making by its action of feminizing an opponent in male combat to manifest victory and achieve self-fulfillment. Because it links the psychological explanation to other meanings grounded in historical and sociological explanation, his thesis deserves a closer look in relation to the others.

Homoeroticism and War

Dundes asserted that the tough demeanor and aggressive contact distinguishing football from other popular American team sports, such as baseball and basketball, was owed to its heightened homosexual display, usually connected psychologically with emasculation. This elicited responses from popular as well as scholarly audiences. Dundes was featured in the popular press and was asked to speak on more talk shows as a result of this one article than for any of his other essays, numbering several hundred (Zumwalt 1995, 33–47). Although Dundes wanted to talk about the link between the game and war, popular interest hinged on the homoerotic components of a sport epitomizing manliness and popularly associated with aggressive heterosexuality (Dundes 1997). It was as if Dundes had blown the whistle on some cover-up, implying that this whole toughness thing with American hypermasculine bodies adored by sexy cheerleaders was one big ruse. He drew attention to the fact that football was the one big-time sport that began and ended every action with intimate male-to-male contact.

Had Dundes outed football players as homosexuals in denial? Hardly, he answered; instead, his point was that, as a metaphor, homosexuality is especially applicable to a situation in which proving masculinity creates anxiety. He might have nodded knowingly (had he lived to see it) at an advertising campaign by Spyware Doctor, a computer security program, that shows a scared, scrawny young man wearing only his underwear and holding a football in front of his groin. A hefty, helmet-clad football player with hands outstretched is in the air, aiming to grab the man's football/phallus, while the young man cowers in fear. The caption for the image reads, "Do you have the right protection?" The advertisement conspicuously draws attention to male castration anxieties with an image of a subordinated man tackled or orally attacked in a homoerotic position. The text even implies repressed homoerotic feelings in the sport by its reference to the football player as hidden, dangerous spyware. "Don't get hit by spyware; protect yourself," the advertisement blares in an obvious appeal to the male fear of rape. If that is not enough, the text closes by reminding viewers that its "OnGuard" real-time protection, with its metaphor of warding off phallic penetration, will "keep your most precious assets covered" (PC Tools Software 2007).

Dundes was not strictly applying the universalist Freudian assumption that males possess a latent homosexual attraction and that its suppression results in socially sanctioned fantasies. Rather, his emphasis was on the cultural context of "proving" masculinity in America. While others maintained that football players convey a hyperheterosexuality, Dundes questioned ways that the homoerotic elements compose this image (Hardin 2000, 36). What separated football in his mind from other sports was its highly ritualized nature, because it provides a socially sanctioned framework for male body contact. "Football, after all," he wrote, "is a so-called 'body contact' sport—is a form of homosexual behavior.... Sexual acts carried out in thinly disguised symbolic form by, and directed toward, males and males only, would seem to constitute ritual homosexuality" (Dundes 1978, 87). Another possibility is that the hyperheterosexuality present in frequent boasts among football players of "sticking it to you" and derisions of "playing like girls" is compensation for the suspicion of homosexuality in a single-sex group. In the wake of the equal rights movement, all-male groups attracted the stigma of being either sexist or gay, yet as men's studies leader Michael Kimmel observes, "Football has gained in popularity in part because it remains so steadfastly single-sex" (Kimmel 2008, 138). Among the major sports, football is also the largest display of same-sex hugs, huddles, and hand-holding.

Dundes understood its controversial nature when he wrote,

> I have no doubt that a good many football players and fans will be skeptical (to say the least) of the analysis proposed here. Even academics with presumably less personal investment in football will probably find implausible, if not downright repugnant, the idea that attempting to assert their masculinity by penetrating the endzones of their rivals.
>
> *(Dundes 1978, 86)*

Although Dundes refers to anthropological literature treating football as a display of ritualized violence and compares it to events elsewhere, including bullfights and cockfights, he and other ethnographers are still at a loss to explain why America's primary text of play should take the form it does. Football in this kind of rhetoric appears to fill a structural slot rather than being a special kind of cultural practice. Dundes's academic complaint was that historical and sociological rhetorics of play are inadequate as meaning because they do not account for a cognition revealed by symbols that presumably guide action. The literal approach of tracing football's origins or positing its social functions offers an interpretation of the consequences of play rather than the motives that explain its action. The question left unanswered or intentionally avoided, Dundes contended, is the psychological rationale leading to the unexpected enthusiasm for the sport in the context of modernization (Dundes 1978, 76–77).

Dundes claimed that the denial of football's homoerotic meaning is proof of its plausibility because of the assumption that it is the kind of disturbing thought that results in disguising or repressing conflict through the projection of symbols into fantasy and play. The meaning he brought to the fore was outside the awareness of participants, so that interviews and oral histories asking players and fans to reflect on the topic are of little consequence. He was less concerned with its Americanness than with the structure of its ritual, which can be cross-culturally compared. He gave scant attention to how the game is played and by whom than with the metaphors associated with play. These tendencies opened him up to criticism on methodological grounds even before dealing with the question of whether the explanation is valid.

The social phenomenon that Dundes addressed from his academic experience is that "in [American] college athletics it is abundantly clear that it is football which counts highest among both enrolled students and alumni" (1978, 75). This led him to observe that despite claims for the national prominence of other sports, "No other American sport consistently draws fans in the numbers which are attracted to football" (1978, 75). Having noted that football strikes, in his words "a most responsive chord in the American psyche," he set out the problem: "What is it about American football that could possibly account for its extraordinary popularity?" He implied that its popularity was indeed surprising in the context of the feminist and civil rights movements, which questioned the social dominance (and what some critics have called the masculinist hegemony or national imperialism) of sport (Stempel 2006).

Constructionist and Ethnographic Interpretations

Prominent among football's academic followers, Michael Oriard provides a historical answer to the question of football's "extraordinary popularity." In *Reading Football* (1993) and *King Football* (2001), he argues that football has risen to the level of spectacle because nineteenth-century newspapers and magazines constructed it—indeed, willed it—as a moral narrative about improving the national character. Although concluding that sport is a place to invest the major issues of the day, he finds the contemporary narrative of football too complex to decode. Unlike the reductionist interpretation for sports writing in the nineteenth century, which set football as the location for showing one's toughness and readiness for adult challenges, today's spectacle has it all, he summarizes in *Reading Football*, and he finds abundant examples of references to race and class in football coverage to show that the sport acts as a lightning rod for national social concerns about inequality. Or, stated another way, as the major American cultural spectacle coming out of a narrative of hardscrabble play and players, football is expected to fulfill the American dream of social equity and mobility, and news is made when it does not live up to that expectation (Lindquist 2006).

Other cultural critics extend the idea of football as a reflection of society to claim that it is an agent of disturbing national trends, including the rise of date rape and sexual coercion; the growing social inequality of race, gender, and class and patriarchal hegemony; and support for the U.S. invasion of Iraq (Forbes, Adams-Curtis, Pakalka, and White 2006; Stempel 2006). Whereas Oriard thinks Americans draw their meanings of sport from myriad media, a host of scholars point the finger at television as the ringleader responsible for imposing, in the words of Carl Stempel, a "masculinist sport-militaristic nationalism complex" (2006, 82; see also Trujillo 1995). Indeed, one instrumental explanation for why football has eclipsed baseball is that it shows better on television, but that still leaves questions about other prime-time sports with continuous, explosive action such as basketball and hockey, which have not been raised to the level of cultural avatar. Countries outside of North America also have sports that draw avid televised attention with "close-up pictures and…slow-motion replays," to quote Michael Mandelbaum (2004). In his opinion, because the action of football occurs far from the stands and appears to the spectator to be merely a tangle of bodies on the field, television "can dissect the action and present each slice of it in a way that the naked eye cannot see" (Mandelbaum 2004, 177).

But during my time in Europe, avid television viewers said the same thing about soccer, especially the World Cup. In Japan, where per capita television ownership rivals that of the United States (678 per 1,000 in Japan, versus 740 per 1,000 in America), baseball, soccer, and sumo matches have a devoted television following (Paolantonio 2008, xii). Mandelbaum responds that football is a winter sport, and cold weather encourages more television viewing (2004, 176), but by that rationale, basketball should be more popular than it is. Football watching is also serious business in warm-weather climates of the Deep South and Texas, as the popular television series *Friday Night Lights*, about a high school football team, attests (running on network television between 2006 and 2011, before syndication; see also Bissinger 1990, on which the series is based). Football is the sport Americans watch rather than play, whereas basketball and baseball top the charts in surveys of American youth for *participation*. The gap between boys' participation in football in the second decade of the twenty-first century and other sports grew despite the growing cultural popularity of American football. In the wake of medical revelations of health problems with concussions and chronic traumatic encephalopathy (CTE) caused by repeated head traumas in football players, the National Federation of High School Associations reported that participation in 11-player football declined around 10 percent between the peak year in 2008–2009 (1,112,303) and 2019 (Cook 2019). Nonetheless, football remains the most prominent sport at many schools and the most popular sport among high school boys by more than 400,000 ahead of outdoor track and field. Attendance at games in high schools and colleges outdistances that for other sports; includes large aggregations of marching bands, flag teams, and spirit clubs; and for many communities the home game with the opening of the school year in the fall is a, or even the, major social event in town. This framing of football as grand spectacle worthy of being televised suggests that football derives its hold from a framed drama unfolding before spectators to which Americans especially relate.

Besides the claim that the mass media make Americans embrace football, other social constructionist approaches have sought to explain football's unlikely rise by following its commercial development. They give credit or blame, through a Gramscian-Marxist lens of crafty elites manipulating the unsuspecting masses, to entrepreneurial figures such as Pete Rozelle or headline-grabbing heroes such as Joe Namath for selling football better than baseball, soccer, or basketball to a consuming public (Oriard 2007). Viewing football as commodity rather than cultural text, some critics reduce its appeal to the fact that sex and violence are good sellers. Stephen Norwood writes, for example, "No NFL team, or college team for that matter, would sell any tickets if it played touch football" (2004, 4). Yet there are problems with this assertion, since a number of upstart football leagues have not sold tickets despite their promotion of sex and violence, and the exaltation of football has hardly been universally embraced, as entrepreneurs' failure to franchise football in Europe attests (Edmundson 2014; Jim Gray 2015; Robertson 1980, 256).

Few critics look to traditions in childhood that contextualize the appeal of football as the epitome of victory culture as adults proceed on the journey of life, although this material provides evidence of a continuity in the speech and ritual surrounding football. Dundes maintains that traditions in childhood undergird ritual male involvement in football. Games such as "king of the hill," "saloogie" (also known as "keep away"), and "piling on" all involve a person who is conferred superior status by the ability to withstand the physical assault of a gang. He asserts that this developmental link provides the basis for football's popularity among sports spectators, as well as establishing the homoerotic elements of the game. To be sure, football's division into a variety of organized "plays," each requiring an offensive plan working against a countering defensive scheme, differentiates it from the folk games. Football's heightened level of organization suggests adult sophistication, but the key competition is still "on the line," where the offense works to create a "hole" and the defense attempts to block it.

A breakdown of football's popularity by participant and spectator suggests that football has different functions for fan and player. According to a national adult poll conducted in 2018, football was the favorite sport to watch of 38 percent of Americans, with baseball and basketball lagging far behind at 12 percent and 10 percent, respectively (Roper Center 2021, PRRI, 1/17–1/21/2018, USPRRI.012518.R01). When asked for the favorite sport in which to participate, 10 percent of adult respondents placed baseball first and football second at 8 percent (Roper Center 2021, Opinion Dynamics, 8/21–8/22/2007 USODFOX.082707.R3). In ethnographies, boys prefer chasing and physical games of social dominance, often exhibit packing behavior, and value toughness, whereas girls gravitate toward cooperative games that involve dyads and triads and value congeniality, repetition, and cooperation (Lever 1976; Pellegrini, Kato, Blatchford, and Baines 2002; Thorne 1993).

Behind-the-scenes glimpses of football teams often seek to answer the question why participants endure extreme pain and suffering for an activity labeled as fun. As children, players might hear from coaches that "Pain is temporary, victory is forever," "the harder the battle, the sweeter the victory," or that "pain is the price of glory" (Doyle, Mieder, and Shapiro 2012, 188). Is the implication that adoring fans confer more glory on football players if they risk injury in battle? Popular writers such as John Feinstein (2006) posit that money is the incentive for players to fight another day, but to get them motivated, they have to buy in to the master narrative of the satisfaction of vanquishing an opponent for a high-stakes triumph. This dominance is translated as a quest to be alone at the top of the standings or to hover over a fallen player, and satisfaction and even regeneration can come from strenuous battle. In *Next Man Up*, Feinstein highlights the message of the Baltimore Ravens' coach to encapsulate this moral imperative:

> Fellas, *this game, this setting is what your whole life is about*....A game like this is about commitment. It's about passion. It's about being willing to give yourself up for the cause if you have to....If it were going to be easy, then nothing would be at stake.
>
> *(2006, 444; emphasis added)*

What makes the sport "hard" rather than easy is the risk of injury. Unlike baseball and basketball, bodily harm from forceful collisions is an expectation of every play. Indeed, in Norwood's compilation of interviews with professional football players, injury is indexed more than commitment, mission, money, or fame. Steve Zabel, one of the athletes interviewed, is especially introspective about whether taking this risk among football players is "normal" or is somehow a reflection of everyday life. He comments:

> Football players in general are not normal people. They don't do normal things. They walk a very fine line between reality and nonreality. If a football player really sat down and tried to introspectively examine what he was about to do, it would frighten the hell out of him. I mean, nobody in his right mind would do something, where the consequences of getting hit in the wrong position might be that you'd be crippled forever or that you might die. There's something that draws people like me to it, whether it's machismo or simply the lure of gratification.
>
> *(Norwood 2004, 260)*

Zabel appears to aver Dundes's point that the obsession with football is often outside of participants' awareness and that their gratification is related to proving masculinity, although he might not agree that in doing so the American football player enacts a homoerotic display more so than other athletes. One might further observe that, as a professional, the player is paid for what he performed ritually as an adolescent.

Ethnographies of adolescents engaged in football often point out the ritual display of masculinity in the staging of high school games. Douglas Foley provides a frequently cited ethnography of football in Texas, a state that prides itself on its passion for the game. According to Foley, for Texas high school football players, the game is about social prominence in and for their community. Foley concludes, "Many of them are willing to endure considerable physical pain and sacrifice to achieve social prominence in their community" (1990, 126). Their discourse shows the game's association with male display when they claim that football "makes a man out of you," and its association with hyperheterosexuality is shown in the statement that it "helps get you a cute chick" (Foley 1990, 126). Foley notes some discourse that reveals "psychological lessons," in his words; however, in what Dundes would call an academic aversion to psychological interpretation, Foley prefers to concentrate on the "contemporary system of class dominance and its archaic system of patriarchal dominance" (1990, 133; see also Foley 1994, 28–62). These lessons, though, support Dundes's query about why particular sexual and violent metaphors are expressed in football. Foley found that coaches' discourse is incorporated into players' folk speech, and what they talk about most is "hitting," "sticking," or "popping" someone. After a hard game, he observes,

> the supreme compliment was having a particular "lick" or "hit" singled out. Folkloric immortality, endless stories about that one great hit in the big game, was what players secretly strove for. For most coaches and players, really "laying a lick on" or "knocking somebody's can off" or "taking a real lick" was that quintessential football moment.
>
> *(1990, 127)*

Players tend to portray themselves as bestial and hypersexualized, referring to themselves in the football play frame as studs, bulls, horses, gorillas, and beasts. As animals, they are different, more powerful, and more manly than in real life, which is associated with the modernist ethics of egalitarianism and feminism. According to Foley, "A stud was a superior physical specimen who fearlessly dished out and took hits, *who liked the physical contact*, who could dominate other players physically" (1990, 127; emphasis added). Foley found that players "talked endlessy" about who is a real stud and whether the coach "really kicks butt" (a phrase similar to being "up his ass" that suggests anal penetration) yet he concludes that all this talk shows only that pain is a badge of honor, rather than having any latent homoerotic component (1990, 127).

Looking for insight from players and the meaning they get from football, one school of thought is that despite primeval elements in football, the sport is not antithetical to modernism (Adams 2001, 30; Norwood 2004, 3–19). The male predilection to be devoted to one or a few team sports, in contradistinction to American girls' attraction to a variety of activities usually involving small groups, suggests the importance of corporate identity and managing multiple roles and specialties, which some academics see as a model of exploitative capitalism. Male players tend to find value in loyalty, camaraderie, and ganging, which are intrinsic and incentive, in their view, to being part of the team. At the same time, this team spirit (exemplified in the saying "there is no *I* in *team*") is underscored by the donning of a uniform, separating the sport from what is seen as the radical individualism and alienation of real life. One has to notice that *teammates*, despite the suggestion of intimacy, "pull together" less by close coordination than by beating an enemy through ritualized violence. In the introduction to *Real Football*, Norwood summarizes that,

> football's appeal derives in large part from its peculiar combination of highly modern qualities—an emphasis on order and precision, coordination within a group, and split-second timing—with more primitive elements, sublimated in bureaucracies, the open display of violence and aggression, which are involved in every play—in the bruising contact on the line, in the blocking and tackling in the open field.
>
> *(2004, 4)*

Mandelbaum extends the argument with a comparative observation about the extreme hierarchy in football:

> Because it unfolds in defined, discrete sequences, and because for each sequence both the offense and the defense must coordinate the action of all eleven players, which cannot occur spontaneously but must be arranged in advance, football both requires and permits coordination from a single, central source, in a way that baseball and basketball do not.
>
> *(2004, 164–65)*

Using an industrial metaphor, the coach is the engineer at the top of the bureaucratic hierarchy whose goal is to run the team like a well-oiled machine (Mandelbaum 2004, 164). Rituals and hollers in the stands, which the spectacle of football supports, provide a different image, though. Spectators root for teams to scrap and fight, much like the collegiate class rushes—melees consisting of freshmen and sophomores colliding in a mass of bodies to push a ball over the line—that fed the campus craze for football in the early twentieth century (Bronner 2012, 114–62; Krout 1929, 235). Contemporary ethnographies of football fan culture tend to reveal more fight than finesse. Shouts of "kill them," "you're getting killed," or "kill the ref" are heard more frequently in any stadium than comments about order and precision (see Smith 1983). References to the clockwork of teams come from the broadcasters or are reserved for the quiet moments of a review upstairs in the booth by sheltered and emasculated, if impartial, "officials," distant from the action on the field.

The Frontier of Football

The theme of regeneration through violence over turf is not just for coaches to spout in halftime pep talks or fans to scream in the heat of battle; it is also familiar from the American saga of frontier expansion (see Chapter 1). Although commonly associated with the colonialist-patriarchal claim of taming virgin land and the frontier experience of nationalist America, the symbolism of land has been shown to permeate the American sense of mission into the modern period, including the notable value-laden slogans of John Kennedy's "new frontier" in politics and "new frontiers" in the popular culture of *Star Trek*, both emerging during the 1960s (Felkins and Goldman 1993; Slotkin 1993; Smith [1950] 1978; Williamson 1987). Yet for all the scholarship produced on football, the idea of virgin land or frontier experience as a context to explain its appeal to Americans receives scant attention. I would venture to say that this is not because it lacks validity but because, in the rush to set football in critical postmodern terms, the Americanness of the game is overlooked. Conversely, historians have typically not made the symbolic connection between sport and frontier experience because they are inclined to look for the notable event or influential person rather than a movement or cultural belief. As wonderful and sweeping a tome as Richard Slotkin's mammoth classic *Gunfighter Nation: The Myth of the Frontier in Twentieth-Century America* (1993) is, it lacks even a single mention of football among its abundant references to the frontier theme in popular culture.

Oriard provides a historical clue to the connection to frontier when he capably traces the sport's roots to the second half of the nineteenth century. He sees the significance of the period as the golden age of print and reads the football coverage of newspapers and magazines as signs of accelerating social changes, especially for the rise of a middle class. Yet popular literature of the period featured dime novels, many of them about the West, and historically, it was a time marked by rapid expansion and then the closing of the frontier. Talk of land, and violence to domesticate the land, pervaded the public's reading material and weighed heavily on the minds of Americans. Earlier, I asserted that football stood at the top of the sports heap after the 1960s, and it is worth noting that this period was replete with "new frontier" and war rhetoric (Engelhardt 2007). Observers of American culture should expect the frontier to be a symbolic part of football if, as Slotkin has insightfully argued, the frontier experience is inextricably tied to American identity, and central to that experience is the acquisition of land as a result of overcoming a hostile enemy in the character of the fearsome Indians.

Historian David Wallace Adams (2001) deserves notice for pointing out that the frontier theme was a factor in the public notoriety of the football team of the Carlisle Indian Industrial School (a boarding school for Native Americans in Pennsylvania under U.S. governmental authority to rapidly assimilate them into white Protestant culture) in the late nineteenth and early twentieth centuries, but he does not extend the analysis to the present day. He contextualizes the popularity of football in colleges during the period in the "cult of manliness" of Victorian America, caused by a desire to counter growing industrialization with activities serving as reminders of

> an older frontier America [where] the opportunities for physical labor, wilderness adventure, and primitive expressions of violence, were not only

available but frequently a precondition for survival. Denied these experiences, the rising generation of young men were in danger of becoming overcivilized, if not feminized.

(Adams 2001, 29)

Journalistic reporting of the highly publicized confrontations between the Carlisle team and major national powers such as Yale, Army, and Harvard blatantly referred to a battle for land between settlers and "the aborigine, the real son of the forest and plain" (Adams 2001, 31; see also Anderson 2007; Jenkins 2007).

Evoking frontier skirmishes in the play of football went well beyond the reporting of contests between the Carlisle Indians and the national collegiate powers of the Northeast. In the early twentieth century, President Theodore Roosevelt, who waxed poetic about the invigorating qualities of the great West, answered critics of the game's brutality by calling for reform of the rules as a national priority, while making sure that the game, in keeping with his vision for maintaining the pioneer American spirit, remained true to the ideals of "the strenuous life." He publicly declared that when he assembled his volunteer cavalry of "Rough Riders" for the foreign adventure of the Spanish–American War, he sought men who had played football because of their character as well as their old-fashioned fight, reminiscent of America's conquest of the frontier (Roosevelt 1899, 8–20; in 1899, the University of Oklahoma adopted the nickname "The Rough Riders" to recognize the cowboys, ranchers, and football players gathered from Oklahoma who joined Roosevelt in war). When the president of Harvard tried to abolish football at the school in 1907, Roosevelt angrily retorted, "As I emphatically disbelieve in seeing Harvard, or any other college, turn out mollycoddles instead of vigorous men I may add I do not in the least object to a sport because it is rough" (quoted in Rudolph [1962] 1990, 377).

Advocates thought of football's action as a throwback to a preindustrial age when one matched one's body and hands against the elements to reap the benefits of the land. Henry Davidson Sheldon, a respected commentator on the collegiate scene, observed that since football had become popular on campuses in the 1880s, it provided an antidote to the physical softness of a new post-frontier, generation of students in elite schools bound for new corporate professions, and it also compensated for the worrisome complexity, mechanization, and standardization in the rapidly industrializing and immigrant America (1901, 251–52). Sheldon complimented football's "mass movements and general attitude of conflict which give zest to the latter," in contrast to "professional baseball in the cities," which "has become a business" (1901, 232). He thought that football owed its rise in the enervating collegiate context to a "human instinct" necessary for "physical combat" (1901, 233). More specific to the American experience, he saw intercollegiate football being adapted to the qualities of a mobile "frontier people—rude, boisterous, and over-assertive," and it matched "the conditions of frontier life favouring versatility and individual initiative" (Sheldon 1901, 90, 107).

Faculties that opposed the game as unbecoming of learned men still understood the communitarian spirit it fostered for the school as a whole. A faculty committee at Yale in 1902, taking up the problems of injury and cheating in football, considered the game's value in promoting selflessness among the students, characteristic of an earlier era of expansion and national feeling: "An impression is very strong and very prevalent that the athlete is working for Yale, the student for himself" (quoted in Rudolph [1962] 1990, 379). Commentaries of this kind led Frederick Rudolph, in his chronicle of the rise of football in the late nineteenth and early twentieth centuries, to pronounce that "the new game of football became an instrument of the past" ([1962] 1990, 379).

Did the frontier rhetoric in football cease with the industrial era and the demise of the Carlisle Indians? Hardly. In professional football, many of the names associated with the dramaturgical fantasy of the game derived from frontier imagery: Braves, Cowboys, Chiefs, Raiders, Forty-niners, Texans, Buffalo Bills. Other teams took their monikers from animals associated with the American wilderness: Eagles, Broncos, Bears, Panthers. In the college ranks, where football is the great symbol of big-time campuses, more than 30 schools' teams are called the Pioneers; others include the (Trail) Blazers, Braves, Cowboys, Highlanders, Hilltoppers, Mavericks, Mountaineers, Raiders, Ramblers, and Rangers. The highest concentration of nonanimal nicknames draws on the frontier experience (Smargon 2008). Typical of these teams are frontiersmen mascots, horses, and wagons that excite the crowd with their movements on the sidelines, especially after a touchdown. Many journalists have also taken notice of the Dallas Cowboys' designation as "America's team," at least in part because of the national appeal of the cowboy and use of the "lone star" in its logo representing its status as an independent republic in 1836. Mandelbaum comments, for example, "In American mythology the Dallas mascot, the cowboy, symbolizes rugged individualism and courage. He is a repository of the virtues that the team itself embodied—or so it sought to suggest to the public, styling itself 'America's Team'" (2004, 187). Even in Harrisburg, Pennsylvania—hardly a western outpost or a landscape that raises frontier images—the public voted in 2008 to call the city's arena football team the Stampede, with a picture of a steer's skull suggesting the western plains (American Indoor Football Association 2008). Opinions left by fans on the team's message board impressed on the owners that football's action reminds them of western mythology involving the unfettered movement across the open range, translated into the modern context as the football field. Further west, professional football teams in St. Louis, Missouri, Sioux City, Iowa, and Forth Worth, Texas, also claim the Stampede name.

The terminology of football is replete with frontier imagery. Football commentators frequently note the importance of the "scout," who checks out the opponent's camp (Mandelbaum 2004, 131–32). The running back, a standout position on the offense, functions, according to Mandelbaum, as "the cavalry of the team—highly mobile agents of swift advance" (2004, 130). A key to success in the game is gaining ground, and the going gets tougher the deeper one moves into the opposition's territory. After a hotly contested game, reporters and players often refer to the game as "a good ol' fashioned Western" or a shoot-out, as Dallas quarterback Tony Romo did following a 41–37 victory on *Monday Night Football* in 2008 (Aron 2008). The previous weekend, Tennessee Titans linebacker Keith Bulluck said of his team's quarterback Kerry Collins, who led a winning march down the field, "I knew the old *gunslinger* was going to go out there and do his thing," even though Collins did not originally hail from the West (Kay 2008; emphasis added). Green Bay Packers quarterback Brett Favre from Mississippi was called "gunslinger" in print at least 5,000 times because, according to biographer Jeff Pearlman, "He did whatever it took to win" (Pearlman 2016, 194). "Did it come with a price?" Favre's business partner reflected:

> Absolutely. I remember the day after one game, both hands were swollen, his knees were swollen, one ankle was the size of a grapefruit, and his back was killing him. You want to know why he needed the drugs? It's easy—he was getting killed.
>
> *(quoted in Pearlman 2016, 194)*

The gunslinger and cowboy terminology for football quarterbacks implied risk-taking and constant rugged toughness. Citing other adventurous quarterbacks who held the title of gunslinger such as George Blanda and Derek Carr (both of whom played for the Oakland Raiders), journalist David Jones reflected, "The term 'gunslinger' is thrown around a lot in reference to lovably reckless quarterbacks" because the football field exudes the feeling of "the Wild West" (Jones 2010).

ESPN correspondent Sal Paolantonio writes that firepower from the Old West is a powerful image for sportswriters because it most vividly connotes for Americans the conquest of land. In fact, he traces football's story line at the moment of important rule changes in 1882, which established the "first down" after gaining a certain number of yards, to the expansionist idea of "Manifest Destiny" (Paolantonio 2008, 7–8). The rule allows the team possessing the ball to advance it while holding on to the territory it has already captured. If it does not, it will be forced to "surrender" the ball. The successful team eliminates the opposing team and has the whole field, from end line to end line, to itself. Invoking the symbolism of four as a complete, expansive life (see Chapter 2), the offense has four tries to get ten yards. Football teams in the United States rely on the methodical running game more than in Canada, where the rules call for three downs, resulting in what Mandelbaum calls "risky, spectacular plays" (2004, 144). With the close of the frontier in 1890, Paolantonio contends, "America, bursting at the seams, needed a game that had a chance to capture this haughtiness [of Manifest Destiny], that moves forward at all costs" (2008, 8).

The influence of land conquest lingered in the game, particularly among early shapers such as Walter Camp and Amos Alonzo Stagg. Many of the early rule changes emphasized advancement of the ball on the ground to emphasize a difference, in Camp's estimation, from the English rugby code, from which American football apparently evolved (Camp 1894, 1–22; Paolantonio 2008, 8). Although related to the action of scrums in English rugby, Camp envisioned the American game, much in keeping with the idea of the American fresh start in the New World, as an independent form of rugged play. For Camp, the central feature that would distinguish the American game as a new one is the measurable, more movable scrimmage *line* rather than the heaps of bodies in the English scrum. The line, he wrote, is "the backbone to which the entire body of American football is attached" (1894, 9). The American game's action is organized around a series of skirmishes in land designated as territory. The quarterback has more control and more options than in the English game and thus is encouraged to create deceptions to advance the ball. To Camp, the American game shows "far more skill in the development of brilliant plays and carefully planned manoeuvres" (1894, 10). Although football has undergone many rule changes since Camp's time, the idea of the scrimmage line—with its function of establishing a movable border, drawing on the memory of the frontier in the late nineteenth century—remains critical to the game. Camp was proud of football's Americanness and the way it broke from the long-held English custom of the relatively immobile pile of bodies of the scrummage. Camp implies that football looks like his country when he writes, "Being bound by no traditions, and having seen no play, the American took the English rules for a starting-point, and almost immediately proceeded to add and subtract, according to what seemed his pressing needs" (1894, 8). Among those needs was a game with quick movement resulting in rewards for gaining ground. Much to Camp's satisfaction, the sport spread westward from the Northeast into the South and West, and he recognized its nationalism by initiating "All-America" honors as a distinctive accolade for football players (Mandelbaum 2004, 161).

Historian James Oliver Robertson explains the resistance to football outside of North America in terms of the centrality of the frontier metaphor to the game. Unlike baseball and basketball, which have been taken up globally, football emphasizes lines that "must be defended, which must be penetrated, which must be moved" (Robertson 1980, 256). He astutely observes:

> In football the entire game is built around the frontier, the line, the boundary. Football ritualizes the moving frontier, and the teamwork, cooperation, and individual heroism necessary to move that frontier; simultaneously, it also ritualizes the teamwork, cooperation, and individual heroism necessary to resist the moving frontier (football players are pioneers *and* Indians at the same time). Ultimate victory in the game comes from moving the frontier more than the others do, crossing the goal line more frequently. There is

little in such a ritual to appeal to the ideals and sensitivities of people who are not Americans.

(Robertson 1980, 256)

Rugged Adolescent Masculinity on the Line

Robertson probably overstates the argument, because using violence to show manliness in response to the feminizing effects of modernization certainly extends beyond America's borders. If this is the case, can this historical consideration be reconciled with Dundes's psychoanalytic perspective, focusing on football's appeal as a demonstration of manliness? One symbolist overlap is the material significance of lines on the field and the conceptual emphasis on advancing linearity (moving forward, expressed in the masculinist value placed on charging "straight ahead," "up the gut," or "up the middle"). As Robertson points out, the football "gridiron" is distinctive in the holy trinity of American sports by its profuse use of lines that players repeatedly cross (1980, 256). The lines structure the game as well as the field, because "plays" begin with the "lining up" of offensive and defensive athletes. The cultural significance of the gridiron is indicated by a commercial aired by wireless communication giant Verizon in 2010. A husky voice narrates a violent collision of football players that causes dirt to fly: "There is a reason it's called a gridiron, because the ground doesn't give up its yards without a fight." Gaining ground is important because an offense stays on the field by acquiring a "first down," measured in ten-yard increments. The division of the 100-yard field into ten-yard segments including crossing the 50-yard line into the opposition's territory, is reminiscent of the visualization of progress on life's journey (see Chapter 2). Gaining the last 50 yards is considered more difficult and past the 20-yard line (or 80 yards from one's home end zone) is called the "red zone," suggesting danger for the opposition toward the end of the advancing team's trek. The offensive team's objective is presented numerically by the number of yards remaining to get a first down, such as "second [down] and eight." Excitement builds when a third-down play has a short distance to go and teams close up their lines in anticipation of grappling bodies. The expectation in such situations is that the running back will be "shot (crash) through the line," suggesting a double meaning of penetrative gun and phallus. The pent-up, potent energy resulting in either a cheered release for the offense or a gutty stop for the defense, thereby showing the offense's impotence, implies a male sexual potency tying the acquisition of property to sexual gratification.

Ample cultural evidence exists for the association of straightness with manliness, which is heightened by football's highly linear gridiron. Men are associated with "directness," in contrast to women's "roundness." For instance, in the military, soldiers (traditionally male) are honored by gaining stripes, and the humorous adage that "size matters" refers to a penile erection (Dundes 2004, 183–84). In contrast, girls' singing games tend to form circles; women are

FIGURE 3.1 "Yale-West Point [Army]: Yale's Line-Up," showing the perpendicular lines forming the "gridiron." October 17, 1908.
Source: George Grantham Bain, photographer. Prints and Photographs Division, Library of Congress.

complimented for being "curvaceous" and are aligned with nature by having menstrual "cycles" (Dundes 2004, 184; Whiting and Ayres 1968, 128). In football strategy, the "end-around," "flea-flicker" (representing back-and-forth movement), and "double-reverse" are considered evasive tactics or even "junk plays." A quarterback who takes the ball ahead rather than handing it off to a halfback, who then rushes forward through the line, is said to dishonestly "sneak" across. In the action of crossing lines, men are arguably conquering nature as well as exhibiting sexual potency (Ortner 1974).

In his critical essay subtitled "Are Freudians Ever Right?" sociologist Gary Alan Fine (1984) raises doubts about the use of linguistic evidence to establish a link between violence and adolescent initiatory behavior in American football. He finds that the expressive evidence is not consistent. Although he agrees that the rhetoric of sacking, making a pass, and penetrating have sexual undertones, he points out that hash marks, guard, punt, and field goal do not. Is it coincidental that all Fine's examples are references to land? He may not make the connection, but we can note the idea of a hash mark for a point on the field to spot the ball, a guard as protection for property, a punt for kicking the ball before it hits the ground, and a field goal for a ball kicked from the ground. Fine's point is that inconsistent symbolism indicates a weakness in the psychoanalytic argument, and he observes even less of a case on the basis of external validity, for he notes that most Americans do not play football and restricts it to a seasonal rather than a year-round activity. "Why," he asks, "aren't these drives present to be expressed throughout the calendar year; are they repressed the other nine months? ... Are there other male activities in American culture which function in the same way?" Fine leaves the questions unanswered; their purpose is to "raise doubt as to the interpretation of football as ritual homosexuality" (Fine 1984, 16), and it appears that others share his skepticism, making Dundes's essay the most quotable citation on football and the article that academics and fans love to hate.

Let me suggest answers to Fine's questions by referring to the importance of the "ground" in football and its autumn play. Unlike other American team sports, the action in football is measured by players advancing across a line. The point of emphasis is the scrimmage line, which is movable. "Football is a game of inches" is a common adage indicating the importance of every piece of ground, and careful records are kept for yards gained (most total yards and yards per play). The defense wants to pin back the offensive players and drive or pound (a sexual double entendre) them to the turf, preferably putting them in a feminine position "on their butts." The defense wants to hold its ground or pin the offense back, "deep in its own territory." No team wants to "give ground" or be pushed around, blown out, knocked down, or thrown for a loss; coaches scream at players to hold their spots and get up. Particularly in American football, teams want to freely move up and down the field. Broadcasters like to talk about a team taking "real estate" or having "property" behind them as a sign of success. On sports talk shows, listeners know that callers are concerned when their team "sucks," in an obvious reference to taking a passive homoerotic position, but they are happy if their team kicks butt. They complain if their losing team looked like boys to the other team's men because they were crushed or, worse, nailed or sacked (with the explanation that the defensive line got "penetration in the *back*field"). In victory, though, spectators charge the field, occupying it with great jubilation, and they may tear down the goalposts as a sign of taking control of the land.

The property metaphor is critical to the drive toward victory. Each of the two teams is said to have "territory," and as a team advances, it acquires ground, even though the designation of territory is nowhere written on the field. A milestone is crossing into the other team's territory past the 50-yard line, acquiring it by pushing the opponent off its turf. Dundes is right that one scores by eventually penetrating the other team's end zone on the ground or by sending a kick through the uprights, but one gains control in the game by "eating up big chunks of yardage." The goal is acquiring a piece of land. Scoring a goal implies that the other team has been eliminated, driven off the field. For the defense, the goal line is protected, and the ultimate test is the goal line stand, treating the end zone as precious ground that is distinguished from the field by stripes or decoration.

Accretion of power occurs as the offense gains ground, suggesting an Oedipal interpretation for the offense. Dundes cites Adrian Stokes's observation of a male Oedipal complex applying to American football because each team defends the goal at their back:

> In front is a new land, the new woman, whom they strive to possess in the interest of preserving the mother inviolate, in order, as it were, to progress from infancy to adulthood: at the same time, the defensive role is the father's; he opposes the forward youth of the opposition.
> *(Dundes 1978, 78–79; Stokes 1956, 185)*

In this view, both teams battle for possession of the father's phallus, that is, the ball, to "steer it through the archetypal vagina, the goal" (Stokes 1956, 187). But this may be too universalist a view, because an American context appears to be at work in observing the battle on the field as one between pioneer foes.

The importance of the ground game is its representation of battle with the goal of driving the other team off its land. This is coupled with a demonstration of social domination by emasculating the opponent in ritual performances of spiking the ball, engaging in war dances, and raising helmets or index fingers. Players are egged on to get the opponent on his back, showing that the team has "kicked ass." Invoking images of hunting, players on the run are chased down, and players are caught in the "open field." In a merger of hunter and soldier, quarterbacks are said to have a "rifle arm" and to be "on target." With the naturalistic image of a brown leather football, the thrower wants to hit his man "in the chest," while the defense, in sports talk, "brings down his prey." With some phallic implication, players in trouble are referred to as being "creamed," "shot down," and "hit hard."

When players are "slammed down to the ground," they are symbolically stuck in the mud or joined to feces. In describing the goal of football as carrying the ball into the end zone, Dundes misses that, on the way, ground is gained without the ball or one's body being brought down. Carriers have to keep the ball "clean"; that is, the ball cannot touch the ground, or else it becomes symbolically contaminated. The player who is dragged down to the turf is not just being overtly feminized; he is "soiled" by being stuck in infantile feces. The contrast is going into the end zone "untouched" or without being thrown down. Manhood is represented in such a case by overcoming the infantile desire to play with dirt or feces. Toughness is shown by "grinding out" or controlling "yards" (equivalent to dirt or land). The end zone is also known as the "house," and the runner who takes off down the field is said to be "bringing it to the house." As a frontier metaphor, this rhetoric suggests the transversal of hostile ground to create a settlement. Skill with the ball means that the prize possession is kept off the ground. Thus, time of possession, represented by control of the ball, allowing the offense to stay on the field, is an all-important statistic.

Historian David Adams insightfully observes that "part of football's appeal was in its capacity to tell stories, to convey meaning" (2001, 30). He suggests that journalistic attachment of the frontier story, as understood by white Americans in the 1890s, to the playing of football helped raise the game's profile (2001, 30–31). How can football be narratively structured? One answer is to trace its plot sequence to see whether it follows the functions of a story. Folklorists have found a common morphology that people recognize as narrative in the dramatic tension created by the establishment of something as missing, or a lack, to the consequence of something being restored, or a lack liquidated (Dundes 1964a, 1964b). In between, a struggle ensues to overcome challenges, summarized as an interdiction and a violation. For football, this morphology takes the form as shown in Table 3.1.

Comparison between this narrative of the game sequence and other children's games is raised because, arguably, football takes on more of a linear sequence than baseball and basketball. In keeping with children's development as independent individuals who desire to move away from the maternal home as a sign of maturity and, at the same time, defend the home as social identity, childhood games frequently involve laying out "sides" that are thrust against each other; examples are "push ball" and "red rover," involving the crossing of an opposing team's line. Games that emphasize linear structures involving pushing and pulling, such as tug-of-war, are particularly associated with masculinity and demonstrations of toughness; it is no coincidence that football's eliminative result of players falling to the ground raises images of war.

Another feature of the linear structure is that crossing a line signals triumph, represented by achieving a higher status or accomplishing a transformation. By doing this, the sequence marks what folklorist Arnold van Gennep (1960) famously identified as a "rite of passage": a four-part structure of a separation from a group, followed by a two-part transition in which a task or ordeal is

TABLE 3.1 Syntagmatic Morphology of American Football

	Lack	*Interdiction*	*Violation*	*Consequence*
Offense	Wants to go forward (into opponent's home or end zone)	Does not want to be stopped (dragged down, tackled to the ground)	Is stopped (or is not stopped, gains ground)	Loses game (or scores and wins game)
Defense	Wants to drive offense back (or recover ball and take it into opponent's home or end zone)	Keeps offense away from defense's home or end zone	Does not stop offense or gives ground (or stops offense)	Loses game (or scores and wins game)

completed, and culminating in an incorporation with the community and elevation to a higher status. This passage is important for the adolescent moving to adulthood who uses the compact play frame to enact a transition period to overcome obstacles (in the agent of a runner) and then becomes reunited with one's peers in celebration of a triumphant maturity. Rather than contradicting the frontier thesis, this developmental perspective fits into the view that football became significant because it was perceived as emboldening at a time when modernization was equated with male infantilization. Yet it is also fair to say that, based on players' testimonies about their experience, the game provides participants with adolescent, masculine functions that are culturally distinct from the context of gaining property for the spectator.

The control of ground as a result of male adolescent initiation or rite of passage may be widespread in the play activities of many cultures, but there is an American social historical context that may help explain the United States' special investment in nationalistic as well as masculinist meanings in football after the 1970s. Much has been made of the loss of national prestige in the wake of the Vietnam War, especially to an Asian enemy that had been characterized in orientalist rhetoric as diminutive, feminine, and sneaky (Jeffords 1989). Associated with subversive guerrilla warfare that was not based on oppositional front lines and control of territory, the Vietcong were a source of frustration because of their use of hidden underground tunnels and their ability to blend into the population. American military leaders nonetheless used football metaphors for America's response, such as bombing campaigns named Operation Linebacker (Secretary of State Henry Kissinger was code-named "Quarterback" at the 1972 Paris peace talks) (MacCambridge 2004, 300). Writing on "post-Vietnam masculinity," Jerry Lembcke argues that the post-Vietnam era was peculiar in accentuating "the identity crises felt by many men." Identified as America's "first lost war," the Vietnam experience was blamed for male insecurities that reached, according to Lembcke, into age cohorts too young or too old for Vietnam (2004, 621). His explanation of how the blow to the male ego extended to national pride is that "military experience is a rite of passage, and for men who were in uniform during a war, there is an urge to connect as directly as possible to combat, the 'real thing' of war" (Lembcke 2004, 620; see also Gibson 1994; Lembcke 1998). War stories told by veterans did not help in the failed cause, especially because 85 percent of soldiers did not see combat, and televised reports on the national news dashed the ability to romanticize the war.

Other factors compounded the crises of masculinity as well as national confidence. In the wake of civil rights legislation, the women's movement came to national attention by targeting the inequities of patriarchy and the dysfunction of the male provider role. Like other social movements of the time, sharing a commitment to progressivism and equity, it linked opposition to the Vietnam War to the failed militaristic policies of the traditional male "establishment." The United States suffered an economic downturn during the 1970s after two decades of prosperity. America's self-assurance as an industrial, commercial giant was shaken by competition from Japan and Germany, defeated foes from World War II. The specter of the Vietnam War loomed large in the search for American heroes who, like the Rambo character from the movies, could go out on their own, in frontier adventurer style, and redeem American pride; Saturday and Sunday heroes such as the superphysical stars of the *National* Football League and college teams seeking a *national* championship filled this void. Professional football catapulted in popularity with single-elimination playoffs that raised the stakes of imperial victory by advancing to the *Super* Bowl. At the local level, many women were attracted to the game, not only because of the publicity and celebrity status given to star players but also because winning elevated the community status of a campus, a region, or a city and appeared to trump the "bragging rights" earned in baseball, basketball, and other institutionalized sports. With the goal of going undefeated always in mind, collegiate and professional football tapped into, and helped expand, America's victory culture. Indeed, in the quest for a national college title, suffering a single loss is considered fatal to one's chances for a championship.

A characteristic of the victory culture is that it is, in military terms, total and unconditional. In other words, the result is the elimination of the enemy. In football terms, it is expressed in the saying, "Winning isn't everything; it's the only thing." Though popularly attributed to legendary Green Bay Packers coach Vince Lombardi, there is evidence that former Vanderbilt and UCLA football coach Henry "Red" Sanders originated the saying in the 1930s (see Belliotti 2008, 7). Lombardi epitomized success, winning three consecutive league championships from 1965 to 1967, and his teams became models of dominance that others aspired to. Into the twenty-first century, John Madden, another coach known for his aggressive attitude on the field, elaborated on Lombardi's words for the society at large in this memorable quotation: "The only yardstick for success our society has is being a champion. No one remembers anything else" (Glenday 2008, 128). The eliminative characteristic of football is apparent in the often-uttered statement that no one remembers who loses the Super Bowl, and after 1974, the National Football League instituted the "sudden death" system to decide a victor if the game ends in a tie (Rolfe 2008). Thus, only one team is left standing. Unlike the "Olympic spirit" of three medalists sharing a victory rostrum, in football, one winner takes all. There is no consolation prize. If this seems harsh, keep in mind that American political races are also run on a winner-takes-all basis, rather than the proportional sharing of power typical of parliamentary systems in Europe and Japan.

I had a chance to view ways that cultural differences shape attitudes toward American football when I lived in Japan. Judging from the country's embrace of American baseball, I thought for sure that the Japanese would take to football fandom as well. The NFL had promoted its brand in Japan with pre-season professional games and football clinics for interested high school players. I had a front-row seat to the development of football at Osaka University because its new team practiced outside the window of my residence. I came down to watch the team's development and also to ask the players and coaches ethnographic questions. The first difference I noticed (besides the smaller size of Japanese players) was the emphasis on practice; the team did not have organized contests, but the game was attractive to participants because of an appeal to *doryoku*, roughly translating to "all-out effort." The Japanese players related the physically demanding drills on the football field to the *gattsu* ("guts") routines in Japanese baseball regimens (Whiting 1990, 65–66).

But in a society that values social harmony, the eliminative characteristic of the game troubled coaches and participants alike. The hostile quality of taking down an opponent seemed "shameful," they told me. Although sumo wrestling involves bodily contact, it is more ritually circumscribed, they observed, than the rough gang tackling of football. They worried about the social repercussions of a "sack" and the disgrace it brought. To be sure, they could be intensely competitive, but in a group-oriented society, they wanted to make sure that feelings of *wa*—a social unity without conflict or ill will, reflecting a social structure in which everyone knows their place—would be maintained. The physical as well as social dominance exuded in American football drew negative comments as unsportsmanlike or, in Japanese parlance, "impolite." In practice, they worked on the discipline of perfecting form, although when they watched games, they commented negatively that the plays looked disordered. They expressed a fondness for baseball's rigid structure of base paths and batting orders; they found the many options for a football "hit" frustrating. Another concern was the game's quick pace. To Americans, I reflected, "momentum" as an unstoppable surge is highly valued, but the Japanese are more cautious and favor the time allowed between innings and pitches in baseball to deliberate at length about strategy and tactics, often as a group (Whiting 1990, 50). Robert Hunt, a former offensive lineman for the Tampa Bay Buccaneers and international player development scout for the NFL, admitted the hard sell of football in Japan. He tried to encourage converts to football by advising youths, "No matter what your position is, you practice what you learned today in everyday life," but the players did not see the connection (Nagatsuka 2007).

Football's Rules of Engagement—Military, Industrial, and Urban

The American victory culture can be viewed in the growth of professional sports and big-time college athletics generally in the post-Vietnam War era, but a significant contribution of American football as it moved into the public limelight was a change in the body image of the athlete. Desirable traits for the modern football player include being large and fast, as well as strong and gritty. In cartoons and humor during football's formative years, players were caricatured as slow, dumb, and flabby, as well as underpaid (Bronner 2012, 94–96). In the new post-Vietnam War context, the imposing sight of young, muscular, wide-bodied linemen in pads and helmets looking like buff titan warriors exudes power rather than grotesqueness. Players at other positions are attributed with "flash" and "cool" and are given nicknames such as "Broadway Joe" Namath (quarterback), "Cool Joe" Montana (quarterback), and "Primetime" or "Neon" Deion Sanders (cornerback). This turn from down-in-the-dirt frontier warfare on the football field to hip urban terms of engagement indicates that football adopted more of an urban sensibility in the post-Vietnam War era.

Mandelbaum credits Bill Walsh, coach of the San Francisco 49ers from 1979 to 1988, with initiating many changes in the game by introducing the "West Coast offense," which relies on short, precisely timed passes distributed among a variety of speedy receivers (2004, 196–97). Walsh's personal laid-back style also drew notice for going against the image of the tough-as-nails authoritarian coach. Other teams at the college and professional levels, though, had already experienced a shift in the makeup of players—from those with rural and European ethnic backgrounds molded to the team's game plan of carefully orchestrated maneuvers to urban, African-American athletes characterized as individualists with improvisational skills. As the change in play swept football programs, commentators referred to a new style of no-huddle hurry-up game they called "basketball in cleats" (Mandelbaum 2004, 198). It valued spontaneity, flexibility, and agility over the "plodding, grinding, rush-oriented style of football that had descended from the methods that Walter Camp had employed" (Mandelbaum 2004, 198).

The basketball reference also could be decoded as referencing the appeal of the game to more urban African-American participants and fans attracted to the sport. According to sports commentator Jeff Greenfield, the sport is not only dominated by African-American athletes (more than 74 percent of National Basketball Association players in 2020) but also expresses a style he called "black ball" which is marked by "leaping agility" (Greenfield 1999). By 2020, people of color accounted for over 70 percent of NFL players. Although to many observers the race of football players was less evident than in other sports because of the extensive body covering they wore, racial tensions in the United States spilled over into the symbolism of and national obsession with football in 2016 when San Francisco 49ers quarterback Colin Kaepernick of African-American background first sat, and then kneeled, during the playing of the National Anthem as a protest of racism in America. Especially since pre-game ceremonies had often been an occasion for patriotic military displays, Kaepernick's gesture became national news. He claimed that he was using his celebrity status in the largest grossing United States professional sports league to draw attention to "people that don't have a platform to talk and have their voices heard, and effect change" (Sandritter 2017). The protest spread and the President called for the firing of players who participated because they were unpatriotic (Bronner 2019, 25). In response, the league allowed players to stay off the field during the playing of the national anthem. But the discourse on race did not stop as attention shifted from systemic oppression of blacks and police brutality to the disparity between the racial composition of players and organizational management with fewer than 10 percent of NFL head coaches with an African-American identity in 2020 (Sinatra 2020; Sonnad 2018).

Hailed as one of the last all-male cultural preserves, professional football made news by breaking down a gender wall when in 2015 the Arizona Cardinals added Jen Welter as an assistant coaching intern. Having played for women's professional football teams, in 2014 she became the first running back to play for a men's professional team. In 2016, the Atlanta Falcons hired Katie Sowers as a wide receiver coach, and became the first openly LGBT coach in the NFL. Female referees began work on the field the same year. At the college level, Vanderbilt University kicker Sarah Fuller made headlines when in 2020 she became the first woman to score in a major conference football game and then was invited to the new U.S. President's inauguration. Aware of her role as a representative for female athletes breaking into men's sports domains, Fuller made her history-making moment less about gender discrimination than about the Americanness of getting ahead, of finding a rising path to success. Her message in football and in life was to "be determined in what you're doing and just be passionate about it. If it's something you really want to accomplish, don't let those down moments and barriers hold you back from what you want to achieve" (Vera 2020). Along with the change in racially inflected style of play, questions of inclusiveness came under increased scrutiny to make football even more of "America's game" and representative of the country's social problems as well as aspirations.

The desire in the revamped game of the twenty-first century for speed on the ends and in the backfield with often smaller, thinner players did not so much eclipse the emphasis on endurance and bulky strength as it added a dimension for spectators in a modern service and information economy. The mechanical grind-it-out game suggested a producer-industrial ethos of moving piles and slow incremental advances to gain ground and acquire territory. Spreading the offense and introducing variable formations and multiple choices (e.g., run-pass options, known with the organizational sounding initialism of RPO) evoked a trajectory life course mindset (see Chapter 2), proliferating bureaucracy with multiple coaches and position "rooms," and rapid pace of an economy tied to time as athletes were constantly "clocked." Defenses also responded with agile, speedy cornerbacks and swift linebackers. They were individualized "skill players" out in the track-sounding "flat" rather than big working-class bodies to move the heavy pile a yard at a time on the line. To the dismay of nostalgic fans who glorified slow pound-it-out games in freezing, snowy weather, a spate of domed stadiums after the Houston Astrodome was built in 1968 that insured dry, temperate field conditions boosted the new emphasis on speedy players in both the ground and passing games. The fullback was hardly used in favor of the lightning quick halfback able to make fast "on-a-dime" turns on the dry turf. By 2020 a third of the

NFL's stadiums had the capacity to be covered and the last two structures—in Las Vegas and Los Angeles—were domed.

Referring to the authority of a head coach overseeing a cadre of assistants, commentators referred to the significance of mini-seconds and clock management to build on the older reference to the "game of inches." A culturally influenced data science of football arose in response with times close to 4 seconds in the 40-yard dash being treated as the gold standard. Reporting on the annual NFL Scouting Combine to test and measure athletes' value in the player draft, Zach Kruse declared in 2013 "No event at the NFL Scouting Combine is more heavily weighed or anticipated than the 40-yard dash." Whereas track and field events stage races to the finish line, the Combine is designed to value explosion and burst in a short area (ten yards from a still start) and over a long distance (with the symbolic number of 40 yards for completeness) for the big quick strike (Kruse 2013).

Just as Walter Camp had been proud of his break with English rugby, 49ers coach Bill Walsh used the moniker "West Coast" to differentiate his new speedy "wide-open" offensive scheme from the tight muscular "up-the-gut" plays of the Northeast. The prominence of California suggested a close of the frontier and invited comparisons with the glitz of popular culture and the anything-goes imagery of Hollywood and the San Francisco Bay Area. The new style defied the strategies of field position and ground control associated with the frontier mentality of military-oriented coaches. The acceleration of the urban pace held more allure, while the battlefield fell into disrepute as a formula for action on the football field as well as in life. Mandelbaum observes the historical shift affecting football play when he writes,

> the decline in the status of war in American society was accompanied by a devaluation of the norms and the practices that war cultivates and that football fosters as well: discipline, self-sacrifice, the acceptance of hierarchy as a principle of organization, and respect for authority. Their antitheses—spontaneity, self-indulgence, an insistence on equality, and the questioning of authority—became more acceptable and more widespread in American society.
>
> *(2004, 196)*

Arguably, the Wild West imagery of the game, with its associated folk narrative of possession, had already weakened by the time Super Bowls marked the ascendancy of the professional leagues. The first Super Bowl was held in Los Angeles in 1967 and was followed by venues in warm-weather climes, usually in major cities such as Miami, Tampa, New Orleans, and San Diego. Cities wanted a football team to represent them, and a number of them, including Indianapolis and St. Louis, erected huge stadiums right in the heart of their downtown districts. Halftime shows no longer stuck to the militaristic tradition of parading marching bands. Linking popular culture to the coolness of the sport, Super

Bowls set the stage with elaborate concerts by megastars such as Bruce Springsteen, the Rolling Stones, and Prince. And what does it say about the commercial element that media attention focuses on the commercials aired during the Super Bowl, as well as the action on the field?

In a show of conspicuous consumption, football players given star status in the post-Vietnam War era were often depicted eating, weightlifting, and spending in excess. They embodied the idea of "to the victor belongs the spoils." Young people admired the apparent pinnacle of glory held by football players, and they aspired to the muscularity and athleticism of the football behemoths, rather than deriding them. Promoting this turn, the National Football League's youth program adopted the slogan "Dream Big, Play Big" to link aspiration with size. Yet it was not bulk but versatility and flexibility that press releases stressed when listing modern players' attributes. Some coaching holdouts of the old control game, featuring a rushing attack based on a few plays that were run and practiced repeatedly, drew criticism for being outmoded, even if they enjoyed success. For example, during the youth rebellion of 1968, arguments between the "Old Man" Woody Hayes at Ohio State University, who preferred the predictable T backfield, and young assistant George Chaump, who preferred the flexible and "sleek" I formation, drew press coverage (Rosenberg 2008, 30). Penn State's coach Joe Paterno, with more than 60 years on the sidelines, was another advocate of "grinding it out." Although he was criticized in his later years, he reportedly adjusted his style in 2008 to an explosive "spread HD" offense—using the parlance (HD stands for "high definition") of modern digital electronics. Along with it, though, his image of authority and running a "clean ship" suffered, with off-the-field issues involving defiant if light and speedy urban players who had run-ins with the law.

Football's metaphorical bow to technology, and its association with unruliness, went beyond the industrial overlays of clockwork precision and machine-like synchronization that marked football teamwork during the industrial era. Standout players made headlines, and individual records began to be kept—something that had never been experienced in the previous era when the team was all, or so it seemed. Mandelbaum sees a connection between the new individualism and the information technology industry of Silicon Valley, near where Walsh devised his eye-popping West Coast offense and suggested the leisure and self-indulgence orientation of a California Dream as a modern revamp of the rags to riches American Dream attained through hard labor (Starr, 2004, 2009). To Mandelbaum, the organizational principles of the new industry emphasize collegiality over hierarchy and flexibility over rigid routine. The industry seeks to break the rules so that one can creatively, often spontaneously, think "outside the box." "Its products were light, versatile machines—personal computers—rather than heavy, bulky, powerful ones such as automobiles," Mandelbaum writes (2004, 198). This also means that American football speaks for organization in the public imagination because it represents the continual changing of rules and strategies, in contrast to the nostalgia and constancy exuded by baseball and basketball. It appears more corporate than sandlot, more income generating than violently regenerative, more about being fully ready than about coming-of-age.

Voices occasionally say that the game needs to return to the tradition of a brutal contest over land. In 2008, Pittsburgh Steelers strong safety Troy Polamalu made headlines when he complained about fines imposed by the corporate NFL on a teammate for unnecessary roughness. Protesting fines is not exactly news, but his choice of words drew a rash of public responses. Polamalu said, "They're taking the physical nature of the game out of the game. It loses so much of its essence, and it really becomes like a *pansy game*" (Bouchette 2008; emphasis added). He laid blame for the game's degeneration on its rising commercialism. His ideal, he said, would be to make football "a real gladiator sport. We go there at a high speed, killing each other" (Bouchette 2008). He expressed admiration for the physical, down-in-the-trenches players of an earlier frontier era, calling them "raw, old-school, pound-it-out football players" (Bouchette 2008). His politically incorrect "pansy" reference drew public ire for its homophobic overtones, and the talk-show airwaves burned with questions of whether the celebrated violence of football is appropriate in a postmodern, post-frontier age.

American Football and the Postmodern Crisis of Masculinity

Regardless of whether it has lost its regenerative qualities from the days of grit, as Polamalu claims, football in the twenty-first century still epitomizes hypermasculine aggression characteristic of war—and is used repeatedly as a metaphor for the triumphant United States generally. Indicative of this metaphor is slang of the US President's "football," referring to a satchel with launch codes for nuclear weapons (Dobbs 2014; Safire 2008, 258). During the second Iraq war, American aggression was pridefully expressed in cartoons with football images. In 2008, a frequently posted cartoon on the Internet showed a hefty football player running through an Iraqi battlefield with a bomb under one arm and a clenched fist. Another photo montage that made the rounds showed an oversized bomber with the caption, "The terrorists have won the toss and elected to receive!" The image of the airplane raised memories of the notorious flying wedge offensive formations in football's early years, which were outlawed because of the injurious force they hurled at defenders (Watterson 2000, 12–13). Football players and huge penetrative bombers became joined as American icons, and both were portrayed as powerful giants that positioned Americans, in socially dominant play terms, as "king of the hill." Regardless of whether football players' positive body image in the post-Vietnam War era had a symbolic component—valuing size and speed because of the suggestion of abundance and control at a time of economic scarcity and political-military threat—the fact is that the appearance and skills of football players became models to aspire to for many growing boys, although perhaps for different reasons than they did in the pre-Vietnam War days.

In a postmodern era of self-development, football, more than other sports, signifies the extremes of training and the possibility of transformation. Brandishing control over young men, larger-than-life football coaches take the role of generals who, through boot/football camp, turn individuals into a winning unit of titans. This has been a frequent theme of movies, literature, and sports journalism. Many Hollywood movies, such as *Necessary Roughness* (1991), *Little Giants* (1994), *Remember the Titans* (2000), *Friday Night Lights* (2004), *Gridiron Gang* (2006), *The Blind Side* (2009), *When the Game Stands Tall* (2014), *My All-American* (2015), and *Greater* (2016) have presented football to adoring audiences as the ultimate coming-of-age experience for boys, who gain confidence and strength through the tough love of an apparently uncaring, steely coach. On television, cameras focus on surly coaches leading their player "armies" as they pace the sidelines with a sense of urgency; like the talented players, they too became the darlings of the press during football's ascendancy. Historian John Sayle Watterson claims that "the Rambos of football already existed in the NFL in the form of Vince Lombardi and George Allen, who emphasized that victory on the gridiron wasn't just important; to paraphrase Lombardi, it was the only thing" (2000, 384). These legendary coaches were honored for their victory-at-all-costs and take-no-prisoners mentality at a time when Americans longed to restore their position at the top of the heap. Such coaches conveyed an image that appeared to run counter to the equal rights movement. They underscored their total patriarchal control of the team and were seen as stern, punishing father figures (epitomized in nicknames such as George "Papa Bear" Halas of the Chicago Bears, Woody "The Old Man" Hayes at Ohio State University, Glenn "Pop" Warner at the University of Pittsburgh and the Carlisle Indian School, and Joe "Pa" Paterno at Penn State University). Also known as authoritarian "field generals," these coaches whipped their boys into shape, linking the meanings of football as a youthful initiation into manhood, military victory by eliminating the enemy, and a control game meant to maximize the possession of territory.

Football as a location to compensate for a crisis of masculinity and a loss of patriarchal tradition in a progressive society continued into the twenty-first century. One indication is William Pollack's 1998 best seller *Real Boys: Rescuing Our Sons from the Myths of Boyhood*, followed by a host of popular titles beseeching the American public not to feminize boys to achieve a civil society (see Gilbert 2002; Iggulden and Iggulden 2007; Mansfield 2006; Sommers 2000). Pollack opens with a dire warning:

> Boys today are in serious trouble, including many who seem "normal" and to be doing just fine. Confused by society's mixed messages about what's expected of them as boys, and later as men, many feel a sadness and disconnection they cannot even name.
>
> *(1998, xxi)*

He strikes a responsive chord by calling for the use of sports to express manly feelings rather than repressing them as overly competitive and hierarchical. Offering a perspective on play as therapy, Pollack underscores the "transformational" quality of sports: "our sons can go from being reserved, detached, and hardened to being expressive, affectionate, resilient" (1998, 274). American Football especially allows for a grand spectacle of an all-male group that has been subjected to opprobrium in public discourse; for fans and players alike, football, more than other sports, is associated with an exuberant expression of emotion and brash display, whether in the chilly stands with shirts off, in a sports bar screaming at the screen, or on the field with war dances and spiked balls upon gaining a touchdown.

Particularly because of its initiatory characteristics, football is important in the American context because of the relative absence of public rites of passage for boys compared with girls. Referring to the apparent disconnection between the primitiveness of traditional male-dominated sports and the progressivism of what he labels "liberated times," sociologist Ray Raphael observes that "the psychic needs of contemporary males have not always been able to keep pace with sex-role liberation and a computerized economy and nuclear warfare, all of which contribute to the apparent obsolescence of traditional initiations" (1988, xii). Although many traditional male initiations such as hazing went underground or disappeared as the twentieth century ended, football as a nationalistic sport became more acceptable as a location to fulfill what Raphael calls "an urge, a yearning, a mysterious drive to prove themselves as men in more primitive terms" (1988, xii). This drive hearkens back to the early days of the game, when reporters wondered about its hold among supposedly elite bastions of gentility at Harvard, Yale, Princeton, Swarthmore, and Columbia. Student chronicles show that the primitive game of contesting a piece of ground held initiatory qualities for players coming of age and, more than other sports, represented the collective identity of the whole class or institution (Bealle 1948, 17–78; Davis 1912, 33–43). For fans, following football was a way to prepare for battle and tell "war stories" after the game in an enactment of ultimate male ritual transformation; it engaged a kind of talk that might be unacceptable in daily life. Indeed, the magazine *Sporting News* distinguished football talk from conversation about other sports by locating it in a "War Room" section (Sporting News 2008; see also Nylund 2007, 40).

Abundant military references are linked to the acquisition and defense of property, which may be viewed as an outgrowth of the frontier experience. In addition to the honor accorded a metaphorical kill, one often hears the football field discussed as a battleground, the scrimmage line as warfare in the trenches, quarterbacks (also called field generals) throwing bombs and rockets, teams marching down the field, and running backs accelerating as if shot out of a cannon. It was not uncommon, particularly during the formative period of football, for journalists to observe that even if young men did not go off to war, they still had a need to engage in combat that could be channeled into football. Writing in *Outing* magazine in 1898, Price Collier observed, "as wars become less frequent, gymnasiums and field sports increase in number and popularity" (1898, 383). David Wallace Adams reports this military metaphor's connection with the frontier in the words of sportswriter Harry Beecher, who wrote of the 1900 Thanksgiving Day game between Carlisle and Columbia, "Now it is brawn, muscle and speed scrapping over a slippery football. Then it was tomahawks and rifles with lives at stake" (Adams 2001, 31). In both cases, being outside on a field of battle vying for turf, particularly during the fall (associated with earth tones and hunting, rather than the feminine fertility of the spring), provided a contrast to the sedentary domestic sphere (*Outing* magazine targeted a male audience and constructed a binary between the exhilarating outdoors and the enervating indoors associated with domestication).

The military rhetoric expanded during the twentieth century with the experience of the world wars in mind. Football strategies came to include blitzes, formations on the front line, and battling linemen in the trenches. There were more references to the modernization of the game as well as war, with the "big strike" forward pass gaining ground quickly, particularly with the modern "spread" and "air raid" offense featuring the quarterback in a "shotgun" formation. As a result, more metaphors for aviation came into play: quarterbacks throwing missiles, receivers catching bullets downfield, and coaches strategizing an aerial attack. Still, the manly guts of football remained the ground game, as evidenced by an often-repeated anecdote told by Purdue head coach Joe Tiller about an encounter with Penn State head coach Joe Paterno, known for his grind-it-out-on-the-ground style of play. As Tiller relates the story,

> Joe looks at me and says, "Tiller, you're not gonna spread the field and throw the ball all over the field today, are ya?" I said, "Coach, we are what we are. We're gonna go out there and play *sissy* ball."
>
> *(Jones 2008b)*

In defense of the pass receiver—who is often viewed in feminine terms as an overly slim, spoiled, and flamboyant diva, contrary to the rough and tumble ethos of the game—Elmo Wright, an end for the Kansas City Chiefs, attempted to symbolically incorporate himself into the game's manly turf war by depicting himself locked in one-on-one combat with a defensive back: "Imagine me running a pattern. I make a break to the middle, and those few seconds that the ball is in the air, my life is on the line" (Craggs 2008).

The sport may have evolved into action taking place all over the field with small, lively encounters erupting simultaneously rather than a tight, forward-moving formation, but possession is still critical to the game's outcome. In the battle for the all-important line, teams are still expected to move oppositional forces; they dig in and get physical, suggesting that they become one with the land. Former coach and sportscaster John Madden became renowned for lauding the kind of player who shows his toughness by getting filthy during play. He praised players for wearing the earth they sought to conquer. His experience inspired a series of wildly popular video games emphasizing bodily collisions in football. The uniform, expected to get grimy, differs from baseball and basketball uniforms by its helmet and pads, which, like military attire, protect participants from attack. In these militaristic references, the contact in the sport is accentuated with instruments of war and violence that use phallic symbols to extend the power of the players and feminize their opponents. The context that makes sense to Americans is the property grab, so that owning land by eliminating its previous occupants is the sign of dominance.

Using animal and frontier names to rally around invokes what Richard Slotkin calls the "myth of the hunter" born out of frontier experience. The myth equates hunting in the wild to a heroic human pursuit involving a national, protective regeneration by destroying natural masters of the land. Slotkin asserts that, according to this worldview, "Every American shares with Boone the love of the chase, the conflict, the kill" (1973, 426). The ground gained and controlled is that of the aggressive hunter figure, not the farmer-cultivator, because it is a representation of vanquishing an opponent, not developing the fertile land. There is a psychoanalytic connection because, as Slotkin notes, the hunted and hunter Indian on the frontier (and I would add the animal or titan in football) takes the image "of the American libido—the primitive source of sexual, conceptual, and creative energy" (1973, 560). In this view, however, people need not hunt to share in the hunter myth. In fact, it becomes more effective to ritualize the hunt by following it in activities such as sport rather than enacting it in a post-frontier society.

The difficulty with Europeans taking up American football, according to at least one European critic, is the construction of football as a spectator spectacle, whereas the version of football known to Americans as soccer is more participatory and not as contact oriented as rugby or American football (Jules Gray 2015). Some scholars consider the ritualization of violence in Europe to be located in the spectators occupying the stands rather than the players on the field. This raises another question about the designation of sporting contests in the United States being either home or away, rather than being played at a neutral site, to emphasize imbalance. The away team is said to be playing in hostile surroundings, and violence tends to be minimized because the home-team crowd is unified behind its team as it immobilizes or crushes the opposition and drives it away (or, in slang, "runs the team out of town").

The neutral setting of the Super Bowl as a culminating event appears to diverge from this model, but it provides background for a grand festival surrounding the crowning of a "world champion" to emphasize the high stakes of elimination. Arguably, the traditionalized celebrations that emerged in homes and bars for viewing the event verify the transgressive quality of football, even if, as

Polamalu claims, the game has lost its "essence" of male combat to the death. The foods served signify unhealthiness and even danger: spicy chili, "hot" wings, sausage, pizza, chips, burgers, beer, and hot dogs. The finger foods emphasize communal sharing and, in many settings, male bonding. Further, among focus-group conversations about male-only activities, I often heard participants say that "spending a Sunday watching football with a bunch of guys is my idea of a perfect day." Hollering at the screen is expected, and attendees are asked, "Who are you going to root for?" suggesting the need for partiality at the event as one's team builds "momentum"—a feeling of mastery and unstoppable progress or forward movement (Letson 2008).

Does football's restriction to one season weaken the symbolist case? It is true that, for most people, fall and winter constitute the football season, but I should point out that in the twenty-first century, football has become more of a year-round event. ESPN, beginning in 2005, has supported arena football, scheduled in the spring, and intra-squad games are another springtime ritual for big-time college sports, attracting as many as 50,000 fans to each event. If virtual play is taken into consideration, year-round involvement becomes even more evident. The Madden NFL football video game, aimed at the hard-core gamer segment of males aged 18 to 35, was the top-selling video game of 2006; almost three million copies were sold, outdistancing Gears of War at 1.8 million and far outpacing the popularity of any other sports game (Glenday 2008, 129; Wagner 2008). In 2007, Madden NFL set a new record by selling two million copies in its first week of release and by 2013 sales topped the 100 million mark (Byrd 2020; Glenday 2008, 128). The Madden series is not alone in the football video market; other popular games include NFL Blitz, ESPN NFL 2K5, and NFL Primetime. In the game versions, sacks and hits tend to be exaggerated with ferocious sound effects. In addition, cable TV and satellite radio stations devoted to football year-round burst on the scene with the dawn of the twenty-first century, enhancing the impact of sports talk rhetoric on the appreciation of football as manly display well beyond when games are played (Eisenstock 2001; Nylund 2007).

More than being limited to a season, football's hold year-round on the American imagination in the postindustrial era derives from its claim as mass spectacle, which is another way of saying that it is something everyone can share in a postmodern era marked by social fragmentation and isolated individualism (Bellah et al. 1996; McLean 2002; Putnam 2000). Football broadcasts a surfeit of social capital with its large teams and spectators in exaggerated proportions housed in oversized stadiums (10,000 for a high school game or 100,000 for a college contest), raising comparisons to classical coliseums as sporting centers of a civilization (Epting 2002; Reid 2008). Besides Polamalu's reference to male warrior combat as football's essence, advertisements and sports journalism broadcast images of football players as "gladiators in the coliseum," suggesting the buildup of vicarious thrills for fans of witnessing death, if only symbolically (Jones 2008a).

At the local high school level, the "big game" has significance in serving as a town commons because of the lack of communal institutions that bring residents—adults and children—together with a local identity. Institutions of church and municipality do not draw people together the way the ritualized football game does, especially in the era of consolidated schools and suburban sprawl. At the game, held outdoors on the "green" or "grounds," fans swirl about the field and socialize. Although the games may not always have the drama depicted in television shows such as *Friday Night Lights*, the message is similar: football cuts across and involves the community. In many regions that do not have major urban centers, the university football team (e.g., Syracuse University in upstate New York, the University of Nebraska in the upper plains, Penn State University in central Pennsylvania) represents the pride of the area; fan devotion, because it is not restricted to students and alumni, is compared to professional-level fervor. The passions that football raises for fans and players in America are reportedly unmatched. Sociologist Harry Edwards, for example, observes, "That kind of intensity brings out relationships, brings out a sense of commitment to each other and the game that you really don't see in other sports" (quoted in Paolantonio 2008, 190). That level of intensity for both fans and players is compared, not coincidentally, with the intensity found in other traditional institutions:

> When those guys say, "Hey, man, I really love you and I'm so happy that you're here," they mean it. I mean they mean it at a level that you don't see in families. They mean it at a level that you only see by guys, from guys who have gone through war together or who will have each other's backs in a police department or fire department.
>
> *(quoted in Paolantonio 2008, 191)*

More Than a Game

If football has a ritual significance of entrenching victory culture in American worldview, then its spectacle should be related to the time it is played as well as its place. Many commentators wonder why, if football is binding and regenerative for players and fans, it is associated with the fall, a season of decay. Football's connection with autumn was apparent in its formative years, even before colleges took it up as a ritual opening of the academic year, often following the campus rushes (mentioned earlier) that set the whole freshmen and sophomore classes against each other. As in football, the rushes or "scraps" often involved brutal contact as players tried to push a ball over a line and therefore declare the campus grounds as theirs (Bronner 2012, 118–34; Krout 1929, 235). Whereas baseball came to be the springtime ritual of going to the well-kept park, bask in the sun, and witness the blossoming greenery as a sign of renewal, football was meant to be dirty, befitting its gritty image of being played on chilly grounds. It marked a time of natural decay, when sustenance would be gained by hunting rather than cultivating. Following the drama of the hunter myth, in the absence of greenery, humans looked beyond their domain and sought to expand. The narrative suggested for autumn endeavors is that adventurers show their courage under conditions of scarcity and decline, and they provide for their families, nations, and communities by venturing out and battling fauna, vying for survival (Paolantonio 2008, 15–32). As is common to hear in football narrative, the goal of the rugged warrior is to be the "last man standing," "laying on a big hit/score," "running roughshod over the opponent," "butting heads," and "dishing dirt" in a particularly "punishing sport." The prominent symbol is not the blooming garden but the dirt below their feet and its association with the untamed field of battle, where men engage in events greater than themselves. Arguably, the culmination of this process is the high-stakes championship or Super Bowl, held after the New Year. The "big game" has a finality to it, along with the anticipation of "next year." The Super Bowl—representing the priority of the professional version of the game, and held after the college championship, whose players will feed into the pros—is culturally marked as the preeminent sporting event with exuberant, even hyperbolic, festivity. It is not held all year but is scheduled in the dead of winter. It regenerates life, with an emphasis on manly control of the land and labor to show the transition from adolescence to adulthood. Football shot up in appeal after the 1960s because it hybridized the regeneration of American frontier exploits with postindustrial characteristics of layered organization and urbane individuality in the midst of a social and political environment in which football provided a bounded cultural scene for an aggressive victory culture, a release from the pressures of routinized everyday life through vicarious spectator experience, and even a location for socially sanctioned immaturity. Rather than plateauing after this boost, football has grown in bursts, at least in the United States, through the enterprises of an advanced consumer culture and responses to deflated national identity and masculinity.

In sum, football—in its historical references to the frontier experience and urban-industrial synchronization; its invocation of tradition in an energetic, competitive, adolescent coming-of-age ritual; and its social context as a masculine response to modernization—is both a reflection and a distortion of American culture. It has undergone many changes in rules as well as descriptive discourse over the years, including a shift from a nineteenth-century regional and campus folk game to a national spectacle of industrial, corporate, urban, and digital power in the twentieth and twenty-first centuries. With this norm of change, the game's reverence for the past is often questioned, suggesting that it lacks the constancy characteristic of tradition and that, more than other big-time sports, it embraces progress (Mandelbaum 2004, 124–26). Yet vital continuities exist between the sport's folk roots and modern versions in terms of the importance of possessing property and pushing occupants off theirs; inflicting bodily punishment with the crushing sack and the psychological humiliation of feminization; the military mindset of intense preparation, strategizing, and battle; its projection of adolescent masculine values and anxieties—and most of all, its glorification of and psychological need for winning. American football has indeed engaged the prescriptive and connotative qualities of victory culture in its ritualization of violence, passionate emotional release, and intense male bonding that connects the narrative of the game's gritty, grimy past to the cutting-edge technological wonders of the widely broadcast and watched present.

"More than a game," American football constitutes for many spectators and participants an event working at various levels and often with contradictory symbolism. This tension within its practice—as modern and antimodern, normal and abnormal, refined and primitive, organized and chaotic—invites speculation not just on the final score but also on the various meanings that the hits, bangs, and blocks of the game entail. Instead of universalizing the end zone as Dundes did, viewers can understand the game structurally in the context of the field and the sidelines; observers can link it historically and socially to Americanness and explain its enactment in mass spectacle as ritual and tradition. Dundes was on to something, though, by drawing attention to the way football provides metaphors to live and fight by on a field of play. Psychologically, the game as a male display related to adolescent development is crucial to its performance by players and the perception of its high stakes by spectators. The idea that football carries an importance greater than other popular sports is evident in the slang of "political football" for a seemingly inconsequential or non-political matter that has been elevated to emotional high-profile political wrangling (Safire 2008, 257–58). In the stands, viewers are hardly passive; they actively engage and help construct the play frame of football that allows for violence and exuberant manly display. Spectators may be said to be framing play to express feelings about life, while players enact a dramatic serious battle over property. Getting down in their stances on the line, titans on both sides of the ball anticipate a clash over turf that they can claim as their own. Whether pushing ahead or pulling back, this is "America's game" and America's paradox. The stadium is a shrine to question America's place in the world, and in the infamous words of Charlie Sheen, experience, "duh, winning" (McCartney 2011). The key to control for the players, and the nation, is gaining ground, and thinking both will emerge victorious.

4
MONEY

Los Angeles journalist Braven Dyer sat in a glitzy Las Vegas casino for the first time and was bowled over by the flashy patrons, their dreams of the big score and getting rich quick at the gambling tables, and excessive *décor* supporting the parade of luxurious goods hawked to visitors. He knew about UCLA football coach Red Sanders' glorification of winning as all-important, and based on what he saw decided to put a twist on the familiar saying for his readers by writing "Of course, money isn't everything. It's the only thing; at Las Vegas, at least" (Dyer 1956, 4:1). What seemed over the top in Las Vegas appeared normalized across the country in succeeding decades. American boxing promoter Floyd "Money" Mayweather, Jr., known for extravagant spending (Lee 2014) and rising out of inner-city poverty to become one of America's richest entrepreneurs, in 2017 received media coverage when he repeated the saying about money being the center of American life (WWE Insider 2017). Unapologetic after purchasing an 18-million-dollar watch, 4.8-million-dollar car, and numerous private jets, Mayweather explained that making money was not enough; he felt compelled to show off his success materially to feel like a "winner in life" (Lane 2019). Mayweather reflected that in the American materialistic system, "Everything you've got to own costs money" (Jim Gray 2015). In his urban world, he explained, people cannot produce the goods or grow their own food, so you have to buy them, and that means making more money. Although the media reported Mayweather's extravagance as unusual, many readers agreed with his basic premise that the ability to consume goods is not only a measure of wealth, it is also a sign of power.

Business provides the goods. And most Americans are familiar with the modern proverb "The business of America is business" (Doyle, Mieder, and Shapiro 2012, 30). It was stated as such in the *New York Times* in 1928 as a quote of President Calvin Coolidge, although his actual words brought out more of the interrelationship

DOI: 10.4324/9780429452970-5

between buying and selling: "the chief business of the American people is business. They are profoundly concerned with producing, buying, selling, investing, and prospering in the world" (Mieder 2020, 177; Terrell 2019). In the original speech delivered to the American Society of Newspaper Editors in 1925 amid boom times, Coolidge underscored the need for a competitive free-market in the nation that in a modern democracy would encourage "the little man" to attain financial success. Critics worried about the effects of business, which years later in the words of entrepreneur Jake Allen under the headline of "Money Isn't Everything; It's the Only Thing" were viewed as: "Money, profit, the-bottom-line, what ever you choose to call them are the sole and driving force" (Isenberg 2011). The sentiment that ethical considerations are secondary is in contrast to Andrew Carnegie's more philanthropic and socially conscious "gospel of wealth" (Carnegie 2006). Using terms of Social Darwinism, Allen emphasized the undemocratic effects of a production-consumption cycle in which "only the strongest survive and they will do so by consuming the weak." Despite the fact that few businesses actually sustain success—20 percent of all businesses fail in their first year and 70 percent before their tenth year—that does not stop Americans from trying or from believing that they will attain wealth. According to the Bureau of Labor Statistics, over 700,000 new businesses begin every year, and the number of American entrepreneurs stands at 11.5 million (Conner 2012; Deane 2020).

After all, in American worldview, wealth is elastic and money is there to be had in what anthropologists call a psychological "image of unlimited good" (Dundes 1971; Hornborg 1992; Khalaf 1992; Mullen 1978). The idea of limitless resources contrasts with other economic systems in which people believe that the amount of wealth is finite and social mobility is restricted, thus leading to an "image of limited good" (Baer 1982; Foster 1965; Piker 1966; Schryer and Foster 1976; Trawick and Hornborg 2015). Many Americans apply this idea of unlimited resources or "super-abundance," according to historian Russel Nye (1966, 277–79), as reason to pursue a fast-track to success in a distinctive version of free-market capitalism, or low-road capitalism, so named because of the reduced worker wages to force lower prices and higher profits (Wright and Rogers 2015, 228–42). Because payment to workers is defined by wages and salaries rather than the ability to produce materials for one's needs, employees need to buy goods to maintain their lives and for profit are encouraged to buy more than they need. Fitting with pressure on workers for time after a busy and long day, especially important to these wage earners is that the products are *instantly* ready to wear, set to be used, and in the digital age programmed to plug and play (Hill 2004, 4–10; Norris 1990, 27–70; Sivulka 2012, 69–78). Advertising, primarily localized in the nineteenth century, boomed to spark consumption on national and international scales in the twentieth century.

In the twenty-first century, the United States rose to become the largest advertising market in the world. America's 240 billion dollars spent on advertising in 2020 is more than double the 106 billion dollars spent in 1980 and almost triple the amount of advertising in China, the second largest advertising market (Guttmann 2021). The figure is expected to grow with more being spent on online advertising. Much of the advertising is aimed at children to acculturate them into a consumer culture. Commercial television programming contains approximately 100 advertisement spots every four hours and the average American child may view as many as 40,000 television commercials annually (Starsburger 2001). Online advertising is taking a larger share of the media advertisement pie from less than ten billion dollars in 2004 to over 125 billion dollars in 2020. This exposure to children, and children-centered consumer holidays such as Halloween and Christmas, according to industry statistics, directly influences the household spending of over 600 billion dollars (Lapierre et al. 2017). An important pitch made by advertisers is to magical thinking in which genies, shamans, giants, and talking animals tout the wondrous, gratifying qualities of products and their transformative, therapeutic power (Assaf 2012; Dégh 1994; Lears 1988; Lears 1994, 40–74). Money, and what it buys, works miracles.

As American adult workers shifted from a producer to service and information economy, business ventures and occupational choices depended more on spending power of consumers (Fox and Lears 1983; Zukin 2005). Although the United States is depicted as an affluent society, the richest 1 percent of Americans own 40 percent of the country's wealth while over 10 percent of the population remains below the poverty rate (Desmond 2019). Nonetheless the rags to riches belief persists, often characterized as the American Dream, that wealth is easily attainable for anyone with ingenuity and hard work (Cullen 2003, 59–102; Gutman 1976; Liberman and Lavine 2000; Tebbel 1963). Thus the tie of commercial capitalism to American consumerism functions paradoxically to both decrease and widen inequality (Graham 2017).

Wealth, Work, and Debt

The United States in the twentieth century became the world's largest consumer market as well as the globe's largest economy (Mitterling, Tomass, and Wu 2020). Yet this boast belies wide disparities in income and social mobility, often along racial and ethnic lines. Frustration over economic inequality and financial insecurity culminated in 2011 with a protest movement called "Occupy Wall Street" that targeted banks and corporate headquarters nationwide. Although street demonstrations had dissipated by 2013, activists turned their attention to the erasure of debt, particularly for higher education and medical expenses for the 99 percent of Americans they claimed had been forced into debt to pay for the basics of life (Patel 2020). Whether forced or willing, Americans across economic classes borrow money to pursue opportunities for growth and maintain consumption of durable goods and services. Folk wisdom associated with a premodern producer economy such as "A penny earned is a penny saved" and "Never spend your money before you have it" hardly seemed to apply in a postindustrial age (Mieder 2020, 160–61). While an American icon of practicality and ingenuity, Benjamin Franklin was not the model for modern living when he advised "spare and have is better than spend and crave," or "frugality keeps you out of bondage, think what you do when you run in debt, you give to another power over your liberty" (Mieder 2020, 163–64). Resonating more with urbanizing Americans beginning in the late nineteenth century were industrialist Andrew Carnegie's pulling-up-by-one's-bootstraps message of "Aim for the highest" drawn from his personal rags to riches story and minister Russell Conwell's performance-lecture on the theme of "acres of diamonds" to be had, insisting that it is the American's duty to get rich to counter the biblical dictum that money is the root of all evil (1 Timothy 6:10; see Barton 1989, 63–64). Writer and motivational speaker Stan Nussbaum in 2005 declared "Shop till you drop" (traced to an auto advertising campaign in 1984) as one of the modern "Ten Commandments of American Culture" along with the admonition to hurry up doing it with "Time is money" and "Just do it" (Nussbaum 2005, 15–21; see also Mieder 2020, 165; Villers and Mieder 2017). Enabling acquisition is the reference to the promise of easy credit in America with "Buy now (today), pay later" introduced in the 1920s and updated in modern parlance to "Live now, pay later" thus equating shopping as a praxis of living (Anderson 2011; Mieder 2020, 170). In modern consumer culture, Americans are likely to acknowledge the desire for wealth and status goods but realize the pressure of debt in satirical stickers pronouncing "I owe, I owe, so off to work I go," a parody of the cheery song "Heigh-Ho" from Walt Disney's happy film *Snow White and the Seven Dwarfs* (1937). In 2020, the average household consumer debt was $145,000 and the total in the United States amounted to a whopping 14 trillion dollars. An average household owed over $7,000 in credit cards alone. Loans for vehicles and education and mortgages for homes were other major sources of debt.

Motivated by a big payoff, and purchasing power expressed in the American proverb "money never sleeps" (Doyle, Mieder, and Shapiro 2012, 169), Americans bemoan through their cultural outlets a frustration with the routinization of service work and the rut or hole one falls into in pursuit of the exalted, "almighty dollar." "Money (That's What I Want)" written by Berry Gordy and Janie Bradford, for example, was the first hit record for the Detroit Motown empire. It was notable for making the American rock magazine *Rolling Stone*'s list of greatest songs of all time. It contained yet another counter to the modern proverb "Money isn't everything" by declaring that what it does not buy, one cannot use. The singer Barrett Strong ends with successive lines that begin with money, then proceeds incrementally to more money, and ends with an infinite amount of money, all of which he wants, thus expressing the image of unlimited good. Contained in the closing lines is the idea that money is available, attainable, and accumulable. The rhythm and blues song was recorded in 1959 and later covered by many popular artists, including the superstar Beatles and Rolling Stones, became an anthem in the twenty-first century for the working man on movie/

television soundtracks (e.g., *Chicago Hope* 1995, *The Wedding Singer* 1998, *My Name is Earl* 2005, *The Simpsons* 2014) and television commercials (ABC television 2015, Old Navy 2014).

While citizens of other countries certainly share a hunger for cash, songwriter Randy Newman underscored the Americanness of pursuing it in "It's Money that Matters" on the Billboard charts in 1988 when he sang "It's money that matters, Hear what I say, It's money that matters, In the U.S.A." His composition was anticipated by the folk proverb "Money talks" (also the title of a popular action comedy movie starring Chris Tucker and Charlie Sheen in 1997). With the rhyming comment "Bullshit walks," the pithy saying is often used in conversation to indicate that occupations associated with high incomes carry undue power (Doyle, Mieder, and Shapiro 2012, 169; Mieder 2020, 179). As revelations of the widening gap between the salaries of corporate executives and office workers became publicly conspicuous, a disillusionment grew in Newman's America. Questioning the traditional work ethic as well as corporate hierarchy was photocopied broadsides tacked to office bulletin boards that blared the idealism of "Work Hard and You Shall Be Rewarded" only to be undermined by an image of a flabby, unattractive white-collar worker with a metal screw through his belly. The cartoonish figure vividly communicated that the worker was symbolically being "screwed" (Dundes and Pagter 1975). The invisible person or force doing the screwing was open to interpretation. Was it the corporate hierarchy "system" of managers because of fear of being replaced preventing people from climbing out of their rung of the hierarchy? Or more broadly was it about power elites who in an ideally egalitarian democratic society need to stay out of sight and control workers through cultural means and thereby establish a cultural if not economic hegemony to retain their power (Artz and Murphy 2000; Lears 1981, 1985; Vallas 2003)? With the power of culture against them, workers had to wonder if responding in often surreptitious cultural expressions such as homegrown broadsides, biting humor, and satirical art could effect change or reinforce the system by acknowledging its entrenchment.

One cultural rallying cry for change that sounded a familiar chord of worker frustration and added feminist themes of a glass ceiling and sexual harassment of women at the office was the successful movie *9 to 5* (1980), which spawned a television series (1982–1983, 1986–1988) and Broadway musical (2008). Dolly Parton's theme song of protest "Nine to Five" sat on top of both pop and country charts, and won a Grammy Award for best country song. The lyrics harped on the disillusionment of begin employed in supposedly prestigious work that is not sufficient to "make a livin'." Reference is made to higher aspirations characterized as dreams, and listeners related to it as the American Dream of success. A strong sentiment in the workers' anthem is one of feeling stuck in a "dead-end" job and prevented from moving up by higher-ups:

9 to 5, for service and devotion
You would think that I

Would deserve a fair promotion
Want to move ahead
But the boss won't seem to let me
I swear sometimes that man is out to get me.
(Words and Music by Dolly Parton, copyright 1982; printed with permission of Lion Fish Music)

The movie aged well because its complaints were still relevant in the twenty-first century. The Broadway musical went on a national tour in 2010–2011 and in regional and international productions afterward. The major Progressive Democratic Senator Elizabeth Warren anthemized Parton's opening song by playing it upon her entrance to announcing her presidential candidacy in 2020 (Torres 2020). The reference to a fixed time clock has changed to a discourse about flexible individualized work arrangements, out of the office as well as in it, and the pressures in a digital age of "service and devotion" 24/7 (which was suggested as a title for a twenty-first-century version of the movie; Clint 2005; see also Woodman and Cook 2019). The opening clicks on a typewriter on the original recording sound dated, but the idea of being stuck to a chair dependent on expanding office technology remains, with the added concern of workers being vulnerable to displacement as a result of automation. In a digital twist, Parton added words to the iconic song and called it "5 to 9" for website company Squarespace, which debuted the new version in a commercial at Super Bowl XLV in 2021. Its pitch was to create websites to get ahead of the intense competition with creative "dreaming" and aggressive "hustling" in response to the new 24/7, 365 days a year, stressful work environment (Mier 2021).

The image of office worker stagnation and disillusion is reinforced in common sayings such as "Another day, another dollar" and "Same shit, different day" (Doyle, Mieder, and Shapiro 2012, 50; Mieder 2020, 175). Laboring to have spending coupled with social power is lamented in a series of popular American songs about middle-class woes. Jackson Browne in 1977 had a pop hit with "The Pretender" whose lyrics described the drudgery of working each day in the struggle to make money. Into the twenty-first century many hip-hop artists who enjoyed a rags to riches transformation waxed poetic about the problems as well as promises of money for a consuming public. Topping the American Billboard Hot 100 in 1997 was "Mo Money Mo Problems" by The Notorious B.I.G. On the recording, he recalls his rise to fame and money, but complains about the government and others who want to bring him down. Another successful rapper, Lil Scrappy, who was born into poverty, acknowledged the drug of acquisitive materialism that threatened to bankrupt him in his 2009 hit "Addicted to Money." It contained a hook line repeating that he has to grab money because he longs to keep buying a bigger house and new and more expensive clothes.

Americans perceive that the way to afford status symbols of house, fashion, and cars in is to start a business, although doing so is risky (Conner 2012; Nye 1966,

104–63). Since 1965 when immigration reopened to the United States, small business creation has been noticeably appealing to immigrants and other marginalized groups that wary of prejudice turn to owning their own shops and services (Conner 2012; Fairlie 2012). Despite the image of the small business in continuity with the Jeffersonian democratic ideal of the yeoman, by the twenty-first century economic reports showed that fewer than 20 firms hold a third of American wealth (Needham 2014; see also Trachtenberg 1982 for the roots of the incorporation trend in the late nineteenth century). Retail sales at the heart of consumerism, however, are dominated by small businesses (98.5 percent). In the early twenty-first century, retail was the top contributor to job gains in the U.S. economy, accounting for 16 percent of the 28 million increase in private sector jobs. Retail, hovering around 6 percent of the gross domestic product (GDP), pushes much of the economy because of its driving influence on manufacturing, marketing, and services (National Retail Federation 2020). Businesses large and small need Americans to keep spending, even when times are tough. "It's everywhere you want to be," the Visa credit card advertised to promise mobility along with indulgence, and Starbucks lured customers by inviting them to pamper or "treat yourself" to justify buying their higher-priced line of coffees.

In a system of acquisitive materialism, ordinary Americans search for luxuries at bargain prices to announce status of a higher economic bracket. In 2016, Apartment.com used the song "Movin' on Up" showing actor Jeff Goldblum being hoisted with a grand piano up the side of a luxury high-rise apartment with different tenants enjoying their space (the penthouse had a football field marking its Americanness; see Chapter 3). The song was originally used on the television show *The Jeffersons* (broadcast from 1975 to 1985) for an African-American family moving up to a deluxe apartment on an upper floor of a high-rise building. The singer uses a traditional metaphor for economic arrival, having a "a piece of the pie." During a downturn in the economy caused by the COVID-19 pandemic in 2020, Haynes Furniture with multiple locations in Virginia recognized this psychology of moving up with an advertisement aimed at consumers to get expensive-looking furniture without guilt: "The Price isn't everything, it's the only thing." The campaign supported the satirical business wisdom that in an acquisitive consumer culture "A bargain is something you don't need at a price you can't resist" (Mieder 2020, 167). Shoppers have in mind, though, the warning that "You get what you pay for," which might also be a motivation to spend more than they intended (Doyle, Mieder, and Shapiro 2012, 171).

Slow and Fast Capitalism

Historically, economists identify a succession of slow capitalist systems in the United States from the regionally competitive (eighteenth and nineteenth centuries), through to the broader and later forms of national and transnational corporate capitalism (twentieth century) (Bowles, Edwards, and Roosevelt 2005, 161). These systems connoted monetary investment in equipment, physical plant, and a labor force to produce saleable goods in quantities that allow for reinvestment and expansion physically and financially (Bowles, Edwards, and Roosevelt 2005, 3–30). Capitalism—particularly in the United States, which has been called "the capitalist country par excellence"—also depends on the institutionalization of private property, accumulation of wealth as profits from enterprises, agencies for credit functions such as banks, and investments to enlarge markets and improve production (Hacker 1957, 10–11; Bowles, Edwards, and Roosevelt 2005, 147–81).

Then how is it possible that a communitarian agrarian group like the Amish can survive, and indeed thrive, in America? They do have private property and accumulate profits from enterprises, but they insist that the pietistic practice of their faith is paramount, and counter capitalist tendencies toward individualism, inequality, and materialism (encapsulated in the idea expressed in the German *Deitsch* dialect of *Hochmut* or self-centered pride and haughtiness) with self-sacrificing religious concepts of *Demut* (humility, related to simplicity and plainness), *Bruderschaft* (brotherhood, or mutual aid within small social units), and *Gelassenheit* (calmness, or submission). Although the Amish in many ways represent a countercultural preindustrial economy born out of political disenfranchisement in Europe, this has not meant socioeconomic stagnation. Prohibited from owning land in Europe, the Amish in North America bought family-sized holdings that could be improved and intensively cultivated (Hostetler 1994, 115–17). As freeholders, the Amish together with their neighbors abandoned the manorial, mercantile practices which had been retarding European feudal agriculture and developed an early capitalist system based upon the entrepreneurial model (Hacker 1957, 11; see also Kulikoff 1992).

While many of the non-Amish farmers sought individual independence and economic-material expansion, the Amish sought ways to maintain communitarianism, that is, living in close proximity to one another and joining together in an unwritten social contract to provide mutual aid rather than the sharing of property and childrearing in the manner of a communal society such as the Hutterites (Bronner 2019, 201–37; Hacker 1957, 11–12; for Hutterite social structure, see Hostetler 1997). According to John Hostetler, who had been raised on an Amish farm with his family, the Amish "wanted to combine agriculture with a preferred way of life, and not farm primarily for commercial gain" (1994, 117). Thus one of the first negotiations for the Amish with the host American society and its economic institutions was over the social and ethical implications of capitalism. And modern tourists flock to Amish farmlands in Central Pennsylvania to reimagine the Amish as American pioneer ancestors. To an extent, John Hostetler claims, tourists assuage their guilt of abandoning the land by giving tribute to the Amish, even though tourist industries threaten Amish folklife (Trollinger 2012). The same farmlands region also features the commercial development of retail outlets to encourage tourists to spend money on commercial goods.

The cultural as well as economic gap grew between the agricultural Amish and industrial-urban America in the late nineteenth century (Brands 2010). Yet the

Amish could maintain their ethnoreligious-linguistic folklife—marked by their "plain" dress and language of Pennsylvania *Deitsch*, among one another, in addition to the speaking of English in commerce—in relative isolation and economic self-sufficiency within the local markets of Central Pennsylvania (Kraybill 2001; Kraybill, Johnson-Weiner, and Nolt 2013). With rural electrification and the expansion of transportation, industry came to the countryside, leading social theorists to contemplate a new stage of capitalism in the twentieth century (Hounshell 1985; see also Contosta 2002, 295–302). Marxist thinkers such as Theodor Adorno and Fredric Jameson referred to this stage as "late capitalism," which featured the accelerated growth of big business and government after World War II (Lowrey 2017). The modifier of "late" suggested that the days of capitalism were numbered. It implied that capitalism had ballooned into a system controlled by super-corporations causing social problems of instability, poverty, and corruption to the point that it might come crashing down and spark sociopolitical revolution (Hannah 2000). Yet while acknowledging that a new economy was developing in the second half of the twentieth century led by the United States, other social commentators spoke of a rising service and information economy that held promise for leveling wealth and increasing the number of enterprises because of wider participation and reduced competitiveness owing to non-material production (Bowles, Edwards, and Roosevelt 2005, 541).

One difference with the old industrial economy in the post-war period was the ascendancy of intellectual property over the physical holdings of manufacturing and agriculture. The white-collar sector of the economy is led by professionals who offer cultivated knowledge, social agency, and political advocacy to clients. Their capital is not location-based as much as it is based on technical expertise and control of information. This professional or "new class" expanded the ranks of the middle class and promised increased social mobility with access to college education and the arts that had formerly been reserved for the elite. Status was conferred by the ability to hire others for their needs (Briggs 1981). Some commentators embraced the growing sector that had advanced furthest in the United States as having a democratizing and diversifying influence because of the opportunity for small-scale entrepreneurship with reduced labor, while others pointed out the tendency for corporate conglomeration of diverse businesses resulting in monopolization and repression (Schettkat and Yocarini 2003). A concomitant trend was an enlarged government (often to serve regulatory functions on corporate excesses), provide more protective services for consumers, and promote entrepreneurship in the service and information economy (Mayer 2012).

Contemplating the increased reliance on intellectual capital at the same time as the informational products of books appeared to be in decline, sociologist Ben Agger (1989) suggested "fast capitalism" to describe a new American work order in which one performs services in the name of gaining social mobility but loses autonomy in the process. Agger theorized that based upon a false premise of gaining an advantage given to global corporations, capitalism "reproduces itself frenetically" instead of imploding, with the socioeconomic repercussion of "replacing profit quickly and degrading reason" (1989, 21). In financial terms, this means that in the new economy more enterprises are possible with a minimum of start-up funding since one does not need to invest in brick-and-mortar buildings and equipment. The expectation, however, is that one gains a quick turnaround of profit, and publicity channeled through media-driven popular culture in America will be necessary. The shelf life of enterprises in the new economy is likely to be shorter, but the consequences of bankruptcy are not as severe, and entrepreneurs are encouraged to establish new mini-enterprises. Sociologist Sharon Zukin criticizes the framing of this American system as democratizing and diversifying by calling it an advertised illusion, a "pseudodemocracy," because of corporate controls of the outlets for providing services and the power to globally merge and manipulate small operations (2005, 250). For Zukin, the "slow" contrast to the new economy was the farmers' market in which multiple vendors relate directly to consumers with their wares (2005, 269–78; see also Bronner 2019, 201–37; Robinson and Hartenfeld 2007). In her view, it struggled to compete with fast capitalism, requiring the ample audiences provided in urban centers.

Pushing the spread of "fast capitalism," and, according to many cultural critics the displacement of "analog" face-to-face communication, was the advent of the Internet and start-up "dot com" businesses in the 1990s (Agger 2016; Bronner 2011, 398–441; Cortada 2004; Hijorth 2015). Agger, in fact, identifies the Internet as ushering in a second stage of fast capitalism that he calls "faster capitalism" (2016, 1–33). "Acceleration" is the keyword in his theory because the *hyper* (or other symbolic equivalents of "mega," "ultra," and "super"; see Raab-Fischer 1994) rate of communicating and doing business on the Internet led to the breakdown of boundaries of all sorts and the quickening pace of everyday life (Agger 2016, 3–4). In his words, the Internet raised expectations of instantaneity, so that people "expect things quickly, instantly, including our fast food, fast cars, fast bodies, fast work, fast reading, and fast writing" (2016, 5). It expanded e-commerce with the promise of ease of use; minimal investment (of time or money); no necessary ties to place (and work from home), community, or physical plant (indeed, many websites do not list addresses); and global instantaneity (an immediate response wherever one is located) and social simultaneity (the boundaries of time and space are immaterial since one can interact with anyone, anytime, anywhere). The Internet became ubiquitous with the imaginary that people are always accessible and able to shop anytime (underscored by the phrase "24/7," meaning the operation is open 24 hours, seven days a week), because they are always connected or "logged in." It suggested an accelerated rate of social change as well as technological innovation. And, for many social theorists, the feature of notifications, alerts, and commands emanating from devices carrying the Internet and carried by people at all times means that it becomes an authority directing everyday life.

A critical difference between slow and fast capitalism, and the defining characteristic of a digital economy in the twenty-first century, is the connection of fast capitalism with "prosumer commerce." Prosumer refers to the simultaneous producing and consuming that people are able to do online and whose mindset of economic fusion carries over to social relations of seamless giving and taking (Ritzer 2015; Zukin 2005, 227–78; the term "prosumer" owes to Toffler 1980). This process is epitomized by eBay, Etsy, Amazon Handmade, and Craigslist, in which every person who logs in can potentially be a seller as well as a shopper. And this can be accomplished without financial or material capital, thus democratizing the economy, at least in principle. It is still capitalist, however, because of the need to attract social capital in the form of "crowd sourcing" that often requires advertising, membership fees, and organizational services. For example, the financial success of the free service of Facebook and YouTube largely owes to the willingness of users to contribute socially, and be tracked and targeted, as both producers and consumers.

Still, the question remains, how can companies that offer free services make a profit? According to sociologists George Ritzer and Nathan Jurgenson (2010, 29), the answer is that:

> the goal of most Web 2.0 companies is to create, and later enhance, the "value" of their site (by, for example, turning it into a well-known brand). They do this by increasing the number of users through publicity and increasing visibility, by expanding what the site has to offer mainly on the basis of what prosumers contribute to it, by having the costs of development (largely labor costs and computer equipment) borne mainly by the prosumers developing the site, by branding the site and perhaps ultimately through the creation of various streams [such as selling user lists and brand-name products].

Even brick-and-mortar stores rely on user labor: supermarkets in the digital age introduced self-checkout in which the shopper scans, bags, and purchases products without the assistance of a clerk. Users are aggregated with the use of "loyalty cards" that offer discounts and allow tracking of their buying habits. Ritzer and Jurgenson claim that in prosumer commerce, corporations "meddle less with the prosumers who are producing and consuming the content" (2010, 31); they concentrate on enlarging use and the creation of effective services.

One such service is ensuring that memorable things do not disappear. With the rate of change accelerating in the digital age, corporations enable their free prosumer labor force to locate, collect, display, and sell objects imbued with sentimental meaning from the past to offset anxieties of obsolescence for themselves as well as their gadgets. Historian Gary Cross finds that

> this stress [of fast capitalism] resulted from a rather distinctly modern phenomenon—people found identity and meaning in specific goods but, as a

result, felt that their selfhoods were threatened when those things disappeared. The nostalgic impulse came from a desire to get them back. Most important, this longing was often rooted in the formative years of consumers—childhood and youth.

(2015, 11)

Ironically, as prosumer commerce built a reliance on improvement of interactive digital devices, it also spurred the creation of outlets for expression, and consumption, of nostalgia, and community, in commodity exchange sites and cultural tourism. Yet these experiences could still feel "virtual" and not "real" or authentic, or what Cross refers to as "the ephemerality of the everyday experience of fast capitalism" (2015, 245).

Within the era of fast capitalism, slow capitalist ventures such as farmers' markets that Zukin lauded emerged as managed commercial establishments rather than community exchanges. They signal, or stage, a historic alternative to corporate, urban America by symbolizing a localized folk agrarian society (see Bronner 2019, 201–37; Hofstadter 1955, 23–59; Robinson and Farmer 2017; Robinson and Hartenfeld 2007). The dramatic growth in the number of farmers' markets nationally in the early twenty-first century, especially after their near-extinction during the 1970s, while countering economic expectations (they defy the rational model of being spurred by profit margins), is explained, at least in part, by the folklorization of the markets in response to the "faster" prosumer economy (cf. McDowell 2010; Norton 2009, 190–216). This is a broad-based phenomenon, but the Amish have played a role in it because of their need for new economic outlets with the decline of farming. For their American neighbors, the Amish spreading across 31 states have been intellectually constructed as icons of the realness, naturalness, and folkness of localism that the markets rely on for their modern or countercultural appeal (Bronner 2019, 201–37; Robinson and Farmer 2017, 101–102; Robinson and Hartenfeld 2007, 48–69).

Although the Amish appear inextricably opposed to the technological basis of prosumer commerce, they have tapped into the perception by Americans of their folklife providing authentic experience of the past in the postmodern present, even if temporarily and only occasionally. Whereas tourism or buying Amish crafts and foods often remains ephemeral, socioeconomic settings in which the Amish appear to operate naturally and provide opportunities for consumption such as farmers' markets appear in the English social imaginary to be "real." At farmers' markets, a symbolic association is built between the vendor dressed in traditional garb and the foods and crafts sold in a way that is not evident for English sellers. The "English," as the Amish call outsiders to their faith, can have direct experiences with the Amish and feel that they are immersed in life as it used to be lived. For the Amish, the farmers' markets frame core values of their folklife including a localized agrarian niche in which they can cooperate with one another and maintain family ties. The Amish might perceive the farmers' market scene, even in urban environments, as Elma did in the Mennonite novel *The Farmers' Market Mishap*:

> The aroma of fresh herbs and ripening berries mingling with fragrances from homemade soaps and creams filled Elma's senses as she drew a deep breath. She appreciated *being able to take part in a rural event that nurtured the feeling of community spirit*.
> (Brunstetter and Brunstetter 2017, 70; emphasis added)

(For the concentration of farmers' markets near urban areas, see Brown 2001.) Not all farmers' markets are appropriate for the Amish, however. They seek out ones that are located close to their settlements and at which they can populate a large, if not dominant, proportion of market stands and have access to transportation. They also prefer ones that exude an old-timey feel in keeping with their value placed on *Das Alt Gebrauch*, or "the Old Way" (Yoder 1950, 84).

The Rise and Reading of Consumer Culture

How did the new way of consumerism take hold in the United States and become ingrained into the American Dream? An especially telling period in American cultural history occurred when the nation, poised in the late nineteenth century, paused to consider its future in the twentieth century. Americans hoped for a unified vision, but confusion appeared to blur the road ahead. The rise of a consumer culture and the wealth that accompanied it created cultural, societal, and individual dilemmas. Wealth was power, and to show this intangible relationship, wealth was made tangible. The accumulation and display of goods expressed the power to manage people by directing production through consumption. It also provided something that the absence of family name and breeding could not—taste. Following an evolutionary model, preachers for wealth argued that affluence lifted culture above ungodly states of barbarism and savagery. They contended that much as conditions and nature propelled the refined human over the primitive ape, so too would the refinement of consumption lead Americans to a new age of ease and abundance. In short, wealth in America promised the flowering of a sprawling, glorious American empire comparable to the classical civilizations of Europe.

Still, there was worry that the humane spirit of the country was submerged beneath the surface allure of having and displaying possessions in the rising consumer culture. Beneath the uniformity of mass consumption, could individuality spring forth? Behind the trappings of "gimcrackeries," as novelist William Dean Howells referred to the new ostentatious goods, could people still touch and inspirit each other? Americans looked to expressive texts such as novels, artifacts, and communities to provide interpretations of unresolved ideas and experiences toward the goal of resolution. The rise of an acquisitive consumer culture provided compelling new images and texts for society to behold and read. These works gained their significance by navigating through ambivalent feelings by putting them into symbols and parables that could be vividly comprehended. By interpreting symbols within images and texts, people had the chance to pause to evaluate the rapid changes occurring around them and to dramatize emotions, extend ideas, and gain an instrument of persuasion. Yet because of the immediacy of these materials, the significance of their metaphors was not always realized. In the rhetoric of accumulation and display, goods increased their roles as mediators and conveyors of cultural values, human emotions, and social priorities.

A character in William Dean Howells's *A Hazard of New Fortunes* (1889) asks, "Does anything from without change us? We're brought up to think so by the novelists, who really have the charge of people's thinking nowadays" (Howells 1980, 422). In the wake of rapid changes—many of them material—felt at the end of the nineteenth century, characters in Howells's popular novel went beyond reading literature for reminders of values to illustrations and things. Indeed, Howells used the establishment of new reading material in the form of a magazine as the organizing principle of the novel. This magazine is different because it has illustrations suited to "the twilight of the nineteenth century." The magazine, expanded to a biweekly, is a hit with consumers. The innocent editor from intellectual Boston transplanted to commercial New York feels the pull of the consumer world and realizes how things—"gimcrackeries," he calls them—were read for values as much as his words. His wife reminds him,

> I remember that when we were looking for a flat you rejected every building that had a bell ratchet or a speaking tube, and would have nothing to do with any that had more than an electric button; you wanted a hallboy, with electric buttons all over him. I don't blame you. I find such things quite as necessary as you do.

He admits that "having and shining" are held up at this time "as the chief good of life." They signify "material civilization…a culture that furnishes showily, that decorates, and that tells" (Howells 1980, 380–81).

In 1899 Thorstein Veblen's *The Theory of the Leisure Class* described a new "leisure class" comprising financiers, manufacturers, and merchants cashing in on the opportunities of industrial America. According to Veblen, the class used consumption to herald a newly attained status by displaying their excesses and by demonstrating the case, idleness, and self-gratification with which wealth and success were enjoyed. Veblen noted that the man's cane conveyed the infirmity associated with idle wealth; the clean-shaven face demonstrated the ample time that a man had to worry about an unnecessary chore and the ability to afford the many accessories needed for the task. As interpreted by Veblen, the upsurge in consumption was driven by the need to clarify uncertain social status by accumulating material things, and it also created a model of fashion for others to follow. The model designated a hierarchy from the leisure class downward: those below would strive toward the position and display of wealth demonstrated by the leisure class; that class, because of its vested interests, would profit further from the consumption created (Veblen [1899] 1979; see also Camic 2020; Diggins 1978; Dorfman [1934] 1961; Riesman 1960).

Although Veblen's view appeared harsh, others calling themselves visionaries saw in the new order opportunities for a more benevolent prosperity and egalitarianism only dreamed of earlier. Personal wealth and stories of consuming wealth abounded by the turn of the century. The rags-to-riches mythology pervaded much of the popular literature, although in reality mobility was rather restricted (Gutman 1976). Still, the image that wealth in America was infinitely expandable, that accumulation of goods provided well-being, and that opportunity was everywhere encouraged "buying into" the system. The "million-dollar corner" in New York City was one engaging popular symbol of success supporting this image and its upscaled consuming vision. In 1912 a widely circulated newspaper story extolled Russian immigrant Robert S. Smith, who had come to New York before the end of the century with $5.75 in his pocket and bought what seemed then to be a remote property at 34th Street and Broadway (the site of Herald Square and Macy's flagship department store advertised as "The World's Largest Store"). Smith eventually sold his tiny parcel for one million dollars, a record price per square foot, to make way for a towering building in what the *New York Sun* called a "peculiarly American story" ("From Pushcart to Affluence" 1912). Meanwhile, Fifth and Sixth avenues in New York became nationally known showcases of the latest fashionable goods available to upwardly aspiring cosmopolitans who lined the avenues wide-eyed and put themselves on display as a stream of consuming shoppers engulfing the avenues (Rich 2015; see also Taylor 1989).

The sentiment of acquisitiveness was a favorite theme of late-Victorian chronicles and novels. The central character in Theodore Dreiser's *Sister Carrie* (1900) finds the "lure of the material" as she wanders around a Chicago department store:

> Carrie passed along the busy aisles, much affected by the remarkable displays of trinkets, dress goods, stationery, and jewelry. Each separate counter was a showplace of dazzling interest and attraction. She could not help feeling the claim of each trinket and valuable upon her personally, and yet she did not stop. There was nothing there which she could not have used-nothing which she did not long to own. The dainty slippers and stockings, the delicately frilled skirts and petticoats, the laces, ribbons, hair-combs, purses, all touched her with individual desire.
>
> *(Dreiser [1900] 1970, 17)*

Entering a restaurant, Carrie noticed:

the tables were not so remarkable in themselves, and yet the imprint of Sherry upon the napery, the name of Tiffany upon the silverware, the name of Haviland upon the china, and over all the glow of the small, red-shaded candelabra and the reflected tints of the walls on garments and faces, made them seem remarkable. Each waiter added an air of exclusiveness and elegance by the manner in which he bowed, scraped, touched, and trifled with things.

(Dreiser [1900] 1970, 235)

Examined alone, Dreiser's writing appears to suggest an unusual preoccupation with habits of accumulation and display, but the attention to the minutest details of consumption carries over to a variety of literary works of the period (see Bowlby 1985). The central theme of Harold Frederic's *The Damnation of Theron Ware*, a bestseller of 1896, is the Hawthorne-like downfall of a Methodist minister who succumbs to various worldly temptations. The name Theron Ware is a clue to the theme of consumption in the novel. Theron is usually linked to an ancient tyrant; Ware suggests salable, often manufactured goods. This is not to suggest that Theron Ware is a tyrant; rather, that he falls prey to many forces, including the material lure of an emerging consumer society. He confronts temptation in a new department store called Thurston's. The name plays on the sense of thirst or consumption it provides for some and drought for others. It is located in the village of Octavius, the Roman name usually associated with wealth and the name of the emperor in whose reign Christ was born. Frederic describes Thurston's turning heads for its new brand of selling, and he in fact draws attention to an old social frame of farmers talking about drought:

"Thurston's" was a place concerning which opinions differed in Octavius. That it typified progress, and helped more than any other feature of the village to bring it up to date, no one indeed disputed. One might move about a great deal, in truth, and hear no other view expressed. But then again one might stumble into conversation with one small storekeeper after another, and learn that they united in resenting the existence of "Thurston's," as rival farmers might join to curse a protracted drought. Each had his special flaming grievance.

(Frederic [1896] 1960, 56–57)

After visiting Thurston's, Ware resolves "to preach a sermon on the subject of the modern idea of admiring the great for crushing the small," but the sermon, presumably inspired by the threat of the department store on town life, is never written. Ware is lured, almost blindly, by the things and the ease of acquiring them in Thurston's, although he feels ignorant about making consumer choices, particularly in selecting a piano for the church. He later returns to buy a piano accompanied by Celia, whose name is an anagram for his loyal wife, Alice, as well as the name of the patron saint of music and the blind. She is the organist of the Catholic church for whom he feels sinful longing: "There were a good many pianos in the big showroom overhead, and Theron found himself almost awed by their size and brilliancy of polish, and the thought of the tremendous sum of money they represented altogether." But Celia cooly declares, "There's nothing here really good. It is always much better to buy of the makers direct." Replying with one of the great romantic lines of Victorian writing, Ware asks, "Do they sell on the installment plan?" (Frederic [1896] 1960, 216–17).

Novelist Harry Leon Wilson produced another, perhaps the ultimate, parable of consumption in *The Spenders* (1902). It is the story of a family fortune made in mining in the rugged but arcadian West, only to be squandered by the younger cosmopolitan generations back East. It joins a host of earlier novels, including Howells's *A Hazard of New Fortunes* ([1889] 1980) and *Rise of Silas Lapham* ([1885] 2018), about moral character and the consequence of new wealth. The novels were popular reading for the way in which they worked through new experiences and values in contrast to the past. Like other novels of the period, *The Spenders* often offers a display-window or catalogue style of narrative to gain its effect. Early in the novel, the contrast of a humble "what-not" in the sitting room and a newly purchased "Empire cabinet" in the parlor commands several pages of commentary. The contrast between these things reflects the differences between the older and newer generations, a reflection of the family strife that wealth has produced:

> The what-not, once the cherished shrine of the American home, sheltered the smaller household gods for which no other resting place could be found. [The] "what-not" [contains] a tender motto worked with the hair of the dead; a "Rock of Ages" in a glass case, with a garland of pink chenille around the base; two dried pine cones brightly varnished; an old daguerreotype in an ornamental case of hard rubber; small old album; two small China vases of the kind that came always in pairs, standing on mats of crocheted worsted; three sea-shells; and the cup and saucer that belonged to grandma....[But] the new cabinet, haughty in its varnished elegance, with its Watteau dames and courtiers, and perhaps the knowledge that it enjoys widespread approval among the elect-this is a different matter. In every American home that is a home, to-day, it demands attention. The visitor, after eyeing it with cautious side-glances, goes jauntily up to it, affecting to have been stirred by the mere impulse of elegant idleness. Under the affectedly careless scrutiny of the hostess he falls dramatically into an attitude of awed entrancement. Reverently he gazes upon the priceless bibelots within: the mother-of-pearl fan, half open; the tiny cup and saucer of Sevres on their brass easel; the miniature Cupid and Psyche in marble; the Japanese wrestlers carved in ivory; the ballet-dancer in bisque; the coral necklace; the souvenir spoon from the Paris Exposition....The what-not is obsolete. The Empire

cabinet is regnant. Yet though one is the lineal descendant of the other-its sophisticated grandchild-they are hostile and irreconcilable.

(Wilson 1902, 34–38)

The connection of "Empire" and "regnant" in the material symbols of the cabinet holding representations of world cultures is not coincidental. At a time when wealth appeared to be expanding, the Empire cabinet replaces the localized, homey what-not. Similarly, department store windows and hotel lobbies become studies in the power and symbolism of things and wealth by showing the unrelenting force of accumulation, the blinding qualities of display, and the commonly fleeting surface rewards. The revealing name "Hightower Hotel" is used in the novel as "an instructive microcosm of New York....It overwhelms with its lavish display of wealth, it stuns with its tireless, battering energy. But it stays always aloof, indifferent if it be loved or hated; if it crush or sustain" (Wilson 1902, 218).

Writers stepped forward during the Gilded Age and Progressive era to point out a disturbing gap between publicly obvious consumers and the often hidden, shunned bottom of the scale. This gap was more distressing because of the republican and Christian ideals of equality that Americans traditionally claimed. Howells brought home the troubling situation to Americans in his biting commentary on the fading vision of a republican past, *A Traveler from Altruria* ([1894] 1957), about an altruistic visitor to the United States from a land where American egalitarian ideals are actually lived out. By setting the reality of urban-dominated life in America against the promise that "money works miracles," as Americans imagined, the book questioned public faith that acquisitive capitalism and urbanism of the new order effected social progress (Howells [1894] 1957, 1971; see also Davis 2005; Engeman 2001; Wendt 2010).

This dilemma of the age was plain to Sir Philip Burne-Jones, an Englishman who recorded his observations of turn-of-the-century America in *Dollars and Democracy* (1904):

> The doctrine of equality, though of course it lends itself...to ridicule or ludicrous satire, is in reality a fine idea, and it lies at the root of all that America once held most sacred when she began the new life a hundred years ago-the theory that every man born in the country should have a fair and equal chance....it is this spirit that has inspired the whole people since it has existed as a separate nation.
>
> (Burne-Jones 1904, 70–71)

Yet matters of money forced elitism and class protectionism upon Americans:

> In snatches of conversation caught in the streets, the restaurants, and the cars, the continual cry is always "dollars-dollars-dollars!" You hear it on all sides

perpetually, and money does truly here, as politics in England, seem to be an end in itself, instead of a means to an end.

(Burne-Jones 1904, 74)

Burne-Jones noted that, unlike in England, where family title and land-based wealth allowed lasting security, in America status was often fleeting. Thus, opulence in the United States had to be displayed materially and reasserted constantly by showing that one is "up to date" and the most modern. In Burne-Jones's view, the power of American wealth was obsessively turned over to the consumption of things that conveyed one's station in life or the station to which one aspired. Even those without money often neglected basic needs to seek things that offered a taste of luxury, he fretted (Burne-Jones 1904, 107–16).

Contrasted with frequent reports of the preoccupation with excess were reformist titles such as Jacob Riis's *How the Other Half Lives* (1890) and Lincoln Steffens's *The Shame of the Cities* (1904), which gave a vivid reminder of how much wealth had been gained and who had been left behind in its acquisition. Waves of immigrants and rural migrants swelled the ranks of the urban poor and appeared starkly captured before the great industrial advance. The growing city sought to reconcile its excessive fortunes and excessive privations. The paradox of conditions that allowed for great wealth while promoting great poverty again forced Americans to contemplate the institutions they had molded for the new age. Questions lingered among reformers over whether the lot of the poor could be improved by teaching them to save or consume better, by having the city and industry serve them better, or by having them become more urbane and industrious (Gallagher 2004; Weinberg 1974; Kesselman 1979; Senter 2019). Often left out of the reformist rhetoric were calls for racial-ethnic equity in wages, and an end to the practice of paying African Americans and immigrants less money.

From his editor's post at *Atlantic Monthly* and later *Harper's Monthly*, William Dean Howells became an observer, a critic, and the conscience of the changing nation. His move from Boston to New York in 1888 drew notice of representing a symbolic shift of the nation's character from its intellectual center in old New England to the commercial colossus. In *A Traveler from Altruria*, Howells cited accumulation as the culprit of a scheme gone awry:

> Men's minds and men's hands were suddenly released to an activity unheard of before. Invention followed invention; our rivers and seas became the warp of commerce where the steam-sped shuttles carried the woof of enterprise to and fro with fireless celerity. Machines to save labor multiplied themselves as if they had been procreative forces; and wares of every sort were produced with incredible swiftness and cheapness.

Accumulation became a force in its own right:

The Accumulation, as we called this power, because we feared to call it by its true name, rewarded its own with gains of twenty, of a hundred, of a thousand per cent, and to satisfy its need, to produce the labor that operated its machines, there came into existence a hapless race of men who bred their kind for its service, and whose little ones were its prey, almost from their cradles.

(Howells [1894] 1957, 274)

Despite Howells's literary influence in warning of the dire consequences of a spreading capitalist-consumer system, the advance of materialism accelerated. At least in part, Americans seemed to be moved more by cultural conventions that averred a faith in consumption. The late-Victorian middle-class interior was overstuffed, filled with manufactured accessories such as layers of drapes and many pillows. Furniture often tended to be excessively ornate and heavy, and popular pieces suited for eclectic display such as étagères, sideboards, and cabinets were used to stuff and layer crowded exhibits of ceramics, souvenirs, novelties, plants, and exotic shells into the Victorian American parlor (Grier 2010; Halttunen 1989).

Equally overstuffed were world's fairs, which attracted millions of people to Philadelphia, Chicago, St. Louis, San Francisco, and other boastful cities to see elaborate, crowded mixtures of commercial spectacles of technological progress and imperial expansion (Rydell 1984; Rydell, Findling, and Pelle 2000). At the 1901 Pan-American Exposition in Buffalo, visitors saw the vision of consumption celebrated at the central "Fountain of Plenty" in the "Court of Abundance." Illustrator Thomas Fleming made a splash by satirizing the consuming vision of "the Plan" with drawings of classical sculptures selling advertising space, pre-industrial "primitives" on the midway doing the bidding of crass Yankees, and commercial exhibits producing comical hypnotizing effects. Fleming drew out a compelling message of the fairs—consumption basked in the glow of "educational" entertainment—while manufacturing radiated the vital energy of a progressive civilization (Fleming 1901, 187).

Economist George Gunton in polemical books *Wealth and Progress* (1888) and *Principles of Social Economics* (1891) in addition to a magazine of "practical economics and political science" titled *Gunton's Magazine* (launched as *The Social Economist* in 1891, published until 1904) chided the obstructionist satirists and critics for mocking the wage-consumer trend and defending the Jeffersonian yeoman ideal. He thought it would promote a democratic value of leveling class differences by expanding the middle class and basing participation on cash in hand rather than social standing. It also would allow for more physical mobility to locations of new industrial opportunities. He argued that for America's workers, many of them immigrants, consumption provided a moral as well as cultural education in saving, planning, and setting goals. Concerned with the image of the United States as "a nation of dollar chasers," Gunton praised the super-rich such as George W. Vanderbilt upon completion of his 250-room Biltmore mansion for "rendering a service to the development of the national taste and civilization of the Republic for the Twentieth Century, no less important than the service his father and grandfather rendered to the industrial development of the Nineteenth Century" (Gunton 1896, 35–36). The difference from Europe, Gunton declared, is that the wealthy in America will not be "separated from the people by an impossible social chasm as in Europe" and in a trickle-down effect, "the social culture, with all it implies, shall percolate down through all the social strata" (Gunton 1896, 35). Using an evolutionary model, Gunton beheld in consumption the promise for America of climbing up from a primitive rung of a cultural ladder into a more advanced stage of industrial and intellectual progress (Horowitz 1985, 45). Gunton argued that by ceding control of production and accepting the social order with the expansion of industrially gained wealth at the top, workers would be rewarded with more leisure and comfort through the ability to consume with their wages than they could in a yeoman model (Horowitz 1980, 314).

The promise of consumption drew considerable comment in the wave of utopian writing during the late nineteenth century. In *Looking Backward* (1888), Edward Bellamy foresaw a contented army who supplied goods to central warehouses for mass distribution to the public of the year 2000 (Bellamy [1888] 1982). Itself a milestone of consumption, Bellamy's book sold more than 125,000 copies within one year of its publication and half a million copies by 1891, making it the best-selling book of its time (Sloat 1988). Bellamy had a vision of progress and abundance, with stores not more than ten minutes away from the new consumers to meet every need. The protagonist Julian West goes to a "consumers' cooperative," which is essentially a modern warehouse club. Bellamy introduced the term "credit card" that entitled residents to shares of the national wealth (the Diner's Club card introduced in 1950 is usually credited with being the first credit card). To make the future more alluring, Bellamy imagined advances in technology representing progress for the benefit of the workers, including electronic broadcasting and electric lighting (Segal 1989). Befitting his nineteenth-century concern over the upheaval of striking tradesmen, Bellamy downplayed the individual productive worker and told of an overarching, formal organization that replaced the old republican localism with a corporate nationalism. He viewed the architectural adornment of nationalism as a "female ideal of Plenty, with her cornucopia," the same emblem that graced the cover of Sears, Roebuck, and Company's catalogues in the late nineteenth century (Bellamy [1888] 1982, 72; see also Kasson 1999, 191–202).

Bradford Peck's *The World a Department Store* (1900) provided another striking illustration of the vision of consumption. Peck's background was that of a merchant of dry goods in Lewiston, Maine, and from humble beginnings rose to wealth. Starting out as an errand boy in the Boston department store of Jordan Marsh, he took advantage of competitive laissez-faire economic policies to establish the largest department store in New England outside of Boston. Yet his book proposed a more centrally controlled, collectivist organization of economic and social life (Davies 1947, 471–72). Like Bellamy's hero, in Peck's novel Percy Brantford (a play on the author's name) falls asleep and wakes up years later to encounter a world where all productive activities, even cooking, are ordered out. Services are paid for and regulated by a credit system: the world "is indebted to the system formerly used in the department stores for our present wise condition of life," and the system is taught to the young through competitions and "object lessons" (on material education, see Bronner 1989; Carter 2018). Dedicated to "suffering toilers in all walks of life," Peck imagined city planning around neat aisles and rows with clear divisions for residences, services, and supply stores (Peck [1900] 1971, 2–45). Brantford eventually exclaims,

> It is like awakening in heaven. All the wonderful changes I have thus far seen, the methods and customs which are now in vogue, shows how systematic all things are. No hurry, no worry, no bustle, yet all laboring for a grand and noble existence.
> *(Peck [1900] 1971, 242–43; see also Cary 1977)*

Objects of Desire

Historians have long held that Americans broke with the agrarian past after the Civil War with their embrace of industrialization, urbanization, and incorporation. Often overlooked is another lasting sign of the times—the flowering of consumer behavior in mass proportions. As more Americans earned wages rather than made or grew products for trade, they increasingly relied on ready-made goods. Having basic goods more widely available because of mass production techniques did not satisfy the craving for useful stuff; rather, it created a demand for more to become available. It did not popularize the traditional ethic of self-sacrifice and saving; instead, the cry went out to bring down the cost of basic goods, and as costs went down more goods became "necessary" to buy (Harris 1981). The "good life" became more materially defined as the accumulation of goods in the home appeared to offer status, mobility, and self-confidence. Luxury items came within the reach and desire of more buyers, and variants of basic goods and "necessary" innovations proliferated. Advertisers and promoters saw to it that demand for more goods, especially novel, high-end, or "improved" ones, continued. In the midst of the rise of consumerism, economist Simon Patten observed, "The new morality does not consist in saving, but in expanding consumption" (1907, 213). Howard Mumford Jones later summarized, "Wealth in this period expressed itself in the acquisition of things" (1971, 17–18).

In unprecedented numbers Americans shopped for standardized, mass-produced goods that were distributed and branded nationally. The department store was the grand palace of the new consumer culture where an abundance of goods was proudly displayed and sold, and where shopping became an emotional experience. Americans beheld the promise and prestige of new goods in advertisements, catalogues, magazine illustrations and stories, novels, theaters, train stations, restaurants, hotels, expositions, and fairs. More than a new way of providing for one's sustenance, consumer behavior spawned new professions, institutions, desires, and outlooks. With new products and gadgets pouring in to replace items of recent vintage that were stigmatized as "old," "undesirable," or "out of fashion," the consumer experience appeared to reinforce the image of unlimited good because if the store did not have it, it would get it for you or you could get it from a mail-order catalogue. More of everything to add to the shoppers' choices was surely to come. One did not want to see empty shelves and consider scarcity. Being served and flattered as a customer was empowering.

Before mass production the prevailing wisdom of business practice late into the nineteenth century was to provide specialized goods on demand for selected customers known to have means to pay, thus ensuring a reputable and secure income. Prices could vary on the basis of what customers could pay. Prospective customers off the street could be excluded. For the protection of their stock, most stores displayed few goods. Select customers asked for merchandise that they often had not seen beforehand. Store managers brought out the goods; sellers treated customers as privileged clients. Department stores were original at their dawning because of their high-volume, fixed-price sale of many varieties of goods available for viewing and handling, which introduced a level of speculation and pandering into business that many economic advisers found shocking.

In Philadelphia on Monday, March 12, 1877, a men's dry-goods merchant named John Wanamaker opened what he called "The Grand Depot," a rhetoric that suggested the mobility and bustle of the railroads crisscrossing the country. While department stores were well known in New York, Chicago, and Paris since the mid-nineteenth century, Wanamaker proposed to expand the scale of the institution and offer more services to customers (Lewis 1983; Nicole Kirk 2018; Leach 1993, 191–224; Whitaker 2011, 8–59). Advertising his department store as a "New Kind of Store," he boasted of open aisles of men's and women's clothing and other items all "under one roof" and "conveniently arranged" by departments. Coming one year after the mass spectacle of the Centennial Exhibition in Philadelphia, the expansion and rearrangement of Wanamaker's business were influenced heavily by the grand exhibits of the world's fair. Later, he would bring to the "Grand Court" of his store a 2,500-pound bronze eagle that had been on display at the 1904 St. Louis World's Fair and became a symbol of the Wanamaker brand (Lisicky 2010, 34; see front cover). The influence of the fairs was not lost on *The Philadelphia Press*, which reported:

> As is very commonly remarked, a view of the main floor from the antique gallery west of the Chestnut entrance strikingly recalls the Centennial Exhibition. There is the same width of display extending about as far as the eye can reach, the riches of the world brought together from all lands, and representing all departments of art and industry, tastefully arranged to be

FIGURE 4.1 Wanamaker's Department Store, Philadelphia, c. 1896. Photographic print on stereo card.
Source: Alfred S. Campbell, photographer. Prints and Photographs Division, Library of Congress.

> shown with advantage. There is the same sense of spaciousness and, what is specially noticeable, the same ample illumination, the whole place being light, bright and cheerful.
>
> (Wanamaker 1911, 71)

The opening of the "Grand Depot" store drew awe for its massive scale and extravagance in an editorial by the Philadelphia *Public Ledger*:

> There are thirty-three blocks of counters, numbering 129 in all, and aggregating two-thirds of a mile in length, and in front of which are 1,400 stools for the convenience of shoppers. There are elegantly fitted rooms for such goods as ladies' finished suits, and other departments, besides parlors, retiring rooms, etc., for the comfort of customers. The store, No. 1313 Chestnut

street, has been purchased by Mr. Wanamaker and entirely demolished in order to make room for a beautiful arcade, leading from Chestnut street into his great store. The entrance is handsomely ornamented, and the arcade is tiled with marble and lighted by day by means of stained glass skylights, and by night by elaborate chandeliers.

(Wanamaker 1911, 51–53)

Small shopkeepers who could not compete with Wanamaker's prices were less impressed. They were in fact worried that they would be forced out of business. To them, Wanamaker stepped over the traditional lines of merchandising by specialties and dividing inventory by the class of customers served (Whitaker 2006, 22). They thought of him as the self-aggrandizing bully attempting to crush the weak, but they thought that maybe he was overly ambitious in his plans and would fail. With moralistic zeal drawing on his experience as the first corresponding secretary in the YMCA movement, Wanamaker posted full-page advertisements in newspapers and distributed illustrated circulars welcoming customers to see for themselves the new concept of a palatial temple of shopping (Nicole Kirk 2018). He gave away calendars, posters, and pamphlets with his signature stamped on them. The technique was suggested by the Centennial Exhibition, which engendered a boom in handouts for the throngs descending on Philadelphia anxious to obtain a souvenir of the fair. Newspapers left the local realm of the city and, with print runs of hundreds of thousands, were scattered throughout the country. Taking a cue from this boosterism, Wanamaker organized special events in his store and offered transportation to the downtown location with glitzy enticements unprecedented in advertising. One month after the store opened, concerned for the disruption of Wanamaker's store to neighborhood patterns, the *Sunday Gazette* hurled the following barb:

> Billions of Millions! more or less, of Ladies and Gentlemen, Boys and Girls, Spitzdogs and Poodles, have visited our Immense Emporium during the first week of its existence and the mammoth headquarters of Monopoly is now an established fact, and must remain a monument to the Gullibility of the Public as long as there is a Public to be gulled.

(Wanamaker 1911, 57–60)

Sunday Mercury predicted that Wanamaker's store and its maverick ideas would fold within three months. Instead the store prospered and expanded into more merchandising lines and provided more customer services. Estimates were that as many as 40,000 shoppers came to the store daily. Wanamaker became an internationally known figure, and his store was proclaimed a progressive, "modern" institution. In 1884 an editorial by Wanamaker declared,

> Seven years ago the winds of old trade customs were dead in our faces. Never did Kansas cyclones blow more fiercely. We could only do our best

and trust the good common sense of the people to set things to rights. We have not been disappointed.

In 1900 Wanamaker announced,

> Where there was one large dry goods store twenty-five years ago there are ten today-so well have the people supported the new codes and practices of business dealing. We have never secured patents on our system; but on the contrary, have given our best strength and experience to educate generals and soldiers of every rank for the mercantile army.

Wanamaker stirred the public imagination by offering the lure of cheaper prices and conveniences (including rest rooms, elevators, and fountains, which were novelties at the time), the promise of equal treatment and fair trading for anyone with cash, and the aura of artistic spectacle and machine-like order. He also made use of mass advertising, grand displays, and educational devices to train and attract enlightened consumers to the abundant world of goods available for viewing and handling. A contemporary of Wanamaker noted:

> The underlying idea of Mr. Wanamaker's great undertaking is to bring the producer and consumer into the closest possible relations; to offer the article wanted with the least possible amount of intermediate handling. This idea of yours has greatly excited the town. I stand by you on the old proverb: "The greatest good to the greatest number."
>
> *(Wanamaker 1911, 61–63)*

That Wanamaker's store set standards for techniques of merchandising, advertising, and store design is not the essential point for analysis. It is that such standards became part of consumer culture and created symbols for the age at a time when there were challenges to the changes that were developing on the grounds that they stifled small businesses and routinized work. These standards moving toward the idea of a national culture with its core in urban capitalistic values found symbolic extension in custom, literature, art, and even city planning. Wanamaker assumed that commerce was "the great civilizer" in altering behavior on a large scale. As consumers, Americans embraced what they were told were "modern" ways of living, seeing, and thinking that centered on providing for their needs, and desires, through purchased products rather than what they produced. The vice-provost of the University of Pennsylvania conveyed the idea in 1909 that Wanamaker's store had become a metaphor for progress, a reference for where the future might lead, when he declared,

> A thorough knowledge of what the Wanamaker Store really represents in its relation to the work of the world is in itself a broad education, for within

this building are found in operation almost every law of political economy, almost every application of scientific knowledge to the service of man, or the results of such application.

(Wanamaker 1911, 133)

Central to the behavior of the new consumers were the connected patterns of accumulation and display. Although reformers during the late nineteenth century sometimes used the pejorative term *materialism* to describe emerging patterns of consumer behavior, others recognized the promise of freedom, abundance, and mobility as the foundations upon which the changing way of American life was built. A well-known Victorian illustration splashed across two full pages of *Harper's Weekly* for November 2, 1878, demonstrated the excitement generated by acquisition of goods, apparently unlimited, for a society that traded in its mythology of pioneer scarcity in favor of material excess. Bragging of the "effective arrangement" of the objects and the way they filled the rooms to abundance, a writer declared,

> A few years ago it would have been impossible to form such a collection in New York; and considering that nearly all these beautiful and interesting objects have been loaned by our citizens at very short notice, and that many persons who would gladly have contributed are absent in Europe, the exhibition certainly speaks well for the art culture and liberality of New Yorkers.
>
> *("Loan Exhibition" 1878)*

New York, proud of its position as the mercantile center of the nation, was not about to stand idly by while Wanamaker built a commercial empire in Philadelphia. New York became a port of entry for developing ideas for the conspicuous display of valued objects in expositions, museums, hotels, and department stores. Interior details of hotels proliferated to flatter guests and build desire for them to spend money. Enterprising Americans were developing tasteful skills in displaying goods on the floors of department stores and in the lobbies of hotels, serving rooms of restaurants, and exhibits of expositions and museums. Historian Alan Trachtenberg has pointed out that "these places created a unique fusion of economic and cultural values; they were staging grounds for the making and confirming of new relations between goods and people" (Trachtenberg 1982, 133). In a 1911 study of the spending habits of working-class women, Sue A. Clark and Edith Wyatt concluded that workers had adopted "the New York show window-display ideal of life manifested everywhere around them" (1911, 23). Far from New York, sociologists Helen and Robert Lynd in their classic study of everyday life in Muncie, Indiana, during the 1920s, titled *Middletown* (1929), observed that consumer culture had swept middle America. During the 1890s Midwestern residents "lived on a series of plateaus as regards standard of living." By the 1920s they found that "the edges of the plateaus have been shaved off, and every one lives on a slope from any point of which desirable things belonging to people all the way to the top are in view" (Lynd and Lynd [1929] 1956, 82–83). Residents were "running for dear life in this business of making the money they earn to keep pace with the even more rapid growth of their subjective wants" (Lynd and Lynd [1929] 1956, 87).

In the Lynds's Middletown of the 1920s, the automobile—a high-ticket, mass-produced technology stressing status and mobility in a consumer culture—was a prime symbol of the town's subjective wants. The way for the marketing of the automobile had been paved by the promotion of the bicycle as a mass-produced product promising freedom of movement and youthfulness during the 1880s. In 1884 a "safety" bicycle had been introduced, and the demand for it, especially among younger members of the middle class, quickly spread. It offered mobility, the thrill of self-propelled speed, the chance to experience fashionable strenuosity in the street and countryside, and, for many courting couples, the chance for an extended excursion away from the watchful eyes of chaperones. The design of the safety bicycle, with two wheels of equal size, abandoned the danger and achievement of the craftsman-like high-wheelers for the style and convenience of a standardized industrial product appealing to a wider audience. And appeal it did with about one million bicycles annually in 1898 and 1899 (Turpin 2018, 3). By 1896, an estimated 2.5 million Americans took to cycling and demand for the vehicles retailing at around 85 dollars (about one tenth of an average annual salary) was supplied by around 250 bicycle factories (Turpin 2018, 9). Still viewed as a luxury item before the end of the nineteenth century, the bicycle did not yet have a standard bearer for its national distribution. At the time, many independent manufacturers distributed the luxury item for local markets. Introducing more assembly-line techniques, many sewing machine and arms manufacturers entered the trade and further fragmented the market. Although some sellers pushed the bicycle as a replacement for a horse, sales were driven by younger middle-class cyclists looking to use it for leisure and courtship. The intense competition for the growing youth craze of romantic bicycle excursions away from watchful eyes of parents and neighbors spawned an advertising war in national magazines. By 1898, 10 percent of all advertising featured bicycles. Frank Presbrey commented,

> Especially is the development of magazine advertising indebted to the bicycle, for the bicycle gave the magazine a measure of recognition as a medium which encouraged the use of large space and more frequent insertions by advertisers in general....It was bicycle manufacturers who first proved that an article of luxury costing $100 could be sold to the mass.
> *(Presbrey 1929, 410–12; see also Hurlihy 2004, 159–308; Norris 1990, 77–80;*
> *Turpin 2018)*

With his keen understanding of the potential of mass consumption, retailing magnate Richard Warren Sears stepped into the bicycle market in the late 1890s with now-familiar techniques. Foreseeing a large market for an already developed product, Sears contracted for huge volume, offered easy installment plans, slashed prices from over $100 to under $10, and advertised profusely in mass circulation outlets. He shifted the prevailing advertising pitch from speed and distance, a kind of manly utilitarian concern, to the popular cultural appeals of style, status, fashion, and easy availability—in short, pushing an object "everybody else has" or should want. Mail-order catalogue rival Montgomery Ward followed suit during the 1890s and like Sears issued special bicycle catalogues appealing to various tastes and featuring different styles. Montgomery Ward blared in his catalogue the message of purchasing a bicycle because others own one: "Bicycles will soon be more common than buggies. Better have one" (Montgomery Ward & Co 1895, 13).

Sears raised the stakes by offering free bicycle trials to consumers before they decide to buy and shipping a bicycle at no cost to anyone who brought in ten orders from his sales circulars. Corporate historians Boris Emmet and John E. Jeuck (1950, 70–72) have claimed that Sears's own hand is evident in a promotion in the guise of an editorial reprinted in a number of newspapers:

> Last year retailers succeeded in reducing the price of all $100 Bicycles to $75, and then they held the trade at home; but what are they going to do now when a new 1898 Bicycle is offered at only $5.00, on easy conditions?-other latest models outright at $13.95 and $19.75, on free trial. It appears the monopoly on the finest grade seamless bicycle tubing has been broken, and where the best tubing alone for a bicycle formerly cost about $18 it is now reduced to less than $4, and Sears, Roebuck and Co., of Chicago, at these special prices, are waging war on all bicycle dealers. They send a Bicycle Catalogue free to anyone who asks for it, and, we are told, shipping several hundred bicycles every day to every state, direct to the riders at $5 to $19.75, on free trial before paying. If Sears, Roebuck and Co. continue to wage their bicycle war throughout the season it will be a boon to all those who want bicycles, but a sad blow to bicycle dealers and manufacturers.
>
> *("Big Drop in Bicycles" 1898)*

Despite touting his products as a victory against the bicycle monopoly, the end result was that Sears virtually formed one of his own. Sales of bicycles topped at 100,000 for the mail-order giant, and he put new models on the market to encourage replacing the buyer's old one with the latest and best Sears had to offer (Cowals 2001).

As a result of success with bicycle sales, advertisers realized the appeal of objects promising independence to a young women's market and promoted other items such as portable cameras and small musical instruments used for social getaways (Norris 1990, 71–94). The safety bicycle was a factor in the breakdown of Victorian restrictions on courtship and also could be used for jaunts to the store and work. Cyclists clamored for improved roads and civic improvements. In 1900 an official of the Census Bureau made the claim that because the bicycle helped to break down isolation and differentiation of the sexes, not to mention limited mobility, "few articles ever used by man have created so great a revolution in social conditions" (Presbrey 1929, 363). Ethnologist W. J. McGee opined that with its arousal of invention and mass production, stimulation of commerce, encouragement of strong character (especially a unified national character), and development of "individuality, judgment, and prompt decision on the part of its users more rapidly and completely than any other device," the bicycle "weighed by its effect on body and mind as well as on material progress must be classed as one of the world's great inventions." Although invented in Europe, the bicycle was "redevised" in the United States, "and native genius made it a practical machine for the multitude; now its users number millions, and it is sold in every country" (McGee 1898, 311–12). By the 1920s, adult consumer attention turned more to automobiles as a mode of transportation and bicycle advertisers focused on the children's market. The techniques of advertising different models with accessories and decorative features started with bicycles carried over to the sale of automobiles. By the 1950s, marketers prepared children and their parents for the idea of investing in transportation technology with the ritual acquisition of the first bicycle.

Although Europe experienced an earlier blossoming of consumer behavior among the middle classes, by the late nineteenth century America boasted a variety of mail-order catalogues, department stores, and world's fairs that reached more people with more ready-made goods than any European counterpart. Even before the full flowering of an American consumer system, Alexis de Tocqueville's classic tome *Democracy in America* (1840) described a distinctive proprietary sense among Americans: "A native of the United States clings to this world's goods as if he were certain never to die." Tocqueville believed the

> passion for physical comforts is essentially a passion of the middle classes; with those classes it grows and spreads, with them it is preponderant. From them it mounts into the higher orders of society and descends into the mass of the people.

Rarely content with their possessions, Americans were quick to replace their goods with "fresh gratifications":

> At first sight there is something surprising in this strange unrest of so many happy men restless in the midst of abundance. The spectacle itself, however, is as old as the world; the novelty is to see a whole people furnish an exemplification of it. Their taste for physical gratifications must be regarded as the original source of that secret disquietude which the actions of Americans betray and of that inconstancy of which they daily afford fresh examples....Besides the good things that he possesses, he every instant fancies a

thousand others that death will prevent him from trying if he does not try them soon.

(Tocqueville [1840] 1981, 422–34)

The lure of goods to not only show social status but also to be cognitively perceived as assigning status informed the growth of credit. It implied an American optimism and future orientation that income would grow but became complicated by the additional goods, the "thousand others" according to Tocqueville, that became unnecessary and even addictive objects of desire. The trouble was that desirable products did not last, became obsolete, and after a short time gave the impression that the owner was old-fashioned. Then new ones needed to be purchased to remain modern and tied in socially. Paradoxically, the consumer capitalist system that promised "fresh" or instant gratification and comfort also produced anxiety that acting on impulse and giving in to an imposed buying habit bring (Roberts 2014, 10).

To be sure, part of the appeal of shopping for something new as a daily experience is that it allows Americans to experience the "fresh start," a personal makeover, many times over without having to relocate (McGee 2005). They could also redefine the home in terms of proximity to stores. Increasingly since the late nineteenth century, home ownership became both the promise and problem of the consumer capitalist system (Clark 1987). The system appeared to expand the affordability of home ownership but it also led to higher debt load from being "house-poor." Average house size increased since the nineteenth century not so as to accommodate larger families, but rather to expand and differentiate private areas in which to amass goods. By 2020, over 65 percent of Americans owned homes, typically the largest purchase that an individual will make, and the figure had been higher before a crippling recession of 2008 that brought out the problem of foreclosures caused by a double whammy of banks giving risky loans and people overextending themselves and being overly optimistic about the future. The surge over the twentieth century was fueled by the house becoming commodified with mass production and more choices for living spaces as a result of advances in communication and transportation technology (see Chapter 1). Another factor in homeownership as well as the consumer culture was the introduction of fully amortized 30-year mortgages covering 80 percent of the house cost (previous to 1954, mortgages covered only about 50 percent), and after 1934, insurance and loans provided by the Federal Housing Authority (Ancestry 2017; Chevan 1989). In 1890 homeownership stood at 47.8 percent but less than 28 percent of homes were covered by a mortgage whereas around 65 percent of homes were covered by the end of the twentieth century (PK 2021a, 2021b).

Despite the image of the United States as a nation of homeowners sharing in the American Dream, the country pales in comparison to rates above 90 percent in Singapore and Bulgaria (Goodman and Mayer 2018, 33). With a substantial population of renters in metropolitan areas where costs are prohibitive, the United States is more comparable to Canada and the United Kingdom (Andrews and Sánchez 2011; Goodman and Mayer 2018). Buttressed by the often-repeated nationalistic motto "The strength of a nation lies in the homes of its people," falsely but symbolically attributed to Abraham Lincoln, most Americans report owning a home as a life goal (and the quotation has become an anthem in advertising home sales and occupational motivation for the realty sector). This belief is partly responsible for rebounds of homeownership rates from economic downturns of the Great Depression of the 1930s and the recession of 2008 (McKnight 2014; Uhlir 2020; for the quotation, see "Common Sense" 1904, 17; Mudge 1896; St. John 1874, 336). The continued investment in homeownership despite the financial risks has sparked a correlative consumer trend of big-box home-improvement super-stores (Borland 2020; Bronner 2011, 192; PK 2021a). In the 1990s, however, a Fannie Mae survey found that 86 percent of Americans believe a person is better off owning a home and 74 percent reported that individuals should buy a home as soon as they could afford it, whether or not they have children (Office of Policy Development and Research 1994). Changes in housing laws as a result of the civil rights movement in the 1960s opened up home ownership to marginalized groups, although critics note remaining cultural and income gaps and the problem of housing for migrant labor (Collins and Margo 2011; Krivo 1986; Lake 1979; Sharp and Hall 2014; Shlay 2006). The U.S. Department of Housing and Urban Development anticipating changing market conditions in the twenty-first century still pronounces that "homeownership remains a firm part of the American Dream" (Office of Policy Development and Research 1994; see also Cullen 2003, 133–58; Goodman and Mayer 2018; Li and Yang 2010; Rohe and Watson 2007).

Homeownership arguably provides a sense of personal control that people might not be able to attain at work in a corporate system. Both home and business ownership are linked to property, although the latter was far riskier in the American capitalist system. Compensating for a decline in the producer-artisan economy, Americans at home could gain a sense of individualizing their prefabricated environments by arranging and altering objects on their lawns, engaging in do-it-yourself home improvements, and furnishing and decorating their interiors. Many technological advances in health (e.g., fitness equipment from gyms), entertainment (e.g., theaters), and food preparation (e.g., ovens from restaurants) that had been created to be public became miniaturized and privatized by moving them into the home and making it a total environment. This trend caused changes in community institutions for social gathering and sharing in public culture. Some observers noted that stores served social functions that visionaries such as John Wanamaker encouraged. Civic leaders expressed concern, though, that traditional neighborhood patterns were disrupted by the consolidation of consumer behavior into shopping palaces. Critics called out the decline of public culture and the tendency in a consumer culture to be alone, and alienated, more easily. That process brings into question the negotiation of the money-making self and the consumption community that I will discuss in the next section with reference to a case study of a town lying between Jefferson's pastoral ideal and Wanamaker's consumer urbanism.

A Consuming Community

Tocqueville's characterization of the restless, impatient American nation intent on expansion is now considered prophetic, but even he might have been surprised at the nation's growth and its move to the cities. Between 1850 and 1900 the population tripled; from 1859 to 1919 manufactured goods increased in value fivefold; from 1860 to 1900 the rail system increased ninefold; between 1800 and 1910 the industrial labor force grew from 2.75 million to over eight million; and the number of cities with populations over 100,000 mounted from nine to 50. Despite rapid urbanization and industrialization that promised dominance over the American landscape, the nation's numbers still gave the edge to the non-urban domain. But the clear trend toward urban lifestyles spurred much reflection, speculation, and debate about a made-over future. Moralists pointed to a vast difference in the character of life and mores between the city and country, and wondered whether the agrarian ideals of family, home, and God could be preserved in the wake of rapid change. With a rhetoric that set the tone for debate, their tracts harped on the contrast between the traditional small town with its easy familiarity and the faceless, mass scale of the urban industrial empire (Barton 1989; Shi 1985; White and White 1962).

The common progression of American residential change—from lone settlement to farm village to market town to city—became a parable of modernization. The organization of the community took on new significance as a visible reminder to outsiders of what to expect. Among the early forms of community, the New England village commons with its towering church steeple suggested communal ownership and a legacy of Christian inspiration. As geographer D. W. Meinig points out, "An idealized image of the New England village became so powerfully impressed upon such a broad readership as to become a national symbol, a model setting for the American community" (Meinig 1979, 165). The village structure suggested the nation's colonial roots, and an older way of viewing land as something spiritual rather than commercial. When the image gave way to other more popular forms of main street, market town, urban grid, and courthouse square with westward expansion, the change—and the recognition of one form differentiated from another—produced commentaries in industrial America on the continuity or break with the past. For example, late nineteenth-century world's fairs in the United States featured rustic "olde tyme" New England kitchens representing nostalgia for domestic harmony and folk authority in the midst of towering commercial exhibition buildings arranged by modern principles of city planning (Roth 1985).

A cultural historical account of Harrisburg, Pennsylvania (designated an "All-American City" in 1985 by the National Municipal League), chronicles a common story of the rise of a cosmopolitan spirit that infused the consumer culture. Often the attention to changes on a mass scale obscures the smaller settings that are replete with cultural dramas and meanings of an immediate and human kind. As a moderate-sized city set against the backdrop of the supposedly frugal Pennsylvania "Dutch" country tracing its roots to agricultural settlement drawn by the promise of religious tolerance in William Penn's colony, old Harrisburg residents in the twentieth century were uneasy about change. By the 1920s in the midst of urban growth sparked by new immigration and southern African-American migration, a threshold literature (in contrast to the futurist utopian literature of the 1880s) came pouring out, chronicling the passing of an old age and the brink of a new one, such as Marian Inglewood's *Then and Now in Harrisburg* (1925) and George P. Donehoo's *Harrisburg: The City Beautiful, Romantic and Historic* (1927). Donehoo reflected: "The old town commenced to sink into the memories of the past and the city of Harrisburg began to materialize" (Donehoo 1927, 175). Its physical and social conversion to the cosmopolitan spirit represented the kind of resolution that swayed the nation. Yet beneath the surface were conflicts between tradition and modernity that renowned columnist Mary McGrory discovered while covering the nationally divisive Harrisburg Seven trial of Vietnam War protesters. The experience led her to write that in places like Harrisburg between the big city and rural village, one finds the "sleeping conscience of America." In its ambivalence, "Harrisburg might indeed be America," she declared in a piece that was widely syndicated (McGrory 1972).

Harrisburg rests along the shores of the Susquehanna River, the longest river on the East Coast of the United States. In its early years it provided an economic lifeline of trading and logging from its source in rural Lake Otsego, New York, in James Fenimore Cooper's setting for the *Leatherstocking Tales* ([1827–1841] 1985) down to the growing metropolis of Baltimore. Harrisburg was founded in 1785 as a frontier outpost, a cluster of three hundred houses, behind which was a host of new farms and mills founded by hearty German and Scots-Irish immigrants. As the concentration of Pennsylvania's population fanned out from the capital of Philadelphia west toward Central Pennsylvania, agitation increased to move the capital of the state inland. After much debate, Harrisburg was chosen as the capital in 1812 and proceeded to grow as a place where government, small industries, and agriculture came together. Additional migration from Baltimore added to the growth and consequently the pattern of consumption changed. In 1925, Marian Inglewood compared the Harrisburg before and after World War I, and reflected:

> When it was still but a frontier village, everybody had his own garden and raised his own fruits and vegetables, but as the place became more thickly settled, the citizens of Harrisburg were forced to depend more and more upon the farmers who lived round about.
>
> *(Inglewood 1925, 51)*

The response was to build market houses, which were considered to be "the first evidences of its trend toward city ways," according to Inglewood. In 1807 the ballyhooed structures, little more than sheds, went up on the central crossroads, named Market Square, for the cost of $915.86 each. Although what the press referred to as the "capacious buildings" of Market Square became the heart of the town, market buildings were erected in each of the neighborhoods of the town. "Most every family, rich and poor alike went to market....This was a way of life," reminisced Ralph "Cub" Huston, an old Harrisburg resident (Barton 1983, 101–2). In addition to carrying regular foodstuffs, the markets provided sources for many regional and ethnic folk foods, particularly Pennsylvania German varieties such as "smier kase" (a kind of soft cheese) and "lep kuche" (a kind of gingerbread) (Inglewood 1925, 52). The exchange of goods and banter in languages other than English gave the city an identity that separated it from eastern and western Pennsylvania.

The markets contributed to the incorporation of Harrisburg as a city in 1860 while preserving the neighborhood and ethnic patterns of the town. They offered unprecedented shopping and serving performances. Huston recalled:

> Practically all the sellers were real farmers or real butchers. In season, each stall would have lettuce, endive, carrots, turnips, beets, eggs, tomatoes, potatoes, cabbage, celery, and corn. These were regular items. Then there were special seasons, including one with the most delectable, sweetest strawberries from York County....Markets also provided opportunities for boys to earn money. Those of us having wagons would park outside the entrances and bid for the chance to haul the baskets to the homes of the shoppers. You had no set rate, as you were at the mercy of the customer. You learned the tricks of the trade. You learned to tip your cap, smile at the right time, how to be careful at curbs, and how to show appreciation. You also learned which customers were generous, and which ones to avoid if you could.
>
> *(Barton 1983, 102–3)*

Permanent grocery stores opened to meet the immediate needs of wage earners, especially after industries such as a steel plant in south Harrisburg (later renamed Steelton) came to Harrisburg after the Civil War. The plant was the first mill in the United States dedicated exclusively to the process of making steel, and it attracted a diverse immigrant workforce primarily from Eastern and Southern Europe (Bodnar [1977] 1990; Barton and Bronner 2008). The stores in the area, including Steelton's, were small establishments entrenched in the class- and ethnic-based neighborhoods. Innovations made by grocery stores included adding consumer goods, such as tableware and clothing, to their regular inventory of food and stocking prepackaged edibles. Grocers

> had long, hard days. They opened their stores at six or seven in the morning. Men coming from their nightshifts would stop to buy the things that had

been written on a list the night before. The grocer's day continued until late at night. Neighborhood stores were seldom longer than a home living room; in fact, many were located in what would have been the parlor. Yet, in that small space you could find everything a family would need for survival.

(Barton 1983, 100)

But as the family bought goods in that small space, the distance between producer and consumer grew. New worlds of assorted choices filled in the gap. Huston recalled the introduction of a new commercial novelty as an example—the candy store:

The Gods with barrels of ambrosia were not any richer than a kid with a penny in a candy store. With a penny one had a choice of a most wonderful assortment. Perhaps the most difficult decisions we made in our lifetime were those made in front of candy counters. You would feast your eyes from left to right, from right to left, from front to back, and even diagonally. You had to decide not only on taste, but also on which items gave the most for your money....Boys had fun buying licorice, because they could emulate their elders by pretending they were chewing tobacco.

(Barton 1983, 100)

The candy store was one of many new specialty stores to sprout around the markets and eventually replace them. Besides carrying a wider assortment of goods in a smaller space, the stores were open almost every day of the week and were more hospitable to youth. Less crowded and less communally oriented than the markets, the stores enabled customers to feel "served" and therefore associated with a higher class. In the quiet, enclosed spaces of the stores, merchants used displays of goods that created an attractive environment for private consumption. The stores offered more of the ready-made goods (besides food) that residents sought for convenience. By changing displays to remind shoppers of new conveniences, the stores conveyed expertise in new fashion trends and technology, and advertised that they offered the latest and most "up-to-date" goods. The stores offered the pull of novelty, the appeal of modernity, and the promise of flattering attention.

By the 1880s a streetscape of small shops lined the avenues and pushed out the markets. The markets and the shopping districts came into conflict, because the markets created crowded neighborhood "centers" within traffic areas. To spur the commercial growth of the cosmopolitan city, civic leaders envisioned "streams" of traffic moving up the citywide avenues. Citing the hazards to traffic that the markets caused, the courts decreed on behalf of the merchants that the central market houses obstructed a highway—the new economic lifeline—and should be removed. Afterward farmers came to the city to buy rather than to sell. The last market day was held January 19, 1889. As Inglewood described the scene,

FIGURE 4.2 In the foreground is the "lower" farmers' market house or "shed" on Market Square, Harrisburg, Pennsylvania, prior to 1889 when the market houses were razed (originally erected around 1792). Behind it is the "upper" house on the north side of square, known as the "butchers market" dominated by sales of meats and sausages.

Source: Photograph Courtesy of the Historical Society of Dauphin County, Harrisburg, PA (ID# PO3172 W).

> it seemed like the passing of old friends when those market houses were torn down, even if every one knew the march of progress made it necessary.... As for the buildings around the Square, they, too, have changed as radically as the Square itself, and have grown up from little log cabins into quite respectable looking semi-skyscrapers.

Among the sights was the hardware store of Kelker and Brother, who had

> just about everything in their large store that was in any way connected with hardware, iron, or steel, from files, nails, and horseshoes up to anvils, circular saws, and Fairbanks scales. They even were agents for Meneely's church bells, something you'd scarcely expect to find in a hardware store of today.
>
> *(Inglewood 1925, 55)*

FIGURE 4.3 Sales clerks and stockroom boys in front of Fahnestock's Department Store on Market Street, downtown Harrisburg, Pennsylvania, probably upon its opening in 1894. Owner William E. Fahnestock is the man with a Bowler hat and bowtie in the middle. In 1922 the property became part of Woolworth department store chain.

Source: Photograph Courtesy of the Historical Society of Dauphin County, Harrisburg, PA (ID# D 00486).

Other stores had things that residents hardly expected, most notably William Fahnestock's shop located on Market Street near Market Square. The Fahnestocks were descended from immigrants who came to Central Pennsylvania in 1726, and with profit earned from a dry goods store in Harrisburg invested in banking and railroads. Although William relocated to New York City to concentrate on the family's financial businesses, he maintained ties to Harrisburg and the family donated the money to build the Harrisburg Y.M.C.A. Originally a ladies' clothing store downtown, Fahnestock's store beginning in 1895 built on its appeal to the influx of women earning wages at new factories in the city ("Harrisburg Great Factories" 1907; "Women Are Forming Clubs" 1907). No longer restricted to sales of clothing, Fahnestock added furniture, bicycles, toys, and rugs to lure the growing numbers of women who accounted for most of the city's consumer purchases. The feminine appeal of shopping at Fahnestock's store was a contrast to the somber manly look of the neighboring Kelkers' hardware store, and as Fahnestock's expanded into a department store, it quickly outdistanced its competitor in business. Taking a cue from Philadelphia department stores, Fahnestock packed his shop windows with bright mannequin-filled displays and hired well-dressed, enthusiastic salesclerks. The store was later taken over by Woolworth's and helped to make the downtown area a lively "shopping district."

FIGURE 4.4 Sales clerks with furniture, toys, and display cases in front of the shop windows of Robinson's Department Store, uptown Harrisburg, Pennsylvania, 1902. A reflection in the window on the right includes the Broad Street Farmers' Market across the street. The site at the end of the twentieth century became part of an independent bookstore complex.
Source: Photograph Courtesy of the Historical Society of Dauphin County, Harrisburg, PA (ID# D 0557).

Harry Robinson went further than Fahnestock in establishing the attraction of consumer dry goods in his department store. His bold step was to move outside the downtown area. The *Harrisburg Telegraph* in 1905 described the uptown neighborhood as "largely a residential section on either side, interspersed here and there with some business places, largely those for local convenience, as corner groceries, bakeries and the like" (Wert 1905). The corner building he occupied had been a dry goods store that drew customers from the Broad Street Market across the street. Robinson pushed the showcase of different departments to three floors, each floor brandishing an airy window display. He invited workers to spend their days off ("dollar days," he called them) leisurely shopping for their labor's rewards and offered "half-price" sales. Unlike his competitors, he openly advertised prices in the newspapers and offered luxurious items as well as bargain items to lure shoppers to the uptown area from every neighborhood. He planted columns in the newspapers disguised as news about the sales as citywide events. Announcing "An Event Up Town That Will Interest the Whole City" in 1909, for example, in the *Harrisburg Daily Independent*, Robinson sounded like a benefactor who "to maintain their reputation for clean, high-class merchandise" would take a loss to clean out his winter inventory. The article emphasized Robinson's growth in physical space and the crowds it would attract:

> As the Robinson store is noted for big value giving and has grown to large dimensions since its opening nineteen years ago, in fact being the largest in that growing business section up town, it is predicted at the prices quoted, the Robinson store will be crowded during the twelve days of the sale with eager buyers who know Robinson values and who realize at what tremendous savings they can purchase real high class merchandise.
>
> *("Robinson & Co's Big Special Sale" 1909)*

The Broad Street Market did not disappear as a result but Robinson's store became more of the magnet for the area as the immigrants who had moved into the downtown 8th ward relocated north. For Robinson to compete with the downtown department stores, though, it was important for him to emphasize in the city dailies that his was a store for the *entire* city.

Other sights and sounds confirmed the movement of the city into the consumer age. The Harrisburg National Bank, founded in 1814, took on a new interior that resembled the designs of grand railroad stations. Established in 1845, Dauphin Deposit Bank off Market Square bragged of its commercial strength by brandishing huge classical pillars at its entrance. A new capitol was erected in 1906 in a Beaux-Arts style with a dome that recalls St. Peter's Basilica in the Vatican. A gilded classically styled statue named "Commonwealth" stands on the dome with a staff topped with a garland and eagle with outstretched wings. The governor at the time declared, "The Capitol which in its mass of granite reigns over the city seems to throw a shadow of power and richness over everything" (Donehoo 1927). Just as the capitol reigned over the city and its eagle suggested soaring heights, the new Commonwealth Hotel towered over Market Square, now cleared of the sheds, and became a center of social activity. When John Wanamaker ran for the United States Senate in 1896, a grand arch announced his entry into town past the hotel. A stately Board of Trade was completed in 1898 on Market Street near the square, and the board shortly thereafter put out a magazine to attract more consumer development. The boom also produced some eccentric organizations like the Sons of Rest, young members of the new leisure class who gathered together to watch others work whenever a large new building was constructed downtown. Members of the uniformed Harrisburg Wheel Club, composed of merchants and professionals, compensated for their sedentary lifestyles by riding the rough old high wheelers on strenuous outings to unspoiled natural outskirts of the city.

Renowned novelist John O'Hara captured the flavor of turn-of-the-century Harrisburg in *A Rage to Live* (1949), which was made into a Hollywood movie in 1965. O'Hara recalled the city from his childhood, and he returned to Market

Square to talk to old-timers about the city's emergence "simply to record reality" (quoted in MacShane 1980, 141–42). In O'Hara's view, Harrisburg was a city turned from the farmers with their strong sense of local-ethnic tradition to the merchants with their vision of the cosmopolitan future; it was a city where the "snappiest," rather than the richest, inhabitants now set the tone in manners, although they were always anxious that the big cities were more in step with modernity than they were. With his eye for family dynamics and hometown details, O'Hara described social changes apparent behind the city's new look: the dining-out that workers felt obliged to do rather than going home for lunch; the increased attention to appearances, and expensive ones at that; the growing concern for having what others had; and the passing of the leisurely ceremonial pipe for the anxiously consumed cigarettes that both men and women now smoked. O'Hara wrote that Harrisburg "went in for a metropolitan social life, with consequent prosperity for dressmakers, tailors, shoemakers, and jewelers at home and away" (O'Hara 1949, 49).

With apparent anxiety over too much change, the city introduced occasions to remember past traditions. It instituted Old Home Week in 1905 to tour and narrate the community buildings of an earlier time. As a result of the tourist development of the Amish settlement toward Lancaster, which included the promotion of markets, city residents were able to escape back to a preindustrial way of life. From the few market houses still left standing,

> people gathered up the bits of wood as mementoes of the good old times they typified, and today in many a Harrisburg home, you'll find a cane, paper weight, or fancy ornament made from the wood of the old market houses on the Square.
>
> *(Inglewood 1925, 54)*

In spite of the romantic stirrings of the old neighborhood and market system, civic leaders facing economic pressure pushed for public works that would transform the city by the 1920s into

> a busy industrial center, in which is made almost every article used by man, from steel and iron to silk and knitted goods, with a valuation of $218,810,400 of the products made. And instead of a hundred Indian traders, representing the total of the industrial employees, they would find an army of 28,258 men and women engaged in the 302 industries in the country.
>
> *(Donehoo 1927, 188)*

The City Beautiful Movement took hold in the city and worker housing was removed to make way for a riverside park that appealed to middle-class walkers and bikers (Pettegrew and LaGrand 2020; Wilson 1980). With the expansion of the State Capitol building, buildings were razed and residents, consisting mostly of minorities, were forced to relocate. By most accounts, they could not re-establish their neighborhood life (Barton and Dorman 2002). Some ethnic pockets maintained cohesion in Steelton but they were challenged when the workforce was cut at the steel plant (Barton and Bronner 2008). Farm communities for which Central Pennsylvania was renowned felt squeezed out by developers and sold their land for commercial strip malls. Suburban tracts and shopping centers arose in bedroom communities across the river from Harrisburg during the 1950s and the transformation of social life as consumers seemed complete. By the 1980s, the city hailed an "Urban Renaissance" driven by a cohort named "young urban professionals" that would bring revenue and night life back to the city. But working-class residents who had been left behind were not sure (Bronner 1986a, 63–86; McCormick 2016; Sauro 2020).

The Consuming Self in Fat City

Sources of images, sounds, and texts varied from the intellectuals who produced novels to the corporate executives who designed new products to the merchants who built a vivid streetscape, but a common agenda can nonetheless be discerned. Judging by what people read in the signs of the times in successive generations after the late nineteenth century, Americans were preoccupied with acquiring money, and holding on to it, because they were lured by the promise of consumer capitalism to provide personal comfort and social progress. Yet they understood the vulnerabilities of resources of this largely economic system that called for speculation on continuous growth in the future (Ehrenreich 1989). Average Americans who were more likely to come from a waged and salaried middle class than a producer economy worked to get money, planned what to do with it, created ways to show it, and contemplated what it meant for the future. They embraced it, but worried about it. Moving into the late twentieth century, they entered a dizzying array of state lotteries and commercial sweepstakes because they envied the super-rich and thought they could get lucky as did the winners they viewed on television. Into the digital age of the twenty-first century, they pondered the world from their computers as never before in a cascade of reports on the effects of globalization while often reaching out to re-establish the local and social in their vicinities.

As Americans looked out into the world more and enjoyed or criticized what they viewed as a culture of excess, they also became more aware of a visible concomitant change on themselves—their bodies, especially compared to those of other Western industrialized nations. They were noticeably fatter, and yet the magazines they read and movies they watched extolled slenderness (Stearns 2002, 127–49). By 2020, the United States had the highest obesity rate at 36.20 percent among industrialized countries well outdistancing those next down on the list of Canada and Australia at less than 30 percent ("Obesity Rates" 2021). In that year, the Centers for Disease Control and Prevention (CDC) counted around 70 percent of American adults as overweight and over 40 percent as obese. That rate had increased 26 percent since 2008, and 21 percent since 1980 (French 2016; U.S. Department of Health and Human Services 2010). The proportion of Americans who tried to lose weight through diets or an exercise program increased from 34 percent at the turn of the millennium to 42 percent in 2015, but the average weight and body-mass index went up anyway (Thompson 2019).

Many health advisers warned against consumer food trends with the rise of an urban service and information economy: increase of fatty foods from fast-food establishments for a nation on the run, heavy advertising for sugar-sweetened beverages and desserts, proliferation of high-calorie snack foods, overeating at buffets and catered events, and high proportion of prepackaged foods with refined carbohydrates and low fiber. The sedentary lifestyle of office work contributes, as does leisure time activities such as television and computer and video game screen time, and occasions for watch parties with "junk food" that involve binge and stress eating/drinking (U.S. Department of Health and Human Services 2010; see also Jones 2017). Indeed, the CDC viewed stress as a contributing factor, which raised a question about pressure in a competitive system to succeed and responses to failure. Historian Peter N. Stearns provided a social historical context by noting that

> Reasonably steady weight gain from the 1920s onward simultaneous with increasingly rigid, widely accepted norms of slenderness add up to a growing tension in personal life, registered daily on the bathroom scales or the furtive aversion to this same ritualist device. In this respect, at least, Americans became more disappointed with themselves.
> *(Stearns 2002, 149)*

Denying oneself goods and foods that were perceived as rewards of American working life proved difficult (LeBesco 2007).

By 2020, one out of every five Americans tried to compensate for the effects of desk jobs and weight gain by signing up for gym memberships. The number of health club members in the United States rose 37.1 percent between 2008 and 2018 (IHRSA 2019). Yet despite fitness centers emerging as important consumer social as well as body shaping destinations, American health report cards did not improve (CDC n.d.). After holiday seasons encouraging indulgence such as New Year's Eve and watching football games on New Year's Day, the rather futile ritual of announcing New Year resolutions annually ensued with getting fit and losing weight topping most lists (see Chapter 2). The U.S. Department of Health and Human Services reported that less than 5 percent of adults participate in 30 minutes of physical activity each day and only one in three adults receive the recommended amount of physical activity each week (President's Council on Sports, Fitness, & Nutrition 2017). Apparently, exercise regimens and equipment that people used at clubs or installed at home in rising numbers were not enough.

Yet fashion in the form of "workout" clothing and specialized athletic shoes became a trend, partly to announce an embrace of leisure time and individual control despite the growing number of hours required for their sedentary work (Klein 2014; Schabner 2006; Schor 2000). Coupled with the trend toward sportswear was the donning of "flip-flops" by adults and children alike as if to declare readiness for leisure time at the beach away from the bustle of city life, even if the flimsy thong sandals went against doctors' orders (Foster 2010).

With children in the twenty-first century spending more than seven and a half hours a day in front of a screen, twenty-first-century studies found that only one in three children is physically active, despite the traditional association of childhood with vigorous physical play. Their data showed that the percentage of children and adolescents affected by obesity (around 20 percent) had more than tripled since the 1970s (Fryar, Carroll, and Ogden 2018). Although following sports is an American obsession, the competitive professionalization of sports has contributed to lower levels of physical activity among youth by conveying the idea that one had to be a superlative athlete to participate. Rather than engage in free play on the playground, part of the visual culture of the early twentieth century, children in the twenty-first century were often shuttled into competitive, adult-managed sports leagues (Friedman 2013). And in a selective process, stellar prospects were placed on "travel teams" and in "all-star" sports camps with the dream of receiving big payoffs as adults in professional sports (Gregory 2017). Many children ended up sitting it out. One alarming twenty-first-century study that drew media attention to the American approach to sport and fitness was a 50-country comparison of differences in physical activity levels by pooling aggregate results of running studies from different nations. The British researchers found that the United States ranked 47th with only Latvia, Peru, and Mexico being worse (Lang et al. 2018, 5). With the news that the United States is not on top of the world in an area that is perceived as a sign of national prosperity, government agencies and commentators announced a crisis and called for policy as well as cultural changes (Bellisari 2013; Hitchcock 2015; Powell 2015).

One distinctively American answer to the global obesity problem is technological and service oriented—cosmetic surgery. The United States leads the world with over four million procedures annually, a figure that is almost double of the next country, Brazil, where many of the customers are in fact American patrons who are attracted there by the lower costs. Accordingly, the United States is home to the most plastic surgeons on the globe. Unlike doctors in Brazil, American surgeons are likely to perform abdominoplasty ("tummy tuck") and liposuction to give their patients a slender, and supposedly youthful, look. Whereas Brazilians spend more money on shaping the buttocks, Americans look to change their girths (Mendible 2009; Simpson 2019). Having the procedures is not cheap, especially since insurance normally does not cover the surgeries, and hence seeking a plastic surgeon is associated with upper-class women and celebrity vanity. Yet the medical sector reports that cosmetic surgery, especially to address portly bodies among men as well as women, became more common among middle-class Americans in the twentieth century (Barry 2003). According to the American Society of Plastic Surgeons, the number of surgical tummy tucks increased 97 percent from 2000 to 2019, and even more non-invasive fat reduction procedures were performed during that time (ASPS 2019, 7–8). Liposuctions and fat reduction procedures are favored more in the West while abdominoplasty is preferred in the Northeast (ASPS 2019, 20–21). The main demographic for cosmetic plastic surgery is white women between the ages of 30 and 54, many of whom also seek breast augmentation (ASPS 2019, 6). The modern popularity of cosmetic surgery represents a shift in thinking of one's body as unalterably sacrosanct. Biblical admonitions remind church-goers, for example, that the "body is a temple of the holy spirit" (Corinthians 6:19–20) and one should "honor God with your bodies" (Genesis 1:26–27). Many Christian guides preached against tampering with the body for cosmetic purposes to avoid ungodly hubris and sexual promiscuity. This was not just a puritanical religious view. During the Victorian period, so-called painted or public women who used cosmetics and body piercings were considered sexually stigmatized and lower-class (Anderson 1993, 2–4).

Contemporary data on American plastic surgery trends verify the often-observed emphasis on a culturally defined body curve of a small waist and full breasts for American women and an instilled self-conscious anxiety that they have to maintain a physical appearance attractive to men (Banner 1983; Hesse-Biber 2006; Holmes 2021). Racial and ethnic difference is evident in women's abilities to "keep their figure"; the Office of Minority Health (2020a) for the U.S. government reports four out of five African-American women are overweight or obese. Non-Hispanic black women were 2.3 times more likely to be overweight as compared to non-Hispanic white females, a figure that is compounded by the statistic that African Americans were 20 percent less likely to engage in physical activity (Office of Minority Health 2020a). Hispanic-American women were 1.8 times more likely to be overweight as compared to non-Hispanic whites. The obesity rate for Asian-American women was the lowest of all the groups (Office of Minority Health 2020b, 2020c). Affecting these rates are cultural aesthetics about preferable body profiles. Historically, traditional blues lyrics by African-American recording artists during the mid-twentieth century often extolled the "big fat mama" with "meat shaking on her bones." In hip-hop culture in the twenty-first century, fat is rendered as "phat" and according to African-American communications scholar Janice Hamlet,

> refers to a person or thing that is excellent and desirable, reflecting the traditional cultural value that human body weight is a good thing and implicitly rejecting the Eurocentric thought which teaches that being skinny is more valued than being fat.
>
> *(Hamlet 2011, 28; see also Strings 2019)*

During the 1990s, teams of researchers from the College of William and Mary and Hampton University confirmed in a psychological study that African-American men viewed the ideal black female body to be heavier than that of white women (Rosen et al. 1993, 601). The researchers did not see a correlation of the preference for a larger body shape with socioeconomic status, however. Historian Peter Stearns interpreted this apparent defiance of mainstream standards as a subcultural manifestation of an ethnic "belief that weight embodied merriment, solidity, and sensuality, though at real cost to health and longevity, which dropped below national averages" (Stearns 2002, 149). Socially, a fatalistic view is implied that with systemic racist oppression keeping people of color from gaining prosperity, that one can express a benevolent social and maternal, if not economic, prosperity through cooking for a grateful hungry crowd. Fatness in African-American discourse can represent nurturing, strength, and sustenance. Adding to the symbolic equation of food with economic as well as therapeutic bodily fulfillment are the American rhetoric of fattening foods being "rich" and the Americanisms of "dough" and "bread" as slang for money (O'Conner and Kellerman 2014). Thinness exemplified in the pejorative term "skinny" or "bony" ass/bitch in African-American slang could represent impoverishment and even whiteness (Pace 2016; Smitherman 1998, 216). Instead of appearing gratifyingly ejective, slenderness from an ethnic perspective can be construed as distressingly inadequate and grotesque (Ingalls 2017; Mendible 2009).

For upper-class white women, a slender, sleek body gives the impression of being healthy, privileged, independent (or childless), and having the time and money to "take care of your *self*." Thinness can suggest a mainstream identity tied into an ethic of "clean," self-controlled living, as well as staying active, busy, and fashionable. From a psychoanalytic perspective, thinness connotes a culturally influenced self-gratifying, ejective symbolism of aggressive power in which internalized money of the "*filthy* rich" is pleasurably expunged from the body, evident in actions of "throwing money around" or spurting "spend" (slang for semen or vaginal secretion as well as an action of spending money, according to the Oxford English Dictionary). By contrast fatness (or "tightness" as in an anally retentive tightwad or tight-ass) indicates uncomfortable retention, or selfish, unnatural, and unhealthy hoarding, of money and food or feces (Ferenczi [1952] 2018; Forrest 1990; see also Bronner 2011, 319–49; Dundes 1962). A fat "booty" in fact can refer in slang to either wide buttocks or money.

Although there is undoubtedly national medical pressure to lose weight for both men and women, noticeably wider girths, usually on men depicted as rich and powerful big-spending "fat cats," held an appeal to people, white and black, because they embodied the symbolism and Americanness of success (Berke 2002; LeBesco 2007). During the Gilded Age, renowned cartoonist Thomas Nast created an image of New York Tammany Hall political bosses with huge bellies and a sack of money popping through the collar (Nast 1871). In 1883, illustrator Bernhard Gillam (n.d.) replaced the stomachs of prominent industrial tycoons such as Jay Gould and Cornelius Vanderbilt in the popular satirical magazine *Puck* with larger bulging sacks of money. J. Keppler, under the heading of "The Bosses of the Senate," exaggerated even more the tubby midsections of top-hat wearing monopolists for the magazine in 1889 (Keppler n.d.). Nast also contributed the modern image of a jolly fat St. Nicholas carrying consumer toys and gifts with his illustrations of "Merry Old Santa Claus" that is the model for mall and advertising Santas through the twenty-first century (Boissoneault 2018; Marling 2000, 197–242).

Santa and the robber barons project a protuberant bodily look that diverges from the statuesque American icons of the exceptional cowboy, G.I. Joe, and Uncle Sam. The former is more evident in a twenty-first-century image of the working-class American in verbal and visual rendering of the "Average Joe," "Regular Joe," "Average Jane," "Ordinary Jane," "Joe Blow," "Joe Schmo," and "Joe Six-Pack" as the authentic working backbone of the nation. Frequently presented as a vehicle to lampoon American culture and specifically the pretension of the cosmopolitan set, the Average Joe folktype could also appear unflattering and might be construed as demonizing the working class in favor of the cultural refinement and political outlook associated with an upwardly mobile professional class (see Butsch 2003; Darowski and Darowski 2017, 69–88; Scharrer 2001, 28). Perhaps the most conspicuous example of suggesting that working-class values and appearances are boorish and outdated was *Queer Eye* (a reboot of *Queer Eye for the Straight Guy* originally airing in 2003) which featured an episode titled "Below Average Joe" (aired February 7, 2018). In it a formerly overweight performer who lives in his parents' basement receives a makeover into a cosmopolitan look from the scrawny urbane metrosexual experts, collectively known as the "Fab Five," with the implication that the average underachieving Joe needs to embrace their economic and aesthetic vision to advance in and conform to the modern world (see Fatphobia Busters 2018; Sender 2006).

Average Joe was the name for a reality television show beginning in 2003 that mocked the privileged fantasy formulas of *The Bachelor* (debuting in 2002) and *Bachelorette* (debuting in 2003). Situation comedies with working-class themes often cast a paunchy central character, an every man (e.g., *King of Queens*, 1998–2007, with a parcel deliverer in New York) and woman (e.g., *Roseanne*, 1988–1997, a line worker at a midwestern plastics company), who struggle to get ahead but take comfort in their families although they are not always cooperative (Grogan 2017, 103–34; LeBesco 2007, 240). Despite showing the economic struggles of the families, often blamed on unseen corporate powers, the shows portrayed resignation to their plight, and the extra pounds of the parents seemed to indicate that they are sitting around gaining weight rather than springing into action, or resistance (Grabowski 2014). Animators often exaggerated the paunch on working-class characters in long-running shows such as *The Flintstones* (1960–1966, set in a Stone-Age town of Bedrock with plump crane operator Fred Flintstone who overeats unhealthy food), *The Simpsons* (debuting in 1989 with the father as the donut-loving nuclear safety inspector Homer, slang for an unintelligent person, living with his family in the Middle America town of Springfield), *Family Guy* (debuting in 1999, with overweight New England blue-collar worker Peter Griffin and his similarly shaped son Chris), and *The Cleveland Show* (2009–2013, featuring Peter Griffin's neighbor, delicatessen owner and postal worker Cleveland Brown, and his porky son Cleveland Jr.) (see Booker 2006, 69–102; Butsch 2003). There is continuity between these themes of seeking upward mobility in a service and information economy and nineteenth century references to the average American Joe as an industrial worker. A letter to *American Machinist* in 1878 related the class-based idea that "the Average Joe" working in the "business, mill, factory, or forge" has to support himself and thus will find college difficult to afford (Lorenz 1879).

Where the Average Joe took on a stout beer belly that represented his plebeian tastes and consumer habits was in the form of Joe Sixpack that dates at least to 1970 (Safire 1998). The moniker and who it represents became an issue in the 2008 presidential election as vice-presidential candidates Sarah Palin and Joe Biden vied to speak for and relate to the pudgy working-class, couch sitting, beef and fried-food eating, television watching, beer guzzling Joe who was mentioned in the same breath with "Main Streeters" and "hockey moms" (Flegenheimer 2020). When the husky columnist Don Russell, using the name "Joe Sixpack" for the low-brow *Philadelphia Daily News*, was asked to name the beer that fits Palin's profile, he answered, "If she did drink one, I suspect she's a light-beer drinker—very thin, no body...After all, the Republican party is not known as a beer-drinking party. They're more of a martini or whiskey party" (Carswell 2008). The name Joe Sixpack stuck around through subsequent national campaigns in reporters' questioning of a vacillating blue-collar vote. Emblematizing a taste-based, working-class consumption community (Boorstin 1974, 145–48; Friedman, Abeele, and De Vos 1993), in 2019 country rock duo Montgomery Gentry from Kentucky released "Joe Sixpack" with lyrics defiantly affirming that the average, out of shape Joe knows how to have a good time with what he has, and does not need the fancy goods of svelte rich and famous city slickers. Joe and Jane College were differentiated from Joe Sixpack, but had similar financial and cultural concerns. The premise of *Ordinary Joe*, an NBC drama hitting the television airwaves in 2021, concerned a single college graduate contemplating the different directions that life will lead if he makes a choice to be a musician, policeman, or nurse, none of which leads to riches or fame (Renault 2020; for the "trajectory" image of the life course, see Chapter 2).

During the 1960s, linguists reported the emergence of the slang term *fat city* among college students on the West Coast, home of the California Dream as the American Dream. They equated it to saying "You've got it made [financially]" and thought it might derive from African-American urban folk speech (Poston and Stillman 1965, 194). Later in the decade, novelist Leonard Gardner's *Fat City* (1969) was a finalist for the National Book Award and drew attention to the term outside the college scene. Set in California, the plot centered on a middling boxer anxious to return to glory. The dark novel was turned into a popular movie in 1972 directed by famed director John Huston who visually captured the push to succeed and the personal obstacles that get in the way. Gardner told an interviewer

> When you say you want to go to Fat City, it means you want the good life. I got the idea for the title after seeing a photograph of a tenement in an exhibit in San Francisco. "Fat City" was scrawled in chalk on a wall. The title is ironic: Fat City is a crazy goal no one is ever going to reach.
>
> *(Durham 1969)*

"Fat City" evoked the equation of fat with opulence; its urban connection was to the "moving on up" image of urban skyscrapers and penthouses that displaced ideas of the biblical "eat [living] off the fat of the land" (Genesis 45:18). Nightclubs and other commercial enterprises took up the "fat city" label through the twenty-first century, especially in locations such as New Orleans and Los Angeles that promoted an identity of the high life (Mouton 2012; Price 2014). Not surprisingly, many restaurants took the "Fat City" name to entice customers to buy oversized fat, juicy steaks as signs of celebrating success.

"Money makes the world go round," Americans are wont to say, and the question is whether more "cash than you know what to do with" makes life better for individuals and signals progress for society. *Progress* and *Success* were keywords in the Americanness of images, sounds, and texts from the nineteenth century on, for in accepting a consumer capitalist system Average Joes and Janes expected that rewards for hard work will be gained in an abundance of goods and ease of life. Regardless of the many plaints about this deceptive promise that emerged during the late nineteenth century, critics moved aside before the inevitable force of progress and success that were defined materially. Progress and success so construed provided a vivid measure of advancement for the society, the culture, and its children. Politicians broached it in every election to comprehend what changes are worth implementing or impeding. The real struggle was ensuring that matters of spirit and human compassion remained part of the essence of life. Within that struggle was the harnessing of wealth to social advantage and welfare while gratifying the self. Not coincidentally charity was often expected during consumer holidays such as Christmas and Thanksgiving as guilt arose about self-indulgence in the hope of reaching fat city. Although people swore that their character did not change with the acquisition of goods, cultural expressions often conveyed the idea that changes were occurring typically outside of one's awareness. Swept up by the tide of goods, Americans from the nineteenth century on became attuned to the consumer culture as the mechanics of the nation. In this they found pause, if not parting. It ironically confirmed the culture even as it questioned its patterns. In text, sounds, and images, consumer selves basked in the glory of attainment and lost something in the process. A major issue was whether progress had created this dilemma—for society, for culture, and for the individual.

The impression of a society of consumers raised images of breaking down the isolation of people. Shared goods meant having more in common; therefore, a scattered society still could be close, even if it meant that strangers could hide behind the facade of their things and more easily build walls around themselves. People could create status differences through their accumulation of luxuries. A society with ready-made goods available to them could also be more expansive. Not tied to the local market and environment, Americans were free to explore new sights. The consumer system reached across the land, advancing in apparent defiance of the constrictions of space and time. Advertisements proclaimed and objects offered that whatever was desired was possible if a rational and efficient way of doing things was adopted, inspired by the very machines that brought this possibility to reality. Freedom of movement and the promise of ease replaced the power of self-reliance. Modern-day Jeremiahs from the industrial era to digital age warned that the power of consumption and its heightened capacity to order goods replaced the power of production and its capacity to produce goods.

As the question for society concerned effects on people, so too do the inquiries into American thought and culture emphasize what happened to socially shared ideas expressed in customs, arts, and institutions. Images, sounds, and texts were more important in a consumer system, since people who were increasingly strangers to one another increasingly relied on signs to communicate. Within the older familiarity of the rooted village, more knowledge was inherited and assumed. People on the move needed more explicit signs to guide them through the changing landscape and their changing lives. And once settled in new situations, people looked to vivid messages to offer advice and tradition. Further, with the broader scope of the consumer capitalist system, the importance of appearance represented a shift from the reliance on handwork and complemented this shift and produced analog and digital worlds of color, light, and spectacle emanating from goods.

Yet as William Dean Howells and others who both took advantage of and simultaneously questioned the new American order in the nineteenth century observed, "it looked a little dull." They saw a veneer on ready-made goods over deep-spirited feelings found formerly in the individuality of handwork and the unrestrained expression of folk song and story. Accepting that the charging behemoth could not be stopped, they sought ways to compensate to keep an ethical egalitarian vision. On Sunday on ritzy Madison Avenue in New York City, according to Howells,

> The men's faces were shrewd and alert, and yet they looked dull; the women's were pretty and knowing, and yet dull. It was probably the holiday expression of the vast, prosperous, commercial class, with unlimited money and no ideals that money could not realize; fashion and comfort were all that they desired to compass.

In contrast, the hardscrabble Bowery had a "gay ugliness-the shapeless, graceless, reckless picturesqueness" (Howells [1889] 1980, 262). Madison Avenue presented a culture of plays and operas; the gritty Bowery culture existed in the style of conversation and books with a "prevailing hideousness that always amused...in that uproar to the eye which the strident forms and colors made" (Howells [1889] 1980, 159). The consumer culture promised a perfection of design and taste to inspire all Americans, but it was the rough-hewn spirit that suggested depth and meaning. And writers and artists avowed, Americanness should involve both. The depth came from the feeling of rooted community and compassion associated with an older system of exchange. The surface quality of consumer goods valued according to cost expanded the sense of community, of belonging to the nation, while at the same time flattering the self of the person who owns the goods and promoting self-centered individualism. Does it matter that if cryptocurrency takes over, there will not be dollar bills to flash? The goods remain and their brand, cost, and status convey meaning, even if they tend to be more fleeting than the handwrought world that the Average Joes and Janes value, Pennsylvania Germans in Harrisburg recalled, and the Amish try to live today.

What of the self, the individual, in the images, sounds, and texts of the consumer culture? In Floyd Mayweather's over-the-top displays of money, the self triumphs over reason to make a point about worth. Many of the American novels of the late nineteenth century include conflicted characters who also declare themselves relevant through the acquisition and display of wealth, but who only realize themselves through the spirit when they have lost everything. The boom in decorating with mirrors during the American Victorian period focused attention on the appearance and flattery of the independent self. In the twenty-first century, the "selfie" photograph captures that feeling and uses it to create a network if not a virtual community (Morel 2021; Veum and Undrum 2017). For some, the selfie rhetorically signals a "selfish" quality while others see it as connection in a digital environment that alienates rather than mediates. Taking selfies in the many photographable scenes of daily life, one's mobility and individuality are valorized. With digital culture crossing boundaries and representing global communication that is instantaneous and simultaneous, resulting in the breakdown of conventional notions of time and space, it is tempting to discard the influence of Americanness. Yet, digital communication in social media and email has also revitalized and diversified group identities that formerly were thought to be ceded to national culture. People are compelled to sort and discern overlapping frames of locality, region, nation, and world as they click away.

Who are the change agents, and scolding Jeremiahs, on the path toward progress and success in the American mentalité? Is it the flashy tycoon because "money is power" and "money talks"? Or is there "strength in numbers" provided by mass grass-roots movements, which was a major question in decades of unrest such as the 1930s, 1960s, and 2020s? In the 2020 presidential primaries, for example, candidate Bernie Sanders questioned the standard of a dollar as part of his American rhetoric of "progress," "revolution," and "movement." To draw attention to racial inequities, he raised the image of African Americans having "ten cents for every dollar white Americans have." His campaign declared that "It's time for America to treat the lives of people of color like they're worth more than *change on the dollar*" (Friends of Bernie Sanders 2020; emphasis added). The double meaning of *change* as lowly but sturdy coins (in contrast to the expandable and manipulable paper dollar) and a process of transformation, if not intentional, certainly was implicit, and identified change as part of a progressive identity. An image of him sitting in ordinary outerwear and handmade mittens, apparently uncomfortable at the formal presidential inauguration, went viral on the Internet in memes as a reminder of the cultural reset of the "Average Joe and Jane" in American life (Ives and Victor 2021; Watercutter 2021).

A target for change was epitomized in the term "Wall Street" broadly representing financial elite pulling strings to get rich at the expense of hard-working average Americans living on the symbolically ordinary "Main Street." In 2021, a dramatic event pitting stock brokers empowered by big money against amateur traders provided a historic saga that begs for decoding variously for American and global contexts. GameStop Corporation was the world's largest video game retailer and yet in the epic battle with Wall Street it was identified as the victimized underdog. Headquartered in a suburb of Dallas, Texas, it had over 5,500 stores in the United States and abroad that sold physical media. As the second decade of the twenty-first century ended, the advent of online services cut into the company's video game market and it faced severe financial losses and possible bankruptcy. Convinced that GameStop's brick-and-mortar business model was doomed, Wall Street investors speculated that the stock would fall, and sold "short," that is, borrowing stock from a lender and then selling it to a buyer at market value expecting the stock to decline in price. When that happens, investors make wads of money by pocketing the difference before returning the stock to the lender (VOA News 2021). Angered by the hegemony of haughty Wall Street brokers, and their manipulation of a product that represented social connection and play in a digital culture that is especially appealing to youth, a popular online financial discussion group, Robinhood Stock Traders, named after a folkloric character who robs from the rich and gives to the poor, encouraged its members to invest in GameStop (Popper Phillips, Kelly, and Bernard 2021). Small traders invested on a mass scale and in a matter of days, GameStop stock rose 1,700 percent, thus destroying chances for the large hedge fund investors who banked on its decline. Because the move by Robinhood disrupted the commercial system, calls went out from financial firms to block the group from investing. Wall Street's clearinghouses that serve to reduce risk forced Robinhood to find emergency cash to continue to be able to trade, but it continued to fight back in a way that the Occupy Wall Street movement could not (Popper Phillips, Kelly, and Bernard 2021). The battle between the "little guy" and the bigwigs drew sympathy from the American public for the underdog in a frame that suggested a one-on-one sports contest with an all-out winner. The odds were against Robinhood but the epic confrontation brought out tensions and systems evolving since the nineteenth century. In rhetoric familiar in the worker anthem of "9 to 5," the U.S. Senate Banking Committee chairman Sherrod Brown released a statement that "American workers have known for years the Wall Street system is broken. They've been *paying the price*" (Ewall-Wice, He, and Hudak 2021; emphasis added). With instant, simultaneous communication on the Internet on a mass scale, would change from the grassroots be possible in ways that the separated individual rags-to-riches model was not?

Howells answered a similar question for his generation of the 1890s facing both financial boom and bust by asking, "Does anything from without change us?" He answered that "Conditions make character" and hoped that people would not surrender to forces that are too mammoth or inscrutable. As a nation whose citizens are often characterized as "restless," the United States fosters criticism of the status quo and the Americanness of political change. Americans also extoll the individual's capacity for change starting with the body while also bemoaning the vastness of social action across space that is as imposing and elusive as the Grand Canyon. The consideration of individual and social change for a fragile mobile and diverse nation also suggests a paradoxical outlook based on the revolutionary heritage of the United States. Every four years in a symbolic quaternary period representing a complete cycle, the country exposes its divisions in the ritualistic presidential election. And in each election, candidates call for change. The system is intended to arrive at a single leader to negotiate a path forward, but unity is never fully possible. That tension, however, keeps the discourse going, and it often centers on the Americanness of, that is, the intellectual and cultural continuity of the past with the future.

While dissent and forcing change are valued as part of the loaded rhetoric of liberty and freedom, the potential for a structural shift is worrisome and conservative measures are often taken to prevent it. An emphasis on the external and the artificial in changing the way people live pervades the texts, sounds, and images of the 1890s as it does in the 2020s. Changing people's minds and culture rather than legislation is the most challenging, and the process of discerning what people think in and of America that I have suggested is a prerequisite of a broader inquiry, and action, for the future. While many of the conditions that Americans viewed then and now raise antimodernist plaints and calls for respect for tradition and heritage, their fundamental faith in progress and success also directs an embrace of "modernity" that involves an accelerated rate of change. Optimistic to a fault, Americans continue to entwine material with social progress and fashion dreams to resolve the basic paradoxes of Americanness.

REFERENCES

Abernethy, Francis Edward, ed. 2010. *Juneteenth Texas: Essays in African-American Folklore.* Denton: University of North Texas Press.

Achenbach, Joel. 2017. "Life Expectancy Improves for Blacks, and the Racial Gap is Closing, CDC Reports." *Washington Post* (May 2). www.washingtonpost.com/news/to-your-health/wp/2017/05/02/cdc-life-expectancy-up-for-blacks-and-the-racial-gap-is-closing/. Accessed January 23, 2021.

Adams, David Wallace. 2001. "More than a Game: The Carlisle Indians Take to the Gridiron, 1893–1917." *Western Historical Quarterly* 32: 25–53.

Adams, Henry. [1918] 1931. *The Education of Henry Adams.* New York: Modern Library.

Adler, Thomas A. 1988. "Bluegrass Music and Meal-Fried Potatoes: Food, Festival, Community." In *"We Gather Together": Food and Festival in American Life,* edited by Theodore C. Humphrey and Lin T. Humphrey, 195–204. Ann Arbor: UMI Research Press.

Agger, Ben. 1989. *Fast Capitalism: A Critical Theory of Significance.* Urbana: University of Illinois Press.

Agger, Ben. 2016. *Speeding Up Fast Capitalism: Cultures, Jobs, Families, Schools, Bodies.* New York: Routledge.

Allen, Erin. 2016. "How Did America Get Its Name." *Library of Congress Blog* (July 4). https://blogs.loc.gov/loc/2016/07/how-did-america-get-its-name/. Accessed December 28, 2020.

Allen, Frederick E. 2000. "Back to the Future: Beyond the Myth of Ever-Faster High-Tech Change and Radical New Breaks from the Past." *American Heritage* 51 (May–June): 18–20.

American Indoor Football Association. 2008. "Harrisburg Stampede to Hold Press Conference Next Tuesday." *OSC: Our Sports Central* (September 15). www.oursportscentral.com/services/releases/harrisburg-stampede-to-hold-press-conference-next-tuesday/n-3718137. Accessed January 25, 2021.

Ames, Kenneth L. 1978. "Meaning in Artifacts: Hall Furnishings in Victorian America." *Journal of Interdisciplinary History* 9: 19–46.

Ancelet, Barry Jean, and Jay Edwards. 1991. *Cajun Country*. Jackson: University Press of Mississippi.

Ancestry. 2017. "Homeownership Through the Ages: A Look at Ownership Then and Now" *ancestry Corporate* (March 23). www.ancestry.com/corporate/blog/homeownership-through-the-ages-a-look-at-ownership-then-and-now. Accessed January 31, 2021.

Anderson, Amanda. 1993. *Tainted Souls and Painted Faces: The Rhetoric of Fallenness in Victorian Culture*. Ithaca, NY: Cornell University Press.

Anderson, Caitlin, curator. 2011. "Buy Now, Pay Later: A History of Personal Credit." *Harvard Business School Historical Collections*. www.library.hbs.edu/hc/credit/credit1a.html. Accessed January 30, 2021.

Anderson, Jay Allan. 2015. "Thanksgiving in the USA: The Meal as Medium and Message." In *The Food and Folklore Reader*, edited by Lucy M. Long, 257–260. New York: Bloomsbury Academic.

Anderson, Lars. 2007. *Carlisle vs. Army: Jim Thorpe, Dwight Eisenhower, Pop Warner and the Forgotten Story of Football's Greatest Battle*. New York: Random House.

Andrews, Dan, and Aida Caldera Sánchez. 2011. "The Evolution of Homeownership: Rates in Selected OECD Countries: Demographic and Public Policy Influences." *OECD Journal: Economic Studies*. www.oecd.org/economy/growth/evolution%20of%20homeownership%20rates.pdf. Accessed January 31, 2021.

Argeros, Grigoris. 2019. "Immigrants and Some People of Color are Moving to the Suburbs—But Life There Isn't as Promising as It Once Was." *The Conversation* (November 20). https://theconversation.com/immigrants-and-some-people-of-color-are-moving-to-the-suburbs-but-life-there-isnt-as-promising-as-it-once-was-126416. Accessed January 10, 2021.

Aron, Jaime. 2008. "Cowboys Win Shootout." *Patriot-News* (Harrisburg, PA) (September 16), Sports 3.

Aronowitz, Stanley. 1992. *False Promises: The Shaping of American Working Class Consciousness*. Durham, NC: Duke University Press.

Artz, Lee, and Bren Ortega Murphy. 2000. *Cultural Hegemony in the United States*. Thousand Oaks, CA: Sage.

Asbury, Susan. 2015. "The Checkered Game of Life: Depictions of the Life Cycle in Board Games." *Midwestern Folklore* 41: 3–19.

ASPS (American Society of Plastic Surgeons). 2019. *Plastic Surgery Statistics Report: ASPA National Clearinghouse of Plastic Surgery Procedural Statistics*. www.plasticsurgery.org/documents/News/Statistics/2019/plastic-surgery-statistics-full-report-2019.pdf. Accessed February 6, 2021.

Assaf, Katya. 2012. "Magical Thinking in Trademark Law." *Law & Social Inquiry* 37: 594–626.

Austin, Michael W., ed. 2008. *Football and Philosophy: Going Deep*. Lexington: University Press of Kentucky.

Ayers, Judith. 2012. "The Rappers Giving the Finger to Fatalism." *Spiked* (April 10). www.spiked-online.com/2012/04/10/the-rappers-giving-the-finger-to-fatalism/. Accessed January 23, 2021.

Babers, Jasmine. 2016. "For Women of Color, the Glass Ceiling is Actually Made of Concrete." *Aspen Institute* (April 19). www.aspeninstitute.org/blog-posts/for-women-of-color-the-glass-ceiling-is-actually-made-of-concrete/. Accessed January 22, 2021.

Baer, Florence E. 1982. "'Give Me...Your Huddled Masses': Anti-Vietnamese Refugee Lore and the 'Image of Limited Good.'" *Western Folklore* 41: 275–291.

Baker, James. 2009. *Thanksgiving: The Biography of an American Holiday*. Lebanon, NH: University of New Hampshire Press.

Baker, Ronald L. 1986. *Jokelore: Humorous Folktales from Indiana*. Bloomington: Indiana University Press.

Banner, Lois W. 1983. *American Beauty*. New York: Knopf.

Barry, Dan, Mike McIntire, and Matthew Rosenberg. 2021. "'Our President Wants Us Here': The Mob that Stormed the Capitol." *New York Times* (January 9). www.nytimes.com/2021/01/09/us/capitol-rioters.html. Accessed January 15, 2021.

Barry, Tom. 2003. "Cosmetic Surgery Gains Points with Middle Class." *Atlanta Business Chronicle* (July 24). www.bizjournals.com/atlanta/stories/2003/07/28/focus2.html. Accessed February 6, 2021.

Barth, Gunther. 1980. *City People: The Rise of Modern City Culture in Nineteenth-Century America*. New York: Oxford University Press.

Barton, Michael. 1982. "The Lonely Crowd in Minnesota: A Psychometric Approach to the Study of the Modern American Character." In *Prospects* 7, edited by Jack Salzman, 365–390. New York: Burt Franklin.

Barton, Michael. 1983. *Life by the Moving Road: An Illustrated History of Greater Harrisburg*. Woodland Hills, CA: Windsor.

Barton, Michael. 1989. "The Victorian Jeremiad: Critics of Accumulation and Display." In *Consuming Visions: Accumulation and Display of Goods in America, 1880–1920*, edited by Simon J. Bronner, 55–72. New York: W. W. Norton.

Barton, Michael, and Jessica Dorman. 2002. *Harrisburg's Old Eighth Ward*. Charleston, SC: Arcadia.

Barton, Michael, and Simon J. Bronner. 2008. *Steelton*. Charleston, SC: Arcadia.

Bartlett, Bruce. 2020. "Donald Trump Truly is the Heir to the Legacy of Andrew Jackson." *New Republic* (August 3). https://newrepublic.com/article/158698/donald-trump-legacy-andrew-jackson. Accessed January 13, 2021.

Baseel, Casey. 2015. "5 Ways College Life is Different in Japan and U.S." *JapanToday* (December 9). https://japantoday.com/category/features/lifestyle/5-ways-college-life-is-different-in-japan-and-u-s. Accessed January 23, 2021.

Baud, Michiel, and Willem van Schendel. 1997. "Toward a Comparative History of Borderlands." *Journal of World History* 8: 211–242.

Bealle, Morris A. 1948. *The History of Football at Harvard, 1874–1948*. Washington, DC: Columbia Publishing.

Beauchamp, Zack. 2021. "Republicans Own This." *Vox* (January 8). www.vox.com/policy-and-politics/22217696/republicans-trump-capitol-hill-storming-mob-responsible. Accessed January 15, 2021.

Bellah, Robert N., Richard Madsen, William M. Sullivan, Ann Swidler, and Steven M. Tipton. 1996. *Habits of the Heart: Individualism and Commitment in American Life*. Updated ed. Berkeley: University of California Press.

Bellamy, Edward. [1888] 1982. *Looking Backward, 2000–1887*. New York: Modern Library.

Belliotti, Raymond Angelo. 2008. "Vince Lombardi and the Philosophy of Winning." In *Football and Philosophy: Going Deep*, edited by Michael W. Austin, 5–17. Lexington: University Press of Kentucky.

Bellisari, Anna W. 2013. *The Obesity Epidemic in North America: Connecting Biology and Culture*. Long Grove, IL: Waveland Press.

Bercovitch, Sacvan. 1975. *The Puritan Origins of the American Self*. New Haven: Yale University Press.

Berke, Richard L. 2002. "Money Talks; Don't Discount the Fat Cats." *New York Times* (February 17). www.nytimes.com/2002/02/17/weekinreview/money-talks-don-t-discount-the-fat-cats.html. Accessed February 7, 2021.

Bethke, Robert D. 1981. *Adirondack Voices: Woodsmen and Woods Lore.* Urbana: University of Illinois Press.

"Big Drop in Bicycles." 1898. "Big Drop in Bicycles." *Weekly Wisconsin* 51 (March 19), 2.

Binderman, Murray B., Ronald B. Newman, and Dennis Wepman. 1976. *The Life: The Lore and Folk Poetry of the Black Hustler.* Philadelphia: University of Pennsylvania Press.

Bissinger, H. G. 1990. *Friday Night Lights: A Town, a Team, and a Dream.* Reading, MA: Addison-Wesley.

Blevins, Cameron. 2014. "Space, Nation, and the Triumph of Region: A View of the World from Houston." *Journal of American History* 101: 122–147.

Bodleian Libraries. n.d. *Broadside Ballads Online.* http://ballads.bodleian.ox.ac.uk/. Accessed January 18, 2021.

Bodnar, John. [1977] 1990. *Steelton: Immigration and Industrialization, 1870–1940.* Pittsburgh: University of Pittsburgh Press.

Boissoneault, Lorraine. 2018. "A Civil War Cartoonist Created the Modern Image of Santa Claus as Union Propaganda." *Smithsonian Magazine* (December 19). www.smithsonianmag.com/history/civil-war-cartoonist-created-modern-image-santa-claus-union-propaganda-180971074/. Accessed February 6, 2021.

Bolles, Richard Nelson. 1978. *The Three Boxes of Life and How to Get Out of Them: An Introduction to Life/Work Planning.* Berkeley, CA: Ten Speed Press.

Booker, Keith M. 2006. *Drawn to Television: Prime-Time Animation from The Flintstones to Family Guy.* Westport, CT: Praeger.

Boorstin, Daniel J. 1974. *The Americans: The Democratic Experience.* New York: Random House.

Borland, Kelsi Maree. 2020. "DIY Boom Continues to Drive Demand for Home Improvement Stores." *GlobeSt.com* (October 2). www.globest.com/2020/10/02/diy-boom-continues-to-drive-demand-for-home-improvement-stores/?slreturn=20210031111848. Accessed January 31, 2021.

Bouchette, Ed. 2008. "Steelers Notebook: Polamalu Criticizes Current State of NFL." *Pittsburgh Post-Gazette* (October 16). www.post-gazette.com/pg/08290/920304-66.stm. Accessed February 10, 2009.

Bowlby, Rachel. 1985. *Just Looking: Consumer Culture in Dreiser, Gissing, and Zola.* New York: Methuen.

Bowles, Samuel, Richard Edwards, and Frank Roosevelt. 2005. *Understanding Capitalism: Competition, Command, and Change,* third edition. New York: Oxford University Press.

Boyer, R. Troy. 2019. "Farm, Town, and Country in American Folklore and Folklife." In *The Oxford Handbook of American Folklore and Folklife Studies,* edited by Simon J. Bronner, 539–554. New York: Oxford University Press.

Brandes, Stanley H. 1987. *Forty: The Age and the Symbol.* Knoxville: University of Tennessee Press.

Brands, H.W. 2004. *Lone Star Nation: How a Ragged Army of Volunteers Won the Battle for Texas Independence, and Changed America.* New York: Doubleday.

Brands, H.W. 2010. *American Colossus: The Triumph of Capitalism, 1865–1900.* New York: Anchor Books.

Briggs, Bruce, ed. 1981. *The New Class?* New York: McGraw Hill.

Bringéus, Nils-Arvid. 1988. "Pictures of the Life Cycle." *Ethnologia Scandinavica*: 5–33.

Bronner, Simon J. 1986a. *Grasping Things: Folk Material Culture and Mass Society in America*. Lexington: University Press of Kentucky.
Bronner, Simon J. 1986b. "Material Culture and Region: Lessons from Folk Studies." *Kentucky Folklore Record* 32: 1–16.
Bronner, Simon J. 1989. "Object Lessons: The Work of Ethnological Museums and Collections." In *Consuming Visions: Accumulation and Display of Goods in America, 1880–1920*, edited by Simon J. Bronner, 217–254. New York: W. W. Norton.
Bronner, Simon J. 1996. *The Carver's Art: Crafting Meaning from Wood*. Lexington: University Press of Kentucky.
Bronner, Simon J. 1998a. *Following Tradition: Folklore in the Discourse of American Culture*. Logan: Utah State University Press.
Bronner, Simon J. 1998b. *Popularizing Pennsylvania: Henry W. Shoemaker and the Progressive Uses of Folklore and History*. University Park: Pennsylvania State University Press.
Bronner, Simon J. 2000. "The American Concept of Tradition: Folklore in the Discourse of Traditional Values." *Western Folklore* 59: 87–104.
Bronner, Simon J. 2002. *Folk Nation: Folklore in the Creation of American Tradition*. Lanham, MD: Rowman & Littlefield.
Bronner, Simon J. 2011. *Explaining Traditions: Folk Behavior in Modern Culture*. Lexington: University Press of Kentucky.
Bronner, Simon J. 2012. *Campus Traditions: Folklore from the Old-Time College to the Modern Mega-University*. Jackson: University Press of Mississippi.
Bronner, Simon J. 2019. *The Practice of Folklore: Essays Toward a Theory of Tradition*. Jackson: University Press of Mississippi.
Bronner, Simon J. 2021. *Jewish Cultural Studies*. Detroit: Wayne State University Press.
Bronstein, Arthur J. 1962. "Let's Take Another Look at New York City Speech." *American Speech* 37: 13–26.
Brown, Allison. 2001. "Counting Farmers Markets." *Geographical Review* 91: 655–674.
Brown, Foxy. 2003. "My Life." In *Cradle 2 The Grave*, produced by Jazz Young. CD audio. New York: Def Jam.
Brown, Jim. 2007. "Is American Football Too Violent?" *Streetdirectory* (April 27). www.streetdirectory.com/travel_guide/46334/recreation_and_sports/is_american_football_too_violent.html. Accessed January 25, 2021.
Brown, Ras Michael. 2012. *African-Atlantic Cultures and the South Carolina Lowcountry*. Cambridge, UK: Cambridge University Press.
Brunstetter, Wanda, and Jean Brunstetter. 2017. *The Farmers' Market Mishap*. Uhrichsville, OH: Shiloh Run Press.
Bryant, Taylor. 2020. "How the Suburbs Became the Perfect Setting for Horror Movies." *Nylon*. www.nylon.com/articles/suburbs-depicted-in-movies. Accessed January 10, 2021.
Buchan, David. 1972. *The Ballad and the Folk*. London: Routledge & Kegan Paul.
Burdan, Amanda C., Betsy Fahlman, Christine Podmaniczky, Jonathan Walz, and Catherine Whitney. 2016. *Rural Modern: American Art Beyond the City*. New York: Rizzoli.
Burne-Jones, SirPhilip. 1904. *Dollars and Democracy*. New York: D. Appleton.
Bush, Harold K., Jr. 1996. "Structural America: The Persistence of Oppositional Paradigm in American Literary Theory." *College Literature* 23: 181–188.
Butsch, Richard. 2003. "Ralph, Fred, Archie, and Homer: Why Television Keeps Re-Creating the White Male Working-Class Buffoon." In *Gender, Race, and Class in Media: A Text Reader*, second edition, edited by Gail Dines and Jean Humez, 547–585. Sage Publications.

Byrd, Matthew. 2020. "Madden NFL 21 Sales Figures Seemingly Unaffected by Negative Reviews." *Den of Geek* (September 16). www.denofgeek.com/games/madden-nfl-21-sales-figures-details/. Accessed January 26, 2021.

Camic, Charles. 2020. *Veblen: The Making of an Economist Who Unmade Economics*. Cambridge, MA: Harvard University Press.

Camp, Charles. 1989. *American Foodways: What, When, Why and How We Eat in America*. Little Rock: August House.

Camp, Walter. 1894. *American Football*. New York: Harper & Brothers.

Campbell, David E., John C. Green, and J. Quin Monson. 2014. *Seeking the Promised Land: Mormons and American Politics*. New York: Cambridge University Press.

Canary, Robert H. 1968. "Playing the Game of Life." *Journal of Popular Culture* 1: 427–432.

Canning, Andrea, Rob Wallace, and Lauren Sher. 2011. "Inside Charlie Sheen's World: Star Says Life with 'Goddesses' Is 'Perfect'." *ABC News* (February 28). https://abcnews.go.com/Entertainment/charlie-sheen-opens-relationship-goddesses-vow-protect-family/story?id=13022500. Accessed January 24, 2021.

Cantú, Norma E. 1999. "La Quinceañera: Towards an Ethnographic Analysis of a Life Cycle Ritual." *Southern Folklore* 56: 73–101.

Cantú, Norma E. 2002. "Chicana Life-Cycle Rituals." In *Chicana Traditions: Continuity and Change*, edited by Norma E. Cantú and Olga Nájera-Ramírez, 15–34. Urbana: University of Illinois Press.

Cantú, Norma E. 2005. "*Muy Macho*: Traditional Practices in the Formation of Latino Masculinity in South Texas Border Culture." In *Manly Traditions: Folk Roots of American Masculinities*, edited by Simon J. Bronner, 116–133. Bloomington: Indiana University Press.

Carnegie, Andrew. 2006. *The "Gospel of Wealth" Essays and Other Writings*. New York: Penguin.

Carswell, Sue. 2008. "Does Palin Realize Joe SixPack is Leaning Toward Obama?" *Vanity Fair* (October 3). www.vanityfair.com/news/2008/10/joe-sixpack-supports-barack-obama. Accessed February 6, 2021.

Carter, Sarah Anne. 2018. *Object Lessons: How Nineteenth-Century Americans Learned to Make Sense of the Material World*. New York: Oxford University Press.

Cary, Francine C. 1977. "The World a Department Store: Bradford Peck and the Utopian Endeavor." *American Quarterly* 29: 370–384.

CDC. n.d. "Health-Related Quality of Life (HRQOL): Report Cards." *Centers for Disease Control and Prevention*. www.cdc.gov/hrqol/applications/report_cards.htm. Accessed February 6, 2021.

Cetron, Marvin, and Owen Davies. 1980. *American Renaissance: Our Lives at the Turn of the 21st Century*. New York: St. Martin's Press.

Cha, Taesuh. 2016. "The Return of Jacksonianism: The International Implications of the Trump Phenomenon." *Washington Quarterly* 39: 83–97.

Chávez, Alex E. 2012. "Ballad of Gregorio Cortez." In *Celebrating Latino Folklore: An Encyclopedia of Cultural Traditions*, edited by María Herrera-Sobek, 85–88. Santa Barbara, CA: ABC-CLIO.

Chavis, Shaun. 2007. "Black-eyed Peas." In *The New Encyclopedia of Southern Culture, Volume 7: Foodways*, edited by John T. Edge, 125–127. Chapel Hill: University of North Carolina Press.

Cherry, Conrad. 1998. "Westward the Course of Destiny." In *God's New Israel: Religious Interpretations of American Destiny*, edited by Conrad Cherry, 113–121. Revised and updated edition. Chapel Hill: University of North Carolina Press.

Chevan, Albert. 1989. "The Growth of Home Ownership: 1940–1980." *Demography* 26: 249–266.

Clark, Clifford Edward. 1987. *The American Family Home, 1800–1960*. Chapel Hill: University of North Carolina Press.

Clark, Sue A., and Edith Wyatt. 1911. *Making Both Ends Meet: The income and Outlay of New York City Working Girls*. New York: Macmillan.

Clements, William M. 1979. "The Folklorist, The Folk, and the Region." *Missouri Folklore Society Journal* 1: 44–54.

Clint, Caffeinated. 2005. "Fonda Agrees to 9 to 5 Sequel." *Moviehole* (July 26). https://moviehole.net/fonda-agrees-to-9-to-5-sequel/. Accessed January 29, 2021.

Cohen, Norm. 2005. *Folk Music: A Regional Exploration*. Westport, CT: Greenwood Press.

Cohn, D'Vera, and Rich Morin. 2008. "Who Moves? Who Stays Put? Where's Home?" *Pew Research Center* (December 17). www.pewsocialtrends.org/2008/12/17/who-moves-who-stays-put-wheres-home. Accessed December 30, 2018.

Cole, Thomas R. 1992. *The Journey of Life: A Cultural History of Aging in America*. Cambridge, UK: Cambridge University Press.

Collier, Price. 1898. "Sport's Place in the Nation's Well-Being." *Outing* 32: 382–388.

Collins, William J., and Robert A. Margo. 2011. "Race and Home Ownership from the End of the civil War to the Present." *American Economic Review* 101: 355–359.

Comenius, John Amos. 1810. *Joh. Amos Coemnii, Orbis Sensualium Pictus: Joh. Amos Comenius's Visible World, or A Nomenclature, and Pictures of All the Chief Things that Are in the World and of Men's Employments Therein*, translated by Charles Hoole. New York: T. & J. Swords.

"Common Sense." 1904. *Common-Sense* (June), 16–18.

Conner, Cheryl. 2012. "Who's Starting America's New Businesses? And Why?" *Forbes* (July 22). www.forbes.com/sites/cherylsnappconner/2012/07/22/whos-starting-americas-new-businesses-and-why/?sh=5b2a3f9e2787. Accessed January 29, 2021.

Contosta, David R. 2002. "Reforming the Commonwealth, 1900–1950." In *Pennsylvania: A History of the Commonwealth*, edited by Randall M. Miller and William Pencak, 257–316. University Park: Pennsylvania State University Press.

Cook, Alex V. 2012. *Saturday Night: Looking for a Good Time in South Louisiana's Juke Joints, Honky-Tonks, and Dance Halls*. Baton Rouge: Louisiana State University Press.

Cook, Bob. 2019. "High School Football Participation is on a Decade-Long Decline." *Forbes* (August 29). www.forbes.com/sites/bobcook/2019/08/29/high-school-football-participation-is-on-a-decade-long-decline/?sh=ca73a1433ded. Accessed January 30, 2021.

Cooper, James Fenimore. [1827–1841] 1985. *The Leatherstocking Tales*, 2 volumes. New York: Library of America.

Cooper, Melissa L. 2017. *Making Gullah: A History of Sapelo Islanders, Race, and the American Imagination*. Chapel Hill: University of North Carolina Press.

Cooper, Richard N., and Richard Layard, eds. 2002. *What the Future Holds: Insights from Social Science*. Cambridge, MA: MIT Press.

Corn, Joseph J., and Brian Horrigan. [1984] 1996. *Yesterday's Tomorrows: Past Visions of the American Future*. Baltimore: Johns Hopkins University Press.

Cornell University. 2001. "What is A US American? Part One." International Students and Scholars Office. www.isso.cornell.edu/students/us1.html. Accessed October 5, 2001.

Cortada, James W. 2004. *The Digital Hand: How Computers Changed the Work of American Manufacturing, Transportation, and Retail Industries*. New York: Oxford University Press.

Cowals, Dennis. 2001. "The Bicycle & the West." https://cliffhanger76.tripod.com/bikewest/1910/index.html. Accessed January 30, 2021.

Cowie, Jefferson R. 2012. *Stayin' Alive: The 1970s and the Last Days of the Working Class*. New York: New Press.

Craggs, Tommy. 2008. "Why Are Wide Receivers Such Flamboyant Egomaniacs?" *Play: The New York Times Sports Magazine* (September), 42–43.

Crèvecoeur, Hector St. John de. [1782] 1971. *Letters from an American Farmer*. New York: Dutton.

Cross, Gary. 2015. *Consumed Nostalgia: Memory in the Age of Fast Capitalism*. New York: Columbia University Press.

Cullen, Jim. 2003. *The American Dream: A Short History of an Idea That Shaped a Nation*. New York: Oxford University Press.

Culler, Jonathan. 2013. "Lévi-Strauss: Good to Think With." *Yale French Studies* 123: 6–13.

Cunningham, Ken. 2004. "True Confessions of an Eight-Year-Old Warrior." *Qualitative Inquiry* 10: 706–714.

Darowski, Joseph J., and Kate Darowski. 2017. *Frasier: A Cultural History*. Lanham, MD: Rowman & Littlefield.

Davies, Wallace Evan. 1947. "A Collectivist Experiment Down East: Bradford Peck and the Coöperative Association of America." *New England Quarterly* 20: 471–491.

Davis, Matthew. 2005. "Remaking the Nation through Brotherhood in the Utopian Fiction of William Dean Howells and Edward Bellamy." *Contemporary Justice Review* 8: 177–192.

Davis, Parke Hill. 1912. *Football: The American Intercollegiate Game*. New York: Scribner's.

Davison, Scott A. 2008. "Virtue and Violence: Can a Good Football Player Be a Good Person?" In *Football and Philosophy: Going Deep*, edited by Michael W. Austin, 67–79. Lexington: University Press of Kentucky.

Deane, Michael T. 2020. "Top 6 Reasons New Businesses Fail." *Investopedia* (February 28). www.investopedia.com/financial-edge/1010/top-6-reasons-new-businesses-fail.aspx#:~:text=According%20to%20the%20U.S.%20Bureau,to%2015%20years%20or%20more. Accessed January 29, 2021.

Dégh, Linda. 1994. *American Folklore and the Mass Media*. Bloomington: Indiana University Press.

Dennis, James M. 1998. *Renegade Regionalists: The Modern Independence of Grant Wood, Thomas Hart Benton, and John Steuart Curry*. Madison: University of Wisconsin Press.

Dennis, Latoya, and Michelle Maternowski. 2017. "Tosa Together Hopes to Create a City Where Everyone Feels They Belong." *WUWM* (March 9). www.wuwm.com/post/tosa-together-hopes-create-city-where-everyone-feels-they-belong. Accessed January 1, 2021.

Desmond, Harry W., and Herbert Croly. 1903. *Stately Homes in America: From Colonial Times to the Present Day*. New York: D. Appleton.

Desmond, Matthew. 2019. "In Order to Understand the Brutality of American Capitalism, You Have to Start on the Plantation." *New York Times Magazine* (August 14). www.nytimes.com/interactive/2019/08/14/magazine/slavery-capitalism.html. Accessed January 29, 2021.

Devine, Jason. 2017. "Births, Deaths, and Migration Transform Communities." *We Are a Changing Nation: A Series on Population Trends* (August 9). www.census.gov/library/stories/2017/08/changing-nation-demographic-trends.html. Accessed December 30, 2018.

Diggins, John P. 1978. *The Bard of Savagery: Thorstein Veblen and Modern Social Theory*. New York: Seabury Press.

Diner, Hasia R. 2000. *Lower East Side Memories: A Jewish Place in America*. Princeton, NJ: Princeton University Press.

Dobbs, Michael. 2014. "The Real Story of the 'Football' that Follows the President Everywhere." *Smithsonian Magazine* (October). www.smithsonianmag.com/history/real-story-football-follows-president-everywhere-180952779/. Accessed April 4, 2021.

Donehoo, George P. 1927. *Harrisburg: The City Beautiful, Romantic and Historic*. Harrisburg, PA: Stackpole Books.

Dorfman, Joseph. [1934] 1961. *Thorstein Veblen and His America*. New York: Viking-Penguin.

Dorson, Richard M., ed. 1964. *Buying the Wind: Regional Folklore in the United States*. Chicago: University of Chicago Press.

Dorson, Richard M. 1966. "The Question of Folklore in a New Nation." *Journal of the Folklore Institute* 3: 277–298.

Dorson, Richard M. 1973. *America in Legend: Folklore from the Colonial Period to the Present*. New York: Random House.

Dorson, Richard M. [1952] 2008. *Bloodstoppers and Bearwalkers: Folk Traditions of Michigan's Upper Peninsula*, edited by James P. Leary. Madison: University of Wisconsin Press.

Douglas, Ann. 1977. *The Feminization of American Culture*. New York: Knopf.

Doyle, Charles Clay, Wolfgang Mieder, and Fred R. Shapiro, comps. 2012. *The Dictionary of Modern Proverbs*. New Haven: Yale University Press.

Dreiser, Theodore. [1900] 1970. *Sister Carrie*. New York: W. W. Norton.

Druckerman, Pamela. 2018. "How the Midlife Crisis Came to Be." *Atlantic* (May 29). www.theatlantic.com/family/archive/2018/05/the-invention-of-the-midlife-crisis/561203/. Accessed January 22, 2021.

Dundes, Alan. 1962. "The Folklore of Wishing Wells." *American Imago* 19: 27–34.

Dundes, Alan. 1964a. "On Game Morphology: A Study of the Structure of Non-Verbal Folklore." *New York Folklore Quarterly* 20: 276–288.

Dundes, Alan. 1964b. *The Morphology of North American Indian Folktales*. Helsinki: Academia Scientiarum Fennica.

Dundes, Alan. 1969. "Thinking Ahead: A Folkloristic Reflection of the Future Orientation in American Worldview." *Anthropological Quarterly* 42: 53–72.

Dundes, Alan. 1971. "Folk Ideas as Units of Worldview." *Journal of American Folklore* 84: 93–103.

Dundes, Alan. 1978. "Into the Endzone for a Touchdown: A Psychoanalytic Consideration of American Football." *Western Folklore* 37: 75–88.

Dundes, Alan. 1981. "Many Hands Make Light Work or Caught in the Act of Screwing in Light Bulbs." *Western Folklore* 40: 261–266.

Dundes, Alan. 1997. *From Game to War and Other Psychoanalytic Essays on Folklore*. Lexington: University Press of Kentucky.

Dundes, Alan. 2004. "As the Crow Flies: A Straightforward Study of Lineal Worldview in American Folk Speech." In *What Goes Around Comes Around: The Circulation of Proverbs in Contemporary Life*, edited by Kimberly J. Lau, Peter Tokofsky, and Stephen D. Winick, 171–187. Logan: Utah State University Press.

Dundes, Alan, and Carl R. Pagter. 1975. *Work Hard and You Shall Be Rewarded: Urban Folklore from the Paperwork Empire*. Bloomington: Indiana University Press.

Durham, Michael. 1969. "A Short Talk with a First Novelist." *Life Magzine* (August 29), 10.

Dyer, Braven. 1956. "Sports Parade." *Los Angeles Times* (April 25). Part 4, 1.

Edison, Carol. 1988. "Roast Beef and Pit-Barbecued Lamb: The Role of Food at Two Utah Homecoming Celebrations." In *"We Gather Together": Food and Festival in American Life*, edited by Theodore C. Humphrey and Lin T. Humphrey, 137–152. Ann Arbor: UMI Research Press.

Edmundson, Mark. 2014. "Op-Ed: Football is America's War Game." *Los Angeles Times* (August 23). www.latimes.com/opinion/op-ed/la-oe-edmundson-americas-and-war-connection-20140824-story.html. Accessed January 25, 2021.

Ehrenreich, Barbara. 1989. *Fear of Falling: The Inner Life of the Middle Class*. New York: Pantheon.

Eisenstock, Alan. 2001. *Sports Talk: A Journey Inside the World of Sports Talk Radio*. New York: Pocket Books.

Elder, Glen H., Jr., and Janet Z. Giele, eds. 2009. *The Craft of Life Course Research*. New York: Guilford.

Elder, Glen H., Jr., and Michael J. Shanahan. 2006. "The Life Course and Human Development." In *Handbook of Child Psychology: Theoretical Models of Human Development*, edited by Richard M. Lerner and William Damon, 665–715. Hoboken, NJ: John Wiley & Sons.

Eliason, Eric. A. 2006. "Mormon Culture Region." In *Encyclopedia of American Folklife*, edited by Simon J. Bronner, 868–871. Armonk, NY: M. E. Sharpe.

Emmet, Boris, and John E. Jeuck. 1950. *Catalogues and Counters: A History of Sears, Roebuck and Company*. Chicago: University of Chicago Press.

Engelhardt, Tom. 2007. *The End of Victory Culture: Cold War America and the Disillusioning of a Generation*. Amherst: University of Massachusetts Press.

Engeman, Thomas S. 2001. "Religion and Politics the American Way: The Exemplary William Dean Howells." *Review of Politics* 63: 107–127.

English Broadside Ballad Archive. n.d. http://ebba.english.ucsb.edu/. Accessed January 18, 2021.

Epting, Chris. 2002. *Los Angeles Memorial Coliseum*. Charleston, SC: Arcadia.

Erlewine, Michael. 2010. *Blues in Black & White: The Landmark Ann Arbor Blues Festivals*. Ann Arbor: University of Michigan Press.

Ewall-Wice, Sarah, Alan He, and Zak Hudak. 2021. "Congress Plans Hearings after GameStop Stock Frenzy and Robinhood Trading Freeze." *CBS News* (January 29). www.cbsnews.com/news/gamestop-robinhood-trading-freeze-congress-hearings/. Accessed January 31, 2021.

Fairlie, Robert. 2012. *Open For Business: How Immigrants are Driving Small Business Creation in the United States*. www.newamericaneconomy.org/wp-content/uploads/2013/07/openforbusiness.pdf. Accessed January 29, 2021.

Falk, Gerhard. 2005. *Football and American Identity*. New York: Haworth Press.

Fatphobia Busters. 2018. "Queer & Fatphobic Eye: S01 E07 'Below Average Joe'." *Fatphobia Busters* (October 7). Blog Post. https://fatphobiabusters.tumblr.com/post/178823996283/queer-fatphobic-eye-s01e07-below-average-joe. Accessed February 7, 2021.

Feinsilber, Mike, and William B. Mead. 1980. *American Averages*. Garden City, NY: Dolphin Books.

Feinstein, John. 2006. *Next Man Up: A Year Behind the Lines in Today's NFL*. New York: Little, Brown.

Felkins, Patricia K., and Irvin Goldman. 1993. "Political Myth as Subjective Narrative: Some Interpretations and Understandings of John F. Kennedy." *Political Psychology* 14: 447–467.

Ferenczi, Sándor. [1952] 2018. "The Ontogenesis of the Interest in Money." In *First Contributions to Psycho-Analysis*, by Sándor Ferenczi, translated by Ernest Jones, 319–331. London: Routledge.
Ferris, William. 1982. *Local Color: A Sense of Place in Folk Art*. New York: McGraw-Hill.
Fife, Austin E. 1988. *Exploring Western Americana*, edited by Alta Fife. Ann Arbor: UMI Research Press.
Fine, Gary Alan. 1984. "Evaluating Psychoanalytic Folklore: Are Freudians Ever Right?" *New York Folklore* 10: 5–20.
Fine, Gary Alan. 1994. *Manufacturing Tales: Sex and Money in Contemporary Legends*. Knoxville: University of Tennessee Press.
Fine, Gary Alan, and Patricia A. Turner. 2001. *Whispers on the Color Line: Rumor and Race in America*. Berkeley: University of California Press.
Fisher, David Hackett. 1989. *Albion's Seed: Four British Folkways in America*. New York: Oxford University Press.
Flegenheimer, Matt. 2020. "Joe Biden's Time in Sarah Palin's Shadow." *New York Times* (May 11). www.nytimes.com/2020/05/11/us/politics/joe-biden-sarah-palin-2008.html. Accessed February 6, 2021.
Fleming, Thomas. 1901. *Around the "Pan" with Uncle Hank: His Trip through the Pan-American Exposition*. New York: Nut Shell Publishing.
Fluhman, J. Spencer. 2012. *"A Peculiar People": Anti-Mormonism and the Making of Religion in Nineteenth-Century America*. Chapel Hill: University of North Carolina Press.
Foley, Douglas E. 1990. "The Great American Football Ritual: Reproducing Race, Class, and Gender Inequality." *Sociology of Sport Journal* 7: 111–135.
Foley, Douglas E. 1994. *Learning Capitalist Culture: Deep in the Heart of Tejas*. Philadelphia: University of Pennsylvania Press.
Forbes, Gordon B., Leah E. Adams-Curtis, Alexis H. Pakalka, and Kay B. White. 2006. "Dating Aggression, Sexual Coercion, and Aggression-Supporting Attitudes Among College Men as a Function of Participation in Aggressive High School Sports." *Violence Among Women* 12: 441–455.
Forrest, David V. 1990. "Further Developmental Stages of the Interest in Money." *American Journal of Psychoanalysis* 50: 319–335.
Forney, Craig A. 2007. *The Holy Trinity of American Sports: Civil Religion in Football, Baseball, and Basketball*. Macon, GA: Mercer University Press.
Foster, George M. 1965. "Peasant Society and the Image of Limited Good." *American Anthropologist* 67: 293–315.
Foster, Jordana Bieze. 2010. "Out on a Limb: Flip-flop Flak." *Lower Extremity Review* (September). https://lermagazine.com/editor_memo/out-on-a-limb-flip-flop-flak. Accessed February 6, 2021.
Fox, Cynthia A. 2007. "Franco-American Voices: French in the Northeastern United States Today." *French Review* 80: 1278–1292.
Fox, Richard Wightman, and T. J. Jackson Lears. 1983. *The Culture of Consumption: Critical Essays in American History, 1880–1980*. New York: Pantheon.
Fox-Genovese, Elizabeth, and Eugene Genovese. 2005. *The Mind of the Master Class: History and Faith in the Southern Slaveholders' Worldview*. Cambridge, UK: Cambridge University Press.
Franklin, John Hope. 2007. "The Cover-Up." *The Atlantic* (November). www.theatlantic.com/magazine/archive/2007/11/the-cover-up/306290/. Accessed January 10, 2021.
Franzen, Axel. 2000. "Does the Internet Make Us Lonely?" *European Sociological Review* 16: 427–438.

Fraser, Donald J. 2018. "Trump Compares Himself to Andrew Jackson. Is it a Fair Comparison?" *History News Network* (April 14). https://historynewsnetwork.org/article/168679. Accessed January 13, 2021.

Frederic, Harold. [1896] 1960. *The Damnation of Theron Ware*, edited by Everett Carter. Cambridge, MA: Harvard University Press.

Freese, Peter. 2013. "The 'Journey of Life' in American Fiction." *Hungarian Journal of English and American Studies* 19: 247–283.

French, Sally. 2016. "How Americans Have Grown More Obese Over Time, In One Depressing Chart." *MarketWatch* (July 5). www.marketwatch.com/story/one-chart-shows-how-americans-grew-larger-over-time-2016-2007-05. Accessed February 5, 2021.

Freud, Sigmund. [1918] 1957. "The Taboo of Virginity." In *The Standard Edition of the Complete Psychological Works of Sigmund Freud, Volume XI*, edited by James Strachey, 191–208. London: Hogarth Press.

Freud, Sigmund. 1959. *Group Psychology and the Analysis of the Ego*, translated and edited by James Strachey. New York: W. W. Norton.

Friedman, Hilary Levey. 2013. "When Did Competitive Sports Take Over American Childhood?" *Atlantic* (September 20). www.theatlantic.com/education/archive/2013/09/when-did-competitive-sports-take-over-american-childhood/279868/. Accessed February 6, 2021.

Friedman, Monroe, Piet Vanden Abeele, and Koen De Vos. 1993. "Boorstin's Consumption Community Concept: A Tale of Two Countries." *Journal of Consumer Policy* 16: 35–60.

Friends of Bernie Sanders. 2020. "Issues: Racial Justice." *Bernie*. https://berniesanders.com/issues/racial-justice/. Accessed February 6, 2021.

"From Pushcart to Affluence: Robert S. Smith Started Thirty Years Ago With $5.75 and Sold a Lot for $1,000,000 the Other Day—Business Philosophy of a Successful Man Who is Sure Opportunities Are as Great Now as Ever They Were." 1912. *Sun Magazine* (New York), October 6, p. 11.

Fryar, Cheryl D., Margaret D. Carroll, and Cynthia L. Ogden. 2018. "Prevalence of Overweight, Obesity, and Severe Obesity Among Children and Adolescents Aged 2–19 Years: United States, 1963–1965 Through 2015–2016." *Health E-States: National Center for Health Statistics* (September). www.cdc.gov/nchs/data/hestat/obesity_child_15_16/obesity_child_15_16.pdf. Accessed February 5, 2021.

Gallagher, Aileen. 2004. *The Muckrakers: American Journalism During the Age of Reform*. New York: Rosen Central.

Garber, Marjorie. 2012. *Loaded Words*. New York: Fordham University Press.

Gardner, Leonard. 1969. *Fat City*. New York: Farrar, Status and Giroux.

Garreau, Joel. 1981. *The Nine Nations of North America*. Boston: Houghton Mifflin.

Garreau, Joel. 2014. "Nine Nations of North America, 30 Years Later." *New York Times*. (July 3). www.nytimes.com/roomfordebate/2014/07/03/where- do-borders-need-to-be-redrawn/nine-nations-of-north-america-30-years-later. Accessed December 30, 2018.

Gastil, Raymond D. 1975. *Cultural Regions of the United States*. Seattle: University of Washington Press.

Gibson, William James. 1994. *Warrior Dreams: Violence and Manhood in Post-Vietnam America*. New York: Hill & Wang.

Gilbert, Elizabeth. 2002. *The Last American Man*. New York: Penguin.

Gillam, Bernhard, artist. n.d. "The Protectors of Our Industries." *Puck* (February 7), 368. www.loc.gov/resource/cph.3g03108/. Accessed February 6, 2021.

Gillespie, Angus. 2002. *Twin Towers: The Life of New York City's World Trade Center*. Revised edition. New York: New American Library.

Gimpel, James G., Nathan Lovin, Bryant Moy, and Andrew Reeves. 2020. "The Urban-Rural Gulf in American Political Behavior." *Political Behavior* 42: 1343–1368.

Glass, Joseph W. 1986. *The Pennsylvania Culture Region: A View from the Barn*. Ann Arbor: UMI Research Press.

Glassie, Henry. 1968. *Pattern in the Material Folk Culture of the Eastern United States*. Philadelphia: University of Pennsylvania Press.

Glassie, Henry, Clifford R. Murphy, and Douglas Dowling Peach. 2015. *Ola Belle Reed and Southern Mountain Music on the Mason-Dixon Line*. Atlanta, GA: Dust-to-Digital.

Gleick, James. 1999. *Faster: The Acceleration of Just About Everything*. New York: Pantheon.

Glenday, Craig, ed. 2008. *Guinness World Records 2008: Gamer's Edition*. London: Guinness World Records Limited.

Goldstein, Diane E., and Amy Shuman. 2012. "The Stigmatized Vernacular: Where Reflexivity Meets Untellability." *Journal of Folklore Research* 49: 113–126.

Gonzalez, Marybel. 2016. "The Quinceañera, a Rite of Passage in Transition." *New York Times* (June 4). www.nytimes.com/2016/06/05/nyregion/the-quinceanera-a-rite-of-passage-in-transition.html. Accessed January 23, 2021.

González-Martín, Rachel. 2016. "Barrio Ritual and Pop Rite: Quinceañeras in the Folklore-Popular Culture Borderlands." In *The Routledge Companion to Latina/o Popular Culture*, edited by Frederick Luis Aldama, 279–290. New York: Routledge.

González-Martín, Rachel. 2020. "Buying the Dream: Relating 'Traditional' Dress to Consumer Practices in US Quinceañeras." In *meXicana Fashions: Politics, Self-Adornment, and Identity Construction*, edited by Aída Hurtado and Norma E. Cantú, 137–157. Austin: University of Texas Press.

Goodman, Laurie S., and Christopher Mayer. 2018. "Homeownership and the American Dream." *Journal of Economic Perspectives* 32: 31–58.

Goodman, Steven. 2003. *Teaching Youth Media: A Critical Guide to Literacy, Video Production and Social Change*. New York: Teachers College Press.

Grabowski, Michael. 2014. "Resignation and Positive Thinking in the Working-class Family Sitcom." *Atlantic Journal of Communication* 22: 124–137.

Graham, Carol. 2017. *Happiness for All? Unequal Hopes and Lives in Pursuit of the American Dream*. Princeton, NJ: Princeton University Press.

Graham, Joe S., ed. 1991. *Hecho en Tejas: Texas-Mexican Folk Arts and Crafts*. Denton: University of North Texas Press.

Grames, Eliza, and Mary Vitcenda. 2012. "Community Festivals—Big Benefits, But Risks, Too." *University of Minnesota Extension*. https://extension.umn.edu/vital-connections/community-festivals-big-benefits-risks-too. Accessed January 24, 2021.

Grantham, Dewey W. 1992. *The Life and Death of the Solid South: A Political History*. Lexington: University Press of Kentucky.

Gray, Jim. 2015. "Interview with Jim Gray." *FloydMayweather* (September 11). www.youtube.com/watch?v=blsBk0XlV4g. Accessed January 29, 2021.

Gray, Jules. 2015. "Can the US Ever Get Europeans to Like American Football?" *BD Health & Fitness* (August 25). www.businessdestinations.com/relax/health-and-fitness/can-the-us-ever-get-europeans-to-like-american-football/. Accessed January 25, 2021.

Greenfield, Jeff. 1999. "The Black and White Truth about Basketball." In *Signifyin(g), Sanctifyin', and Slam Dunking: A Reader in African American Expressive Culture*, edited by Gena Dagel Caponi, 373–378. Amherst: University of Massachusetts Press.

Gregory, Sean. 2017. "How Kids' Sports Became a $15 Billion Industry." *Time* (August 24). https://time.com/4913687/how-kids-sports-became-15-billion-industry/. Accessed February 6, 2021.

Grider, Sylvia. 2001. "Epics of Defeat: Texas' Alamo and Scotland's Culloden." In *2001: A Texas Folklore Odyssey*, edited by Francis Edward Abernethy, 74–89. Denton: University of North Texas Press.

Grier, Katherine C. 2010. *Culture & Comfort: Parlor Making and Middle-Class Identity, 1850–1930*. Revised edition. Washington, DC: Smithsonian Books.

Griffith, James S. 1995. *A Shared Space: Folklife in the Arizona-Sonora Borderlands*. Logan: Utah State University Press.

Griffith, James S. 2011. *A Border Runs Through It: Journeys in Regional History and Folklore*. Tucson: Rio Nuevo.

Grogan, Sarah. 2017. *Body Image: Understanding Body Dissatisfaction in Men, Women and Children*, third edition. New York: Routledge.

Gunderson, Robert Gray. 1957. *The Log Cabin Campaign*. Lexington: University of Kentucky Press.

Gunton, George. 1888. *Wealth and Progress: A Critical Examination of the Wages Question and Its Economic Relation to Social Reform*. London: Macmillan.

Gunton, George. 1891. *Principles of Social Economics, Inductively Considered and Practically Applied, with Criticisms on Current Theories*. New York: G. P. Putnam's Sons.

Gunton, George. 1896. "The Opening of Biltmore." *Gunton's Magazine* (January) 10: 33–36.

Gutman, Herbert. 1976. "The Reality of the Rags-to-Riches 'Myth': The Case of Paterson, New Jersey Locomotive, Iron and Machinery Manufacturers, 1830–1880." In *Work, Culture, and Society in Industrializing America: Essays in America's Working Class and Social History*, by Herbert Gutman, 211–233. New York: Alfred A. Knopf.

Guttmann, A. 2021. "U.S. Advertising Industry-Statistics and Facts." *Statista* (January 18). www.statista.com/topics/979/advertising-in-the-us/. Accessed January 30, 2021.

Haas, Heather A. 2008. "Proverb Familiarity in the United States: Cross-Regional Comparisons of the Paremiological Minimum." *Journal of American Folklore* 121: 319–347.

Hacker, Louis M. 1957. *American Capitalism*. New York: Krieger.

Hagen, Jeff. 1999. *Fry Me to the Moon: An Illustrated Journey to Wisconsin's Famous Friday Night Fish Fry and Beyond*. Madison, WI: Prairie Oak Press.

Hallgren, Sören, and Bengt Söderberg. 1970. *Mellan Himmel och Helvete*. Stockholm: Rabén & Sjögren.

Halttunen, Karen. 1989. "From Parlor to Living Room: Domestic Space, Interior Decoration, and the Culture of Personality." In *Consuming Visions: Accumulation and Display of Goods in America, 1880–1920*, edited by Simon J. Bronner, 157–190. New York: W. W. Norton.

Hamilton, Mark. 2008. "Is the Gridiron Holy Ground?" In *Football and Philosophy: Going Deep*, edited by Michael W. Austin, 183–195. Lexington: University Press of Kentucky.

Hamlet, Janice D. 2011. "Word! The African American Oral Tradition and its Rhetorical Impact on American Popular Culture." *Black History Bulletin* 74: 27–31.

Hannah, Matthew G. 2000. "The Moral Imperative of Late Capitalism." In *Worldview Flux: Perplexed Values Among Postmodern Peoples*, edited by Jim Norwine and Jonathan M. Smith, 217–232. Lanham, MD: Lexington Books.

Hardin, Michael. 2000. "What Is the Word at Logos College? Homosocial Ritual or Homosexual Denial in Don Delillo's *End Zone?*" *Journal of Homosexuality* 40: 31–50.
Harris, Lynn B. 2014. *Patroons and Periaguas: Enslaved Watermen and Watercraft of the Lowcountry*. Columbia: University of South Carolina Press.
Harris, Marlys J. 1987. "The Theory of the Busy Class." *Money* 16 (April): 203–220.
Harris, Neil. 1981. "The Drama of Consumer Desire." In *Yankee Enterprise: The Rise of the American System of Manufactures*, edited by Otto Mayr and Robert C. Post, 189–216. Washington, DC: Smithsonian Institution Press.
"Harrisburg Great Factories Employ Thousands of Girls." 1907. *Board of Trade Journal* 2, no. 11 (October): 13.
Hartmann, Douglas. 2003. "The Sanctity of Sunday Afternoon Football: Why Men Love Sports." *Contexts* 2: 13–21.
Heilbroner, Robert L. 1960. *The Future as History: The Historic Currents of Our Time and the Direction in Which They Are Taking America*. New York: Harper and Brothers.
Henderson, Al, and Simon J. Bronner. 2013. "Reunions." In *Encyclopedia of American Folklife*, edited by Simon J. Bronner, 1097–1100. Armonk, NY: M.E. Sharpe.
Hennepin, Louis. 1950. "Myths." In *America Begins: Early American Writing*, edited by Richard M. Dorson, 292–294. New York: Pantheon.
Herrera-Sobek, María. 1993. *Northward Bound: The Mexican Immigrant Experience in Ballad and Song*. Bloomington: Indiana University Press.
Hesse-Biber, Sharlene. 2006. *The Cult of Thinness*, second edition. New York: Oxford University Press.
Higginson, Francis. 1950. "New England's Plantation." In *America Begins: Early American Writing*, edited by Richard M. Dorson, 71–79. New York: Pantheon.
Hijorth, Larissa. 2015. "Locating the Mobile and Social: A Preliminary Discussion of Camera Phones and Locative Media." In *Between Humanities and the Digital*, edited by Patrik Svensoon and David Theo Goldberg, 229–242. Cambridge, MA: MIT Press.
Hill, Denise Delis. 2004. *In Vogue: A Century of American Fashion in Advertising*. Lubbock: Texas Tech University Press.
Hines, Tesa Rigel. 2019. "At Work, Women and People of Color Still Have Not Broken the Glass Ceiling." *The Conversation* (April 29). https://theconversation.com/at-work-women-and-people-of-color-still-have-not-broken-the-glass-ceiling-115688. Accessed January 22, 2021.
Hitchcock, Karen. 2015. *Fat City*. Collingwood, VIC: Black.
Hlavaty, Craig. 2018. "Where Does 'Houston' Begin and End?" *Houston Chronicle* (August 7). www.chron.com/news/houston-texas/houston/article/Where-does-Houston-begin-and-end-13130575.php. Accessed January 1, 2021.
Hofstadter, Richard. 1955. *The Age of Reform*. New York: Vintage.
Hofstadter, Richard. 1968. *The Progressive Historians: Turner, Beard, Parrington*. New York: Knopf.
Hofstadter, Richard. 1997. "The Agrarian Myth." In *Myth America: A Historical Anthology*, edited by Patrick Gerster and Nicholas Cords, 16–21. St. James, New York: Brandywine.
Holden, Stephen. 2006. "'Quinceañera': Turning Sweet 15 in Los Angeles's Immigrant Stew." *New York Times* (August 4). www.nytimes.com/2006/08/04/movies/04quin.html?_r=0. Accessed January 23, 2021.
Holland, Jack, and Ben Fermor. 2020. "The Discursive Hegemony of Trump's Jacksonian Populism: Race, Class, and Gender in Constructions and Contestations of US National

Identity, 2016–2018." *Politics* (July). https://doi.org/10.1177/0263395720936867. Accessed January 13, 2021.

Holmes, Kathryn Marjorie. 2021. "*Your Religion is Showing: Negotiating the Culture of the Church of Jesus Christ of Latter-day Saints Through the Body.*" PhD diss. Pennsylvania State University.

Hornborg, Alf. 1992. "Machine Fetishism, Value, and the Image of Unlimited Good: Towards a Thermodynamics of Imperialism." *Man* 27: 1–18.

Horowitz, Daniel. 1980. "Consumption and Its Discontents: Simon N. Patten, Thorstein Veblen, and George Gunton." *Journal of American History* 67: 301–317.

Horowitz, Daniel. 1985. *The Morality of Spending: Attitudes toward the Consumer Society in America, 1875–1940*. Baltimore: Johns Hopkins University Press.

Horowitz, Juliana Menace, Anna Brown, and Kiana Cox. 2019. *Race in America 2019*. Washington, DC: Pew Research Center.

Hostetler, John A. 1994. *Amish Society*, fourth edition. Baltimore: Johns Hopkins University Press.

Hostetler, John A. 1997. *Hutterite Society*, second edition. Baltimore: Johns Hopkins University Press.

Hounshell, David A. 1985. *From the American System to Mass Production, 1800–1932: The Development of Manufacturing Technology in the United States*. Baltimore: Johns Hopkins University Press.

Howells, William Dean. [1894] 1957. *A Traveler from Altruria*. New York: Sagamore Press.

Howells, William Dean. 1971. *The Altrurian Romances*. New York: Arno Press.

Howells, William Dean. [1889] 1980. *A Hazard of New Fortunes*. New York: New American Library.

Howells, William Dean. [1885] 2018. *The Rise of Silas Lapham: Authoritative Text, Contexts, Criticism*, edited by Paul R. Petrie. New York: W. W. Norton.

Hubbard, William. 1981. "The Meaning of Buildings." *New Republic* 185 (November 18): 29–30.

Hubbell, Allan Forbes. 1950. *The Pronunciation of English in New York City: Consonants and Vowels*. New York: King's Crown Press.

Hubka, Thomas C. 1984. *Big House, Little House, Back House, Barn: The Connected Farm Buildings of New England*. Lebanon, NH: University Press of New England.

Hufford, Mary. 1986. *One Space, Many Places: Folklife and Land Use in New Jersey's Pinelands National Reserve*. Washington, DC: American Folklife Center, Library of Congress.

Hume, Mike. 2008. *Falls Church News-Press* (December 18). https://fcnp.com/2008/12/18/picking-splinters-the-birth-of-sudden-death/. Accessed January 25, 2021.

Humphrey, Lin T. 1979. "Small Group Festive Gatherings." *Journal of the Folklore Institute* 16: 190–201.

Humphrey, Theodore C., Sue Samuelson, and Lin T. Humphrey. 1991. "Introduction: Food and Festivity in American Life." In *"We Gather Together": Food and Festival in American Life*, edited by Theodore C. Humphrey and Lin T. Humphrey, 1–18. Logan: Utah State University Press.

Hunnicutt, Trevor, Patricia Zengerle, and Jarrett Renshaw. 2021. "Assuming U.S. Presidency, Biden Calls for End to 'Uncivil War'." *Reuters* (January 20). https://news.trust.org/item/20210120162146-fk12e/. Accessed April 8, 2021.

Hurlihy, David V. 2004. *Bicycle: The History*. New Haven: Yale University Press.

Hurtado, Albert L. 1996. "The Spanish Borderlands." *OAH Magazine of History* 10: 13–14.

Hyra, Derek. 2014. "The Back-to-the-City Movement: Neighbourhood Redevelopment and Processes of Political and Cultural Displacement." *Urban Studies* 52: 1–21.

Iggulden, Gonn, and Hal Iggulden. 2007. *The Dangerous Book for Boys*. New York: HarperCollins.

IHRSA. 2019. "2018 Shows Continuing Uptrend of U.S. Health Club Industry." *IHRSA* (April 12). www.ihrsa.org/improve-your-club/industry-news/2018-shows-continuing-uptrend-of-u-s-health-club-industry/. Accessed February 5, 2021.

Ingalls, Rebecca. 2017. *Reconstructing the Female Food-Body: Profanity, Purity, and the Bakhtinian Grotesque in Food, Feminisms, Rhetorics*, edited by Melissa A. Goldthwaite, 222–236. Carbondale: Southern Illinois University Press.

Inglewood, Marian. 1925. *Then and Now in Harrisburg*. Harrisburg, PA: Minnie I. Etzewiler.

Inkeles, Alex. 1989. "National Character: A Key to Understanding the USA" in *Understanding the USA*, edited by Peter Funke, 150–175. Tübingen: Gunter Narr.

Inskeep, Steve. 2016. "Donald Trump and the Legacy of Andrew Jackson." *The Atlantic* (November 30). www.theatlantic.com/politics/archive/2016/11/trump-and-andrew-jackson/508973/. Accessed January 13, 2021.

International Harvester. 1918. "Make the Place Homelike." Advertisement. *Reclamation Record* (December): 567.

Isenberg, David. 2011. "Money Isn't Everything; It's the Only Thing." *HuffPost* (March 25). www.huffpost.com/entry/money-isnt-everything-its_b_405089. Accessed January 29, 2021.

Ives, Mike, and Daniel Victor. 2021. "Bernie Sanders is Once Again the Star of a Meme." *New York Times* (January 21). www.nytimes.com/2021/01/21/us/politics/bernie-sanders-meme.html. Accessed February 6, 2021.

Jabbour, Alan, and Karen Singer Jabbour. 2010. *Decoration Day in the Mountains: Traditions of Cemetery Decoration in the Southern Appalachians*. Chapel Hill: University of North Carolina Press.

Jackson, Mark. 2020. "Life Begins at 40: The Demographic and Cultural Roots of the Midlife Crisis." *Notes and Records: The Royal Society Journal of the History of Science* 74: 345–364.

Jeffords, Susan. 1989. *The Remasculinization of America: Gender and the Vietnam War*. Bloomington: Indiana University Press.

Jenkins, Sally. 2007. *The Real All Americans: The Team that Changed a Game, a People, a Nation*. New York: Doubleday.

Jenkins, Virginia Scott. 1994. *The Lawn: A History of an American Obsession*. Washington, DC: Smithsonian Institution Press.

Jones, Suzi. 1976. "Regionalization: A Rhetorical Strategy." *Journal of the Folklore Institute* 13: 105–120.

Jones, David. 2008a. "Gap Widens between Players, Fans." *Patriot-News* (Harrisburg, PA) (September 26), Sports 20.

Jones, David. 2008b. "2 Joes Match Wits for Final Time." *Patriot-News* (Harrisburg, PA) (October 3), Sports 20.

Jones, David. 2010. "Blanda Defined AFL Era." *Patriot-News* (Harrisburg, PA) (October 1), Sports 28.

Jones, Howard Mumford. 1971. *The Age of Energy: Varieties of American Experience, 1865–1915*. New York: Viking Press.

Jones, Michael Owen. 2017. "'Stressed' Spelled Backwards is 'Desserts': Self-Medicating Moods with Foods." In *Comfort Food: Meanings and Memories*, edited by Michael Owen Jones and Lucy M. Long, 17–41. Jackson: University Press of Mississippi.

Jones, Tanya K. 2018. "Football is the New Religion in America." *Sport in American History* (September 3). https://ussporthistory.com/2018/09/03/football-is-the-new-religion-in-america/. Accessed February 9, 2021.

Jones-Jackson, Patricia. 1997. *When Roots Die: Endangered Traditions on the Sea Islands.* Athens: University of Georgia Press.

Joyner, Charles W. 1985. *Down by the Riverside: A South Carolina Slave Community.* Urbana: University of Illinois Press.

Kammen, Michael. 1972. *People of Paradox: An Inquiry Concerning the Origins of American Civilization.* New York: Knopf.

Kammen, Michael. 1979. "Changing Perceptions of the Life Cycle in American Thought and Culture." *Proceedings of the Massachusetts Historical Society,* Third Series, 91: 35–66.

Kammen, Michael. 2004. *A Time to Every Purpose: The Four Seasons in American Culture.* Chapel Hill: University of North Carolina Press.

Kassabova, Kapka. 2018. "Border Ghosts." *World Literature Today* 92: 35–39.

Kasson, John F. 1999. *Civilizing the Machine: Technology and Republican Values in America, 1776–1900.* Revised edition. New York: Hill and Wang.

Katz, James, and Philip Aspden. 1997. "A Nation of Strangers?" *Communications of the ACM* 40: 81–86.

Kay, Joe. 2008. "Collins Lead Titans Over Bengals 24-7 in Wind." *Yahoo! Sports* (September 14). sports.yahoo.com/nfl/recap?gid=20080914004. Accessed September 16, 2008.

Kemper, Kurt Edward. 2009. *College Football and American Culture in the Cold War Era.* Urbana: University of Illinois Press.

Keppler, J., artist. n.d. "The Bosses of the Senate." *Puck* (January 23). www.loc.gov/pictures/item/2002718861/. Accessed February 6, 2021.

Kesselman, Steven. 1979. *The Modernization of American Reform.* New York: Garland Publishing.

Khalaf, Sulayman N. 1992. "Gulf Societies and the Image of Unlimited Good." *Dialectical Anthropology* 17: 53–84.

Kimmel, Michael. 2008. *Guyland: The Perilous World Where Boys Become Men.* New York: HarperCollins.

Kirk, Dan. 2018. "Portrait of a Forest: Men and Machine." *Vermont Folklife Center.* www.vermontfolklifecenter.org/exhibits-feed/portrait-of-a-forest-men-and-machine. Accessed January 30, 2021.

Kirk, Nicole C. 2018. *Wanamaker's Temple: The Business of Religion in an Iconic Department Store.* New York: NYU Press.

Klein, Alyssa Vingan. 2014. "Why Fitness is Having a Moment in Fashion." *Fashionista* (May 1). https://fashionista.com/2014/05/fitness-fashion-trend-2014. Accessed February 6, 2021.

Klein, Matthew C., and Michael Pettis. 2020. *Trade Wars are Class Wars: How Rising Inequality Distorts the Global Economy and Threatens International Peace.* New Haven: Yale University Press.

Kluckhohn, Florence Rockwood. 1953. "Dominant and Variant Value Orientations." In *Personality in Nature, Society and Culture,* edited by Clyde Kluckhohn, Henry A. Murray, and David M. Schneider, 342–357. New York: Alfred A. Knopf.

Klymasz, Robert B. 1983. "Folklore of the Canadian-American Border." In *Handbook of American Folklore,* edited by Richard M. Dorson, 227–232. Bloomington: Indiana University Press.

Koppell, Jonathan. 2019. "We Make Deals with the Devil Sometimes. It's What Makes America Great." *azcentral* (October 24). www.azcentral.com/story/opinion/op-ed/2019/09/12/what-makes-america-great-we-put-pragmatism-over-ideological-purity/2293361001/. Accessed January 30, 2021.

Kraybill, Donald B. 2001. *The Riddle of Amish Culture*, revised edition. Baltimore: Johns Hopkins University Press.

Kraybill, Donald B., Karen Johnson-Weiner, and Steven M. Nolt. 2013. *The Amish*. Baltimore: Johns Hopkins University Press.

Krivo, Lauren J. 1986. "Home Ownership Differences between Hispanics and Anglos in the United States." *Social Problems* 33: 319–334.

Krout, John Allen. 1929. *Annals of American Sport*. New Haven, CT: Yale University Press.

Kruse, Zach. 2013. "The Anatomy and Importance of the 40-Yard Dash at the NFL Scouting Combine." *Bleacher Report* (February 20). https://bleacherreport.com/articles/1537023-the-anatomy-and-importance-of-the-40-yard-dash. Accessed January 30, 2021.

Kulikoff, Allan. 1992. *The Agrarian Origins of American Capitalism*. Charlottesville: University Press of Virginia.

Kunzelman, Michael, and Amanda Seitz. 2021. "Experts: Capitol Riot Product of Years of Hateful Rhetoric." *U.S. News & World Report* (January 6). www.npr.org/2021/01/06/954149242/a-look-at-the-rhetoric-around-the-storming-of-u-s-capitol. Accessed January 12, 2021.

Labov, William, Sharon Ash, and Charles Boberg. 2006. *The Atlas of North American English: Phonetics, Phonology and Sound Change*. Berlin: Mouton de Gruyter.

Lake, Robert W. 1979. "Racial Transition and Black Homeownership in American Suburbs." *Annals of the American Academy of Political and Social Science* 441: 142–156.

Landau, L. 1920. "Some Parallels to Shakespeare's 'Seven Ages'." *Journal of English and Germanic Philology* 19: 382–396.

Lands, LeeAnn. 2008. "Be a Patriot, Buy a Home: Re-Imagining Home Owners and Home Ownership in Early 20th Century Atlanta." *Journal of Social History* 41: 943–965.

Lane, Barnaby. 2019. "The 11 Most Extravagant Things Floyd Mayweather Has Spent His Millions On." (October 19). www.businessinsider.com/floyd-mayweather-most-extravagant-purchases-2019-10#:~:text=Amongst%20his%20lavish%20purchases%20over,fighter%20has%20ever%20paid%20for. Accessed January 29, 2021.

Lang, Justin J., Mark S. Tremblay, Luc Léger, Tim Olds, and Grant R. Tomkinson. 2018. "International Variability in 20 m Shuttle Run Performance in Children and Youth: Who Are the Fittest from a 50-country Comparison? A Systematic Literature Review with Pooling of Aggregate Results." *British Journal of Sports Medicine* 52: 276.

Lapierre, Matthew A., Frances Fleming-Milici, Esther Rozendaal, Anna R. McAlister, and Jessica Castonguay. 2017. "The Effect of Advertising on Children and Adolescents." *Pediatrics* (November), 140 (Supplement 2): S152–S156. https://pediatrics.aappublications.org/content/pediatrics/140/Supplement_2/S152.full.pdf. Accessed January 30, 2021.

Leach, Edmund. 1989. *Claude Lévi-Strauss*. Chicago: University of Chicago Press.

Leach, MacEdward. [1966] 2002. "Folklore and American Regionalism." In *Folk Nation: Folklore in the Creation of American Tradition*, edited by Simon J. Bronner, 189–198. Lanham, MD: Rowman & Littlefield.

Leach, William. 1993. *Land of Desire: Merchants, Power, and the Rise of a New American Culture*. New York: Vintage.

Lears, T. J. Jackson. 1981. *No Place of Grace: Antimodernism and the Transformation of American Culture, 1880–1920*. New York: Pantheon.
Lears, T. J. Jackson. 1985. "The Concept of Cultural Hegemony: Problems and Possibilities." *American Historical Review* 90: 567–593.
Lears, T. J. Jackson. 1988. "Packaging the Folk: Tradition and Amnesia in American Advertising, 1880–1940." In *Folk Roots, New Roots: Folklore in American Life*, edited by Jane S. Becker and Barbara Franco, 103–140. Lexington, MA: Museum of Our National Heritage.
Lears, T. J. Jackson. 1994. *Fables of Abundance: A Cultural History of Advertising in America*. New York: BasicBooks.
LeBesco, Kathleen. 2007. "Fatness as the Embodiment of Working-Class Rhetoric." In *Who Says? Working-Class Rhetoric, Class Consciousness, and Community*, edited by William DeGenaro, 238–255. Pittsburgh: University of Pittsburgh Press.
Lee, Amber. 2014. "Most Ridiculous Ways Floyd Mayweather Has Spent Money." *Bleacher Report* (April 29). https://bleacherreport.com/articles/2045890-most-ridiculous-ways-floyd-mayweather-has-spent-money. Accessed January 29, 2021.
Lee, Dorothy. 1950. "Lineal and Non-lineal Codifications of Reality." *Psychosomatic Medicine* 12: 89–97.
Lembcke, Jerry. 1998. *The Spitting Image: Myth, Memory, and the Legacy of Vietnam*. New York: New York University Press.
Lembcke, Jerry. 2004. "Post-Vietnam Masculinity." In *Men and Masculinities: A Social, Cultural, and Historical Encyclopedia*, edited by Michael Kimmel and Amy Aronson, 620–622. Santa Barbara, CA: ABC-CLIO.
Lepore, Jill. 1999. *The Name of War: King Philip's War and the Origins of American Identity*. New York: Knopf.
Lepore, Jill. 2007. "The Meaning of Life: What Milton Bradley Started." *New Yorker* (May 14). www.newyorker.com/magazine/2007/05/21/the-meaning-of-life. Accessed January 22, 2021.
Letson, Ben. 2008. "Feeling the Big Mo'." In *Football and Philosophy: Going Deep*, edited by Michael W. Austin, 209–218. Lexington: University Press of Kentucky.
Lever, Janet. 1976. "Sex Differences in the Games Children Play." *Social Problems* 23: 478–487.
Levin, Patricia. 2006. "Little Egypt." In *Encyclopedia of American Folklife*, edited by Simon J. Bronner, 736–738. Armonk, NY: M.E. Sharpe.
Lévi-Strauss, Claude. 1963. *Totemism*, translated by Rodney Needham. Boston: Beacon Press.
Lewis, Russell. 1983. "Everything under One Roof: World's Fairs and Department Stores in Paris and Chicago." *Chicago History* 13: 28–47.
Li, Wei. 1998. "Anatomy of a New Ethnic Settlement: The Chinese *Ethnoburb* in Los Angeles." *Urban Studies* 35: 479–501.
Li, Wei. 2012. *Ethnoburb: The New Ethnic Community in Urban America*. Honolulu: University of Hawaii Press.
Li, Wenli, and Fang Yang. 2010. "American Dream or American Obsession? The Economic Benefits and Costs of Homeownership." *Business Review* (third Quarter), 20–30.
Liberman, Gail, and Alan Lavine. 2000. *Rags to Riches: Motivating Stories of How Ordinary People Achieved Extraordinary Wealth*. Chicago: Dearborn.
Limón, José E. 1983. "Folklore, Social Conflict, and the United States-Mexico Border." In *Handbook of American Folklore*, edited by Richard M. Dorson, 216–226. Bloomington: Indiana University Press.

Lindquist, Danille Christensen. 2006. "'Locating' the Nation: Football Game Day and American Dreams in Central Ohio." *Journal of American Folklore* 119: 444–488.
Lipset, Seymour Martin. 1996. *American Exceptionalism*. New York: W. W. Norton.
Lisicky, Michael J. 2010. *Wanamaker's: Meet Me at the Eagle*. Charleston, SC: History Press.
Litan, Robert E. 2000. "The 'Globalization' Challenge: The U.S. Role in Shaping World Trade and Investment." *Brookings* (March 1). www.brookings.edu/articles/the-globalization-challenge-the-u-s-role-in-shaping-world-trade-and-investment/. Accessed January 24, 2021.
"Loan Exhibition, The." 1878. *Harper's Weekly* 22 (November 2), 872–874.
Lorenz, W.A. 1879. "Letter to the Editor." *American Machinist* (December 27), 6–7.
Lowrey, Annie. 2017. "Why the Phrase 'Late Capitalism' Is Suddenly Everywhere." *Atlantic* (May 1). www.theatlantic.com/business/archive/2017/05/late-capitalism/524943/. Accessed January 29, 2021.
Lowry, James D., Jr., and Leo E. Zonn. 1989. "Cognitive Images of the South: The Insider's View." *Southeastern Geographer* 29: 42–54.
Lutey, Tom. 2016. "Trump: 'We're Going to Win So Much, You're Going to be So Sick and Tired of Winning.'" *Billings Gazette* (May 26). https://billingsgazette.com/news/state-and-regional/govt-and-politics/trump-we-re-going-to-win-so-much-you-re-going-to-be-so-sick/article_2f346f38-37e7-5711-ae07-d1fd000f4c38.html. Accessed January 24, 2021.
Lynd, Robert S., and Helen M. Lynd. [1929] 1956. *Middletown: A Study in American Culture*. New York: Harcourt Brace Jovanovich.
MacCambridge, Michael. 2004. *America's Game: The Epic Story of How Pro Football Captured a Nation*. New York: Random House.
MacShane, Frank. 1980. *The Life of John O'Hara*. New York: E.P. Dutton.
Malone, Bill C. 2018. *Country Music USA*. 50th anniversary edition. Austin: University of Texas Press.
Mandelbaum, Michael. 2004. *The Meaning of Sports: Why Americans Watch Baseball, Football, and Basketball and What They See When They Do*. New York: Public Affairs.
Mansfield, Harvey C. 2006. *Manliness*. New Haven, CT: Yale University Press.
Marling, Karal Ann. 2000. *Merry Christmas!: Celebrating America's Greatest Holiday*. Cambridge, MA: Harvard University Press.
Marshall, Howard Wight. 1981. *Folk Architecture in Little Dixie: A Regional Culture in Missouri*. Columbia: University of Missouri Press.
Marshall, Howard Wight, and John Michael Vlach. 1973. "Toward a Folklife Approach to American Dialects." *American Speech* 48: 163–191.
Martinez, Michael, Jaqueline Hurtado, CNN, and CNN en Espanol. 2015. "'Narcocorridos': El Chapo's Jailbreak Inspires New Round of Folk Songs." *CNN* (July 25). www.cnn.com/2015/07/25/us/el-chapo-escape-narcocorridos/. Accessed December 29, 2018.
Mayer, Robert N. 2012. "The US Consumer Movement: A New Era Amid Old Challenges." *Journal of Consumer Affairs* 46: 171–189.
Mazareanu, E. 2019. "Landscaping Services in the U.S.—Statistics & Facts." *Statista* (July 9). www.statista.com/topics/4798/landscaping-services-in-the-us/. Accessed January 9, 2021.
McCarthy, Niall. 2020. "Potential Lockdowns Will Affect People Differently." *Statista* (March 25). www.statista.com/chart/21238/average-living-area-per-person-in-selected-countries/. Accessed January 9, 2021.
McCartney, Anthony. 2011. "'Duh, Winning': Charlie Sheen Moves to Trademark Phrases." *Daily Herald* (April 7). www.heraldextra.com/entertainment/people/duh-winning-charlie-sheen-moves-to-trademark-phrases/article_604a0da0-a4d0-5b44-8466-232b2c6e60d1.html. Accessed January 26, 2021.

McCoral, Greg. 2009. "Success Kid/I Hate Sandcastles." *Know Your Meme*. https://knowyourmeme.com/memes/success-kid-i-hate-sandcastles. Accessed January 24, 2021.

McCormick, M. Diane. 2016. "From Burbs to Burg: For Decades, Companies Headed in One Direction—From Harrisburg to the Suburbs. Welcome Back!" *Burg* (July 29). https://theburgnews.com/in-the-burg/from-burbs-to-burg-for-decades-companies-headed-in-one-direction-from-harrisburg-to-the-suburbs-welcome-back. Accessed January 31, 2021.

McDowell, John H. 2010. "Rethinking Folklorization in Ecuador: Multivocality in the Expressive Contact Zone." *Western Folklore* 69: 181–209.

McDowell, John H. 2012. "The Ballad of Narcomexico." *Journal of Folklore Research* 49: 249–274.

McGee, Micki. 2005. *Self-Help, Inc.: Makeover Culture in American Life*. New York: Oxford University Press.

McGee, W.J. 1898. "Fifty Years of American Science." *Atlantic Monthly* 82 (September), 307–320.

McGreal, Chris. 2021. "Condemnation—and Support: Trump's Midwest Base Split by Capitol Attack." *Guardian* (January 10). www.theguardian.com/us-news/2021/jan/10/trump-midwest-base-split-capitol-attack-condemnation-support. Accessed January 15, 2021.

McGrory, Mary. 1972. "The Sleeping Conscience of America." *Boston Globe* (February 20), A6.

McKenzie, Shelly. 2013. *Getting Physical: The Rise of Fitness Culture in America*. Lawrence: University Press of Kansas.

McKnight, Anne. 2014. "The Strength of a Nation Lies in the Homes of Its People." *Williamson Herald* (April 7). www.williamsonherald.com/features/real_estate/the-strength-of-a-nation-lies-in-the-homes-of/article_18dcd46d-65ad-50ea-bda5-3538b4a2ec25.html#:~:text=Spoken%20by%20Abraham%20Lincoln%20more,their%20value%20is%20virtually%20immeasurable. Accessed January 31, 2021.

McLean, Scott L. 2002. *Social Capital: Critical Perspectives on Community and "Bowling Alone."* New York: New York University Press.

McNeil, W.K., ed. 1995a. *Appalachian Images in Folk and Popular Culture*. Knoxville: University of Tennessee Press.

McNeil, W.K. 1995b. *Ozark Country*. Jackson: University Press of Mississippi.

Mead, Margaret. 1951. "The Study of National Character." In *The Policy Sciences: Recent Developments in Scope and Method*, edited by Daniel Lerner, 70–85. Stanford, CA: Stanford University Press.

Mead, Walter Russell. 2017. "The Jacksonian Revolt: American Populism and the Liberal Order." *Foreign Affairs* 96: 2–7.

Meinig, D. W. 1965. "The Mormon Culture Region: Strategies and Patterns in the Geography of the American West, 1847–1964." *Annals of the Association of American Geographers* 55: 191–220.

Meinig, D. W. 1979. "Symbolic Landscapes: Some Idealizations of American Communities." In *Interpretation of Ordinary Landscapes*, edited by D. W. Meinig, 164–192. New York: Oxford University Press.

Mendible, Myra. 2009. "Big Booty Beauty and the New Sexual Aesthetic." *American Sexuality Magazine* (January 5). www.researchgate.net/profile/Myra_Mendible/publication/256497105_Big_Booty_and_the_New_Sexual_Aesthetic/links/561d201808ae50795afd75c8/Big-Booty-and-the-New-Sexual-Aesthetic.pdf. Accessed February 9, 2021.

Mesch, Gustavo S. 2001. "Social Relationships and Internet Use among Adolescents in Israel." *Social Science Quarterly* 82: 329–339.

Mieder, Wolfgang. 2012. "Language and Vernacular Culture: Why Folklorists Should Read the Dictionary of American Regional English." *Journal of Folklore Research* 49: 107–112.

Mieder, Wolfgang. 2020. *The Worldview of Modern American Proverbs*. New York: Peter Lang.

Mier, Tomás. 2021. "Dolly Parton Hilariously Recreates '9 to 5' for New Super Bowl Ad: 'Cause It's Hustlin' Time!" *People* (February 2). https://people.com/country/super-bowl-2021-dolly-parton-recreates-9-to-5/. Accessed February 8, 2021.

Miller, Aaron. 2020. "Idealism Without Illusion." *Carnegie Endowment for International Peace* (August 4). https://carnegieendowment.org/2020/08/04/idealism-without-illusion-pub-82433. Accessed January 10, 2021.

Miller, Perry. 1956. *Errand into the Wilderness*. New York: Harper.

Mills, Jarrod. 2020. "Tips for Making Sure Your New Year's Resolutions Stick." *Times-Tribune* (January 3). www.thetimestribune.com/news/local_news/tips-for-making-sure-your-new-years-resolutions-stick/article_8cd14b54-17fd-51a9-ab5a-89859e6e34c4.html. Accessed January 24, 2021.

Milspaw, Yvonne. 1997. "Regional Style in Quilt Design." *Journal of American Folklore* 110: 363–390.

Mitterling, Thomas, Nirai Tomass, and Kelsey Wu. 2020. "The Decline and Recovery of Consumer Spending in the US." *Brookings* (December 14). www.brookings.edu/blog/future-development/2020/12/14/the-decline-and-recovery-of-consumer-spending-in-the-us/. Accessed January 29, 2021.

Montgomery Ward & Co. 1895. *Catalogue and Buyers' Guide*. Chicago: Montgomery Ward.

Morel, Annamaire. 2021. "*Glamour, Guns, and Glitter: Selfie-Empowerment and Self-Representation Online*." PhD diss. Pennsylvania State University.

Morgan, Philip D. 2010. *African American Life in the Georgia Lowcountry: The Atlantic World and the Gullah Geechee*. Athens: University of Georgia Press.

Morrison, Amanda Maria. 2008. "Musical Trafficking: Urban Youth and the Narcocorrido-Hardcore Rap Nexus." *Western Folklore* 67: 379–396.

Moskowitz, Peter. 2018. *How to Kill a City: Gentrification, Inequality, and the Fight for the Neighborhood*. New York: Nation Books.

Mouton, Stephen, director. 2012. *Fat City New Orleans*. DVD. Los Angeles: Vanguard Cinema.

Mudge, G.O. 1896. "The Signs of the Times: The Homes of the Nation." *Twentieth Century* (June 4), 9.

Mullen, Patrick B. 1978. "The Folk Idea of Unlimited Good in American Buried Treasure Legends." *Journal of the Folklore Institute* 15: 209–220.

Muresan, Adela. 2016. "Who Lives Largest? The Growth of Urban American Homes in the Last 100 Years." *PropertyShark* (September 8). www.propertyshark.com/Real-Estate-Reports/2016/09/08/the-growth-of-urban-american-homes-in-the-last-100-years/. Accessed January 9, 2021.

Murphey, Murray G. 1965. "An Approach to the Historical Study of National Character." In *Context and Meaning in Cultural Anthropology*, edited by Melford E. Spiro, 144–163. New York: Free Press.

Murray, Patrick. 2020. "National: COVID Concerns Increase as Schools Open." *Monmouth University Poll* (September 9). Press Release.

Muzzio, Douglas, and Thomas Halper. 2002. "Pleasantville?: The Suburb and Its Representation in American Movies." *Urban Affairs Review* 37: 543–574.

Nagatsuka, Kaz. 2007. "NFL Japan Raising Level of Play: High School Students Tackle Football's Fundamentals." *Japan Times* (January 25). http://search.japantimes.co.jp/cgi-bin/sf20070125a1.html. Accessed September 24, 2008.

Naisbitt, John. 1982. *Megatrends*. New York: Avon.

Naisbitt, John, and Patricia Aburdene. 1990. *Megatrends 2000*. New York: Avon.

Nájera-Ramírez, Olga, Norma E. Cantú, and Brenda M. Romero. 2009. *Dancing across Borders: Danzas y bailes Mexicanos*. Urbana: University of Illinois Press.

Nast, Thomas, artist. 1871. "The Brains" That Achieved the Tammany Victory at the Rochester Democratic Convention." *Harper's Weekly* (October 21), 992. www.loc.gov/item/2002723257/.

National Football League. 2009. "NFL: America's Choice." *National Football League Report* (January). www.coldhardfootballfacts.com/Documents/Super_Bowl_1–09_popularity.pdf. Accessed February 10, 2009.

National Retail Federation. 2020. *The Economic Impact of the US Retail Industry*. https://cdn.nrf.com/sites/default/files/2020-06/RS-118304%20NRF%20Retail%20Impact%20Report%20.pdf. Accessed January 29, 2021.

Needham, Vicki. 2014. "Report: 18 Firms Hold a Third of US Wealth." *The Hill* (August 9). https://thehill.com/policy/finance/economy/214757-report-18-companies-hold-over-a-third-of-us-wealth. Accessed January 29, 2021.

Nelson, Maria Burton. 1994. *The Stronger Women Get, the More Men Love Football: Sexism and the American Culture of Sports*. New York: Avon.

"New York Gossip: New Developments in Architecture—The High-Building Craze." 1883. *Chicago Tribune* (February 25), 9.

Nicolaisen, W.F.H. 1976a. "The Folk and the Region." *New York Folklore*: 143–149.

Nicolaisen, W.F.H. 1976b. "Place-Name Legends: An Onomastic Mythology." *Folklore* 87: 146–159.

Nicolaisen, W.F.H. 1977. "Some Humorous Folk-Etymological Narratives." *New York Folklore* 3: 1–14.

Norris, James D. 1990. *Advertising and the Transformation of American Society, 1865–1920*. New York: Greenwood Press.

Norton, Barley. 2009. *Songs for the Spirits: Music and Mediums in Modern Vietnam*. Urbana: University of Illinois Press.

Norwine, Jim, Michael Bruner, Allen Ketcham, and Michael Preda. 2000. "'I Love You, Man': Values in Flux." In *Worldview Flux: Perplexed Values among Postmodern Peoples*, edited by Jim Norwine and Jonathan M. Smith, 21–64. Lanham, MD: Lexington Books.

Norwood, Stephen H. 2004. *Real Football: Conversations on America's Game*. Jackson: University Press of Mississippi.

Nostrand, Richard L. 1992. *The Hispano Homeland*. Norman: University of Oklahoma Press.

Nostrand, Richard L., and Lawrence E. Estaville. 2001. "Introduction: Free Land, Dry Land, Homeland." In *Homelands: A Geography of Culture and Place across America*, edited by Richard L. Nostrand and Lawrence E. Estaville, xiii–xxiii. Baltimore: Johns Hopkins University Press.

Nussbaum, Stan. 2005. *American Cultural Baggage: How to Recognize and Deal With It*. Maryknoll, NY: Orbis Books.

Nye, Russel B. 1966. *This Almost Chosen People: Essays in the History of American Ideas*. East Lansing: Michigan State University Press.

Nylund, David. 2007. *Beer, Babes, and Balls: Masculinity and Sports Talk Radio.* Albany: State University of New York Press.

Oates, Thomas P., and Kyle W. Kusz. 2019. "'My Whole Life is about Winning': The Trump Brand and the Political/Commercial Uses of Sport." In *Sport, Rhetoric, and Political Struggle,* edited by Daniel A. Grano and Michael L. Butterworth, 207–222. New York: Peter Lang.

Oberhauser, Ann M., Daniel Krier, and Abdi M. Kusow. 2019. "Political Moderation and Polarization in the Heartland: Economics, Rurality, and Social Identity in the 2016 U.S. Presidential Election." *Sociological Quarterly* 60: 224–244.

"Obesity Rates by Country 2021." 2021. *World Population Review.* https://worldpopulationreview.com/country-rankings/obesity-rates-by-country. Accessed February 5, 2021.

Ochonicky, Adam R. 2020. *The American Midwest in Film and Literature: Nostalgia, Violence, and Regionalism.* Bloomington: Indiana University Press.

O'Conner, Patricia T., and Stewart Kellerman. 2014. "Monetizing 'Dough' and 'Bread.'" *Grammarphobia* (June 16). www.grammarphobia.com/blog/2014/06/dough-bread.html. Accessed February 7, 2021.

Office of Minority Health. 2020a. "Obesity and African Americans." *HHS.gov.* https://minorityhealth.hhs.gov/omh/browse.aspx?lvl=4&lvlid=25. Accessed February 6, 2021.

Office of Minority Health. 2020b. "Obesity and Asian Americans." *HHS.gov.* https://minorityhealth.hhs.gov/omh/browse.aspx?lvl=4&lvlid=55. Accessed February 6, 2021.

Office of Minority Health. 2020c. "Obesity and Hispanic Americans." *HHS.gov.* https://minorityhealth.hhs.gov/omh/browse.aspx?lvl=4&lvlid=70. Accessed February 6, 2021.

Office of Policy Development and Research. 1994. "U.S. Housing Market Conditions Summary." *U.S. Department of Housing and Urban Development* (August). www.huduser.gov/periodicals/ushmc/summer94/summer94.html#:~:text=In%20the%201890%2D1940%20period,%2D%20to%2048%2Dpercent%20range. Accessed January 31, 2021.

O'Hara, John. 1949. *A Rage to Live.* New York: Random House.

Omrčanin, Margaret Stewart. 1972. *Ruth Suckow: A Critical Study of Her Fiction.* Philadelphia: Dorrance.

Oriard, Michael. 1993. *Reading Football: How the Popular Press Created an American Spectacle.* Chapel Hill: University of North Carolina Press.

Oriard, Michael. 2001. *King Football: Sport and Spectacle in the Golden Age of Radio and Newsreels, Movies and Magazines, the Weekly and the Daily Press.* Chapel Hill: University of North Carolina Press.

Oriard, Michael. 2007. *Brand NFL: Making and Selling America's Favorite Sport.* Chapel Hill: University of North Carolina Press.

Ortega, Veronica. 2017. "TV Sales Spike Before Super Bowl Sunday." *WSBT* (February 2). https://wsbt.com/news/local/tv-sales-spike-before-super-bowl-sunday. Accessed January 24, 2021.

Ortner, Sherry B. 1974. "Is Female to Male as Nature Is to Culture?" In *Women, Culture and Society,* edited by Michelle Zimbalist Rosaldo and Louise Lamphere, 67–87. Stanford, CA: Stanford University Press.

O'Sullivan, John L. 1839. "The Great Nation of Futurity." *United States Magazine and Democratic Review* 6, no. 23 (November): 426–430.

O'Sullivan, John L. 1845a. "Annexation." *United States Magazine and Democratic Review* 17, no. 85 (July–August): 5–10.

O'Sullivan, John L. 1845b. "The True Title." *Morning News* (New York) (December 27): 1.

Owens, Linus. 2018. "Why Has Halloween Become So Popular Among Adults?" *The Conversation* (October 26). https://theconversation.com/why-has-halloween-become-so-popular-among-adults-104896. Accessed January 24, 2021.

Pace, Donielle. 2016. "*'You Look Like a Skinny White Girl'*: Black Cultural Effects on the Body Image of Thin Black Women." M.A. thesis, University of Houston. https://uh-ir.tdl.org/bitstream/handle/10657/1518/PACE-THESIS-2016.pdf?sequence=1&isAllowed=y. Accessed February 9, 2021.

Paolantonio, Sal. 2008. *How Football Explains America*. Chicago: Triumph Books.

Paredes, Américo. 1958. *"With His Pistol in His Hand": A Border Ballad and Its Hero*. Austin: University of Texas Press.

Paredes, Américo. 1995. *A Texas-Mexican Cancionero: Folksongs of the Lower Border*. Austin: University of Texas Press.

Paredes, Américo. [1978] 2002. "Border Identity: Culture Conflict and Convergence along the Lower Rio Grande." In *Folk Nation: Folklore in the Creation of American Tradition*, edited by Simon J. Bronner, 199–214. Lanham, MD: Rowman & Littlefield.

Parish, John Carl. 1932. *The Emergence of the Idea of Manifest Destiny*. Berkeley: University of California Press.

Parrington, Vernon Louis. 1927–1930. *Main Currents in American Thought: An Interpretation of American Literature from the Beginnings to 1920*. New York: Harcourt.

Patel, Vimal. 2020. "Look Who's Talking About Canceling Debt: How a Fringe Idea Went Mainstream." *Chronicle of Higher Education* (January 23). www.chronicle.com/article/look-whos-talking-about-canceling-debt/. Accessed January 29, 2021.

Patten, Simon N. 1907. *The New Basis of Civilization*. New York: Macmillan.

Payne, Keith, Heidi A. Vuletich, and Kristjen B. Lundberg. 2017. "The Bias of Crowds: How Implicit Bias Bridges Personal and Systemic Prejudice." *Psychological Inquiry* 28: 233–248.

PC Tools Software. 2007. "Do You Have the Right Protection?" Advertisement for Spyware Doctor security program. *Game Informer* 176 (December), 15.

Pearl, Jonathan, and Judith Pearl. 1999. *The Chosen Image: Television's Portrayal of Jewish Themes and Characters*. Jefferson, NC: McFarland.

Pearlman, Jeff. 2016. *Gunslinger: The Remarkable, Improbable, Iconic Life of Brett Favre*. Boston: Mariner Books.

Peck, Bradford. [1900] 1971. *The World a Department Store*. New York: Arno Press.

Pelligrini, Anthony, Kentaro Kato, Peter Blatchford, and Ed Baines. 2002. "A Short-Term Longitudinal Study of Children's Playground Games across the First Year of School: Implications for Social Competence and Adjustment to School." *American Educational Research Journal* 39: 991–1015.

Pessen, Edward. 1986. *The Log Cabin Myth: The Social Backgrounds of the Presidents*. New Haven: Yale University Press.

Peterson, Merrill D. 1954. "Parrington and American Liberalism." *Virginia Quarterly Review* 30: 35–49.

Pettegrew, David, and James B. LaGrand. 2020. "Harrisburg, the City Beautiful: Recasting the History of Urban Reform in a Small American Capital." *Pennsylvania History* 87: 1–10.

Pettigrew, Thomas F. 2017. "Social Psychological Perspectives on Trump Supporters." *Journal of Social and Political Psychology* 5: 107–116.

Pew Research Center. 1999. "Americans Look to the 21st Century, Millennium Survey." http://208.240.91.18/mill2rpt.htm. Accessed July 2, 2002.

Piker, Steven. 1966. "'The Image of Limited Good': Comments on an Exercise in Description and Interpretation." *American Anthropologist* 68: 1202–1211.

Pinsker, Sanford. 2000. "Henry Adams and Our New Century." *Partisan Review* 62 (Spring): 270–281.

PK. 2021a. "Historical Homeownership Rate in the United States, 1890-Present." *DQYDJ.com*. https://dqydj.com/historical-homeownership-rate-united-states/. Accessed January 31, 2021.

PK. 2021b. "The 30 Year Mortgage, Mortgage Insurance, and Housing Accessibility." *DQYDJ.com*. https://dqydj.com/history-30-year-mortgage/. Accessed January 31, 2021.

Pliska, Jonathan. 2016. "'A Beautiful Spot Capable of Every Improvement': Introduction to 'A Garden for the President: A History of the White House Grounds.'" *White House Historical Association*. www.whitehousehistory.org/a-beautiful-spot-capable-of-every-improvement. Accessed January 9, 2021.

Poe, Edgar Allan. 1838. *The Narrative of Arthur Gordon Pym of Nantucket: Comprising the Details of a Mutiny and Atrocious Butchery on Board the American brig Grampus, on Her Way to the South Seas in the Month of June, 1827*. New York: Harper & Brothers.

Pollack, William. 1998. *Real Boys: Rescuing Our Sons from the Myths of Boyhood*. New York: Henry Holt.

Popper, Nathaniel, Matt Phillips, Kate Kelly, and Tara Siegel Bernard. 2021. "The Silicon Valley Start-Up That Caused Wall Street Chaos." *New York Times* (January 30). www.nytimes.com/2021/01/30/business/robinhood-wall-street-gamestop.html. Accessed January 31, 2021.

Poston, Lawrence, III, and Francis J. Stillman. 1965. "Notes on Campus Vocabulary, 1964." *American Speech* 40: 193–195.

Potter, David M. 1954. *People of Plenty: Economic Abundance and the American Character*. Chicago: University of Chicago Press.

Powell, Matt. 2015. "Sneakernomics: America's Real Health Crisis." *Forbes* (November 2). www.forbes.com/sites/mattpowell/2015/11/02/sneakernomics-americas-real-health-crisis/?sh=1b1576b92910. Accessed February 6, 2021.

Pratt, Julius W. 1927. "The Origin of 'Manifest Destiny.'" *American Historical Review* 32: 795–798.

Presbrey, Frank. 1929. *The History and Development of Advertising*. New York: Doubleday, Doran.

Preserve at Little Pine, The. 2020. "About Us: The Days Are Fuller Here." *The Preserve at Little Pine*. https://thepreserveatlittlepine.com/about-us/. Accessed January 10, 2021.

President's Council on Sports, Fitness, & Nutritions. 2017. "Facts & Statistics: Physical Activity." *HHS.gov*. www.hhs.gov/fitness/resource-center/facts-and-statistics/index.html. Accessed February 6, 2021.

Price, John E. 2016. "The Super Bowl: America's Holiday." *Sport in American History* (February 1). https://ussporthistory.com/2016/02/01/the-super-bowl-americas-holiday/?fbclid=IwAR1qZCfNHjbqZt0ZfeiYwBuuQuqYuJsFjsD2VGGKQzwchCnqt54CXAcBZHU. Accessed February 7, 2021.

Price, Joseph L., ed. 2001. *From Season to Season: Sports as American Religion*. Macon, GA: Mercer University Press.

Price, Todd A. 2014. "Fat City's Restaurants Are on the Rise." *Times-Picayune* (New Orleans, LA) (February 20). www.nola.com/entertainment_life/eat-drink/article_366c9952-9203-5d67-bb47-896f23e53bc3.html. Accessed February 6, 2021.

Pucin, Diane. 2008. "3-D TD Jumps Off Screen." *Los Angeles Times* (December 5). http://articles.latimes.com/2008/dec/05/sports/sp-media5. Accessed September 12, 2010.

Purnell, Brian. 2020. "Racism, Policing and Black Lives Matter Protests." *The Conversation* (November 7). https://theconversation.com/biden-wins-experts-on-what-it-means-for-race-relations-us-foreign-policy-and-the-supreme-court-149327. Accessed January 10, 2021.

Putnam, Robert D. 2000. *Bowling Alone: The Collapse and Revival of American Community*. New York: Touchstone.

Raab-Fischer, Roswitha. 1994. "A Hyperinflation of Lexical Mega-Monsters? Eine korpusgestützte Analyse zum Gebrauch der Wortbildungselemente mega-, ultra-, super- und hyper- im heutigen Englisch." *AAA: Arbeiten aus Anglistik und Amerikanistik* 19: 83–111.

Rader, Benjamin G. 1999. *American Sports: From the Age of Folk Games to the Age of Televised Sports*. Upper Saddle River, NJ: Prentice-Hall.

Raphael, Ray. 1988. *The Men from the Boys: Rites of Passage in Male America*. Lincoln: University of Nebraska Press.

Rauch, Jonathan. 2014. "The Real Roots of Midlife Crisis." *Atlantic* (December). www.theatlantic.com/magazine/archive/2014/12/the-real-roots-of-midlife-crisis/382235/. Accessed January 22, 2021.

Reid, Heather L. 2008. "Heroes of the Coliseum." In *Football and Philosophy: Going Deep*, edited by Michael W. Austin, 128–140. Lexington: University Press of Kentucky.

Reinitz, Richard. 1977. "Vernon Louis Parrington as Historical Ironist." *Pacific Northwest Quarterly* 68: 113–119.

Renault, Jean-Maxime. 2020. "Pilot Script Review of *Ordinary Joe*." *Primetimer* (March 30). www.primetimer.com/pilots/pilotpreviews/ordinary-joe. Accessed February 7, 2021.

Rich, Nathaniel. 2015. "The History of a City Underfoot." *New York Times Magazine* (April 23). www.nytimes.com/2015/04/26/magazine/the-history-of-a-city-underfoot.html. Accessed January 29, 2021.

Riesman, David. 1960. *Thorstein Veblen: A Critical Interpretation*. New York: Charles Scribner's Sons.

Riesman, David, and Reuel Denney. 1951. "Football in America: A Study in Cultural Diffusion." *American Quarterly* 3: 309–325.

Riis, Jacob. 1890. *How the Other Half Lives: Studies Among the Tenements of New York*. New York: Charles Scribner's Sons.

Riismandel, Kyle. 2020. *Neighborhood of Fear: The Suburban Crisis in American Culture, 1975–2001*. Baltimore: Johns Hopkins University Press.

Ritzer, George. 2015. "Prosumer Capitalism." *Sociological Quarterly* 56: 413–445.

Ritzer, George, and Nathan Jurgenson. 2010. "Production, Consumption, Prosumption: The Nature of Capitalism in the Age of the Digital 'Prosumer'." *Journal of Consumer Culture* 10: 13–36.

Roberts, Paul. 2014. *The Impulse Society: America in the Age of Instant Gratification*. New York: Bloomsbury.

Roberts, Sam. 1995. *Who We Are*. New York: Times Books.

Roberts, Sam. 2010. "Region is Reshaped as Minorities Go to Suburbs." *New York Times* (December 14). www.nytimes.com/2010/12/15/nyregion/15nycensus.html. Accessed January 10, 2021.

Robertson, James Oliver. 1980. *American Myth, American Reality*. New York: Hill & Wang.

Robinson, Jennifer Meta, and James Robert Farmer. 2017. *Selling Local: Why Local Food Movements Matter*. Bloomington: Indiana University Press.

"Robinson & Co's Big Special Sale: An Event Up Town That Will Interest the Whole City." 1909. *Harrisburg Daily Independent* (February 9), 9.

Robinson, Jennifer Meta, and J.A. Hartenfeld. 2007. *The Farmers' Market Book: Growing Food, Cultivating Community*. Bloomington: Indiana University Press.

Rogers, Kim Lacy. 2006. "Aging, the Life Course, and Oral History: African American Narratives of Struggle, Social Change, and Decline." In *Handbook of Oral History*, edited by Thomas L. Charlton, Lois E. Myers, and Rebecca Sharpless, 297–335. Lanham, MD: AltaMira Press.

Rohe, William M., and Harry L. Watson, eds. 2007. *Chasing the American Dream: New Perspectives on Affordable Homeownership*. Ithaca, NY: Cornell University Press.

Rolfe, John. 2008. "Beautiful Losers: Immortality Can Come with Losing the Super Bowl." *Sports Illustrated* (January 22). http://sportsillustrated.cnn.com/2008/writers/john_rolfe/01/22/super.bowl.losers/index.html. Accessed September 19, 2008.

Roosevelt, Theodore. 1899. *The Rough Riders*. New York: Review of Reviews.

Roper Center. 2021. Roper iPoll. https://ropercenter-cornell-edu.ezaccess.libraries.psu.edu/ipoll/#. Ithaca: Cornell University. Accessed April 5, 2021.

Rosen, Ellen F., Adolph Brown, Jennifer Braden, Herman W. Dorsett, Dawna N. Franklin, Ronald A. Garlington, Valerie E. Kent, Tonya T. Lewis, and Linda C. Petty. 1993. "African-American Males Prefer a Larger Female Body Silhouette than Do Whites." *Bulletin of the Psychonomic Society* 31: 599–601.

Rosenberg, Michael. 2008. *War as They Knew It: Woody Hayes, Bo Schembechler, and America in a Time of Unrest*. New York: Grand Central Publishing.

Rosenberg, Neil. 2005. *Bluegrass: A History*. Revised edition. Urbana: University of Illinois Press.

Rosenzweig, Roy, and David Thelen. 1998. *The Presence of the Past: Popular Uses of History in American Life*. New York: Columbia University Press.

Roth, Radris. 1985. "The New England, or 'Olde Tyme,' Kitchen Exhibit at Nineteenth-Century Fairs." In *The Colonial Revival in America*, edited by Alan Axelrod, 159–183. New York: W. W. Norton.

Roud Folk Song Index. n.d. *Vaughn Williams Memorial Library*. www.vwml.org/roudnumber/. Accessed January 18, 2021.

Rudolph, Frederick. [1962] 1990. *The American College & University: A History*. Athens: University of Georgia Press.

Rydell, Robert W. 1984. *All the World's A Fair: Visions of Empire at American International Expositions, 1876–1916*. Chicago: University of Chicago Press.

Rydell, Robert W., John E. Findling, and Kimberly D. Pelle. 2000. *Fair America: World's Fairs in the United States*. Washington, DC: Smithsonian Books.

Ryden, Kent C. 1993. *Mapping the Invisible Landscape: Folklore, Writing, and the Sense of Place*. Iowa City: University of Iowa Press.

Safire, William. 1998. "On Language; The Return of Joe Six-Pack." *New York Times Magazine* (May 3). www.nytimes.com/1998/05/03/magazine/on-language-the-return-of-joe-six-pack.html. Accessed February 6, 2021.

Safire, William. 2008. *Safire's Political Dictionary*, revised edition. New York: Oxford University Press.

Salter, Phia S., Glenn Adams, and Michael J. Perez. 2017. "Racism in the Structure of Everyday Worlds: A Cultural-Psychological Perspective." *European Journal of Personality* 27: 150–155.

Sanburn, Josh. 2014. "The Top of America." *Time* (March 6). https://time.com/13828/the-top-of-america/. Accessed January 3, 2021.

Sandritter, Mark. 2017. "A Timeline of Colin Kaepernick's National Anthem Protest and the Athletes Who Joined Him." *SBNation* (September 25). www.sbnation.com/2016/9/11/12869726/colin-kaepernick-national-anthem-protest-seahawks-brandon-marshall-nfl. Accessed February 4, 2021.

Santino, Jack. 1994. *All Around the Year: Holidays and Celebrations in American Life*. Urbana: University of Illinois Press.

Sauro, Sean. 2020. "Millennials Eagerly Move Into Downtown Harrisburg But Does That Equal Growth and Change?" *Patriot-News* (Harrisburg, PA) (February 10). www.pennlive.com/news/2020/02/millennials-eagerly-move-into-downtown-harrisburg-but-does-that-equal-growth-and-change.html. Accessed April 6, 2021.

Scala, Dante J., and Kenneth M. Johnson. 2017. "Political Polarization along the Rural-Urban Continuum? The Geography of the Presidential Vote, 2000–2016." *Annals of the American Academy of Political and Social Science* 672: 162–187.

Schabner, Dean. 2006. "American Work More than Anyone." *abcNews* (January 7). https://abcnews.go.com/US/story?id=93364&page=1. Accessed February 6, 2021.

Scharrer, Erica. 2001. "From Wise to Foolish: The Portrayal of the Sitcom Father, 1950s–1990s." *Journal of Broadcasting & Electronic Media* 45: 23–40.

Schettkat, Ronald, and Lara Yocarini. 2003. "The Shift to Services: A Review of the Literature." *Structural Change and Economic Dynamics* 17: 127–147.

Schor, Juliet. 2000. *The Overworked American: The Unexpected Decline of Leisure*. New York: Basic Books.

Schryer, Frans J., and George M. Foster. 1976. "A Reinterpretation of Treasure Tales and the Image of Limited Good." *Current Anthropology* 17: 708–713.

Schuerman, Matthew L. 2019. *Newcomers: Gentrification and Its Discontents*. Chicago: University of Chicago Press.

Scrapbooker. 2017. "Donald Trump-Winning." *Know Your Meme*. https://knowyourmeme.com/photos/1277365-donald-trump. Accessed January 24, 2021.

Sears, Elizabeth. 1986. *The Ages of Man: Medieval Interpretations of the Life Cycle*. Princeton, NJ: Princeton University Press.

Segal, Howard P. 1989. "Edward Bellamy's 'Looking Backward' and the American Ideology of Progress through Technology." *OAH Magazine of History* 4(2): 20–24.

Sender, Katherine. 2006. "Queens for a Day: Queer Eye for the Straight Guy and the Neoliberal Project." *Critical Studies in Media Communication* 23: 131–151.

Senter, Jacqueline Conciatore. 2019. *Muckrakers and Progressive Reformers*. New York: Cavendish Square.

Serwer, Adam. 2020. "The New Reconstruction." *The Atlantic* (October 2020). www.theatlantic.com/magazine/archive/2020/10/the-next-reconstruction/615475/. Accessed January 10, 2021.

Sharp, Gregory, and Matthew Hall. 2014. "Emerging Forms of Racial Inequality in Homeownership Exit, 1968–2009." *Social Problems* 61: 427–447.

Sheldon, Henry Davidson. 1901. *The History and Pedagogy of American Students Societies*. New York: D. Appleton.

Shi, David E. 1985. *The Simple Life: Plain Living and High Thinking in American Culture*. New York: Oxford University Press.

Shlay, Anne B. 2006. "Low-income Homeownership: American Dream or Delusion?" *Urban Studies* 43: 511–531.

Siegel, Lee. 2008. "Why Does Hollywood Hate the Suburbs?" *Wall Street Journal* (December 27). www.wsj.com/articles/SB123033369595836301. Accessed January 10, 2021.

Silverman, David J. 2020. *This Land is Their Land: The Wampanoag Indians, Plymouth Colony, and the Troubled History of Thanksgiving.* New York: Bloomsbury.

Simpson, Stephen D. 2019. "Plastic Surgery Worldwide: Which Countries Nip and Tuck the Most?" *Investopedia* (June 25). www.investopedia.com/financial-edge/0712/plastic-surgery-worldwide-which-countries-nip-and-tuck-the-most.aspx. Accessed February 6, 2021.

Sinatra, Alex. 2020. "Studies Show that the NFL Is Not as Diverse as It Wants You to Think." *USA Today Sports* (June 17). https://touchdownwire.usatoday.com/2020/06/17/studies-show-that-the-nfl-is-not-as-diverse-as-it-wants-you-to-think/. Accessed February 4, 2021.

Sivulka, Juliann. 2012. *Soap, Sex, and Cigarettes: A Cultural History*, second edition. Boston: Wadsworth.

Sloat, Warren. 1988. "Looking Back at 'Looking Backward': We Have Seen the Future and It Didn't Work." *New York Times* (January 17). www.nytimes.com/1988/01/17/books/looking-back-at-looking-backward-we-have-seen-the-future-and-it-didn-t-work.html. Accessed January 30, 2021.

Slotkin, Richard. 1973. *Regeneration through Violence: The Mythology of the American Frontier, 1600–1860.* Middletown, CT: Wesleyan University Press.

Slotkin, Richard. 1993. *Gunfighter Nation: The Myth of the Frontier in Twentieth-Century America.* New York: HarperCollins.

Slowe, Peter M. 1991. "The Geography of Borderlands: The Case of the Quebec-US Borderlands." *Geographic Journal* 157: 191–198.

Smargon, Adam Joshua. 2018. "College Nicknames." (May 21). www.smargon.net/nicknames. Accessed April 8, 2021.

Smirke, Robert. 1864. *The Seven Ages of Man.* London: L. Booth.

Smith, Bubba. 1983. *Kill, Bubba, Kill.* New York: Simon & Schuster.

Smith, Henry Nash. [1950] 1978. *Virgin Land: The American West as Symbol and Myth.* Cambridge, MA: Harvard University Press.

Smitherman, Geneva. 1998. "Word From the Hood: The Lexicon of African-American Vernacular English." In *African-American English: Structure, History and Use*, edited by Slikoko S. Mufwene, John R. Rickford, Guy Bailey, and John Baugh, 203–226. London: Routledge.

Smithsonian Institution. 1969. *1969 Festival of American Folklife.* Washington, DC: Smithsonian Institution.

Sommers, Christina Hoff. 2000. *The War Against Boys: How Misguided Feminism Is Harming Our Young Men.* New York: Simon & Schuster.

Sonnad, Nikhil. 2018. "The NFL's Racial Divide, In One Chart." *Quartz* (May 24). https://qz.com/1287915/the-nfls-racial-makeup-explains-much-of-its-national-anthem-problems/. Accessed February 4, 2021.

Sporting News. 2008. "Pro Football War Room." http://warroom.sportingnews.com/promo.html. Accessed September 12, 2008.

Stannard, David. 1971. "American Historians and the Idea of National Character: Some Problems and Prospects." *American Quarterly* 23: 202–220.

Stanton, Zack. 2020. "Trump Doesn't Understand Today's Suburbs—And Neither Do You." *Politico* (August 6). www.politico.com/news/magazine/2020/08/06/suburbs-history-race-politics-391966. Accessed January 10, 2021.

Staples, Andy. 2010. "Shift to 3-D TV Broadcasts Will Begin with College Football Fans." *SI.com* (March 3). http://sportsillustrated.cnn.com/2010/writers/andy_staples/03/02/3d-tv/index.html. Accessed September 12, 2010.

Starr, Kevin. 2004. *Coast of Dreams: California on the Edge, 1990–2003*. New York: Knopf.
Starr, Kevin. 2009. *Golden Dream: California in an Age of Abundance, 1950–1963*. New York: Oxford University Press.
Starsburger, Victor C. 2001. "Children and TV Advertising: Nowhere to Run, Nowhere to Hide." *Journal of Developmental and Behavioral Pediatrics* 22: 185–187.
Stearns, Peter N. 2002. *Fat History: Bodies and Beauty in the Modern West*. Revised edition. New York: New York University Press.
Steffens, Lincoln. 1904. *The Shame of the Cities*. New York: McClure, Phillips.
Steinberg, Ted. 2006. *American Green: The Obsessive Quest for the Perfect Lawn*. New York: W. W. Norton.
Steinmetz, Katy. 2011. "Top 10 Buzzwords: 2. Winning/Winner." *Time* (December 7). http://content.time.com/time/specials/packages/article/0,28804,2101344_2100571_2100573,00.html. Accessed January 24, 2021.
Stempel, Carl. 2006. "Televised Sports, Masculinist Moral Capital, and Support for the U. S. Invasion of Iraq." *Journal of Sport and Social Issues* 30: 79–106.
St. John, Eugenia. 1874. *The Cradle of Liberty: A Story of Insane Asylums*. Boston: N.D. Berry.
Stokes, Adrian. 1956. "Psycho-Analytic Reflections on the Development of Ball Games, Particularly Cricket." *International Journal of Psycho-Analysis* 37: 185–192.
Stonebeck, Diane. 2018. "Why Eat Pork and Sauerkraut for New Year's Day?" *Morning Call* (January 1). www.mcall.com/entertainment/dining/mc-why-eat-pork-and-sauerkraut-for-new-years-day-20171229-story.html. Accessed December 27, 2018.
Strings, Sabrina. 2019. *Fearing the Black Body: The Racial Origins of Fat Phobia*. New York: New York University Press.
Suckow, Ruth. 1924. *Country People*. New York: Knopf.
Suckow, Ruth. [1930] 2002. "The Folk Idea in American Life." In *Folk Nation: Folklore in the Creation of American Tradition*, edited by Simon J. Bronner, 145–160. Lanham, MD: Rowman & Littlefield.
Sullivan, Louis H. 1896. "The Tall Office Building Artistically Considered." *Lippincott's Monthly Magazine* (March), 403–409.
TAUNY. 2016. "TAUNY Presents Programs on French Heritage Starting October 15." *TAUNY: Traditional Arts in Upstate New York*. (October 7). http://tauny.org/post/307/tauny-presents-programs-on-french-heritage-starting-october-15. Accessed January 2, 2021.
Taylor, William R. 1961. *Cavalier and Yankee: The Old South and American National Character*. New York: Braziller.
Taylor, William R. 1989. "The Evolution of Public Space in New York City: The Commercial Showcase of America." In *Consuming Visions: Accumulation and Display of Goods in America, 1880–1920*, edited by Simon J. Bronner, 287–310. New York: W. W. Norton.
Tebbel, John. 1963. *From Rags to Riches: Horatio Alger and the American Dream*. New York: Macmillan.
Terrell, Ellen. 2019. "When a Quote is Not (Exactly) a Quote: The Business of America is Business Edition." *Inside Adams: Science, Technology & Business* (January 17). https://blogs.loc.gov/inside_adams/2019/01/when-a-quote-is-not-exactly-a-quote-the-business-of-america-is-business-edition/. Accessed January 29, 2021.
Thomas, C.K. 1932. "Jewish Dialect and New York Dialect." *American Speech* 7: 321–326.

Thompson, Dennis. 2019. *WebMD* (November 13). www.webmd.com/diet/obesity/news/20191113/more-americans-trying-to-lose-weight-but-few-succeeding#1. Accessed February 5, 2021.

Thorne, Barrie. 1993. *Gender Play: Girls and Boys in School*. New Brunswick, NJ: Rutgers University Press.

Thug Life. 1994. *Thug Life*: Volume 1. CD audio. Santa Monica, CA: Interscope.

Tocqueville, Alexis de. [1840] 1981. *Democracy in America*. New York: Modern Library.

Toffler, Alvin. 1980. *The Third Wave*. New York: William Morrow.

Torres, Monica. 2020. "The 1980 Movie '9 to 5' Is Still Depressingly Relevant for Women at Work." *HuffPost* (August 18). www.huffpost.com/entry/movie-9-to-5-film-dolly-parton_l_5db6fa34e4b079eb95a7299a. Accessed January 29, 2021.

Trachtenberg, Alan. 1982. *The Incorporation of America: Culture and Society in the Gilded Age*. New York: Hill and Wang.

Trawick, Pal, and Alf Hornborg. 2015. "Revisiting the Image of Limited Good: On Sustainability, Thermodynamics, and the Illusion of Creating Wealth." *Current Anthropology* 56: 1–27.

Trollinger, Susan L. 2012. *Selling the Amish: The Tourism of Nostalgia*. Baltimore: Johns Hopkins University Press.

Trujillo, Nick. 1995. "Machines, Missiles, and Men: Images of the Male Body on ABC's Monday Night Football." *Sociology of Sport Journal* 12: 403–423.

Turner, Frederick Jackson. [1920] 1996. *The Frontier in American History*. New York: Dover.

Turpin, Robert J. 2018. *First Taste of Freedom: A Cultural History of Bicycle Marketing in the United States*. Syracuse, NY: Syracuse University Press.

Uhlir, Kurt. 2020. "112 Uplifting Real Estate Quotes That Will Inspire You to Grow This Year." *Showcase IDX Blog*. https://showcaseidx.com/real-estate-quotes/. Accessed January 31, 2021.

United States Census Bureau. 2016. "Americans Moving at Historically Low Rates, Census Bureau Reports." *Census.gov Newsroom* (November 16). www.census.gov/newsroom/press-releases/2016/cb16-189.html. Accessed December 30, 2018.

United States Census Bureau. 2018. "Urban Areas Facts." *Geography Program* (May 15). www.census.gov/programs-surveys/geography/guidance/geo-areas/urban-rural/ua-facts.html. Accessed January 1, 2021.

Urban Land Institute. 2016. *Housing in the Evolving American Suburb*. Washington, DC: Urban Land Institute.

U.S. Department of Health and Human Services. 2010. *The Surgeon General's Vision for a Healthy and Fit Nation*. Rockville, MD: U.S. Department of Health and Human Services, Office of the Surgeon General.

Vallas, Steven P. 2003. "The Adventures of Managerial Hegemony: Teamwork, Ideology, and Worker Resistance." *Social Problems* 50: 204–225.

van Gennep, Arnold. 1960. *The Rites of Passage*, translated by Monika B. Vizedom and Gabrielle L. Caffee. Chicago: University of Chicago Press.

Veblen, Thorstein. 1899. *The Theory of the Leisure Class: An Economic Study of Institutions*. New York: Macmillan.

Veblen, Thorstein. [1899] 1979. *The Theory of the Leisure Class*. New York: Penguin.

Vellinga, Marcel. 2011. "The End of the Vernacular: Anthropology and the Architecture of the Other." *Etnofoor* 23: 171–192.

Vera, Amir. 2020. "Vanderbilt's Sarah Fuller Tells Young Girls 'The Path to Success Is a Lot of Ups and Downs'." *CNN* (December 2). www.cnn.com/2020/12/01/us/sarah-fuller-anderson-cooper-full-circle-trnd/index.html. Accessed February 4, 2021.

Veum, Aslaug, and Linda Victoria Moland Undrum. 2017. "The Selfie as a Global Discourse." *Discourse & Society* 29: 86–103.

Villarino, José, and Arturo Ramírez. 1992. *Chicano Border Culture and Folklore*, second edition. San Diego: Marin.

Villers, Damien, and Wolfgang Mieder. 2017. "'Time is Money': Benjamin Franklin and the Vexing Problem of Proverb Origins." *Proverbium* 34: 391–404.

VOA News. 2021. "Controversy Over GameStop's Stock Market Saga Explained." *VOA News* (January 30). www.voanews.com/economy-business/controversy-over-gamestops-stock-market-saga-explained. Accessed January 31, 2021.

Vogt, Evon Z. 1955. *Modern Homesteaders: The Life of a Twentieth-Century Frontier Community*. Cambridge, MA: Harvard University Press.

Wachs, Eleanor. 1988. "'To Toast the Bake': The Johnston Family Clambake." In *"We Gather Together": Food and Festival in American Life*, edited by Theodore C. Humphrey and Lin T. Humphrey, 75–88. Ann Arbor: UMI Research Press.

Wagner, James. 2008. "Top-Selling Video Games Show Growing Casual/Crossover Trend." *Gigaom*. http://gigaom.com/2008/01/24/top-selling-video-games-show-growing-casualcrossover-trend/. Accessed April 2, 2008.

Wagner, Kate. 2017. "The Rise of the McModern." *Curbed* (June 30). https://archive.curbed.com/2017/6/30/15893836/what-is-mcmansion-hell-modern-suburbs-history. Accessed January 9, 2021.

Wald, Elijah. 2001. *Narcocorrido: A Journey into the Music of Drugs, Guns, and Guerillas*. New York: Rayo.

Wanamaker, John. 1911. *Golden Book of the Wanamaker Stores*. Philadelphia: John Wanamaker.

Watercutter, Angela. 2021. "The Bernie Sanders Meme Proves the Internet is Resetting." *Wired* (January 22). www.wired.com/story/bernie-sanders-meme-shift/. Accessed February 6, 2021.

Wattenberg, Ben. 1995. *Values Matter Most*. Washington, DC: Regnery.

Watterson, John Sayle. 2000. *College Football: History, Spectacle, Controversy*. Baltimore: Johns Hopkins University Press.

Weaver, William Woys. 2013. *As American as Shoofly Pie: The Foodlore and Fakelore of Pennsylvania Dutch Cuisine*. Philadelphia: University of Pennsylvania Press.

Webb, Walter Prescott. [1931] 1959. *The Great Plains*. Lincoln: University of Nebraska Press.

Wehse, Rainer. 2014. "Blason Populaire." In *Encyclopedia of Humor Studies*, edited by Salvatore Attardo, 85–87. Thousand Oaks, CA: SAGE.

Weinberg, Arthur Myron, ed. 1974. *The Muckrakers: The Era in Journalism that Moved America to Reform*. New York: Van Nostrand.

Weisman, Alan, and Jay Dusard. 1991. *La Frontera: The United States Border with Mexico*. Tucson: University of Arizona Press.

Wendt, Michael. 2010. "Howells vs. Capitalism." *ESSAI* 7, Article 43. https://dc.cod.edu/essai/vol7/iss1/43/. Accessed January 30, 2021.

Wert, J. Howard. 1905. "Walks Around Harrisburg." *Harrisburg Telegraph* (December 13), 7.

Wethington, Elaine. 2000. "Expecting Stress: American and the 'Midlife Crisis'." *Motivation and Emotion* 24: 85–103.

Whitaker, Jan. 2006. *Service and Style: How the American Department Store Fashioned the Middle Class*. New York: St. Martin's Press.

Whitaker, Jan. 2011. *The World of Department Stores*. New York: Vendome Press.
White, O. Kendall, Jr. 1978. "Mormonism in America and Canada: Accommodation to the Nation-State." *Canadian Journal of Sociology* 3: 161–181.
White, Merry. 1994. *The Material Child: Coming of Age in Japan and America*. Berkeley: University of California Press.
White, Morton, and Lucia White. 1962. *The Intellectual versus the City: From Thomas Jefferson to Frank Lloyd Wright*. Cambridge, MA: Harvard University Press.
Whiting, John W.M., and Barbara Ayres. 1968. "Inferences from the Shape of Dwellings." In *Settlement Archaeology*, edited by K.C. Chang, 117–133. Palo Alto, CA: National Book Press.
Whiting, Robert. 1990. *You Gotta Have Wa*. New York: Vintage.
Wiggins, William H., Jr., and Douglas DeNatale, eds. 1993. *Jubilation!: African American Celebrations in the Southeast*. Columbia, SC: MicKissick Museum.
Wike, Richard, Janell Fetterolf, and Mara Mordecai. 2020. "U.S. Image Plummets Internationally as Most Say Country Has Handled Coronavirus Badly." *Pew Research Center* (September 15). www.pewresearch.org/global/2020/09/15/us-image-plummets-internationally-as-most-say-country-has-handled-coronavirus-badly/. Accessed January 3, 2020.
Wilkerson, Isabel. 2011. *The Warmth of Other Suns: The Epic Story of America's Great Migration*. New York: Vintage.
Wilkie, Christina. 2020. "Trump Tries to Claim Victory Even as Ballots Are Being Counted in Several States—NBC Has Not Made a Call." *CNBC* (November 4). www.cnbc.com/2020/11/04/trump-tries-to-claim-victory-even-as-ballots-are-being-counted-in-several-states-nbc-has-not-made-a-call.html. Accessed January 24, 2021.
Williams, Michael Ann. 2004. *Homeplace: The Social Use and Meaning of the Folk Dwelling in Southwestern North Carolina*. Charlottesville: University of Virginia Press.
Williams, Robin M., Jr. 1952. *American Society: A Sociological Interpretation*. New York: Alfred A. Knopf.
Williams, Roger. 1643. *A Key into the Language of America*. London: Gregory Dexter.
Williamson, Ray A. 1987. "Outer Space as Frontier: Lessons for Today." *Western Folklore* 46: 255–267.
Willis Tower. 2020. "History and Facts." www.willistower.com/history-and-facts. Accessed January 3, 2021.
Wilsey, John D. 2017. "'Our Country is Destined to be the Great Nation of Futurity': John L. O'Sullivan's Manifest Destiny and Christian Nationalism, 1837–1846." *Religions* 8 (4), 68. doi:10.3390/rel8040068. Accessed December 31, 2020.
Wilson, Harry Leon. 1902. *The Spenders*. Boston: Lothrop.
Wilson, William H. 1980. "Harrisburg's Successful City Beautiful Movement, 1900–1915." *Pennsylvania History* 47: 213–233.
"Women Are Forming Clubs to Patronize Clean Shops." 1907. *Board of Trade Journal* 2, no. 11 (November): 20
Woodard, Colin. 2011. *American Nations: A History of the Eleven Rival Regional Cultures of North America*. New York: Penguin.
Woodman, Dan, and Julia Cook. 2019. "As the 9-to-5 work day disappears, Our Lives Are Growing More Out of Sync." *The Conversation* (October 29). https://theconversation.com/as-the-9-to-5-work-day-disappears-our-lives-are-growing-more-out-of-sync-125800. Accessed January 29, 2021.
Wright, Erik Olin, and Joel Rogers. 2015. *American Society: How It Really Works*, second edition. New York: W. W. Norton.

WWE Insider. 2017. "Floyd Mayweather-'Money Isn't Everything, Money is the Only Thing .'" (October 12). Video. www.youtube.com/watch?v=WJyhjtKf3mc. Accessed January 29, 2021.

Yates, Gayle Graham. 2006. "Family Reunions." In *The New Encyclopedia of Southern Culture, Volume 4: Myth, Manners and Memory*, edited by Charles Reagan Wilson, 222–223. Chapel Hill: University of North Carolina Press.

Yoder, Joseph W. 1950. *Amish Traditions*. Huntingdon, PA: Yoder Publishing.

Yorgason, Ethan R. 2003. *Transformation of the Mormon Culture Region*. Urbana: University of Illinois Press.

Zelinsky, Wilbur. 1973. *The Cultural Geography of the United States*. Revised ed. Englewood Cliffs, NJ: Prentice-Hall.

Zelinsky, Wilbur. 1980. "North America's Vernacular Regions." *Annals of the Association of American Geographers* 70: 1–16.

Zuckerman, Michael. 2000. "The Presence of the Present, The End of History." *Public Historian* 22: 19–22.

Zukin, Sharon. 2005. *Point of Purchase: How Shopping Changed American Culture*. New York: Routledge.

Zumwalt, Rosemary Lévy. 1995. "Alan Dundes: Folklorist and Mentor." In *Folklore Interpreted: Essays in Honor of Alan Dundes*, edited by Regina Bendix and Rosemary Lévy Zumwalt, 1–48. New York: Garland.

INDEX

abundance 51, 85, 93, 97, 133, 154, 161–63, 168, 171–72; of goods 163, 190; super- 143
Acadia 20, 43; *see also* Cajun culture; Maine
Adam and Eve 11
Adams, David Wallace (historian) 116–17, 125, 136
Adams, Henry 51
adolescence 69–70, 73, 81, 84, 95, 105, 107, 113, 140–41; ethnographies of 113–14; masculinity 121–28, 140; and obesity 185; *see also* childhood; life course
Adorno, Theodor 150
advertising 33, 78, 93, 94, 96, 104, 138, 143–44, 148, 152, 156, 161, 173, 177, 184, 188, 191; aimed at children 144; bicycle 169–71; magical thinking in 144; Robinson, Harry 180–81; Spyware Doctor, of 108; Wanamaker, John, of 164, 166–67; *see also* consumerism
African Americans 37, 40, 65, 67, 79, 81, 88, 90–91, 129–30, 148, 160, 175, 186–87, 189, 193
Africans 18
"Age and Life of Man, The" (Fancy) 70, 71–72; *see also* "Life and Age of Man, The"; "Life and Age of Woman, The"
Agger, Ben (sociologist) 150–51
agrarian myth 68–69
agriculture 13–14
Alger, Horatio 28

"Allegory of Human Life" (Cole) *see* "Voyage of Life, The"
Allen, George (coach) 134
Allen, Jake (entrepreneur) 143
almanacs 75
America, idea of x
American Dream 8, 29, 34, 84, 172, 173; of success 146; *see also* American Promise; dream home
Americanness 5, 8, 66, 76–77, 85, 87, 116; cognitive concept of, 1–2, 3, 6; definition of 1–2; of getting ahead 130; of inequities 66; of mobility 44–46; of political change 194; of pursuing money 146; of suburbs 29–35; of success 187–90; of winning 7–8, 101–4
American Promise 23, 34; *see also* American Dream
Amish 13, 149–50, 153–54, 182, 192; *see also* Pennsylvania, Germans
animal rights movement 97
anthropology 2, 109, 143
anti-Semitism 66
Appalachian Mountains 11, 12, 15, 17, 37–39
"Are Freudians Ever Right?" (Fine) 122–23
Arizona 23, 35; Cardinals 130
Arkansas 16, 19
Asian Americans 59, 65, 67, 186; Southeast 85; *see also* Chinese; Japan
As You Like It (Shakespeare) 70
Atlantic World 20–21

Australia 183
authority 82, 131–32, 151; folk 174; governmental 116; parental 31, 61
automobile 1, 31, 77, 132, 145, 169, 171
Average Joe folktype 188–89, 192, 193
Average Joe (reality television show) 188

Bachelor, The (television show) 188
Bachelorette, The (television show) 188
Baker, Ronald L. (folklorist) 17
ballad 37, 41–42, 71, 72; see also *corridos*
balloon-frame construction 29
Baltimore 13, 23, 175
barbecue 1
bar mitzvah 82–83
basketball 104, 105, 108, 111–12, 113, 115, 120, 125, 127, 129, 133, 137; see also sports
beaches 33, 36, 90, 185
Beecher, Harry (sportswriter) 136
beliefs 10–11, 49
Bellamy, Edward 162
Benton, Thomas Hart (artist) 28
Bercovitch, Sacvan (historian) 14
bicycle 169–71, 181
Biden, Joseph 64, 102, 189
birthday 17, 40, 84, 91
Black Lives Matter movement 66
Black Thought 81
Bland, James 88
blason populaire 17; see also jokes, Kentucky-Indiana
bluegrass (music) 37
Blue Ridge Mountains 35
blues (music) 37, 186
body 7–8, 183–91; see also obesity; thinness
Bolles, Richard 78
Boone, Daniel 44, 137
Bootheel region (Missouri) 16
borderlands 40–44
"Bosses of the Senate, The" (illustration) 188
Boxes of Life, The (Bolles) 78
broadsides 70, 71–72, 75; photocopied 146
Brooklyn 28, 86, 93; accent 23; Coney Island section of 93
Brown, Foxy (rapper) 80–81
Browne, Jackson 147
Bull, John 93
'Burbs, The (movie) 33
Burne-Jones, Philip 159–60
Burns, Robert (poet) 86

Cajun culture 16, 20; see also Acadia; Louisiana
California 11–12, 17, 41, 131; Dream 132, 189; see also West Coast
Camp, Walter 120, 129, 131
campaigns, political 2, 24, 46; see also slogans, political
Canada 16, 44, 119, 173, 183; border with United States 42–43; maritime provinces of 16, 43
can-do attitude 48, 53, 65; see also optimism, American
candy store 177
Cape Cod 18; house 29; see also Levittown; Plymouth
capitalism 8, 106, 114, 143–44, 159; consumer 172, 183, 190–91; slow and fast 148–54; see also consumerism; corporate organization; money
Capitol, U.S., January 6, 2021 siege of 66–67
Caribbean 13, 44
Carnegie, Andrew (industrialist) 143, 145
Carlisle Indian Industrial School 116–17, 118, 134
Census, U.S. 15, 24, 45, 171
Centers for Disease Control and Prevention (CDC) 183–84
Chaump, George 132
Checkered Game of Life (board game) 77
Chicago 25, 37, 161
childhood 31, 34, 37, 52, 58, 62, 69, 72–74, 75, 78, 79, 84, 88, 94, 99, 112, 153, 171, 185; games 94, 103, 107, 112, 125; of John O'Hara 181–82; see also adolescence
children *see* childhood
China 31, 61, 102, 144; see also Chinatowns: Chinese Americans
Chinatowns 28
Chinese Americans 34, 86; see also Asian Americans; Chinatowns
Chosen Image, The (Pearl) 82
Christianity 7, 10–11; see also religion
Christmas 85, 95, 96, 98, 144, 188, 190
Church of Latter-day Saints *see* Mormons
circularity 69–70, 85, 121–22; see also linearity
cities 23–24, 27–29, 174, 175–83; modernist label of 27; see also City Beautiful Movement; suburbs; urbanization
City Beautiful Movement 182

civil religion 76, 107
civil rights 12, 30, 65, 90, 103, 110, 126, 173; *see also* African Americans; women, social movement of
Civil War and Reconstruction era 12, 77, 88, 96, 163, 176
class, social 5, 29, 51, 70, 110, 114, 144, 159–61, 166, 176–77, 189, 191; leisure 155–56, 181; lower (under) 15, 186; middle 29, 32–33, 74, 77, 79, 116, 147, 161, 169, 171, 182–83, 186; professional (new) 29, 150; upper 33, 105, 185, 187; working 89, 92, 130, 168, 183, 188
Cleveland Show, The (television show) 189
Clinton, Bill 47
Cole, Thomas (painter) 73
Collier, Price 136
colonialism 12, 14, 18–19, 32, 41, 93, 115–16, 174; *see also* imperialism
Columbus, Christopher 7
Comenius, John Amos 75
commercial culture 4–5, 7, 24, 26, 44, 84, 87, 161, 177, 181, 183, 190, 191, 193; *see also* advertising; consumerism; popular culture
conservation movement 22
conservatism 25, 66–67, 102, 194
conspicuous consumption, concept of 32, 132
consumerism 57, 79, 83, 87, 89, 94, 97, 144–48, 150–54, 163; and consumer culture 96–97, 99, 140, 144, 150–94; and football 104; and individualism 79; and middle class 74; urban-industrial 70; *see also* capitalism; materialism
Conwell, Russell (minister) 145
Coolidge, Calvin 142–43
Cooper, James Fenimore 175
Corn, Joseph (historian) 51
corporate organization 27, 106, 146, 150, 173; *see also* commercial culture
corridos 41–42; narco- 42
Cortez, Gregorio 41–42
cosmetic surgery 185–86
Country People (Suckow) 28
COVID-19 *see* pandemic
cowboy 117, 118, 119, 188; *see also* Great Plains
Cradle 2 the Grave (movie) 81
"Cradle to the Grave" (Thug Life) 80
credit card 77, 148, 162; debt 145
creolization 16, 20, 39,
Crèvocoeur, Hector St. John de 50

Croly, Herbert 32
Cross, Gary (historian) 152–53
cultural 3–5; construction 3, 69; decoration 3; definition of 3–5; form 3; landscape 5, 10–15, 21–24, 29–35, 40–41, 46, 118, 191; stylization 3
Currier and Ives lithographs 73–75, 77
Curry, John Steuart (artist) 28
cyberlore *see* digital culture

Damnation of Theron Ware, The (Frederic) 157–58
Darwinism, Social 143
Decoration Day 17, 88
Delmarva 16
Democracy in America (Tocqueville) 171–72
department stores 156, 157, 159, 162–63, 164, 168, 171, 179–81; Gimbel's 98; Macy's 98; *see also* Wanamaker, John
Desmond, Harry W. (editor) 32
Detroit 94, 98, 99, 145
digital culture 17, 45, 132, 142, 143, 152–53, 183, 192–93; *see also* Internet; websites
discourse 2
Disney, Walt 145
Doctrine of First Effective Settlement 19
Dollars and Democracy (Burne-Jones) 159–60
Donehoo, George P. 175
Dorson, Richard M. (folklorist) 12, 13, 43–44
Douglass, Frederick 90
dream home 33–34
Dreiser, Theodore 156–57
Dundes, Alan (folklorist) 49, 62–63, 107–110, 112–14, 121–24, 141; *see also* Freud, Sigmund
Dyer, Braven (journalist) 142

Eastern Seaboard 13, 18, 21
Eastern Shore *see* Delmarva
economy 13, 43, 52, 55, 58, 103, 135, 144, 148, 150–53; globalized 8, 34, 57; industrial 150; plantation 13–14; preindustrial 149; producer 8, 144–45, 173, 183; rural (agrarian) 32, 89; service and information 6, 29, 45, 78, 89, 106, 130, 144, 150, 184, 189; *see also* commercial culture
Edmundson, Mark 104
Education of Henry Adams, The (Adams) 51
Edwards, Harry (sociologist) 139
elite culture 5

emic (native) views 6, 12
Emmet, Boris (historian) 170
Empire cabinet 158–59
England 9, 19, 41, 70, 160; Church of 18; farming system of 13–14; *see also* Puritans
esoteric and exoteric, concept 16, 17
ESPN 119, 138; video games 138
Estaville, Lawrence E. 39
ethnoburbs 34; *see also* suburbs
ethnography 6–7, 13, 17, 38, 50, 62–63, 84, 109–15; *see also* folk culture
Europe 1, 5, 111, 127, 137, 162, 171; classical civilizations of 154; feudal 70; industrialized 14
expansionism 18, 21–23, 48, 119, 161, 174; *see also* imperialism

Fahnestock, William 179–80
Fahnestock's store 179
family 31, 35, 37–39, 40, 51, 58, 60–64, 74–75, 81, 87, 89–90, 95, 98–99, 154, 158, 160; African-American 148; agrarian ideals of 174; Amish 153–54; German-American 28; picnics 37, 90; reunions 17, 40
Family Guy (television show) 189
Fancy, Peter (composer) 70
farmers' markets 153–54
farms 14, 20, 23, 24, 149; *see also* agrarian myth
Faster: The Acceleration of Just About Everything (Gleick) 51
fatalism 70, 81, 187; male 80
Fat City (Gardner) 189–90
fatness *see* obesity
Feinstein, John 112–13
femininity 107–8, 117, 121, 123–24, 126, 134, 136–37, 140, 179; *see also* gender; masculinity
feminism 110, 114, 146
Festival of American Folklife *see* Smithsonian Folklife Festival
Fine, Gary Alan (sociologist) 122–23
"Fire, The" (Black Thought) 81
Fisk Jubilee Singers 88
Fleming, Thomas (illustrator) 161
Flintstones, The (television show) 188
flip-flops 185
Florida 44, 45, 96; Miami 86, 94, 131
Foley, Douglas 113–14
folklore 2, 11, 12, 17, 41, 43, 49, 153; *see also* folk culture; folksongs; folktales

folk culture 4–5, 39, 68–69, 79, 149–50, 153; *see also* folklore; folksongs; folktales
folklife *see* folk culture
folksongs 37–39, 191
folktales 5, 17, 20, 44, 80; *see also* jokes
folkways *see* folk culture
food, American 1, 20, 36–37, 40, 90, 93–94, 96–98, 138, 176, 184, 187; *see also* hamburgers; hot dogs; material culture; picnics
football 87, 89, 98, 99, 101–42, 148, 184; *see also* sports
"Four Seasons of Life" (lithograph) 73
Fourth of July *see* Independence Day
frame, concept of 3, 6, 7, 35, 36, 38–39, 40, 43, 76, 84, 107, 109, 111, 153, 157, 192, 193; play 114, 126, 141; *see also* ethnography
France, New 10, 43
Francophone *see* French-Canadians
Franklin, Benjamin 145
Franklin, John Hope (historian) 65–66
Frederic, Harold 157–58
French Canadians 43; *see also* New France
fresh start, concept of 23, 49–50, 75, 85, 87, 120, 172; *see also* New and Old World, concept of
Freud, Sigmund 17, 108, 122; *see also* psychoanalytic perspective
Friday Night Lights (television series) 111, 134, 139
frontier 7, 12, 22, 23, 41, 50–51, 92–93, 175; theme in football 115–21, 124–27, 129, 131, 135–37, 140; *see also* cowboy; rhetoric, frontier; wilderness
Fuller, Sarah 130
future orientation 8, 21, 44, 47–69
futurity *see* O'Sullivan, John

Gallup polls 33–34, 52–54, 61, 63
Game of District Messenger Boy or Merit Rewarded, The (board game) 77
Game of Life (board game) 77
games 78, 87, 90, 94, 103, 107, 112; baseball 90, 93; board 77, 80; bowl 87; Highland 87; and narrative 125; singing 121; video 137–38, 193; *see also* football; sports
GameStop Corporation 193–94
Garden of Eden 7, 10–11
Gardner, Leonard (novelist) 189
Garreau, Joel (journalist) 44

gender 2, 7–8, 40, 59, 68, 84, 110; discrimination 130; and family roles 98; wall 130; *see also* masculinity; women
geographers, cultural 12, 22
Germany 5, 31, 64, 127; Frankfurt 93; *see also* Pennsylvania, Germans
G.I. Joe 188
Gilded Age 159, 187; *see also* Progressive era
Gillam, Bernhard 187–88
Girvin, Clarence "Doc" 38
Girvin, Eva (Owen) 38
Glassie, Henry (folklorist) 20
Gleick, James (journalist) 51
globalization x, 8, 18, 34, 57, 88, 103, 120, 150–51, 183, 192
Goodman, Steven (film critic) 73
Gould, Jay 188
Great Plains 16, 21, 40
Greenfield, Jeff (sports commentator) 129
Grimm, Jacob and Wilhelm 5
grocers 176–77
Groundhog Day 17
Gullah and Geechee cultures 20
Gunfighter Nation: The Myth of the Frontier in Twentieth-Century America (Slotkin) 116
Gunton, George (economist) 161–62
Guzman, Joaquin "El Chapo" 42

Halas, George 134
Halloween 94–95, 144
hamburgers 1, 2, 93; McDonald's 31
Hamilton, Alexander 66–67
Hamlet, Janice (communications scholar) 186
Harris poll 33, 61, 64
Harrisburg (Pennsylvania) 16, 31, 118, 175–83
Harrisburg: The City Beautiful, Romantic and Historic (Donehoo) 175
Harvest Home 96
Hayes, Woody (coach) 132, 134
Hazard of New Fortunes, A (Howells) 155, 158
health clubs 184–85
Heilbroner, Robert (economist) 49
Hennepin, Louis (Belgian Franciscan missionary) 10
Herder, Johann Gottfried von 5
heritage 15, 34, 49, 51, 94; Appalachian Mountain 37; and homelands 39; national 51, 65–66, 90, 99; pioneer 95;

revolutionary 194; southern 17; *see also* tradition
heroes 44, 127; folk 41–42; football 111, 120–21, 127; frontier 24, 44, 137; gladiator 104–5; super- 99
Higginson, Francis (Puritan minister) 9
higher education 81–82, 144
high schools 50, 62, 81, 105; football in 105, 113, 127, 138
Hill, Lauryn 81
hip-hop (music) 80–81, 147, 186
Hispanics 34, 59, 65, 67, 186, 190; and Quinceañera 84–85
Hofstadter, Richard 68–69
Holden, Stephen (film critic) 84
holidays 1, 19, 36, 84–99, 144, 184; *see also* ritual year
home, cognitive idea of 38–39, 45–46, 99, 125, 158, 172–74; and Thanksgiving 99
homelands, concept of 39–40, 46
homeownership, 172–74
homophobia 66
homosexuals *see* LGBT
Hoosier 17
Horrigan, Brian (historian) 51
Hostetler, John 149
hot dogs 1, 2, 93, 94, 138
Houston 24, 91
Howells, William Dean 154–55, 160–61, 191, 194
How the Other Half Lives (Riis) 27, 160
Hubbard, William (architect) 31
Huber-Owen family 37–39
humor 18
Humphrey, Lin T. 38
Huston, John (director) 190
Huston, Ralph "Cub" 176

idealism, American 66, 146; *see also* optimism, American
identity 2, 5, 12, 28, 39, 45, 99, 116, 125, 135, 139, 152–53, 187, 190; African-American 130; borderlands 40–44; corporate 114; eastern 16; ethnic 28–29, 41, 82–83, 88; family 39; masculine 126, 140; national 5, 12, 140; place-based 16; progressive 193; regional 12–13, 15–18, 20, 36–37, 45, 87–88; southern 15; urban 87, 176; *see also* gender; race and ethnicity
Illinois 12–13; nation 10–11

immigrants 2, 12, 14, 19, 21, 23, 34, 84, 93–94, 96, 98, 148, 156, 160, 161, 175, 176, 179, 181; *see also* race and ethnicity
immigration *see* immigrants
imperialism 22, 92–93, 110, 127, 161; *see also* expansionism
Independence Day 1, 89–90, 91, 92–93, 102
Indiana 17, 20, 36; Indianapolis 131; -Kentucky jokes 17–18; Muncie 168
indigenous population 2, 9, 12, 18, 21, 22, 42, 43, 97; *see also* Native Americans
individualism 5, 7, 8, 14, 38, 49, 62, 69, 85, 95, 114, 132, 138, 192; capitalist 14, 149; competitive 79; and future orientation 63; and polling 68; private property and 31; rugged 44, 118
industrialization 6, 14, 44–45, 50–51, 62, 68–69, 105, 106, 116, 117, 163, 174, 183; *see also* urbanization
infantilization 81, 103, 124, 126; *see also* childhood; femininity
Inglewood, Marian 175, 177–78
International Harvester Company 33
Internet 57, 68, 101–2, 133, 151, 152, 193, 194; *see also* digital culture; websites
Islamophobia 66
isoglosses 16, 20

Jacksonian political philosophy 66
Jameson, Fredric 150
Jamestown 18
Japan 61, 64, 111, 127–28, 158; Coming of Age Day in 82; *see also* Asian Americans
Jay Treaty of 1795 42
Jefferson, Thomas 66–67, 148, 174
Jeuck, John E. 170
Jews 10, 23, 63, 82–83, 85
Jim Crow laws 15
Joe Sixpack folktype 189
jokes 17, 36, 78–79, 82; Kentucky-Indiana 17–18; riddle- 11; *see also* folktales
Johnson, James Weldon 90
Johnson, Samuel 73
Jones, Howard Mumford 163
Jones, Suzi (folklorist) 35–36
journalism 21, 44, 51, 104, 117, 118, 125, 142, 166, 170, 180; sports 110, 116, 134–35, 138
Juneteenth 17, 90–91
Jurgenson, Nathan (sociologist) 152

Kaepernick, Colin 129
Kennedy, John 116

Kentucky 17, 20, 37, 189
Keppler, J. 188
King Football (Oriard)
King, Martin Luther, Jr. 91
Kissinger, Henry 126
Kluckhohn, Florence (sociologist) 48–49
Klymasz, Robert (folklorist) 42
Kruse, Zach 131

Labor Day 89, 91, 94
labor, indentured 15
land 12, 14–15, 28, 46; lure of 22; pasture 32
La Salle, René-Robert Cavelier, Sieur 10
Latinx *see* Hispanics
Las Vegas 131, 142
lawn 29, 30, 31, 32–33, 173
Leatherstocking Tales (Cooper) 175
legend 35–36, 42, 44
Leidens Ontzet 96
lesbians *see* LGBT
Lévi-Strauss, Claude 2
Levitt, William J. 29–30
Levittown 30–31
LGBT 108, 130, 188
Li, Wei (geographer) 34
liberalism 25, 66, 67, 102; of New Yorkers 168; and pluralism 103; *see also* progressivism
"Life and Age of Man, The" (Baillie) 76; *see also* "Age and Life of Man, The"
"Life and Age of Woman, The" (Baillie) 77–78; *see also* "Age and Life of Man, The"; "Life and Age of Man, The"
life course 69–84; four-phase 73
"Lift Every Voice" (song) 90
Lil Scrappy (rapper) 147
limited good, image of 143; *see also* unlimited good, image of
Lincoln, Abraham 27, 90, 96, 173
linearity 69–73, 77, 81, 99, 121; *see also* circularity; symbolism, of lines
Little Dixie (Missouri) 16
Little Egypt (southern Illinois) 12–13
localism 2, 153, 162
Lombardi, Vince (coach) 101, 127
Looking Backward (Bellamy) 162
Los Angeles 24, 28, 34, 94, 131
lost tribes of Israel 10
Louisiana 16, 20, 37
Lowcountry region (South Carolina and Georgia) 20
Lynd, Helen 168–69
Lynd, Robert 168–69

Madden, John (coach) 127, 137; video game 138
Maine 16, 18, 43; Down Easters 18; Lewiston 162
Mandelbaum, Michael 111, 115, 119, 129, 131, 132
Manifest Destiny 21–22, 35, 48, 119
manor house 32–33, 35, 149
Mansion of Happiness (board game) 77
manufacturing 14
market houses 176, 177–78, 181
Marxism 111, 150
masculinity 82, 107–9, 113, 121–28, 133–39; and Victorian cult of manliness 116; hyper- 104, 107; and national identity 140; *see also* gender
maritime culture 16, 20, 44
Mason-Dixon Line 11
mass culture 5, 44; *see also* massification; popular culture
massification 20, 36, 44, 106; *see* mass culture
Massachusetts 21; Bay Colony 9, 18, 96
master-planned community (MPC) 35
material culture 19, 29, 35, 155, 161; *see also* food, American; materialism
materialism 83, 142, 149, 161, 168; acquisitive 147, 148; *see also* consumerism; wealth
Mayweather, Floyd, Jr. (boxing promoter) 142, 192
McDonaldization 8, 31, 32
McGee, W. J. (ethnologist) 171
McGrory, Mary (journalist) 104, 175
McMansions 31, 32
Meinig, D.W. (geographer) 174
memes 18; *see also* digital culture
Memorial Day 88, 89
metaphors 2
Mexico 13, 40–42, 44, 83–84, 185; *see also corridos*
Michaelmas 96
Michigan 104; Upper Peninsula of 13
middle age 70, 74, 79; *see also* midlife crisis
Middle Atlantic region 16, 20
Middletown (Lynd) 168–69
midlife crisis 78–79
Midwest 20, 44, 67, 168
millennial thinking 7, 47, 51, 53, 55–56, 63–64
Milwaukee 24
Minneapolis 91
Mississippi Delta region 16, 37

Mississippi River 11, 13, 20
Missouri 16, 20; St. Louis 26, 93, 118, 131, 161, 164
mobility 7, 36, 44–46, 51–52, 65, 85, 110, 148, 156, 163, 168–69, 171; economic 23, 60, 144, 189; and individuality 192; physical 13, 44–46, 161, 164, 169; social 5, 8, 15, 28, 34–35, 70, 77, 79, 89, 93, 143–44, 150–51; *see also* American Dream; American Promise
modernization 105, 109, 121, 126, 140, 174, 194; of football 136; *see also* progress
money 36, 142–94; *see also* capitalism
"Money (That's What I Want)" (song) 145
Montgomery Ward (catalogue) 170
Mormon Culture Region (MCR) 16, 22–23, 39
Mormons 17, 22–23
morphology 125–26; *see also* structuralism
Morton, George 96
Mourt's Relation (Morton) 95–96
movies 33, 73, 107, 127, 134, 181, 183; of 1950s 73; bar/bat mitzvah in 82
"Movin' on Up" (song) 148
multiculturalism 23, 25, 29, 84; *see also* pluralism
Mummer's Parade 88
music, hillbilly 4
mythology 10–11, 43–44, 72, 118, 168; frontier 7, 41; of the hunter 137, 139; Pilgrim 95, 97; Roman 85; *see also* agrarian myth; rags-to-riches mythology

Namath, Joe, 111–12, 129
names 13, 22, 30, 31, 34–35, 118, 119, 134, 137; place 12, 36–37
narcissism of minor differences 17; *see also* Freud, Sigmund
Narrative of Arthur Gordon Pym of Nantucket, The (Poe) 72
Nast, Thomas (cartoonist) 187, 188
National Football League (NFL) 105–6, 112, 127, 128, 129–32, 133, 134; *see also* football
nationalism 2, 5, 42–43, 162, 192; cultural 5; philosophy of Romantic 5
National Opinion Research Center 52–53
Native Americans 9, 14, 21, 43, 95–96; National Day of Mourning for 97
nature 7, 22, 24–25, 33, 49, 76, 122; and cycles 122; *see also* conservation movement

Neighbors (movie) 33
Netherlands 96; *see also* New Netherland
New England 10, 14, 16, 18, 19, 20, 23, 44, 96, 98, 160, 162, 174, 189; Pilgrims 95
New Hampshire 43
New Jersey 13, 16, 23
Newman, Randy (songwriter) 146
New Netherland 19, 23, 96
New and Old world, concept of 7, 9, 10, 14, 50, 96
New Orleans 20, 87, 131, 190
New Republic 12, 43–44, 72, 96
newspapers and magazines *see* journalism
New Year 36–37, 85–88, 91, 96–97, 184; resolutions 87, 184
New York 16, 43, 93; City 24, 27, 30, 36, 98, 156, 159, 191–92; Metropolitan 16, 23–24; North Country of 43; Tammany Hall 187; *see also* Times Square
Nile River 13
9 to 5 (movie) 146, 147
"Nine to Five" (song) 146–47, 194
North Carolina 20, 35, 37–39, 86
Norwood, Stephen 112, 113, 115
Nostrand, Richard 39
Notorious B.I.G., The (rapper) 147
Nussbaum, Stan 145

obesity 8, 183–91; *see also* thinness
Occupy Wall Street movement 101, 193
"Oh Dem Golden Slippers" (song) 88
O'Hara, John (novelist) 181–82
Ohio 16, 20, 22; State University 132, 134
Oklahoma 16; University of 117
old age 37, 45, 70, 73–75, 77, 78, 175; old 70
Olmstead, Frederick Law 32–33
optimism, American 7, 44, 50, 53, 59–60, 63–64, 87; and aspiration 93; and future orientation 172; *see also* can-do attitude
Orbis Sensualium Pictus (Comenius) 75
Ordinary Joe (television show) 189
Oregon 21–22, 36
Oriard Michael 110, 116
O'Sullivan, John (journalist) 21–22
Owen, Philip 37–39
Ozark region 16, 20

Pacific Northwest 23, 36, 44; *see also* Oregon
Palin, Sarah 189
pandemic 1, 44, 64–65, 148

Paolantonio, Sal (correspondent) 119
Paredes, Américo (folklorist), 41
Parish, John Carl (historian) 22
Parrington, Vernon Louis 66
Parton, Dolly 146
past, sense of the 5, 21, 36–37, 47, 49–53, 58, 60–62, 64, 68–69, 75, 85–87, 152–53, 158, 174, 182; agrarian 163; republican 159; and sports 118, 140–41; *see also* future orientation; tradition
pastoral ideal 7, 12, 23–24, 73, 94, 174; *see also* agriculture; farms; yeoman ideal
Paterno, Joe 132, 134, 136
patriarchy 110, 114–16, 126, 134; *see also* family; feminism; masculinity
Patten, Simon (economist) 163
Pearl, Jonathan 82
Pearl, Judith 82
Peck, Bradford 162–63
People of Plenty (Potter) 51
Pennsylvania 19, 36, 37–39, 67, 98; Colony 18; Culture Region (PCR) 16, 36, 44; Germans 36, 96, 175, 176, 192; Harrisburg 16, 31, 118, 175–83; Lancaster 36, 37–38, 182; State Capitol 181, 182–83; *see also* Amish
Pew Research Center 34, 45, 65; Millennium Survey 63
Philadelphia (Pennsylvania) 13, 23, 88, 89, 98, 99, 164, 168, 175; Centennial Exhibition (world's fair) 161, 164, 166
photography 4, 25, 27, 38, 62, 82; selfie 192
picnics 37, 40, 90; *see also* food
Pinchot, Gifford 22
Pine Barrens region (New Jersey) 13
Pinsker, Sanford 51
Pioneer Day 17
place, sense of 12, 13, 35, 37, 40, 44–45
plantation 13–15; South 39
Pleasantville (movie) 33
Plimoth Plantation 14; *see also* Plymouth
pluralism 5, 24–25, 28, 43, 66–67, 103; *see also* multiculturalism
Plymouth (Massachusetts) 18, 96
Pioneer Day 17
Poe, Edgar Allan 72
Polamalu, Troy 133, 138
politicians 2, 47, 190
Pollack, William 134–35
polls, opinion 48–69
popular culture 4–5, 33, 48, 73, 75, 83, 151; bar mitzvah in 83; California in

131, 189–90; frontier theme in 116; Quinceañera in 84; and sport 131–32; *Star Trek* in 116
Potter, David (historian) 51
practicality, American trait of 39, 54, 145
pragmatism *see* practicality, American trait of
Presence of the Past, The (Rosenzweig and Thelen) 61–62
Principles of Social Economics (Gunton) 161
privacy 29, 57
progress 22, 60, 61, 63, 65–66, 99, 138, 140, 157, 159, 162, 167, 174, 178, 190, 193–94; American confidence in 87; on life's journey 121, 124; material 74–75, 77–78, 171; social 23, 159, 183, 194; and success 190–92; technological 161
Progressive era 92, 159
progressivism 126, 134–35, 147, 161–62, 193–94
property 9–10, 14, 32–35, 66, 121–23, 126, 135, 140–41, 149, 156, 173; grab 14, 137; and individualism 31; intellectual 4, 150; *see also* farms; plantation; suburbs
prosumer commerce 152–53; *see also* consumerism
proverbs 49, 79, 101, 144–45; of "the business of America is business" 142–43; of "the greatest good to the greatest number" 167; of "the harder the battle, the sweeter the victory" 112; of "money isn't everything" 142, 145; of "money makes the world go round" 190; of "money is power" 192; of "money never sleeps" 145; of "money talks" 146, 192; of "pain is the price of glory" 112; of "pain is temporary, victory is forever" 112; of "a penny earned is a penny saved" 144; of "to the victor belong the spoils" 132; of "time is money" 145; of "winning isn't everything, it's the only thing" 101; *see also* sayings; speech, folk
psychoanalytic perspective 121, 123–24, 137, 140, 187; on male Oedipal complex 124; *see also* Freud, Sigmund
psychology 12, 17, 36, 38, 39, 52, 65, 67, 79, 107–9, 114, 140–41, 143, 148, 187; *see also* Freud, Sigmund; psychoanalytic perspective
Puritans 9–10, 13–14, 95–96; *see also* mythology, Pilgrim; Plimoth Plantation

Quakers 18
Quebec 43
Queer Eye (television series) 188
Quinceañera (rite of passage) 83–84
Quinceañera (movie) 84

race and ethnicity 2, 7–8, 12, 20, 23, 28, 40, 44, 48, 59–60, 65, 68, 129–30; and class 110; *see also* immigrants; racialization; racism
racialization 10, 15, 33, 41
racism 28, 55, 65–66, 79–80, 107, 129
radio 42, 138
Rage to Live, A (O'Hara) 181
Ragged Dick novels (Alger) 28
rags-to-riches mythology 28, 42, 77, 132, 144, 145, 147, 156, 194; *see also* class; mobility; wealth
ranch house 29–31; *see also* Levittown
Raphael, Ray 135
Reading Football (Oriard) 110
Reagan, Ronald 50
Real Boys: Rescuing Our Sons from the Myths of Boyhood (Pollack) 134–35
region 11, 12, 35–46, 44–46; folk 13, and homelands 13; rivalries 18; *see also* regionalism
regionalism 12, 27–28, 40–44; western 22; *see also* region
Regionalist art 27–28, 29, 68–69; *see also* regionalism
religion 22, 55, 58, 70, 71, 83, 107, 149–50, 175, 186; *see also* Christianity; Jews; Mormons
rhetoric 6, 39; of *American,* x, 1, 2; biblical 7, 56, 70, 72, 186, 190; frontier 12, 22, 23, 41, 50–51, 92–93, 116, 119; 175; of gunslinger and cowboy 119; of liberty and freedom 21, 22, 25, 35, 54, 65, 89, 93, 145, 194; of war 116; *see also* frontier, theme in football; symbolism; values
riddle-joke 11–12
Riis, Jacob 27, 160
Rise of Silas Lapham (Howells) 158
rites of passage 7, 79, 82, 125, 135
ritual American year 84–99
Ritzer, George (sociologist) 152
Robertson, James Oliver (historian) 120–21
Robinhood Stock Traders 193–94
Robinson, Harry 180–81
Roosevelt, Theodore 117

Roper Center for Opinion Research 48, 52, 55, 60, 99fn1
Rosenzweig, Roy (historian) 61
Rough Riders 117
Rousseau, Jean-Jacques 5
Rudolph, Frederick 118
Russell Don (columnist) 189; *see also* Joe Sixpack folktype

Sanders, Bernie 192–93
Sanders, Henry (coach) 101, 142
Santa Claus 98, 188; *see also* Christmas
sayings 2, 49, 69, 101; of "another day, another dollar" 147; of "bullshit walks" 146; of "cradle to the grave" 69; of "let bygone be bygones" 49; of "runs the team out of town" 137; of "there is not *I* in team" 114; of "there's just winning and losing" 101; of "the strength of a nation lies in the homes of its people" 173; of "winning isn't everything; it's the only thing" 127, 142; *see also* proverbs; speech, folk science *see* technology
Sears, Richard Warren 169–70
sectionalism 12, 22; *see also* region
self-help books 78, 80
senescence *see* old age
"Seven Ages of Man" (Smirke) 70–71
sexism 66, 107, 109
Shakespeare, William 70
Shame of the Cities, The (Steffens) 160
Sheen, Charlie (actor) 101–2, 141, 146
Sheldon, Henry Davidson 117
Shoemaker, Henry W. 22
Simpsons, The (television show) 188–89
Sister Carrie (Dreiser) 156–57
skyscrapers 25–27, 28, 29
slang *see* speech, folk
slavery 15
slogans 2, 132; advertising 145; political 2, 102, 116; *see also* sayings
Slotkin, Richard 116, 137
Slowe, Peter M. (cultural geographer) 43
small group festive gathering (SGFS) 38
Smirke, Robert 70–71
Smith, Robert S. 156
Smithsonian Folklife Festival 38, 90
smuggling 42, 43
Snow White and the Seven Dwarfs (movie) 145
social change 3, 116, 151, 182, 194
soil *see* land

songs 37–38, 41–42, 90, 145, 147; patriotic 90; *see also* folksongs
South, American 13–15, 16, 36, 44
Sowers, Katie (coach) 130
Southwest, American 16, 41–42; Spanish 13
space, American sense of 9–46; living 30–31
speech, folk 12, 17, 35–36, 107–8, 112, 114, 187, 189; African American 186–87, 189; of "fat city" 189–90; *see also* proverbs; sayings
Spenders, The (Wilson) 158
sports 7, 89, 103–141, 184–85, 194; youth 185; *see also* football; games
stages of life *see* stairway of life
stairway of life 75–77; *see also* life course
Stearns, Peter N. (historian) 184, 187
Steelton (Pennsylvania) 176, 183
Steffens, Lincoln 160
stock brokers 193
Stokes, Adrian 124
Strong, Barrett (singer) 145
structuralism 107, 109, 141; *see also* morphology
suburbs 29–35, 183; *see also* cities; ethnoburbs
Suckow, Ruth 28, 29
Sullivan, Louis 25–28
Sun Belt 45
Super Bowl 85, 87, 103, 106, 127, 131–32, 137, 140, 147; *see also* football
surveillance culture *see* privacy
Swedish colony 18–19
symbolism 2, 6; of animals 76; of December 85; of dynamo 51; of four 72, 75, 81; of forty 75, 78; of land 116; of lines 69, 77, 121, 125; microchip 51; of New England village 174; of seven 70; of ten 70; *see also* psychoanalytic perspective; rhetoric

technology 4, 8, 22, 31–32, 41, 45, 51, 52–54, 68, 141, 151, 153, 161, 162, 169; communication 60; consumer 35; digital 45, 56, 151, 153; and fashion trends 177; and football 132; in health 58, 173, 185; information 132; office 147; photographic and broadcasting 4; and science 58; transportation 171–72
teenagers *see* adolescence
television 42, 70, 87, 94, 98, 103, 105, 110–11, 134, 138, 139, 144, 146, 148,

183, 184, 188–89; bar/bat mitzvah on 82; networks 68; *see also* radio
"Ten Commandments of American Culture" (Nussbaum) 145
Texas 16, 21, 37, 40–41, 50, 90, 113–14, 193
Thanksgiving 19, 95–97; as homecoming 99; Macy's Parade on 98–99
Thelen, David (historian) 61
Then and Now in Harrisburg (Inglewood) 175
Theory of the Leisure Class (Veblen) 32, 155–56; *see also* conspicuous consumption
thinness 104, 183–84, 185, 187; and speed 104; *see also* obesity
Thug Life (hip hop group) 80
Tiller, Joe (coach) 136
time, American sense of 47–100, 151, 155, 191, 192; at work 143, 145, 146–47
Times Square (New York City) 36, 86
toasts 79–80, 81
Tocqueville, Alexis de 171–72, 174
Trachtenberg, Alan (Americanist) 6
tradition 3–4, 7, 17, 35–40, 46, 49, 51, 60–61, 87, 104, 137–38; and family values 60–61; Western 5, 49, 79, 85, 183; *see also* heritage; past, sense of the
transnationalism 43, 148
Traveler from Altruria, A (Howells) 159, 160–61
Trump, Donald 64–67, 102
Trumpism 66–67
Turner, Frederick Jackson (historian) 50
two-party election system 66–68, 102, 194

Uncle Sam 91–93, 188
United Kingdom 64, 173; *see also* England
universities *see* higher education
unlimited good, image of 143, 145, 164; *see also* abundance; limited good, image of
urbanization 23–24, 51, 69, 106, 163, 174; *see also* cities; industrialization
Utah 17, 22–23; *see also* Mormon Culture Region (MCR); West, American

values 3, 22, 42, 52, 54–55, 58, 60–61, 85, 97, 99, 102–3, 105–7, 153, 155, 158, 168; capitalist 167; of citizenship 94; ethnic 84, 97; family 60; of freedom, equality, and justice 65–66; manly 104, 140; national 105; traditional 28, 50, 61; working-class 188; *see also* beliefs;

rhetoric, of liberty and freedom; tradition
Vanderbilt, George W. 161–62, 188
van Gennep, Arnold (folklorist) 125–26
Veblen, Thorstein (sociologist) 32, 155–56
Vermont 18, 43
vernacular, concept of 4
Vespucci, Amerigo (Italian explorer) 7
victory culture 7, 101–41
violence 33, 44, 97, 103, 116–17, 121, 133, 137; and adolescent initiatory behavior 122; racial 44, 65, 79; regeneration through 115–16, 139; ritualized 109, 115, 141; sex and 112; war and 106, 137; *see also* football; war
Virginia 96, 148; colony of 14, 18
visual culture 70, 185; of "cradle to the grave" 79
Vogt, Evon 50
"Voyage of Life, The" (Cole) 73
"Voyage of Life, The" (Johnson) 73

Waldseemüller, Martin (German cartographer) 7
Walsh, Bill (coach) 129, 131
Wanamaker, John 164–68, 173–74, 181
war 52–54, 88, 102, 104, 107–8, 131; advertising 169–70; Civil 77, 88, 96, 163, 176; Cold 52, 57, 106; dances 124, 135; and football 104, 106, 108–10; 133–39; and homoeroticism 108–10; Iraq 133; Napoleonic 90; nuclear 63, 135; of 1812 90, 93; protesting 89, 91, 175; on poverty 12; Revolutionary 89, 93, 102; Spanish-American 92–93, 117; stories 126, 135, 140; tug-of- 125; Vietnam 126–27, 129, 132–33, 175; world 52, 104, 127, 136, 150, 175; *see also* violence
Warner, Glenn "Pop" (coach) 134
Warren, Elizabeth (Senator) 147
Washington, D.C. 32, 89, 90
Washington, George 44, 96
wealth 9, 14, 28–29, 92, 142–50, 154, 157, 158–60, 162, 190, 192; land-based 160; and materialism 58, 142, 163; and success 155–56; *see also* capitalism; money; property
Wealth and Progress (Gunton) 161
Webb, Walter Prescott (historian) 40, 44
websites 45, 147, 151; *see also* digital culture; Internet
Welter, Jen 130

West, American 16, 44, 117, 119
West Coast 98, 189; offense 129, 131–32; *see also* California
West Virginia 16
wheel of fortune 70–71
White House 32–33, 64
whiteness 116, 186–187
wilderness 9, 14
Williams, Roger (Puritan minister) 10
Wilson, Harry Leon (novelist) 158
winning *see* victory culture
Winthrop, Robert C. 21–22
Wisconsin 4; fish-fry 4
women 79, 80, 107, 121–22, 164, 170, 179, 182, 186; bodies of 186–87; sexual harassment 146; social movement of 126; and sports 104, 127, 130; upper-class 185, 187; working-class 168; *see also* femininity; feminism
Wood, Grant (artist) 28
work, office 27, 29, 143–47

"Work Hard and You Shall Be Rewarded" (photocopied broadside) 146
World a Department Store, The (Peck) 162–63
world's fairs 51, 93, 158, 161, 166
World Trade Center 25, 63; attack on 63–64
worldview 2, 15–16, 22–23, 27, 34, 48, 137, 139, 143; progressive 22, 64; regionalist 28

yeoman ideal 13, 14, 24, 148, 161, 162; *see also* pastoral ideal
YMCA movement 166, 179
Yoopers 13, 18
yuppies (young urban professionals) 29, 183

Zabel, Steve (athlete) 113
Zelinsky, Wilbur (cultural geographer) 16, 19
Zuckerman, Michael (historian) 62
Zukin, Sharon (sociologist) 151, 153